A Preface to Marketing Management

THE IRWIN SERIES IN MARKETING

Gilbert A. Churchill, Jr., Consulting Editor
University of Wisconsin, Madison

SIXTH EDITION

A Preface to Marketing Management

J. Paul Peter
McManus–Bascom Professor of Marketing
University of Wisconsin—Madison

James H. Donnelly, Jr.
Thomas C. Simons Professor of Business
University of Kentucky

IRWIN

Burr Ridge, Illinois
Boston, Massachusetts
Sydney, Australia

© RICHARD D. IRWIN, INC., 1979, 1982, 1985, 1988, 1991, and 1994

Senior sponsoring editor: Stephen M. Patterson
Senior developmental editor: Andy Winston
Marketing manager: Scott J. Timian
Project editor: Lynne Basler
Production manager: Laurie Kersch
Cover designer: Randy Scott
Interior designer: Keith J. McPherson / Crispin Prebys
Art manager: Kim Meriwether
Compositor: Graphic World, Inc.
Typeface: 10/12 Bembo
Printer: R.R. Donnelley & Sons Company

Library of Congress Cataloging-in-Publication Data

Peter, J. Paul
    A preface to marketing management / J. Paul Peter, James H. Donnelly, Jr. — 6th ed.
        p.   cm. — (The Irwin series in marketing)
    Includes indexes.
    ISBN 0-256-12251-2
    1. Marketing—Management.   I. Donnelly, James H.   II. Title.
III. Series.
HF5415. 13.P388   1994
658.8—dc20   93–19853

Printed in the United States of America
1 2 3 4 5 6 7 8 9 0 DOC 0 9 8 7 6 5 4 3

PREFACE

A Preface to Marketing Management was a market success from the beginning. However, as students of marketing we knew that continued success would come not from resting on the success of the past, but from forging ahead. Our goal is that students and teachers of marketing management find the current edition of our book to be a useful and valuable resource.

Consequently we have done more than tinker with each new edition. The basic structure has been kept much as it was originally, but we have significantly expanded the content and depth of the chapters. And, of course, we continually update all the information.

As the title indicates, this book is intended to serve as an overview of the critical aspects of marketing management. Because it was developed with several potential uses in mind, one of our major concerns was to achieve a balance between theory and practice. We believe we have achieved this balance through the use of chapter materials, supplemental sections with very focused purposes, and our "highlight" features.

The result of our efforts has been used successfully as a supplement in undergraduate and MBA-level marketing management courses that focus on case problems, and in short courses, executive development programs, and continuing education seminars. More recently, perhaps because of the rising prices of introductory marketing texts, our book has been used successfully as a primary introductory text. One reviewer commented that our book is "pound-for-pound, the best introductory marketing text available." Both the content and the structure of the book have proved to be useful for the above purposes.

This edition of the book has five major sections:

Section 1. Essentials of marketing management. This section consists of 14 chapters that present what we believe to be the essentials of marketing management. Our objective in this section is to present material that could be useful in analyzing a marketing case or problem. While the chapters are necessarily broad in scope, relevant research and review literature serve as the bases for the concepts presented. Whenever possible, the reader is directed to relevant research literature and is also provided with additional sources of information at the end of each chapter.

In this edition, important new material has been added to this section. Also, some changes begun in the previous edition have, based on user feedback, been carried even further in this edition. While all chapters were revised and updated, the following changes deserve special mention:

1. Chapter 10, "Distribution Strategy" includes a new discussion of vertical marketing systems. As more and more organizations have recognized their practicality, vertical marketing systems have increased in popularity. For this reason we believe expanded coverage was necessary.

2. Chapter 12, "The Marketing of Services" completes a major revision begun in the previous edition. We believe this chapter reflects both the increased emphasis on marketing in many service industries, as well as the challenges they face.

3. In today's marketing environment, a text chapter on global marketing must reflect the latest thinking. Recognizing the tremendous importance of global marketing, we have further revised and updated Chapter 13, "International Marketing," which was the focus of a major revision in the previous edition.

A feature of our book that has received very positive feedback from both students and teachers is the occasional "highlights" that are included throughout. Not the usual "news" items found in other texts, these highlights emphasize important new information and are handy references when analyzing cases and problems. We have retained those that have proved successful and have added many new ones to this edition.

Section II. Analyzing marketing problems and cases. This section presents an approach to analyzing, writing, and presenting case analyses. It has received widespread praise from both faculty and students and we believe it is the best presentation available on the topic. In this edition, the section has been completely revised in order to integrate Michael Porter's "Five Forces Model" into our case analysis framework.

It is important to note that this section could have been placed at the beginning of the book because it is designed to be read at the start of a course using cases. However, since it is usually referred to throughout the semester, it was placed after the text material for convenience. Also, for those courses or training seminars that do not employ cases, the text may be used without reference to this section.

Section III. Financial analysis for marketing decisions. The ultimate objectives of marketing activities are usually expressed in financial terms. This section presents some important financial calculations that can be useful in evaluating the financial position of a firm and the financial impact of various marketing strategies.

Section IV. Developing marketing plans. This section contains an approach to developing marketing plans. In keeping with our concept of this book and the needs of intended users, the purpose of the section is to help readers develop practical planning skills by providing a general format for structuring actual marketing plans. Section IV also offers sources where important marketing information can be found and explains what types of information to include in various parts of the plan.

Section V. Secondary data sources. This section contains an annotated bibliography of numerous relevant secondary sources, which can be used as a resource for the analysis of many types of marketing problems. We have found this section to be extremely valuable. It can increase the depth of case analysis as well as expose readers to important secondary sources that will be useful to them in their careers. Eight specific classifications of secondary sources are presented: selected periodicals, general marketing information sources, selected marketing information services, selected retail trade publications, financial information sources, basic U.S. statistical sources, general business and industry sources, and indexes and abstracts.

Throughout this edition we have implemented the suggestions and ideas of those individuals who have served as reviewers of this and previous editions. We would also like to publicly acknowledge their assistance.

Reviewers of previous editions

Catherine Axinn, Syracuse University
Linda M. Delene, Western Michigen University
Robert Finney, California State University, Hayward
David Horne, Wayne State University
Edward J. Mayo, Western Michigan University
Johannah Jones Nolan, University of Alabama, Birmingham
Debu Purohit, Duke University
Matthew H. Sauber, Eastern Michigan University
Ann Marie Thompson, Northern Illinois University
John R. Thompson, Memphis State University
J. B. Wilkinson, University of Akron

Reviewers of the present edition

Stephen Goldberg, Fordham University
Sol Klein, Northeastern University
Vernon R. Stauble, California State Polytechnic University
Ronald L. Schill, Brigham Young University
Kathleen R. Whitney, Central Michigan University

Finally, we acknowledge Andrew Policano, Dean of the School of Business at the University of Wisconsin; and Richard Furst, Dean of the College of Business and Economics, University of Kentucky, who have always supported our efforts. Dr. Geoffrey Gordon of Northern Illinois University deserves special thanks for his contributions to our book. We would also like to thank Steve Patterson, Senior Sponsoring Editor; Andy Winston, Senior Developmental Editor; and Lynne Basler, Project Editor, for their contributions in bringing this new edition to print.

J. Paul Peter
James H. Donnelly, Jr.

CONTENTS

SECTION I

Essentials of Marketing Management

Introduction

Chapter 1
Strategic Planning and the Marketing Management Process

Chapter 1

Strategic Planning and the Marketing Management Process

The purpose of this introductory chapter is to present the marketing management process and outline what marketing managers must *manage* if they are to be effective. In doing so, it will also present a framework around which the remaining chapters are organized. Our first task is to review the organizational philosophy known as the marketing concept, since it underlies much of the thinking presented in this book. The remainder of this chapter will focus on the process of strategic planning and its relationship to the process of marketing planning.

THE MARKETING CONCEPT

Simply stated, the marketing concept means that *an organization should seek to make a profit by serving the needs of customer groups.* The concept is very straightforward and has a great deal of commonsense validity. Perhaps this is why it is often misunderstood, forgotten, or overlooked.

The purpose of the marketing concept is to rivet the attention of marketing managers on serving broad classes of customer needs (customer orientation), rather than on the firm's current products (production orientation) or on devising methods to attract customers to current products (selling orientation). Thus, effective marketing starts with the recognition of customer needs and then works backward to devise products and services to satisfy these needs. In this way, marketing managers can satisfy customers more efficiently in the present and anticipate changes in customer needs more accurately in the future. It is hoped that the end result is a more efficient market in which the customer is better satisfied and the firm is more profitable.

HIGHLIGHT 1–1

Basic Elements of the Marketing Concept

1. Companywide managerial awareness and appreciation of the consumer's role as it is related to the firm's existence, growth, and stability. As Drucker has noted, business enterprise is an organ of society; thus, its basic purpose lies outside the business itself. And the valid definition of business purpose is the creation of customers.

2. Active, companywide managerial awareness of, and concern with, interdepartmental implications of decisions and actions of an individual department. That is, the firm is viewed as a network of forces focused on meeting defined customer needs, and comprising a system within which actions taken in one department or area frequently result in significant repercussions in other areas of the firm. Also, it is recognized that such actions may affect the company's equilibrium with its external environment, for example, its customers, its competitors.

3. Active, companywide managerial concern with innovation of products and services designed to solve selected consumer problems.

4. General managerial concern with the effect of new products and service introduction on the firm's profit position, both present and future, and recognition of the potential rewards which may accrue from new product planning, including profits and profit stability.

5. General managerial appreciation of the role of marketing intelligence and other fact-finding and reporting units within, and adjacent to the firm, in translating the general statements presented above into detailed statements of profitable market potentials, targets, and action. Implicit in this statement is not only an expansion of the traditional function and scope of formal marketing research, but also assimilation of other sources of marketing data, such as the firm's distribution system and its advertising agency counsel, into a potential marketing intelligence service.

6. Companywide managerial effort, based on participation and interaction of company officers, in establishing corporate and departmental objectives that are understood by and acceptable to these officers, and that are consistent with enhancement of the firm's profit position.

Source: Robert L. King, "The Marketing Concept: Fact or Intelligent Platitude," *The Marketing Concept in Action,* Proceedings of the 47th National Conference (Chicago: American Marketing Association, 1964), p. 657. For an up-to-date discussion of the marketing concept, see Franklin S. Houston, "The Marketing Concept: What It Is and What It Is Not," *Journal of Marketing,* April 1986, pp. 81–87.

The principle task of the marketing function operating under the marketing concept is not to manipulate customers to do what suits the interests of the firm, but rather to find effective and efficient means of making the business do what suits the interests of customers. This is not to say that all firms practice marketing in this way. Clearly, many firms still emphasize only production and sales. However, effective marketing, as defined in this text, requires that consumer needs come first in organizational decision making.

One qualification to this statement deals with the question of a conflict between consumer wants and societal needs and wants. For example, if society deems clean air and water as necessary for survival, this need may well take precedence over a consumer's want for goods and services that pollute the environment.

WHAT IS MARKETING?

One of the most persistent conceptual problems in marketing is its definition.[1] The American Marketing Association has recently defined marketing as "the process of planning and executing conception, pricing, promotion, and distribution of ideas, goods, and services to create exchanges that satisfy individual and organizational objectives."[2] Although this broad definition allows the inclusion of nonbusiness exchange processes (i.e., persons, places, organizations, ideas) as part of marketing, the primary emphasis in this text is on marketing in the business environment. However, this emphasis is not meant to imply that marketing concepts, principles, and techniques cannot be fruitfully employed in other areas of exchange. In fact, some discussions of nonbusiness marketing take place later in the text.

WHAT IS STRATEGIC PLANNING?

Before a production manager, marketing manager, and personnel manager can develop plans for their individual departments, hopefully, some larger plan or blueprint for the *entire* organization has been developed. Otherwise, on what would the individual departmental plans be based?

In other words, there is a larger context for planning activities. Let us assume that we are dealing with a large business organization that has several business divisions and several product lines within each division (e.g., General Electric, Philip Morris). Before any marketing planning can be done by individual divisions or departments, a plan has to be developed for the *entire* organization.[3]

---

[1] See Reinhard Angelmar and Christian Pinson, "The Meaning of Marketing," *Philosophy of Science,* June 1975, pp. 208–14.

[2] Peter D. Bennett, *Dictionary of Marketing Terms* (Chicago: American Marketing Association, 1988), p. 115.

[3] John H. Grant and William R. King, *The Logic of Strategic Planning* (Boston: Little, Brown, 1982), chap. 1. This section is based on J. H. Donnelly, Jr., J. L. Gibson, and J. M. Ivancevich, *Fundamentals of Management,* 7th ed. (Homewood., Ill.: Richard D. Irwin, 1990), chap. 5.

(HIGHLIGHT 1–2)

Ten Key Principles for Marketing Success

Principle 1. Create Customer Want Satisfaction.

Principle 2. Know Your Buyer Characteristics.

Principle 3. Divide the Market into Segments.

Principle 4. Strive for High Market Share.

Principle 5. Develop Deep and Wide Product Lines.

Principle 6. Price Position Products and Upgrade Markets.

Principle 7. Treat Channels as Intermediate Buyers.

Principle 8. Coordinate Elements of Physical Distribution.

Principle 9. Promote Performance Features.

Principle 10. Use Information to Improve Decisions.

Source: Fred C. Allvine, Excerpt from *Marketing: Principles and Practices,* p. viii, by Fred C. Allvine, copyright © 1987 by Harcourt Brace Jovanovich, Inc., reprinted by permission of the publisher.

Then objectives and strategies established at the top level provide the context for planning in each of the divisions and departments by divisional and departmental managers. These lower-level managers develop their plans within the constraints developed at the higher levels.[4]

Strategic Planning and Marketing Management

Some of the most successful business organizations are here today because many years ago they offered the right product at the right time to a rapidly growing market. The same can also be said for nonprofit and governmental organizations. Many of the critical decisions of the past were made without the benefit of strategic thinking or planning. Whether these decisions were based on wisdom or were just luck is not important; they worked for these organizations. However, a worse fate befell countless other organizations. Over three quarters of the 100 largest U.S. corporations of 70 years ago have fallen from the list.[5] These corporations at one time dominated their markets,

---

[4]L. Rosenberg and C. D. Schewe, "Strategic Planning: Fulfilling the Promise," *Business Horizons,* July–August 1985, pp. 54–63.

[5]Joe Dodson, "Strategic Repositioning through the Customer Connection," *The Journal of Business Strategy,* May/June 1991, pp. 4–7.

controlled vast resources, and had the best-trained workers. In the end, they all made the same critical mistake. Their managements failed to recognize that business strategies must reflect changing environments. Instead, they attempted to carry on business as usual.

Present day managers are increasingly recognizing that wisdom and innovation alone are no longer sufficient to guide the destinies of organizations, both large and small. Over the course of the past decade, markets have become increasingly global, technology has evolved at an accelerated pace, novel forms of distributing products and services have proliferated, and firms have continually invented new organizational forms—all occurring as customer needs and preferences continually shift in sometimes unpredictable ways.[6] Fifteen years ago, few would have predicted that Sears, the world's largest retailer for over half a century, would be struggling for survival while two relative newcomers, Wal-Mart and Kmart, would become market leaders.[7] Likewise, few would have thought that IBM and General Motors would be engaged in fierce competition for market supremacy with such companies as Microsoft and Toyota. Organizations today need not only function in a competitive and hostile environment but must also be able to cooperate with other companies, perhaps even with ones that in other respects may be competitors.[8] For these and countless other reasons, managers have turned to strategic planning as a means to ensure competitive viability.[9]

Strategic planning includes all of the activities that lead to the development of a clear organizational mission, organizational objectives, and appropriate strategies to achieve the objectives for the entire organization. Successful strategic planning plays a key role in achieving an equilibrium between the short and the long term by balancing acceptable financial performance with preparation for the inevitable changes in markets, technology, and competition, as well as in economic and even political factors.[10] Figure 1–1 presents the process of strategic planning. It indicates that the organization gathers information about the changing elements of its environment. This information is useful in aiding the organization to adapt better to these changes through the process

---

[6]G. S. Day, K. E. Jocz, and H. P. Root, "Domains of Ignorance: What We Most Need to Know," *Marketing Management,* Winter 1992, pp. 9–14.

[7]H. H. Beam, "Strategic Discontinuities: When Being Good May Not Be Enough," *Business Horizons,* July–August 1990, pp. 10–14.

[8]Peter Lorange and Johan Roos, "Why Some Strategic Alliances Succeed and Others Fail," *The Journal of Business Strategy,* January–February 1991, pp. 25–30.

[9]C. Anderson and C. P. Zeithaml, "Stage of the Product Life Cycle, Business Strategy, and Business Performance," *Academy of Management Journal,* March 1984, pp. 5–24.

[10]F. Paul Carlson, "The Long and Short of Strategic Planning," *The Journal of Business Strategy,* May/June 1990, pp. 15–19.

Figure 1–1   *The Strategic Planning Process*

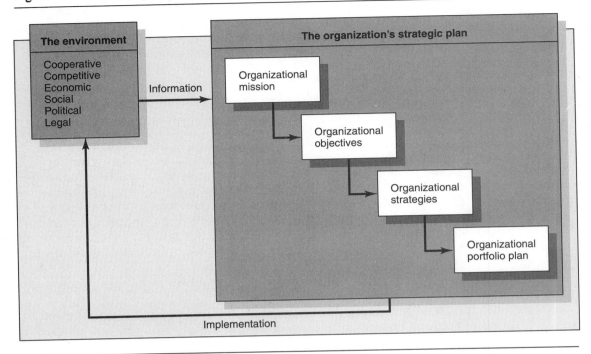

of strategic planning.[11] The strategic plan(s)[12] and supporting plan are then implemented in the environment. The results of this implementation are fed back as new information so that continuous adaptation can take place.

The Strategic Planning Process

The output of the strategic planning process is the development of a strategic plan. Figure 1–1 indicates four components of a strategic plan: mission, objectives, strategies, and portfolio plan. Let us carefully examine each one.

[11]The process depicted in Figure 1–1 is a generally agreed upon model of the strategic planning process, although some may include or exclude a particular element. For example, see A. A. Thompson and A. J. Strickland III, *Strategic Management: Concepts and Cases,* 6th ed. (Homewood, Ill.: Richard D. Irwin, 1990), and Philip Kotler, *Marketing Management: Analysis, Planning, and Control,* 6th ed. (Englewood Cliffs, N.J.: Prentice Hall 1988).

[12]The process may differ depending on the type of organization or management approach, or both. For certain types of organizations, one strategic plan will be sufficient. Some manufacturers with similar product lines or limited product lines will develop only one strategic plan. However, organizations with widely diversified product lines and widely diversified markets may develop strategic plans for units or divisions. These plans usually are combined into a master strategic plan.

Organizational mission

Every organization's environment supplies the resources that sustain the organization, whether it is a business organization, a college or university, or a governmental agency. In exchange for these resources, the organization must supply the environment with goods and services at an acceptable price and quality. In other words, every organization exists to accomplish something in the larger environment, and that purpose or mission is usually clear at the start. However, as time passes and the organization expands, the environment changes, and managerial personnel change, one or more things are likely to occur. First, the original purpose may become irrelevant as the organization expands into new products, new markets, and even new industries. Second, the original mission remains relevant but some managers begin to lose interest in it. Finally, changes in environment may make the original mission inappropriate. The result of any or all of these three conditions is a "drifting" organization, without a clear mission or purpose to guide critical decisions. When this occurs, management must search for a purpose or restate the original purpose.

The mission statement of an organization should be a long-run vision of what the organization is trying to become: the unique aim that differentiates the organization from similar ones. Note that the need is not a stated purpose, such as "to fulfill the educational needs of college students," that will enable stockholders and managers to feel good or to use for good public relations. The need is for a stated mission that will provide direction and significance to all members of the organization regardless of their level in the organization.

The basic questions that must be answered when an organization decides to examine and restate its mission are: "What is our business?" "What should it be?" While such questions may appear simple, they are in fact such difficult and critical ones that the major responsibility for answering them must lie with top management.[13] In developing a statement of mission, management must take into account three key elements:[14]

1. *The organization's history*. Every organization—large or small, profit or nonprofit—has a history of objectives, accomplishments, mistakes, and policies. In formulating a mission, the critical characteristics and events of the past must be considered.

2. *The organization's distinctive competencies*. While there are many things an organization may be able to do, it should seek to do what it can do best. Distinctive competencies are things that an organization does well: so well in fact that they give it an advantage over similar organizations. Procter & Gamble could probably enter the synthetic fuel business, but such a decision

---

[13]Lewis W. Walker, "The CEO and Corporate Strategy in the Eighties: Back to Basics," *Interfaces*, January–February 1984, pp. 3–9; Peter Drucker, *Management: Tasks, Responsibilities, Practices* (New York: Harper & Row, 1974), chap. 7.

[14]Kotler, *Marketing Management*, chap. 2.

HIGHLIGHT 1–3

Some Actual Mission Statements

Organization	Mission
1. Office equipment manufacturer	We are in the business of problem solving. Our business is to help solve administrative, scientific, and human problems.
2. Credit union	To produce a selected range of quality services to organizations and individuals to fulfill their continuing financial needs.
3. Large conglomerate	Translating new technologies into commercially salable products.
4. Consumer products paper company	The development and marketing of inedible food store products.
5. State department of health	Administering all provisions of law relating to public health laws and regulations of the State Board of Health, supervising and assisting county and regional boards and departments of health, and doing all other things reasonably necessary to protect and improve the health of the people.
6. Appliance manufacturer	A willingness to invest in any area of suitable profit and growth potential in which the organization has or can acquire the capabilities.

---

would certainly not take advantage of its major distinctive competence: knowledge of the market for low-priced, repetitively purchased consumer products. No matter how appealing an opportunity may be, the organization must have the competencies to capitalize on that opportunity.[15]

3. *The organization's environment.* The organization's environment dictates the opportunities, constraints, and threats that must be identified before a mission statement is developed. Technological developments in the communications field may have a negative impact on travel and should certainly be considered in the mission statement of a large motel chain.[16]

---

[15]For a study of the relationship between corporate distinctive competencies and performance in 185 firms, see M. A. Hitt and R. D. Ireland, "Corporate Distinctive Competence, Strategy and Performance," *Strategic Management Journal,* July–September 1985, pp. 273–93.

[16]See C. Smart and I. Vertinsky, "Strategy and the Environment: A Study of Corporate Responses to Crises," *Strategic Management Journal,* April–June 1984, pp. 199–214. This study of the largest U.S. and Canadian companies examines the relationship between a firm's external environment and its repertoire of strategic responses to cope with crisis.

However, it is extremely difficult to write a useful and effective mission statement. It is not uncommon for an organization to spend one or two years developing a useful mission statement. When completed, an effective mission statement will be: *focused on markets rather than products, achievable, motivating, and specific.*[17]

Focused on markets rather than products. The customers or clients of an organization are critical in determining its mission. Traditionally, many organizations defined their business in terms of what they made, "our business is glass," and in many cases they named the organization for the product or service (e.g., National Cash Register, Harbor View Savings and Loan Association). Many of these organizations have found that, when products and technologies become obsolete, their mission is no longer relevant and the name of the organization may no longer describe what it does. Thus, a more enduring way of defining the mission is needed. In recent years, therefore, a key feature of mission statements has been an *external* rather than *internal* focus. In other words, the mission statement should focus on the broad class of needs that the organization is seeking to satisfy (external focus), *not* on the physical product or service that the organization is offering at present (internal focus). This has been clearly stated by Peter Drucker. He argues:

> A business is not defined by the company's name, statutes, or articles of incorporation. It is defined by the want the customer satisfies when he buys a product or service. To satisfy the customer is the mission and purpose of every business. The question "What is our business?" can, therefore, be answered only by looking at the business from the outside, from the point of view of customer and market.[18]

While Drucker was referring to business organizations, the same necessity exists for both nonprofit and governmental organizations.[19] That necessity is to state the mission in terms of serving a particular group of clients or customers and meeting a particular class of need.

Achievable. While the mission statement should "stretch" the organization toward more effective performance, it should, at the same time, be realistic and achievable. In other words, it should open a vision of new opportunities but should not lead the organization into unrealistic ventures far beyond its competencies.

Motivational. One of the side (but very important) benefits of a well-defined mission is the guidance it provides employees and managers working in geographically dispersed units and on independent tasks. It provides a shared sense of purpose outside the various activities taking place within the organization.

---

[17]Drucker, *Management*, pp. 77–89; Kotler, *Marketing Management*, chap. 2.

[18]Drucker, *Management*, p. 79.

[19]Paul C. Nutt, "A Strategic Planning Network for Nonprofit Organizations," *Strategic Management Journal*, January–March 1984, pp. 57–76; Peter Smith Ring and James L. Perry, "Strategic Management in Public and Private Organizations: Implications of Distinctive Contexts and Constraints," *Academy of Management Review*, April 1985, pp. 276–86.

Therefore, such end results as sales, patients cared for, and reduction in violent crimes can then be viewed as the result of careful pursuit and accomplishment of the mission and not as the mission itself.[20]

Specific. As we mentioned earlier, public relations should not be the primary purpose of a statement of mission. It must be specific to provide direction and guidelines to management when they are choosing between alternative courses of action.[21] In other words, "to produce the highest quality products at the lowest possible cost" sounds very good, but it does not provide direction for management.

Organizational objectives

Organizational objectives are the end points of an organization's mission and are what it seeks through the ongoing, long-run operations of the organization. The organizational mission is distilled into a finer set of specific and achievable organizational objectives. These objectives must be *specific, measurable, action commitments* by which the mission of the organization is to be achieved.

As with the statement of mission, organizational objectives are more than good intentions. In fact, if formulated properly, they can accomplish the following:

1. They can be converted into specific actions.
2. They will provide direction. That is, they can serve as a starting point for more specific and detailed objectives at lower levels in the organization. Each manager will then know how his or her objectives relate to those at higher levels.
3. They can establish long-run priorities for the organization.
4. They can facilitate management control because they serve as standards against which overall organizational performance can be evaluated.

Organizational objectives are necessary in any and all areas that may influence the performance and long-run survival of the organization. Peter Drucker believes that objectives should be established in at least eight areas of organizational performance. These are market standing, innovations, productivity, physical and financial resources, profitability, manager performance and responsibility, worker performance and attitude, and social responsibility.[22]

The above list of objectives is by no means exhaustive. An organization may very well have additional ones. The important point is that management must translate the organizational mission into specific objectives that will support the realization of the mission. The objectives may flow directly from the mission or be considered subordinate necessities for carrying out the mission

---

[20]"Who's Excellent Now," *Business Week*, November 5, 1984, pp. 76–88.

[21]Drucker, *Management*, p. 87.

[22]Peter Drucker, *The Practice of Management* (New York: Harper & Row, 1954); and reemphasized in Drucker's *Management*.

Figure 1–2 *Sample Organizational Objectives* (manufacturing firm)

Area of Performance	Possible Objective
1. Market standing	To make our brands number one in their field in terms of market share.
2. Innovations	To be a leader in introducing new products by spending no less than 7 percent of sales for research and development.
3. Productivity	To manufacture all products efficiently as measured by the productivity of the work force.
4. Physical and financial resources	To protect and maintain all resources—equipment, buildings, inventory, and funds.
5. Profitability	To achieve an annual rate of return on investment of at least 15 percent.
6. Manager performance and responsibility	To identify critical areas of management depth and succession.
7. Worker performance and attitude	To maintain levels of employee satisfaction consistent with our own and similar industries.
8. Social responsibility	To respond appropriately whenever possible to societal expectations and environmental needs.

of the organization. Figure 1–2 presents some examples of organizational objectives. Note that they are broad statements that serve as guides and that they are of a continuing nature. They specify the end points of an organization's mission and the results that it seeks in the long run both externally and internally. Most important, however, the objectives in Figure 1–2 are *specific, measurable, action commitments* on the part of the organization.

Organizational strategies

Hopefully, when an organization has formulated its mission and developed its objectives, it knows where it wants to go. The next managerial task is to develop a "grand design" to get there. This grand design constitutes the organizational strategies. The role of strategy in strategic planning is to provide a clear, realistic articulation of a desired competitive position and the underlying core strategic goals and objectives related to achieving this position and enhancing it over time.[23] Strategy involves the choice of major directions the organization will take in pursuing its objectives.

Achieving organizational objectives comes about in two ways. It is accomplished by better managing what the organization is presently doing and/or finding new things to do. In choosing either or both of these paths, the organization then must decide whether to concentrate on present customers or to seek new ones, or both. Figure 1–3 presents the available strategic choices.

---

[23]Donald K. Yee, "Pass or Fail? How to Grade Strategic Progress," *The Journal of Business Strategy*, May/June 1990, pp. 10–14.

Figure 1–3 *Organizational Growth Strategies*

Products / Markets	Present Products	New Products
Present customers	Market penetration	Product development
New customers	Market development	Diversification

It is known as a product/market matrix and indicates the strategic alternatives available to an organization for achieving its objectives. It indicates that an organization can grow in a variety of ways by concentrating on present or new products and on present or new customers.[24]

Market penetration strategies. These organizational strategies focus on improving the position of the organization's present products with its present customers. For example:

— A dairy concentrates on getting its present customers to purchase more of its products.
— A charity seeks to increase contributions from present contributors.
— A bank concentrates on getting present depositors to use additional services.

A market penetration strategy might involve devising a marketing plan to encourage customers to purchase more of a product. Tactics used to carry out the strategy could include price reductions, advertising that stresses the many benefits of the product, packaging the product in different-sized packages, or making the product available at more locations. For example, Procter & Gamble recently decided to implement an everyday low pricing strategy, slashing prices on over 40 percent of its product offerings, in order to stimulate consumer demand. Likewise a production plan might be developed to produce more efficiently what is being produced at present. Implementation of such a plan could include increased production runs, the substitution of preassembled components for individual product parts, or the automation of a process that previously was performed manually. In other words, market penetration strategies concentrate on improving the efficiency of various functional areas in the organization.

---

[24]Originally discussed in the classic H. Igor Ansoff, *Corporate Strategy* (New York: McGraw-Hill, 1965).

Market development strategies. Following this strategy, an organization would seek to find new customers for its present products. For example:

— A manufacturer of industrial products may decide to develop products for entrance into consumer markets.
— A governmental social service agency may seek individuals and families who have never utilized the agency's services.
— A manufacturer of automobiles decides to sell automobiles in Eastern Europe because of the recent transition to a free market system.
— An athletic clothing and footwear company decides to develop a line of fitness clothing for women.

Product development strategies. In choosing either of the remaining two strategies, the organization in effect seeks new things to do. With this particular strategy, the new products developed would be directed to present customers. For example:

— A candy manufacturer may decide to offer a low-calorie candy.
— A social service agency may offer additional services to present client families.
— A college or university may develop programs for senior citizens.
— A soft drink manufacturer develops a clear cola.

Diversification. An organization diversifies when it seeks new products for customers it is not serving at present. For example:

— A discount store purchases a savings and loan association.
— A cigarette manufacturer diversifies into real estate development.
— A college or university establishes a corporation to find commercial uses for the results of faculty research efforts.
— A cosmetics manufacturer acquires a baby-care products company.

On what basis does an organization choose one (or all) of its strategies? Of extreme importance are the directions set by the mission statement. Management should select those strategies consistent with its mission and capitalize on the organization's distinctive competencies which will lead to a sustainable competitive advantage.[25] A sustainable competitive advantage can be based on either the assets or skills of the organization. Technical superiority, low-cost production, customer service/product support, location, financial resources, continuing product innovation, and overall marketing skills are all examples of distinctive competencies that can lead to a sustainable competitive

---

[25]N. Venkatramen and J. C. Camillus, "Exploring the Concept of 'Fit' in Strategic Management," *Academy of Management Review*, July 1984, pp. 513–25; H. Mintzberg and J. A. Waters, "Of Strategies, Deliberate and Emergent," *Strategic Management Journal*, July–September 1985, pp. 257–72.

HIGHLIGHT 1–4

Some Commonly Used Performance Standards

Effectiveness Standards

A. Sales Criteria.
1. Total sales.
2. Sales by product or product line.
3. Sales by geographic region.
4. Sales by salesperson.
5. Sales by customer type.
6. Sales by market segment.
7. Sales by size of order.
8. Sales by sales territory.
9. Sales by intermediary.
10. Market share.
11. Percentage change in sales.

B. Customer Satisfaction.
1. Quantity purchased.
2. Degree of brand loyalty.
3. Repeat purchase rates.
4. Perceived product quality.
5. Brand image.
6. Number of letters of complaint.

Efficiency Standards

C. Costs.
1. Total costs.
2. Costs by product or product line.
3. Costs by geographic region.
4. Costs by salesperson.
5. Costs by customer type.
6. Costs by market segment.
7. Costs by size of order.
8. Costs by sales territory.
9. Costs by intermediary.
10. Percentage change in costs.

Effectiveness-Efficiency Standards

D. Profits.
1. Total profits.
2. Profits by product or product line.
3. Profits by geographic region.
4. Profits by salesperson.
5. Profits by customer type.
6. Profits by market segment.
7. Profits by size of order.
8. Profits by sales territory.
9. Profits by intermediary.

Source: Charles D. Schewe, *Marketing: Principles and Strategies* © 1987, New York, McGraw-Hill, Inc., p. 593. With the permission of the publisher.

---

advantage.[26] For example, Honda is known for providing quality automobiles at a reasonable price. Each succeeding generation of Honda cars has shown marked quality improvement over previous generations. This, in turn, has led to the Honda Accord's becoming the leading selling car in the United States. The key to sustaining a competitive advantage is to continually focus and build on the assets and skills that will lead to long-term performance gains.

---

[26]D. Aaker, "Managing Assets and Skills: The Key to a Sustainable Competitive Advantage," *California Management Review,* Winter 1989, pp. 91–106.

Organizational portfolio plan

The final phase of the strategic planning process is the formulation of the organizational portfolio plan. In reality, most organizations at a particular time are a portfolio of businesses, that is, product lines, divisions, schools. To illustrate, an appliance manufacturer may have several product lines (e.g., televisions, washers and dryers, refrigerators, stereos) as well as two divisions, consumer appliances and industrial appliances. A college or university will have numerous schools (e.g., education, business, law, architecture) and several programs within each school. Some widely diversified organizations such as Philip Morris are in numerous unrelated businesses, such as cigarettes, food products, land development, industrial paper products, and a brewery.

Managing such groups of businesses is made a little easier if resources are plentiful, cash is plentiful, and each is experiencing growth and profits. Unfortunately, providing larger and larger budgets each year to all businesses is seldom feasible. Many are not experiencing growth, and profits and resources (financial and nonfinancial) are becoming more and more scarce. In such a situation, choices must be made, and some method is necessary to help management make the choices. Management must decide which businesses to build, maintain, or eliminate, or which new businesses to add.[27] Indeed, much of the recent activity in corporate restructuring has centered around decisions relating to which groups of businesses management should focus on.

Obviously, the first step in this approach is to identify the various division's product lines and so on that can be considered a "business." When identified, these are referred to as *strategic business units* (SBUs) and have the following characteristics:

— They have a distinct mission.
— They have their own competitors.
— They are a single business or collection of related businesses.
— They can be planned independently of the other businesses of the total organization.

Thus, depending on the type of organization, an SBU could be a single product, product line, or division; a department of business administration; or a state mental health agency. Once the organization has identified and classified all of its SBUs, some method must be established to determine how resources should be allocated among the various SBUs. These methods are known as *portfolio models*. For those readers interested, the appendix of this chapter presents two of the most popular portfolio models, the Boston Consulting group model and the General Electric model.

---

[27]There are several portfolio models; each has its detractors and supporters. The interested reader should consult Richard G. Hamermesh and Roderick E. White, "Manage Beyond Portfolio Analysis," *Harvard Business Review*, January–February 1984, pp. 103–9, and J. A. Seeger, "Revising the Images of BCG's Growth/Share Matrix," *Strategic Management Journal*, January–March 1984, pp. 93–97.

The SBU concept is a powerful tool because SBUs partition a company according to the principal markets served.[28] A critical element of successful planning involves an organization possessing an outward orientation. However, such an orientation must remain flexible. Last year's SBU may not be the best unit for planning next year's strategy. It is all too common for larger companies to overlook an important new competitor, technology, or customer segment for several planning cycles, simply because it does not show up clearly in the company's reports. Managers must be aware that the optimal form of any individual SBU is likely to change over time.

The Complete Strategic Plan

Figure 1–1 indicates that at this point the strategic planning process is complete, and the organization has a time-phased blueprint that outlines its mission, objectives, and strategies. Completion of the strategic plan facilitates the development of marketing plans for each product, product line, or division of the organization. The marketing plan serves as a subset of the strategic plan in that it allows for detailed planning at a target market level. Several marketing plans, each one targeted toward a specific market, will evolve from the strategic plan. For example, separate marketing plans would be developed for the various markets that a firm, which produces consumer appliances and industrial electrical products, competes in. Given a completed strategic plan, each area knows exactly where the organization wishes to go and can then develop objectives, strategies, and programs that are consistent with the strategic plan.[29] This important relationship between strategic planning and marketing planning is the subject of the final section of this chapter.

THE MARKETING MANAGEMENT PROCESS

Marketing management can be defined as "the analysis, planning, implementation, and control of programs designed to bring about desired exchanges with target markets for the purpose of achieving organizational objectives. It relies heavily on designing the organization's offering in terms of the target market's needs and desires and on using effective pricing, communication, and distribution to inform, motivate, and service the market."[30] It should be noted that this definition is entirely consistent with the marketing concept, since it

---

[28]See Alexander Hiam, "Exposing Four Myths of Strategic Planning," *The Journal of Business Strategy*, September/October 1990, pp. 23–28, for a discussion of this topic.

[29]R. A. Linneman and H. E. Klein, "Using Scenarios in Strategic Decision Making," *Business Horizons*, January–February 1985, pp. 64–74.

[30]Kotler, *Marketing Management*, p. 14.

Figure 1–4   *Strategic Planning and Marketing Planning*

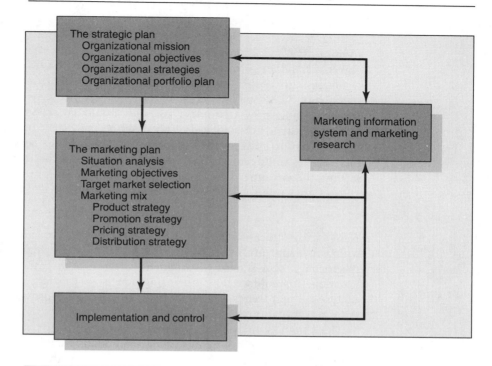

emphasizes the serving of target market needs as the key to achieving organizational objectives. The remainder of this section will be devoted to a discussion of the marketing management process in terms of the model in Figure 1–4.

Organizational Mission and Objectives

Marketing activities should start with a clear understanding of the organization's mission and objectives. These factors provide marketing management direction by specifying the industry, the desired role of the firm in the industry (such as research-oriented innovator, custom-batch specialist, or mass producer), and hopefully, a precise statement of what the firm is trying to accomplish. However, since written mission statements and objectives are often ambiguous or ill-defined, the marketing manager may have to consult with other members of top management to determine precisely what the firm is trying to accomplish, both overall and during a specific planning period. For example, a commonly stated organizational objective is "growth." Obviously, this objective is so general that it is practically useless. On the other hand, a statement such as "sustained growth of 14 percent in profits before taxes" provides a quantitative goal which the marketing manager can use for determining desired sales levels and the marketing strategies to achieve them. In addition, the marketing manager must monitor any changes in mission or objectives and adapt marketing strategies to meet them.

Increasingly, organizations are also developing customer-service mission statements. These statements can outline which dimensions of customer service are important, how customers are and should be served, define customer service performance standards, and describe the extent of the organization's commitment to customer service.[31] In effect, a customer service mission statement serves to direct management attention toward the all-important goal of serving the customer.

Situation Analysis

With a clear understanding of organizational objectives and mission, the marketing manager must then analyze and monitor the position of the firm and, specifically, the marketing department, in terms of its past, present, and future situation. Of course, the future situation is of primary concern. However, analyses of past trends and the current situation are most useful for predicting the future situation.

The situation analysis can be divided into six major areas of concern: (1) the cooperative environment; (2) the competitive environment; (3) the economic environment; (4) the social environment; (5) the political environment; and (6) the legal environment. In analyzing each of these environments, the marketing executive must search both for opportunities and for constraints or threats to achieving objectives. Opportunities for profitable marketing often arise from changes in these environments that bring about new sets of needs to be satisfied. Constraints on marketing activities, such as limited supplies of scarce resources, also arise from these environments.

The cooperative environment. The cooperative environment includes all firms and individuals who have a vested interest in the firm's accomplishing its objectives. Parties of primary interest to the marketing executive in this environment are (1) suppliers; (2) resellers; (3) other departments in the firm; and (4) subdepartments and employees of the marketing department. Opportunities in this environment are primarily related to methods of increasing efficiency. For example, a company might decide to switch from a competitive bid process of obtaining materials to a single source that is located near the

---

[31]For a more complete discussion of customer service and the mission statement, see Richard Germain and M. Bixby Cooper, "How a Customer Mission Statement Affects Company Performance," *Industrial Marketing Management,* February, 1990, pp. 47–54, and Harvey N. Shycon, "Improved Customer Service: Measuring the Payoff," *The Journal of Business Strategy,* January / February 1992, pp. 13–17.

company's plant. Likewise, members of the marketing, engineering, and manufacturing functions may utilize a teamwork approach to developing new products versus a sequential approach. Constraints consist of such things as unresolved conflicts and shortages of materials. For example, a company manager may believe that a distributor is doing an insufficient job of promoting and selling the product, or a marketing manager may feel that manufacturing is not taking the steps needed to produce a quality product.

The competitive environment. The competitive environment includes primarily other firms in the industry that rival the organization for both resources and sales. Opportunities in this environment include such things as (1) acquiring competing firms; (2) offering demonstrably better value to consumers and attracting them away from competitors; and (3) in some cases, driving competitors out of the industry. For example, one airline purchases another airline, a bank offers depositors a free checking account with no minimum balance requirements, or a grocery chain engages in an everyday low-price strategy that competitors can't meet. The primary constraints in these environments are the demand stimulation activities of competing firms and the number of consumers who cannot be lured away from competition.

The economic environment. The state of the macroeconomy and changes in it also bring about marketing opportunities and constraints. For example, such factors as high inflation and unemployment levels can limit the size of the market that can afford to purchase a firm's top-of-the-line product. At the same time, these factors may offer a profitable opportunity to develop rental services for such products or to develop less expensive models of the product. In addition, changes in technology can provide significant threats and opportunities. For example, in the communications industry, technology has developed to a level where it is now possible to provide cable television using phone lines. Obviously such a system poses a severe threat to the existence of the cable industry as it exists today.

The social environment. This environment includes general cultural and social traditions, norms, and attitudes. While these values change slowly, such changes often bring about the need for new products and services. For example, a change in values concerning the desirability of large families brought about an opportunity to market better methods of birth control. On the other hand, cultural and social values also place constraints on marketing activities. As a rule, business practices that are contrary to social values become political issues, which are often resolved by legal constraints. For example, public demand for a cleaner environment has caused the government to require that automobile manufacturers' products meet certain average gas mileage and emission standards.

The political environment. The political environment includes the attitudes and reactions of the general public, social and business critics, and other organizations, such as the Better Business Bureau. Dissatisfaction with such business and marketing practices as unsafe products, products that waste resources, and unethical sales procedures can have adverse effects on corporation image and

---

> ## HIGHLIGHT 1–5
>
> ### *Key Elements in the Marketing Plan*
>
> *People* — What is the target market for the firm's product(s)? What is its size and growth potential?
>
> *Profit* — What is the expected profit from implementing the marketing plan? What are the other objectives of the marketing plan, and how will their achievement be evaluated?
>
> *Personnel* — What personnel will be involved in implementing the marketing plan? Will only intrafirm personnel be involved, or will other firms, such as advertising agencies or marketing research firms, also be employed?
>
> *Product* — What product(s) will be offered? What variations in the product will be offered in terms of style, features, quality, branding, packaging, and terms of sale and service? How should products be positioned in the market?
>
> *Price* — What price or prices will products be sold for?
>
> *Promotion* — How will information about the firm's offerings be communicated to the target market?
>
> *Place* — How, when, and where will the firm's offerings be delivered for sale to the target market?
>
> *Policy* — What is the overall marketing policy for dealing with anticipated problems in the marketing plan? How will unanticipated problems be handled?
>
> *Period* — For how long a time is the marketing plan to be in effect? When should the plan be implemented, and what is the schedule for executing and evaluating marketing activities?

---

customer loyalty. However, adapting business and marketing practices to these attitudes can be an opportunity. For example, these attitudes have brought about markets for such products as unbreakable children's toys, high-efficiency air conditioners, and more economical automobiles.

The legal environment. This environment includes a host of federal, state, and local legislation directed at protecting both business competition and consumer rights. In past years legislation reflected social and political attitudes and has been primarily directed at constraining business practices. Such legislation usually acts as a constraint on business behavior, but again can be viewed as providing opportunities for marketing safer and more efficient products. In recent years, there has been less emphasis on creating new laws for constraining business practices. As an example, deregulation has become more common as evidenced by recent events in the airlines, financial services, and telecommunications industries.

HIGHLIGHT 1–6

Criteria for Setting Marketing Objectives

Criteria	Poor Goal	Good Goal
Overall marketing objectives are clearly stated.	To get people to buy our new Betty Crocker Microwave Bread Shop products.	To obtain 5 percent of the fresh-baked bread market in 12 months.
Behavioral objectives are clearly stated.	To have sales increase.	To stimulate 30 percent of all U.S. households to try one loaf of Betty Crocker Microwave bread.
Expectations are realistic.	To obtain half the fresh-baked bread market.	Given the strong name of Betty Crocker in the baked bread goods market and that Americans consume 50 lbs of bread a year, we hope to achieve an 18 percent share of the fresh baked bread market.
Adequate support exists for the program.	No mention of budget dollars in the program statement. No check to make sure the program meshes with corporate goals.	Given the commitment by General Mills to grow in the baked goods market, the budget for Betty Crocker's Microwave Bread Shop over the next three years is $45 million, $41 million, and $35 million, respectively.

Source: Charles W. Lamb, Jr., Joseph F. Hair, Jr., and Carl McDaniel, *Principles of Marketing* (Cincinnati: South-Western Publishing, 1992), p. 27.

In addition, political leaders are increasingly going to bat for their own multinational organizations.[32] For example, the U.S. vice president recently lobbied on behalf of such organizations as AT&T and Guardian Industries, trying to get foreign countries to open their markets to American companies.

---

[32]David A. Heenan, "Why the U.S. Government Should Go to Bat for Business," *The Journal of Business Strategy,* March/April 1990, pp. 46–48.

Marketing Planning

In the previous sections it was emphasized that (1) marketing activities must be aligned with organizational objectives; and (2) marketing opportunities are often found by systematically analyzing situational environments. Once an opportunity is recognized, the marketing executive must then plan an appropriate strategy for taking advantage of the opportunity. This process can be viewed in terms of three interrelated tasks: (1) establishing marketing objectives; (2) selecting the target market; and (3) developing the marketing mix.

Establishing objectives. Marketing objectives usually are derived from organizational objectives; in some cases where the firm is totally marketing-oriented, the two are identical. In either case, objectives must be specified and performance in achieving them should be measurable. Marketing objectives are usually stated as standards of performance (e.g., a certain percentage of market share or sales volume) or as tasks to be achieved by given dates. While such objectives are useful, the marketing concept emphasizes that profits rather than sales should be the overriding objective of the firm and marketing department. In any case, these objectives provide the framework for the marketing plan.

Selecting the target markets. The success of any marketing plan hinges on how well it can identify customer needs and organize its resources to satisfy them profitably. Thus, a crucial element of the marketing plan is selecting the groups or segments of potential customers the firm is going to serve with each of its products. Four important questions must be answered:

1. What do customers want and/or need?
2. What must be done to satisfy these wants and/or needs?
3. What is the size of the market?
4. What is its growth profile?

Present target markets and potential target markets are then ranked according to (a) profitability; (b) present and future sales volume; and (c) the match between what it takes to appeal successfully to the segment and the organization's capabilities. Those that appear to offer the greatest potential are selected. Chapters 3, 4, and 5 are devoted to discussing consumer behavior, industrial buyers, and market segmentation.

Developing the marketing mix. The marketing mix is the set of controllable variables that must be managed to satisfy the target market and achieve organizational objectives. These controllable variables are usually classified according to four major decision areas: product, price, promotion, and place (or channels of distribution). The importance of these decision areas cannot be overstated and, in fact, the major portion of this text is devoted to analyzing them. Chapters 6 and 7 are devoted to product and new product strategies; Chapters 8 and 9 to promotion strategies in terms of both nonpersonal and personal selling; Chapter 10 to distribution strategies; and Chapter 11 to pricing strategies. In addition, marketing mix variables are the focus of analysis in two chapters on marketing in special fields, that is, the marketing of services (Chapter 12) and international marketing (Chapter 13). Thus, it should be clear to the reader that the marketing mix is the core of the marketing management process.

The output of the foregoing process is the marketing plan. It is a formal statement of decisions that have been made on marketing activities; it is a blueprint of the objectives, strategies, and tasks to be performed.

Implementation and Control of the Marketing Plan

Implementing the market plan involves putting the plan into action and performing marketing tasks according to the predefined schedule. Even the most carefully developed plans often cannot be executed with perfect timing. Thus, the marketing executive must closely monitor and coordinate implementation of the plan. In some cases, adjustments may have to be made in the basic plan because of changes in any of the situational environments. For example, competitors may introduce a new product. In this event, it may be desirable to speed up or delay implementation of the plan. In almost all cases, some minor adjustments or "fine tuning" will be necessary in implementation.

Controlling the marketing plan involves three basic steps. First, the results of the implemented marketing plan are measured. Second, these results are compared with objectives. Third, decisions are made on whether the plan is achieving objectives. If serious deviations exist between actual and planned results, adjustments may have to be made to redirect the plan toward achieving objectives.

Marketing Information Systems and Marketing Research

Throughout the marketing management process, current, reliable, and valid information is needed to make effective marketing decisions. Providing this information is the task of the marketing decision support system (MDSS) and marketing research. These topics are discussed in detail in Chapter 2.

THE RELATIONSHIP BETWEEN THE STRATEGIC PLAN AND THE MARKETING PLAN

Strategic planning is clearly a top-management responsibility. However, there has been an increasing shift towards more active participation of marketing professionals in corporate strategic analysis and planning.[33] Management is finding that a key strategic challenge is deciding how to best position a com-

---

[33]See D. W. Cravens and S. S. Shipp, "Market-Driven Strategies for Competitive Advantage," *Business Horizons,* January–February 1991, pp. 53–61 for a discussion of the relationship between strategic and market planning.

Figure 1–5 *Relating the Marketing Plan to the Strategic Plan*

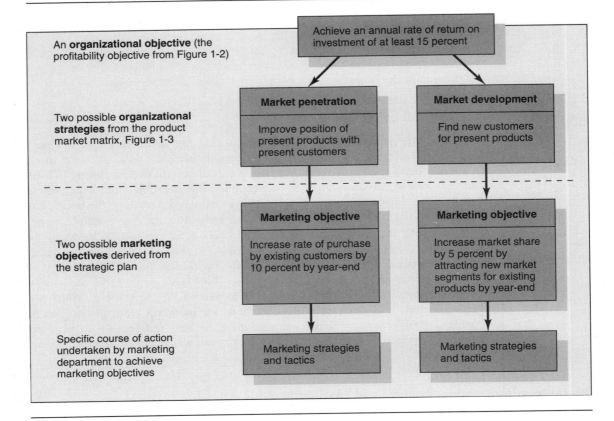

An **organizational objective** (the profitability objective from Figure 1-2)

Achieve an annual rate of return on investment of at least 15 percent

Two possible **organizational strategies** from the product market matrix, Figure 1-3

Market penetration

Improve position of present products with present customers

Market development

Find new customers for present products

Two possible **marketing objectives** derived from the strategic plan

Marketing objective

Increase rate of purchase by existing customers by 10 percent by year-end

Marketing objective

Increase market share by 5 percent by attracting new market segments for existing products by year-end

Specific course of action undertaken by marketing department to achieve marketing objectives

Marketing strategies and tactics

Marketing strategies and tactics

pany in a market to gain the greatest advantage over the competition. A critical prerequisite to making successful decisions is gaining the necessary information regarding each market opportunity. Toward this end, marketing managers are involved in the strategic planning process in two important ways: (1) they often influence the strategic planning process by providing inputs in the form of information and suggestions relating to their particular products, product lines, and areas of responsibility; and (2) they must be aware of what the process of strategic planning involves as well as the results because everything they do, the marketing objectives and strategies they develop, must be derived from the strategic plan. There is rarely a strategic planning question or decision that does not have marketing implications.

Thus, if strategic planning is done properly, it will result in a clearly defined blueprint for managerial action at all levels in the organization. Figure 1–5 illustrates the hierarchy of objectives and strategies using one possible objective and two strategies from the strategic plan (above the dotted line) and illustrating how these relate to elements of the marketing plan (below the dotted line). Many others could have been developed, but our purpose is to illustrate how the marketing plan must be derived from and contribute to the achievement of the strategic plan.

CONCLUSION

This chapter has described the marketing management process and provided an outline for many of the remaining chapters in this text. At this point it would be useful for the reader to review Figure 1–4 as well as the Table of Contents. This review will enable you to relate the content and progression of material to the marketing management process.

ADDITIONAL READINGS

Curren, Mary T.; Valerie S. Folkes; and Joel H. Steckel. "Explanations for Successful and Unsuccessful Marketing Decisions: The Decision Maker's Perspective." *Journal of Marketing,* April 1992, pp. 18–31.

German, Myna; Donald A. Donohue, Jr.; and Steven P. Schnaars. "A Chink in Marketing's Armor: Strategy above Tactics." *Business Horizons,* March–April 1991, pp. 74–78.

Kaplan, Robert S., and David P. Norton. "The Balanced Scorecard—Measures That Drive Performance." *Harvard Business Review,* January–February 1992, pp. 71–79.

Kohli, Ajay K., and Bernard J. Jaworski. "Market Orientation: The Construct, Research Propositions, and Managerial Implications." *Journal of Marketing,* April 1990, pp. 1–18.

Lichtenthal, J. David, and David T. Wilson. "Becoming Market Oriented." *Journal of Business Research* volume 24 (1992), pp. 191–207.

McDonald, Malcolm H. B. "Ten Barriers to Marketing Planning." *Journal of Business and Industrial Marketing,* Winter 1992, pp. 5–18.

Narver, John C., and Stanley F. Slater. "The Effect of a Market Orientation on Business Profitability." *Journal of Marketing,* October 1990, pp. 20–35.

Turpin, Dominique V. "The Strategic Persistence of the Japanese Firm." *The Journal of Business Strategy,* January/February 1992, pp. 49–52.

Portfolio Models

Portfolio models have become a valuable aid to marketing managers in their efforts to develop effective marketing plans. The use of these models has become widespread as marketing managers face a situation that can best be described as "more products, less time, and less money." More specifically, (1) as the number of products a firm produces expands, the time available for developing marketing plans for each product decreases; (2) at a strategic level, management must make resource allocation decisions across lines of products and, in diversified organizations, across different lines of business; and (3) when resources are limited (which they usually are), the process of deciding which strategic business units (SBUs) to emphasize becomes very complex. In such situations, portfolio models can be very useful.

Portfolio analysis is not a new idea. Banks manage loan portfolios seeking to balance risks and yields. Individuals who are serious investors usually have a portfolio of various kinds of investments (common stocks, preferred stocks, bank accounts, and the like), each with different characteristics of risk, growth, and rate of return. The investor seeks to manage the portfolio to maximize whatever objectives he or she might have. Applying this same idea, most organizations have a wide range of products, product lines, and businesses, each with different growth rates and returns. Similar to the investor, managers should seek a desirable balance among alternative SBUs. Specifically, management should seek to develop a business portfolio that will assure long-run profits and cash flow.

Portfolio models can be used to classify SBUs to determine the future cash contributions that can be expected from each SBU as well as the future resource requirements that each will require. Remember, depending on the organization, an SBU could be a single product, product line, division, or distinct business. While there are many different types of portfolio models, they generally examine the competitive position of the SBU and the chances for improving the SBU's contribution to profitability and cash flow.

There are several portfolio analysis techniques. Two of the most widely used are discussed in this appendix. To truly appreciate the concept of portfolio analysis, however, we must briefly review the development of portfolio theory.

A REVIEW OF PORTFOLIO THEORY

The interest in developing aids for managers in the selection of strategy was spurred by an organization known as the Boston Consulting Group over 25 years ago. Its ideas, which will be discussed shortly, and many of those that followed were based on the concept of experience curves.

Experience curves are similar in concept to learning curves. Learning curves were developed to express the idea that the number of labor hours it takes to produce one unit of a particular product declines in a predictable manner as the number of units produced increases. Hence, an accurate estimation of how long it takes to produce the 100th unit is possible if the production time for the 1st and 10th units are known.

The concept of experience curves was derived from the concept of learning curves. Experience curves were first widely discussed in the ongoing Profit Impact of Marketing Strategies (PIMS) study conducted by the Strategic Planning Institute. The PIMS project studies 150 firms with more than 1,000 individual business units. Its major focus is on determining which environmental and internal firm variables influence the firm's return on investment (ROI) and cash flow. The researchers have concluded that seven categories of variables appear to influence the return on investment: (1) competitive position; (2) industry/market environment; (3) budget allocation; (4) capital structure; (5) production processes; (6) company characteristics; and (7) "change action" factors.[34]

The experience curve includes all costs associated with a product and implies that the per-unit cost of a product should fall, due to cumulative experience, as production volume increases. In a given industry, therefore, the producer with the largest volume and corresponding market share should have the lowest marginal cost. This leader in market share should be able to underprice competitors, discourage entry into the market by potential competitors, and, as a result, achieve an acceptable return on investment. The linkage of experience to cost to price to market share to ROI is exhibited in Figure A–1. The Boston Consulting Group's view of the experience curve led the members to develop what has become known as the BCG Portfolio Model.

THE BCG MODEL

The BCG is based on the assumption that profitability and cash flow will be closely related to sales volume. Thus, in this model, SBUs are classified in terms of their relative market share and the growth rate of the market the SBU is in. Using these dimensions, products are either classified as stars, cash cows, dogs, or question marks. The BCG model is presented in Figure A–2.

---

[34]George S. Day and David B. Montgomery, "Diagnosing the Experience Curve," *Journal of Marketing,* Spring 1983, pp. 44–58.

Figure A–1 *Experience Curve and Resulting Profit Curve*

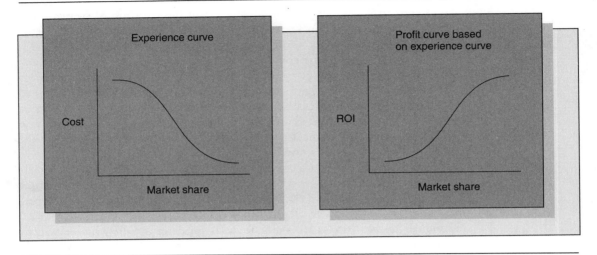

— *Stars* are SBUs with a high share of a high-growth market. Because high-growth markets attract competition, such SBUs are usually cash users because they are growing and because the firm needs to protect their market share position.

— *Cash cows* are often market leaders, but the market they are in is not growing rapidly. Because these SBUs have a high share of a low-growth market, they are cash generators for the firm.

— *Dogs* are SBUs that have a low share of a low-growth market. If the SBU has a very loyal group of customers, it may be a source of profits and cash. Usually, dogs are not large sources of cash.

— *Question marks* are SBUs with a low share of a high-growth market. They have great potential but require great resources if the firm is to successfully build market share.

As you can see, a firm with 10 SBUs will usually have a portfolio that includes some of each of the above. Having developed this analysis, management must determine what role each SBU should assume. Four basic objectives are possible:

1. *Build share*. This objective sacrifices immediate earnings to improve market share. It is appropriate for promising question marks whose share has to grow if they are ever to become stars.

2. *Hold share*. This objective seeks to preserve the SBU's market share. It is very appropriate for strong cash cows to ensure that they can continue to yield a large cash flow.

3. *Harvest*. Here, the objective seeks to increase the product's short-term cash flow without concern for the long-run impact. It allows market share to

Figure A–2   *The Boston Consulting Group Portfolio Model*

Relative Market Share

	High	Low
High (Market Growth Rate)	Stars	Question marks
Low	Cash cows	Dogs

decline in order to maximize earnings and cash flow. It is an appropriate objective for weak cash cows, weak question marks, and dogs.

4. *Divest.* This objective involves selling or divesting the SBU because better investment opportunities exist elsewhere. It is very appropriate for dogs and those question marks the firm cannot afford to finance for growth.

There have been several major criticisms of the BCG Portfolio Model, revolving around its focus on market share and market growth as the primary indicators of preference. First, the BCG model assumes market growth is uncontrollable.[35] As a result, managers can become preoccupied with setting market share objectives, instead of trying to grow the market. Second, assumptions regarding market share as a critical factor affecting firm performance may not hold true, especially in international markets.[36] Third, the BCG model assumes that the major source of SBU financing comes from internal means. While the above criticisms are valid ones, the usefulness of the BCG model in assessing the strategic position of SBUs has enabled it to continue to be utilized by managers, especially of large firms, across all industries.[37]

---

[35]P. Rajan Varadarajan, Terry Clark, and William M. Pride, "Controlling the Uncontrollable: Managing Your Market Environment," *Sloan Management Review,* Winter 1992, pp. 39–47.

[36]Reed E. Nelson, "Is There Strategy in Brazil?" *Business Horizons,* July–August 1992, pp. 15–23.

[37]Donald L. McCabe and V. K. Narayanan, "The Life Cycle of the PIMS and BCG Models," *Industrial Marketing Management,* November 1991, pp. 347–352.

THE GENERAL ELECTRIC MODEL

Although the BCG model can be useful, it does assume that market share is the sole determinant of an SBU's profitability. Also, in projecting market growth rates, a manager should carefully analyze the factors that influence sales and any opportunities for influencing industry sales.

Some firms have developed alternative portfolio models to incorporate more information about market opportunities and competitive positions. The GE model is one of these. The GE model emphasizes all the potential sources of strength, not just market share, and all of the factors that influence the long-

Figure A–3 *The General Electric Portfolio Model*

		Business Strength		
		Strong	**Average**	**Weak**
	High	A	A	B
Industry Attractiveness	**Medium**	A	B	C
	Low	B	C	C

Figure A–4 *Components of Industry Attractiveness and Business Strength at GE*

Industry Attractiveness	**Business Strength**

Market size.
Market growth.
Profitability.
Cyclicality.
Ability to recover from inflation.
World scope.
	Market position:
	  Domestic market share.
	  World market share.
	  Share growth.
	  Share compared with leading
	    competitor.
	
	Competitive strengths:
	  Quality leadership.
	  Technology.
	  Marketing.
	  Relative profitability.

term attractiveness of a market, not just its growth rate. As Figure A–3 indicates, all SBUs are classified in terms of *business strength and industry attractiveness*. Figure A–4 presents a list of items that can be used to position SBUs in the matrix.

Industry attractiveness is a composite index made up of such factors as those listed in Figure A–4. For example: *market size*—the larger the market, the more attractive it would be; *market growth*—high-growth markets are more attractive than low-growth markets; *profitability*—high-profit-margin markets are more attractive than low-profit-margin industries.

Business strength is a composite index made up of such factors as those listed in Figure A–4. For example: *market share*—the higher the SBU's share of market, the greater its business strength; *quality leadership*—the higher the SBU's quality compared to competitors, the greater its business strength; *share compared with leading competitor*—the closer the SBU's share to the market leader, the greater its business strength.

Once the SBUs are classified, they are placed on the grid (Figure A–3). Priority "A" SBUs (often called *the green zone*) are those in the three cells at the upper left, indicating that these are SBUs high in both industry attractiveness and business strength, and that the firm should "build share." Priority "B" SBUs (often called *the yellow zone*) are those medium in both industry attractiveness and business strength. The firm will usually decide to "hold share" on these SBUs. Priority "C" SBUs are those in the three cells at the lower right (often called *the red zone*). These SBUs are low in both industry attractiveness and business strength. The firm will usually decide to *harvest* or *divest* these SBUs.

Whether the BCG, the GE model, or a variation of these models is used, some analyses must be made of the firm's current portfolio of SBUs as part of any strategic planning effort. Marketing must get its direction from the organization's strategic plan.

Marketing Information, Research, and Understanding the Target Market

Chapter 2

Marketing Decision Support Systems and Marketing Research

It is obvious that the American business system has been capable of producing a vast quantity of goods and services. However, in the past two decades the American business system has also become extremely capable of producing massive amounts of information and data. In fact, the last few decades have been referred to as the "Information Era" and the "Age of Information."

This situation is a complete reversal from what previously existed. In the past, marketing executives did not have to deal with an oversupply of information for decision-making purposes. In most cases they gathered what little data they could and hoped that their decisions would be reasonably good. In fact, it was for this reason that marketing research came to be recognized as an extremely valuable staff function. It provided marketing management with information where previously there had been little or none and, thereby, alleviated to a great extent the paucity of information for marketing decision making. However, marketing management in many companies has failed to store marketing information, and much valuable marketing information is lost when marketing personnel change jobs or companies.

Today, some marketing managers feel buried by the deluge of information and data that comes across their desks. How can it be, then, that marketing managers complain that they have insufficient or inappropriate information on which to base their everyday operating decisions? Specifically, managers complain that:

1. There is too much marketing information of the wrong kind and not enough of the right kind.
2. Marketing information is so dispersed throughout the company that great effort is usually needed to locate simple facts.

3. Vital information is sometimes suppressed by other executives or subordinates for personal reasons.
4. Vital information often arrives too late to be useful.
5. Information often arrives in a form that provides no idea of its accuracy, and there is no one to turn to for confirmation.

Marketing management requires current, reliable information before it can function efficiently. Because of this need, and the information explosion of past decades, many large corporations have banked their total marketing knowledge in computers. Well-designed marketing decision support systems (MDSS) can eliminate corporate losses of millions of dollars from lost information and lost opportunities.

This chapter is concerned with marketing decision support systems and marketing research. Since the two concepts are easily confused, it is important initially to distinguish one from the other. In general terms, a marketing decision support system is concerned with the continuous gathering, processing, and utilization of pertinent information for decision-making purposes. The primary objective of the MDSS is to ensure that the right information is available to the right decision maker at the right time. Marketing research, on the other hand, usually focuses on a specific marketing problem with the objective of providing information for a particular decision. As such, marketing research is an integral part of the overall marketing decision support system but usually is project oriented rather than a continuous process.

MARKETING DECISION SUPPORT SYSTEMS

A marketing decision support system is a new type of marketing information system. This type of information system is designed to support all phases of marketing decision making—from problem identification to choosing the relevant data to work with, picking the approach to be used in making the decision, and evaluating alternative courses of action. This type of information system can be defined as:

> a coordinated collection of data, system tools, and techniques with supporting software and hardware by which an organization gathers and interprets relevant information from business and the environment and turns it into a basis for making management decisions.[1]

Figure 2–1 illustrates the concept of an MDSS. There are two main changes depicted in this figure: (1) the conversion of data to information; and (2) the conversion of information to action. The first conversion is the task of the marketing information center, while the second is the major purpose of marketing decision making.

---

[1]Peter D. Bennett, ed., *Dictionary of Marketing Terms* (Chicago: American Marketing Association, 1988), p. 53.

HIGHLIGHT 2–1

Suggestions for Developing an MDSS

The following is a list of suggestions to aid in the effective implementation of an MDSS.

1. Develop small systems first before coordinating them into an overall system.
2. Develop systems relevant to current management practices and organizational structures.
3. Develop decision support system skills internally and do not rely too heavily on outside experts.
4. Involve users of the system in its design and implementation.

5. Build a flexible system to meet the information needs of various levels of management and types of managers.
6. Monitor early usage of the system to ensure success and make sure future users of the system are aware of the success.
7. Build the system in an evolutionary manner, adding complex models only after data storage and retrieval systems are successfully in place.

Source: From *Principles of Marketing,* 3rd ed., pp. 218–19 by Thomas C. Kinnear and Kenneth L. Bernhardt. Copyright © 1990, 1986 by Scott, Foresman and Company. Reprinted by permission of Harper Collins, Publishers.

Figure 2–1   *The Marketing Decision Support System*

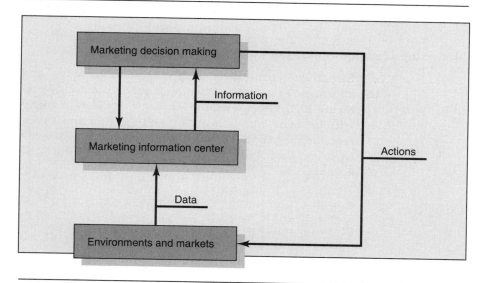

The Marketing Information Center

Although the growth of the concept of a marketing decision support system has been fairly recent, most experts agree that a single, separate marketing information center must exist to centralize responsibility for marketing information within the firm. This is necessary because both the users and suppliers of such information are widely scattered throughout the organization, and some unit is needed to oversee the entire operation.

The general purpose of this organizational unit is to maintain, as well as to improve and upgrade, the accuracy, completeness, and timeliness of information for marketing management decisions. Operationally, this means that the information center must gather raw data from various environments and markets and process them so they can be obtained and analyzed by marketing executives. Data must be gathered from both internal and external sources. Internally, such data as sales, costs, and profits, as well as other company reports, need to be converted to information and stored in the computer. Externally, data from trade journals, magazines, newspapers, government publications, and other sources of pertinent information used by marketing executives for decision making also must be converted and stored.

A critical point here is that the MDSS converts raw data into information that marketing management can actually use for making intelligent decisions. An MDSS must produce information in a form marketing executives can understand when it is needed and have it under the manager's control. In other words, a key distinction that separates an MDSS from other types of marketing information systems is that an MDSS has the direct and primary objective of supporting marketing management decision making.[2] Figure 2–2 provides examples of two firms with conventional MISs and two firms with MDSSs to illustrate this important difference.

Marketing Decision Making

Earlier we stated that the main purpose of marketing executives is to convert information to actions through the process of decision making. Note that, in Figure 2–1, two up-and-down arrows connect marketing decision making with the marketing information center. These arrows represent an important aspect of the MDSS (i.e., it is an *interactive system* in which marketing executives sit at computer terminals and actively analyze information and convert it to actions).

---

[2]See Gilbert A. Churchill, Jr., *Marketing Research: Methodological Foundations* 5th ed. (Hinsdale, Ill.: Dryden Press, 1991), chap. 18. Also see George M. Zinkhan, Erich A. Joachimsthaler, and Thomas C. Kinnear, "Individual Differences and Marketing Decision Support System Usage and Satisfaction," *Journal of Marketing Research*, May 1987, pp. 208–14.

Figure 2–2 *Examples of MISs and MDSSs*

A Marketing Information System (MIS) at Savin Corporation

Savin Corporation has installed a computer terminal in each of its warehouses to keep track of every item in its inventory. The system identifies the quantity on hand, the location and movement of stock, and the status of all orders. The system is used to plan shipments, locate single items in inventory, and locate customer records.

A Marketing Information System (MIS) at United Services Automobile Association

The United Services Automobile Association, the nation's eighth largest insurer of passenger cars, purchased a $4 million system that now contains virtually all of the company's written records. When a customer reports an accident, an adjuster can call up the customer's file, check the coverage, and keep track of all the paperwork through the final settlement of the claim. The company figures that it used to take five people a day-and-a-half to perform tasks that one person now handles in 20 minutes.

A Marketing Decision Support System (MDSS) at Crocker National Bank

The Crocker National Bank in San Francisco has purchased desktop terminals for most of its top-level executives. Each terminal is tapped into the huge computers that record all bank transactions. The executives are able to make comparisons, analyze problems, and prepare charts and tables in response to simple commands. For example, they can analyze emerging trends in deposits and loans and monitor the influence of various interest rates and loan maturities.

A Marketing Decision Support System (MDSS) at Gould, Inc.

Gould, Inc., has developed a decision support system to help managers retrieve, manipulate, and display information needed for making decisions. The system combines large visual display and video terminals with a computerized information system. The system is designed solely to assist managers to make comparisons and analyze problems for decision-making purposes. The MDSS instantly prepares tables and color charts in response to simple commands.

In previous types of marketing information systems, the information center often attempted to prepare reports to meet the individual needs of different marketing executives at different levels in the organization. More often than not, such attempts provided too much information of the wrong kind and not enough information of the right kind. However, in addition to the flexibility, timeliness, and detail provided by an MDSS, such problems do not occur because marketing executives themselves retrieve and manipulate the information.

Many experts believe that, in a few years, most marketing executives will be sharing their desk space with a personal computer. Personal computers have the capability of increasing both the productivity of marketing managers and the quality of their decisions. First, the capacity of the computers to extract, process, and analyze data swiftly and accurately is awesome. Second, computers have gotten smaller, faster, and smarter in a shorter time than any other technological innovation in history. A desktop personal computer can solve ordinary arithmetic problems 18 times faster than the world's first large-scale computer built less than 50 years ago (weighing 30 tons). Finally, computers have become extremely inexpensive in comparison to earlier models. Just 30 years ago a medium-sized computer cost a quarter of a million dollars. A firm can now buy a desktop computer with three times the memory capacity for less than $2,000. While it may take some time for marketing executives to learn to use the equipment, the potential for better, more profitable decision making may outweigh the brief inconvenience.

MARKETING RESEARCH

Marketing research should be an integral part of a marketing decision support system. In essence, marketing research combines insights and intuition with the research process to provide information for making marketing decisions. In general, marketing research can be defined as:

> the function that links the consumer, customer, and public to the marketer through information—information used to identify and define marketing opportunities and problems; generate, refine, and evaluate marketing actions; monitor marketing performance; and improve understanding of marketing as a process. Marketing research specifies the information required to address these issues; designs the method for collecting information; manages and implements the data collection process; analyzes the results; and communicates the findings and their implications.[3]

Today's marketing managers should understand the role of research in decision making. It cannot be overstated that *marketing research is an aid to decision making and not a substitute for it.* In other words, marketing research does not make decisions but it can substantially increase the probability that the best decision will be made. Unfortunately, too often marketing managers view marketing research reports as the final answer to their problems. Instead, marketing managers should recognize that (1) even the most carefully controlled research projects can be fraught with pitfalls and (2) decisions should be made in the light of their own knowledge and experience and other factors that are not explicitly considered in the research project. The problems that the Coca-Cola Company faced when it dropped its original formula and introduced New Coke were brought about by both faulty marketing research and a failure of Coke executives to use sound judgment in interpreting the research results.[4]

---

[3]Peter D. Bennett, ed., *Dictionary of Marketing Terms* (Chicago: American Marketing Association, 1988), pp. 117–18.

[4]For a complete discussion of these issues, see Robert F. Hartley, *Marketing Mistakes,* 4th ed. (New York: John Wiley & Sons, 1989), pp. 221–36.

HIGHLIGHT 2–2

Marketing Research that Influenced Marketing Strategies

Marketing research can be a useful aid in decision making. Below are several examples of marketing research that helped firms develop their marketing strategies.

Fischer-Price

In an attempt to expand its product line, Fisher-Price, the very successful toy maker, had some of its executives peer through a one-way mirror and eavesdrop for four hours as a dozen women in Cleveland complained about their battles with the zippers, buckles, buttons, and snaps on kids' clothing. The subsidiary of Quaker Oats used this information and the results of other similar focus groups to design a line of preschool playwear that does not include a button or zipper; rather, just about all of the fasteners are Velcro. The new line is consistent with the company's philosophy of identifying areas in which small children are not being well served and then designing a nearly indestructible product that is easy to use.

Eastman Kodak

The Eastman Kodak Company, interested in altering a relatively flat sales curve and knowing that amateur photographers goof on more than 2 billion pictures a year, had its technical researchers look at 10,000 photos to see what kinds of things users were doing wrong. The study led to a number of design ideas for the Kodak disc camera that helped eliminate almost one-half of the out-of-focus and underexposed shots. First introduced in 1982, the disc camera has been one of the most successful new products in Kodak history.

Coca-Cola

As a part of Coca-Cola's age-old strategy of making its soft drinks available as widely as possible, the company test-marketed BreakMate in 30 U.S. cities and overseas. BreakMate is a compact machine that chills water, carbonates it, mixes it with Coca-Cola syrup, and dispenses it into a 6½-ounce cup. The test marketing involved placing the dispensers in small offices, which heretofore had been largely unserved by soft-drink companies. Standard soft-drink vending machines are profitable only where there are at least 45 employees because of the cost of servicing them in comparison to the volume of sales they generate. Even in some big offices, vending machines are a long walk or an elevator ride from many departments. Coke executives believed that BreakMate could be profitable in offices or departments with as few as five workers. If the soft drink was immediately at hand, people would drink more of it. One of the purposes of the test was to examine that belief as well as to check how the machine performed in a largely unmonitored environment.

Source: Adapted excerpts from *Marketing Research: Methodological Foundations,* Fifth Edition by Gilbert A. Churchill, Jr., copyright © 1991 by Holt, Rinehart and Winston, Inc., p. 3–4 reprinted by permission of the publisher.

Although marketing research does not make decisions, it is a direct means of reducing risks associated with managing the marketing mix and long-term marketing planning. In fact, a company's return on investment from marketing research is a function of the extent to which research output reduces the risk inherent in decision making. For example, marketing research can play an important role in reducing new product failure costs by evaluating consumer acceptance of a product prior to full-scale introduction.

In a highly competitive economy, a firm's survival depends on the marketing manager's ability to make sound decisions, to outguess competitors, to anticipate consumer needs, to forecast business conditions, and to plan for company growth. Marketing research is one tool to help accomplish these tasks. Research is also vital for managerial control, because without appropriate data, the validity of past decisions on the performance of certain elements in the marketing system (e.g., the performance of the sales force or advertising) cannot be evaluated reliably.

Although many of the technical aspects of marketing research, such as sampling design or statistical analysis, can be delegated to experts, the process of marketing research begins and ends with the marketing manager. In the beginning of a research project, it is the marketing manager's responsibility to work with researchers to define the problem carefully. When the research project is completed, the application of the results in terms of decision alternatives rests primarily with the marketing manager.[5] For these reasons, and since the marketing manager must be able to communicate with researchers throughout the course of the project, it is vital for managers to understand the research process from the researcher's point of view.

The Research Process

Marketing research can be viewed as a systematic process for obtaining information to aid in decision making. Although there are many different types of marketing research, the framework illustrated in Figure 2–3 represents a general approach to defining the research process. Each element of this process will be briefly discussed.

Purpose of the research

The first step in the research process is to determine explicitly the purpose of the research. This may well be much more difficult than it sounds. Quite often a situation or problem is recognized as needing research, yet the nature of the problem is not clear or well defined. Thus, an investigation is required

[5]For a discussion of the use of research findings in marketing decision making, see Rohit Deshpande, "The Organizational Context of Market Research Use," *Journal of Marketing,* Fall 1982, pp. 91–101. Also see Rohit Deshpande and Gerald Zaltman, "A Comparison of Factors Affecting Use of Marketing Information in Consumer and Industrial Firms," *Journal of Marketing Research,* February 1987, pp. 114–19.

Figure 2-3   *The Five Ps of the Research Process*

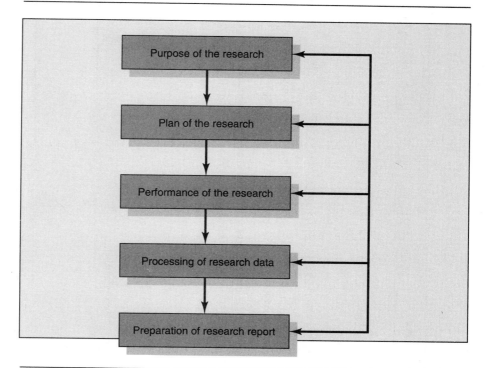

to clarify the problem or situation. This investigation includes such things as interviewing corporate executives, reviewing records, and studying existing information related to the problem. At the end of this stage the researcher should know (1) the current situation; (2) the nature of the problem; and (3) the specific question or questions the research is to find answers to—that is, why the research is being conducted.

Plan of the research

The first step in the research plan is to formalize the specific purpose of the study. Once this is accomplished, the sequencing of tasks and responsibilities for accomplishing the research are spelled out in detail. This stage is critical since decisions are made that determine the who, what, when, where, and how of the research study.

An initial decision in this stage of the process is the type of data that will be required. The two major types of data are primary and secondary. Primary data is data that must be collected from original sources for the purposes of the study. Secondary data is information that has been previously collected for some other purpose but can be used for the purposes of the study.

HIGHLIGHT 2–3

A Comparison of Five Methods of Marketing Research

	Definition	Advantages	Disadvantages
Observation	Systematic description of behavior.	Documents the variety of ongoing behavior. Unobtrusive observation captures what happens naturally, when no experimenter is present.	Time consuming. Requires careful training of observers. Observer may interfere with behavior and alter what is happening.
Case study	In-depth description of a single person, family, or organization.	Focuses on the complexity and uniqueness of the individual.	May lack generalizability. Data may reflect the interests and perspective of the investigator.
Survey research	Asking questions to a comparatively large number of people about their opinions, attitudes, or behavior.	Permits data collection from large numbers of subjects.	The way questions are asked can influence the answers. Survey response may not be directly related to behavior.
Experimentation	An analysis of cause-effect relations by manipulating some conditions and holding others constant.	Permits statements about causality. Permits control and isolation of specific variables.	Laboratory findings may not be applicable to other settings.
Correlational research	Assessing the strength of relationship among variables.	Determines whether information on variable A can be used to predict variable B.	Difficult to infer causality. Cannot detect nonlinear relationships.

Source: Adapted from P. R. Newman and B. M. Newman, *Principles of Psychology* (Homewood, Ill.: Dorsey Press, 1983), p. 28.

HIGHLIGHT 2–4

Types of Questions that Marketing Research Can Help Answer

I. *Planning.*
  A. What kinds of people buy our product? Where do they live? How much do they earn? How many of them are there?
  B. Is the market for our product increasing or decreasing? Are there promising markets that we have not yet reached?
  C. Are there markets for our products in other countries?

II. *Problem Solving.*
  A. Product
    1. Which, of various product designs, is likely to be the most successful?
    2. What kind of packaging should we use for our product?
  B. Price
    1. What price should we charge for our new product?
    2. As production costs decline, should we lower our prices or try to develop a higher-quality product?
  C. Place
    1. Where, and by whom, should our product be sold?

    2. What kinds of incentives should we offer to induce dealers to push our product?
  D. Promotion
    1. How effective is our advertising? Are the right people seeing it? How does it compare with the competition's advertising?
    2. What kinds of sales promotional devices—coupons, contests, rebates, and so forth—should we employ?
    3. What combination of media—newspapers, radio, television, magazines—should we use?

III. *Control.*
  A. What is our market share overall? In each geographic area? By each customer type?
  B. Are customers satisfied with our product? How is our record for service? Are there many returns?
  C. How does the public perceive our company? What is our reputation with dealers?

Source: Gilbert A. Churchill, Jr., *Basic Marketing Research* 2nd ed. (Hinsdale, Ill.: Dryden Press, 1992), p. 9.

If the research project requires primary data, decisions have to be made concerning the following issues:

1. How will the data be collected? Personal interviews? Mail questionnaires? Telephone interviews?
2. How much data is needed?
3. What measures will be used, and how will they be checked for reliability and validity?
4. Who will design the measures and collect the data?

Figure 2–4 *Sample Research Plan*

I *Tentative projective title.*

II *Statement of the problem.*

One or two sentences to outline or to describe the general problem under consideration.

III *Define and delimit the problem.*

Here the writer states the purpose(s) and scope of the problem. *Purpose* refers to goals or objectives. Closely related to this is *justification*. Sometimes this is a separate step, depending on the urgency of the task. *Scope* refers to the actual limitations of the research effort; in other words, what is *not* going to be investigated. Here is the point where the writer spells out the various hypotheses to be investigated or the questions to be answered.

IV *Outline.*

Generally, this is a tentative framework for the entire project by topics. It should be flexible enough to accommodate unforeseen difficulties, show statistical tables in outline form, and also show graphs planned. Tables should reflect the hypotheses.

V *Method and data sources.*

The types of data to be sought (primary, secondary) are briefly identified. A brief explanation of how the necessary information or data will be gathered (e.g., surveys, experiments, library sources) is given. *Sources* refer to the actual depositories for the information, whether from government publications, company records, actual people, and so forth. If measurements are involved, such as consumers' attitudes, the techniques for making such measurements are stated. All of the techniques (statistical and nonstatistical) should be mentioned and discussed about their relevance for the task at hand. The nature of the problem will probably indicate the types of technqiues to be employed, such as factor analysis, depth interviews, or focus groups.

VI *Sample design.*

This provides the limits of the universe or population to be studied and how it will be listed (or prepared). The writer specifies the population, states the sample size, whether sample stratification will be employed, and how. If a nonrandom sample is to be used, the justification and the type of sampling strategy to be employed, such as convenience sample, are stated.

VII *Data collection forms.*

The forms to be employed in gathering the data should be discussed and, if possible, included in the plan. For surveys, this will involve either a questionnaire or an interview schedule. For other types of methods, the forms could include IBM cards, inventory forms, psychological tests, and so forth. The plan should state how these instruments have been or will be validated, and the reader should be given some indication of their reliability and validity.

VIII *Personnel requirements.*

This provides a complete list of all personnel who will be required, indicating exact jobs, time duration, and expected rate of pay. Assignments should be made indicating each person's responsibility and authority.

IX *Phases of the study with a time schedule.*

This is a detailed outline of the plan to complete the study. The entire study should be broken into workable pieces. Then, considering the person who will be employed in each phase, their qualifications and experience, and so forth, the time in months for the job is estimated. Some jobs may overlap. This plan will help in estimating the work months required. The overall time for the project should allow for time overlaps on some jobs.

Figure 2–4 *(continued)*

IX Phases of the study with a time schedule—cont'd.
Illustration:
1. Preliminary investigation—two months.
2. Final test of questionnaire—one month.
3. Sample selection—one month.
4. Mail questionnaires, field follow-up, and so forth—four months.
5. Additional phases.

X *Tabulation plans.*
This is a discussion of editing and proof of questionnaires, card punching, and the type of computer analysis. An outline of some of the major tables required is very important.

XI *Cost estimate for doing the study.*
Personnel requirements are combined with time on different phases to estimate total personnel costs. Estimates on travel, materials, supplies, drafting, computer charges, and printing and mailing costs must also be included. If an overhead charge is required by the administration, it should be calculated and added to the subtotal of the above items.

---

5. Where will the data be collected? Nationally? Regionally? Locally? At home? At work?

6. When and for how long will data be collected?

If secondary data will suffice for the research question(s), similar decisions have to be made. However, since the data are already in existence, the task is much simpler (and cheaper). For example, most of the sources of secondary data listed in Section 5 of this text are available in a public or university library.

In addition to determining data requirements, the research plan also specifies the method of data analysis, procedures for processing and interpreting the data, and the structure of the final report. In other words, the entire research project is sequenced, and responsibility for the various tasks is assigned. Thus, the research plan provides the framework for the coordination and control of the entire project.

When the research plan is fully specified, the time and money costs of the project are estimated. If management views the benefits of the research as worth the costs, the project proceeds to the next phase. A sample research plan is presented in Figure 2–4.

Performance of the research

Performance is used here in the narrow sense: of preparing for data collection and actually collecting the data. It is at this point that the research plan is put into action.

The preparations obviously depend on the type of data desired and method of data collection. For primary research, questions and questionnaire items must be pretested and validated. In addition, preparations for mail surveys include such things as sample selection, questionnaire printing, and envelope

Figure 2–5 *Six Criteria for Evaluating Marketing Research Reports*

1. Under what conditions was the study made? The report should provide:
   a. Full statement of the problems to be investigated by the study.
   b. Source of financing for the study.
   c. Names of organizations participating in the study, together with their qualifications and vested interests.
   d. Exact time period covered in data collection.
   e. Definitions of terms employed.
   f. Copies of data collection instruments.
   g. Source of collateral data.
   h. Complete statement of method.
2. Has the questionnaire been well designed?
3. Has the interviewing been adequately and reliably done?
4. Has the best sampling plan been followed, or has the best experimental design been used?
5. Was there adequate supervision and control over the editing, coding, and tabulating?
6. Have the conclusions been drawn in a logical and forthright manner?

and postage considerations. For telephone or personal interviews, such things as interviewer scoring forms, instructions, and scheduling must be taken care of. For secondary data, such things as data recording procedures and instructions need attention.

In terms of actual data collection, a cardinal rule is to obtain and record the maximal amount of useful information, subject to the constraints of time, money, and interviewee privacy. Failure to obtain and record data clearly can obviously lead to a poor research study, while failure to consider the rights of subjects or interviewees raises both ethical and practical questions. Thus, both the objectives and constraints of data collection must be closely monitored.

Processing research data

Processing research data includes the preparation of data for analysis and the actual analysis of the data. Preparations include such things as editing and structuring the data, and perhaps coding and preparing it for computer analysis. Data sets should be clearly labeled to ensure that they are not misinterpreted or misplaced. The data are then analyzed according to the procedure specified in the research plan and are interpreted according to standard norms of the analysis.

Preparation of research report

The research report is a complete statement of everything accomplished relative to the research project and includes a writeup of each of the previous stages. Figure 2–5 illustrates the types of questions the researcher should ask prior to submitting the report to the appropriate decision maker.

HIGHLIGHT 2-5

A Comparison of Survey Data Collection Techniques

Basis of comparison	Mail surveys	Telephone surveys	Personal interview surveys
Cost per completed survey	Usually the least expensive, assuming adequate return rate	Moderately expensive, assuming reasonable completion rate	Most expensive because of interviewer's time and travel expenses
Ability to probe and ask complex questions	Little, since self-administered format must be short and simple	Some, since interviewer can probe and elaborate on questions to a degree	Much, since interviewer can show visual materials, gain rapport, and probe
Opportunity for interviewer to bias results	None, since form is completed without interviewer	Some because of voice inflection of interviewer	Significant because of voice and facial expressions of interviewer
Anonymity given respondent	Complete, since no signature is required	Some because of telephone contact	Little because of face-to-face contact

Source: Eric N. Berkowitz, Roger A. Kerin, Steven W. Hartley, and William Rudelius, *Marketing,* 3rd ed. (Homewood Ill.: Richard D. Irwin, 1992), p. 182.

The importance of clear and unambiguous report writing cannot be overstressed, since the research is meaningless if it cannot be communicated. Often the researcher must trade off the apparent precision of scientific jargon for everyday language that the decision maker can understand. It should always be remembered that research is an aid for decision making and not a substitute for it.

Problems in the research process

Although the foregoing discussion presented the research process in a simplified framework, this does not mean that conducting research is a simple task. There are many problems and difficulties that must be overcome if a research study is to be of value. For example, consider the difficulties in one type of marketing research, *test marketing*.

The major goal of most test marketing is to measure new product sales on a limited basis where competitive retaliation and other factors are allowed to operate freely. In this way, future sales potential can be estimated. Test market research is a vital element in new product marketing. Listed below are a number of problem areas that can invalidate test market study results.[6]

1. Representative test areas are improperly selected from the standpoint of size, geographical location, population characteristics, and promotional facilities.
2. Sample size and design are incorrectly formulated because of ignorance, budget constraints, or an improper understanding of the test problem.
3. Pretest measurements of competitive brand's sales are not made, which means that the researcher has no realistic base to use for comparison purposes.
4. Attempts are not made to control the cooperation and support of test stores. Consequently, certain package sizes might not be carried, or pricing policies might not be adhered to.
5. Test market products are overadvertised or overpromoted during the test.
6. The full effect of such sales-influencing factors as sales force, season, weather conditions, competitive retaliation, shelf space, and so forth are not fully evaluated.
7. Market test periods are too short to determine whether the product is fully accepted by consumers or only tried on a limited basis.

Similar problems could be listed for almost any type of marketing research. However, the important point to be recognized is that careful planning, coordination, and control are imperative if the research study is to accomplish its objective.

CONCLUSION

This chapter has been concerned with marketing decision support systems and with marketing research. In terms of marketing decision support systems, one of the major reasons for increased interest has been the rapid growth in information-handling technology. However, as we have seen in this chapter, the study of MDSSs is not the study of computers. The study of MDSSs is part of a much larger task: the study of more efficient methods for marketing management decision making.

In terms of marketing research, this chapter has emphasized the importance of research as an aid for marketing decision making. Just as planning is integral for marketing management, the research plan is critical for marketing research.

---

[6]For a discussion of some general problems in marketing research, see Alan G. Sawyer and J. Paul Peter, "The Significance of Statistical Significance Testing in Marketing Research," *Journal of Marketing Research*, May 1983, pp. 122–33.

A research plan not only formalizes the objectives of the study but also details the tasks and responsibilities of the research team as well as cost estimates. Conducting research is a matter of following the research plan and reporting the events of each stage clearly and unambiguously. Finally, emphasis was placed on the extreme care that must be taken to avoid research difficulties and pitfalls.

ADDITIONAL READINGS

Aaker, David A., and George S. Day. *Marketing Research*. 4th ed. New York: John Wiley, 1990.

Boyd, Harper W., Jr.; Ralph Westfall; and Stanley F. Stasch. *Marketing Research: Text and Cases*. 7th ed. Homewood, Ill.: Richard D. Irwin, 1989.

Churchill, Gilbert A. Jr., *Marketing Research: Methodological Foundations*. 5th ed. Hinsdale, Ill.: Dryden Press, 1991.

———. *Basic Marketing Research*. 2nd ed. Hinsdale, Ill.: Dryden Press, 1992.

Dillon, William R.; Thomas J. Madden; and Neil H. Firtle. *Marketing Research in a Marketing Environment*. 2nd ed. Homewood, Ill.: Richard D. Irwin, 1990.

Green, Paul E.; Donald S. Tull; and Gerald Albaum. *Research for Marketing Decisions*. 5th ed. Englewood Cliffs, N.J.: Prentice Hall, Inc., 1988.

Kinnear, Thomas C., and James R. Taylor. *Marketing Research: An Applied Approach*. 4th ed. New York: McGraw-Hill, 1991.

O'Brien, James A. *Management Information Systems*. Homewood, Ill.: Richard D. Irwin, 1993.

Peterson, Robert A. *Marketing Research*. 2nd ed. Plano, Tex.: Business Publications Inc., 1988.

Tull, Donald S., and Del I. Hawkins. *Marketing Research: Measurement and Method*. 5th ed. New York: Macmillan, 1990.

Chapter 3

Consumer Behavior

The marketing concept emphasizes that profitable marketing begins with the discovery and understanding of consumer needs and then develops a marketing mix to satisfy these needs. Thus, an understanding of consumers and their needs and purchasing behavior is integral to successful marketing.

Unfortunately, there is no single theory of consumer behavior that can totally explain why consumers behave as they do. Instead, there are numerous theories, models, and concepts making up the field. In addition, the majority of these notions have been borrowed from a variety of other disciplines, such as sociology, psychology, social psychology, and economics, and must be integrated to understand consumer behavior.

In this chapter some of the many influences on consumer behavior will be examined in terms of the buying process. The reader may wish to examine Figure 3–1 closely, since it provides the basis for this discussion.

The chapter will proceed by first examining the buying process and then discussing the group, product class, and situational influences on this process.

THE BUYING PROCESS

The buying process can be viewed as a series of five stages: need, recognition, alternative search, alternative evaluation, purchase decision, and postpurchase feelings. In this section, each of these stages will be discussed. It should be noted at the outset that this is a general model for depicting a logical sequence of buying behavior. Clearly, individuals will vary from this model because of

Figure 3–1 *An Overview of the Buying Process*

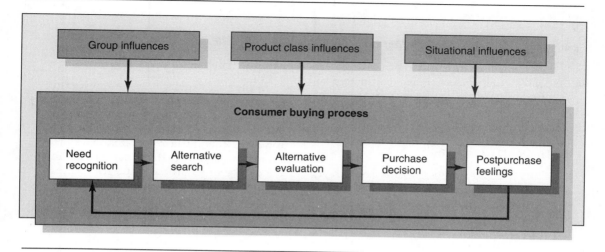

personal differences in such things as personality, self-concept, subjective perceptions of information, the product, and the purchasing situation. However, the model provides a useful framework for organizing our discussion of consumer behavior.

Need Recognition

The starting point for this model of the buying process is the recognition of an unsatisfied need by the consumer. Any number of either internal or external stimuli may activate needs or wants and recognition of them. Internal stimuli are such things as feeling hungry and wanting some food, feeling a headache coming on and wanting some Excedrin, or feeling bored and looking for a movie to go to. External stimuli are such things as seeing a McDonald's sign and then feeling hungry or seeing a sale sign for winter parkas and remembering that last year's coat is worn out.

It is the task of marketing managers to find out what needs and wants a particular product can and does satisfy and what unsatisfied needs and wants consumers have for which a new product could be developed. In order to do so, marketing managers should understand what types of needs consumers may have. A well-known classification of needs was developed many years ago by Abraham Maslow and includes five types.[1] Maslow's view is that lower-

---

[1] A. H. Maslow, *Motivation and Personality* (New York: Harper & Row, 1954); also see James F. Engel, Roger D. Blackwell, and Paul W. Miniard, *Consumer Behavior,* 7th ed. (Hinsdale, Ill.: Dryden Press, 1993), chap. 16 for further discussion of need recognition.

HIGHLIGHT 3–1

Getting Close and Staying Close to Customers

A number of leading companies have recognized that understanding consumers and offering them the products and services that they want is the key to success. Below are several examples

Harley-Davidson, Inc.

By the early 1980s, Japanese motorcycle manufacturers dominated the U.S. market. The Japanese bikes were more sophisticated, of better quality, and cheaper than Harleys. Harley-Davidson was days away from filing for bankruptcy by the end of 1985. However, it got refinanced and continued to work hard to improve the quality of its motorcycles through bettering the design, getting employees more committed to quality, working with dealers, and interacting continuously with consumers to get feedback on its products and ideas for improvements. By 1990, Harley-Davidson dominated the super-heavyweight motorcycle market with a market share of over 62 percent.

Source: J. Paul Peter and Jerry C. Olson, *Consumer Behavior and Marketing Strategy,* 3rd ed., Homewood, Ill.: Richard D. Irwin, 1993, p. 6.

Monroe Auto Equipment

In the past decade, nine companies from Japan and Europe stormed the U.S. market for shock absorbers and struts—under-the-body parts that give cars a smooth ride. Monroe Auto Equipment recognized that to survive in this mature market, it had to increase the quality of its products and reduce costs. Since 1986, productivity in its 36 plants increased 26 percent, annual sales increased 70 percent to $900 million, and profits increased 20 percent. In the $1.5 billion-a-year market, Monroe sells more than half of all the replacement shocks and close to one third of those put on new cars. Monroe learned how to build better quality products by studying Japanese methods and focused on having zero defects, which satisfies both organizational and consumer buyers.

Nike

While there are many strong competitors in the sports shoe market, Nike is at the top.

---

level needs, starting with physiological and safety, must be attended to before higher-level needs can be satisfied. Maslow's hierarchy is described below.

Physiological needs. This category consists of the primary needs of the human body, such as food, water, and sex. Physiological needs will dominate when all needs are unsatisfied. In such a case, none of the other needs will serve as a basis for motivation.

Safety needs. With the physiological needs met, the next higher level assumes importance. Safety needs consist of such things as protection from physical harm, ill health, economic disaster, and avoidance of the unexpected.

Belongingness and love needs. These needs are related to the social and gregarious nature of humans and the need for companionship. This level in the

In 1990, sales jumped 31 percent to $2.2 billion, about $75 million higher than archrival Reebok International. Nike's profits were $243 million compared to $177 million for Reebok. The company sells over 800 models for use in about 25 sports. It makes three lines of basketball shoes, each expressing what Nike calls a different attitude. The Air Jordan (retail price $125) is for consumers who want to follow in the footsteps of the Chicago Bulls superstar. The Flight (up to $115) is for players who value the lightest Nikes, while the Force (up to $150) incorporates the latest designs, such as a custom air bladder, for consumers who want a snug fit. The company updates its shoes at least every six months to tempt new customers to lace on new pairs before last year's wear out. By carefully segmenting the market, coming out with frequent innovations and style changes, and continually researching to develop the most effective and stylish athletic shoes, Nike offers quality products that consumers want.

Wal-Mart

Sam Walton, founder of Wal-Mart, had a simple idea on how to be a successful retailer: be an agent for consumers, find out what they want, and sell it to them for the lowest possible price. To do so effectively, Wal-Mart has developed a corporate culture focused on consumers. The company has a sophisticated computerized warehouse and inventory system that carefully tracks sales and communicates sales data with manufacturers to ensure stores remain well stocked with high-demand merchandise. Wal-Mart bargains hard with manufacturers to get the lowest possible price and keeps overhead low, in fact, the lowest in the industry. Wal-Mart stays close to customers. Is it any wonder that in 1991 it became the number one retailer in the United States, with sales of over $32 billion?

hierarchy is the point of departure from the physical or quasi-physical needs of the two previous levels. Nonsatisfaction of this level of need may affect the mental health of the individual.

Esteem needs. These needs consist of both the need for the self-awareness of importance to others (self-esteem) and actual esteem from others. Satisfaction of these needs leads to feelings of self-confidence and prestige.

Self-actualization needs. This need can be defined as the desire to become more and more what one is, to become everything one is capable of becoming. This means that the individual will fully realize the potentialities of given talents and capabilities. Maslow assumes that satisfaction of these needs is only possible after the satisfaction of all the needs lower in the hierarchy.

HIGHLIGHT 3–2

Factors Affecting Information Search by Consumers

Influencing Factor	Increasing the Influencing Factor Causes Search to:
I. Market characteristics	
A. Number of alternatives	Increase
B. Price range	Increase
C. Store concentration	Increase
D. Information availability	Increase
1. Advertising	
2. Point-of-purchase	
3. Sales personnel	
4. Packaging	
5. Experienced consumers	
6. Independent sources	
II. Product characteristics	
A. Price	Increase
B. Differentiation	Increase
C. Positive products	Increase
III. Consumer characteristics	
A. Learning and experience	Decrease
B. Shopping orientation	Mixed
C. Social status	Increase
D. Age, gender, and household life cycle	Mixed
E. Perceived risk	Increase
IV. Situational characteristics	
A. Time availability	Increase
B. Purchase for self	Decrease
C. Pleasant surroundings	Increase
D. Social surroundings	Mixed
E. Physical / mental energy	Increase

Source: Del I. Hawkins, Kenneth A. Coney and Roger Best, Jr., *Consumer Behavior: Implications for Marketing Strategy,* 5th ed., Homewood, Ill.: Richard D. Irwin, 1992, p. 478.

While the hierarchy arrangement of Maslow presents a convenient explanation, it is probably more realistic to assume that the various need categories overlap. Thus, in affluent societies, many products may satisfy more than one of these needs. For example, gourmet foods may satisfy both the basic physiological need of hunger as well as esteem and status needs for those who serve gourmet foods to their guests.

Alternative Search

Once a need is recognized, the individual then searches for alternatives for satisfying the need. There are five basic sources from which the individual can collect information for a particular purchase decision.

1. *Internal sources.* In most cases the individual has had some previous experience in dealing with a particular need. Thus, the individual will usually "search" through whatever stored information and experience is in his or her mind for dealing with the need. If a previously acceptable product for satisfying the need is remembered, the individual may purchase with little or no additional information search or evaluation. This is quite common for routine or habitual purchases.

2. *Group sources.* A common source of information for purchase decisions comes from communication with other people, such as family, friends, neighbors, and acquaintances. Generally, some of these (i.e., relevant others) are selected which the individual views as having particular expertise for the purchase decision. Although it may be quite difficult for the marketing manager to determine the exact nature of this source of information, group sources of information often are considered to be the most powerful influence on purchase decisions.

3. *Marketing sources.* Marketing sources of information include such factors as advertising, salespeople, dealers, packaging, and displays. Generally, this is the primary source of information about a particular product. These sources of information will be discussed in detail in the promotion chapters of this text.

4. *Public sources.* Public sources of information include publicity, such as a newspaper article about the product, and independent ratings of the product, such as *Consumer Reports*. Here product quality is a highly important marketing management consideration, since such articles and reports often discuss such features as dependability and service requirements.

5. *Experiential sources.* Experiential sources refer to handling, examining, and perhaps trying the product while shopping. This usually requires an actual shopping trip by the individual and may be the final source consulted before purchase.

Information collected from these sources is then processed by the consumer.[2] However, the exact nature of how individuals process information to form evaluations of products is not fully understood. In general, information pro-

---

[2]For a detailed review of research on external search, see Sharon E. Beatty and Scott M. Smith, "External Search Effort: An Investigation Across Several Product Categories," *Journal of Consumer Research,* June 1987, pp. 83–95. Also see Narasimhan Srinivasan and Brian T. Ratchford, "An Empirical Test of a Model of External Search for Automobiles," *Journal of Consumer Research,* September 1991, pp. 233–42; Julie L. Ozanne, Merrie Brucks and Dhruv Grewal, "A Study of Information Search Behavior during the Categorization of New Products," *Journal of Consumer Research,* March 1992, pp. 452–63.

cessing is viewed as a four-step process in which the individual is (1) exposed to information; (2) becomes attentive to the information; (3) understands the information; and (4) retains the information.[3]

Alternative Evaluation

During the process of collecting information or, in some cases, after information is acquired, the consumer then evaluates alternatives based on what has been learned. One approach to describing the evaluation process can be found in the logic of attitude modeling.[4] The basic logic can be described as follows:

1. The consumer has information about a number of brands in a product class.
2. The consumer perceives that at least some of the brands in a product class are viable alternatives for satisfying a recognized need.
3. Each of these brands has a set of attributes (color, quality, size, and so forth).
4. A set of these attributes is relevant to the consumer, and the consumer perceives that different brands vary in terms of how much of each attribute they possess.
5. The brand that is perceived as offering the greatest number of desired attributes in the desired amounts and desired order will be the brand the consumer will like best.
6. The brand the consumer likes best is the brand the consumer will intend to purchase.

Purchase Decision

If no other factors intervene after the consumer has decided on the brand that is intended for purchase, the actual purchase is a common result of search and evaluation. Actually, a purchase involves many decisions, which include product type, brand, model, dealer selection, and method of payment, among other factors. In addition, rather than purchasing, the consumer may make a decision to modify, postpone, or avoid purchase based on an inhibitor to purchase or a perceived risk.

---

[3]For further discussion of information processing, see J. Paul Peter and Jerry C. Olson, *Consumer Behavior and Marketing Strategy,* 3rd ed. (Homewood, Ill.: Richard D. Irwin, 1993), Chap. 3.

[4]For a summary of research on attitude modeling, see Blair H. Sheppard, Jon Hartwick, and Paul R. Warshaw, "The Theory of Reasoned Action: A Meta-Analysis of Past Research with Recommendations for Modification and Future Research," *Journal of Consumer Research,* December 1988, pp. 325–43.

Traditional risk theorists believe that consumers tend to make risk-minimizing decisions based on their *perceived* definition of the particular purchase. The perception of risk is based upon the possible consequences and uncertainties involved. Consequences may range from economic loss, to embarrassment if a new food product does not turn out well, to actual physical harm. Perceived risk may be either functional (related to financial and performance considerations) or psychosocial (related to whether the product will further one's self- or reference group image). The amount of risk a consumer perceives in a particular product depends on such things as the price of the product and whether other people will see the individual using the product.

The perceived risk literature emphasizes that consumers generally try to reduce risk in their decision making. This can be done by either reducing the possible negative consequences or by reducing the uncertainty. The possible consequences of a purchase might be minimized by purchasing in small quantities or by lowering the individual's aspiration level to expect less in the way of results from the product. However, this cannot always be done. Thus, reducing risk by attempting to increase the certainty of the purchase outcome may be the more widely used strategy. This can be done by seeking additional information regarding the proposed purchase. In general, the more information the consumer collects prior to purchase, the less likely postpurchase dissonance is to occur.

Postpurchase Feelings

In general, if the individual finds that a certain response achieves a desired goal or satisfies a need, the success of this cue–response pattern will be remembered. The probability of responding in a like manner to the same or similar situation in the future is increased. In other words, the response has a higher probability of being repeated when the need and cue appear together again, and thus it can be said that learning has taken place. Frequent reinforcement increases the habit potential of the particular response. Likewise, if a response does not satisfy the need adequately, the probability that the same response will be repeated is reduced.

For some marketers this means that if an individual finds a particular product fulfills the need for which it was purchased, the probability is high that the product will be repurchased the next time the need arises. The firm's promotional efforts often act as the cue. If an individual repeatedly purchases a product with favorable results, loyalty may develop toward the particular product or brand. This loyalty can result in habitual purchases, and such habits are often extremely difficult for competing firms to alter.

Although many studies in the area of buyer behavior center around the buyer's attitudes, motives, and behavior before and during the purchase decision, emphasis has also been given to study of behavior after the purchase. Specifically, studies have been undertaken to investigate postpurchase dissonance, as well as postpurchase satisfaction.[5]

The occurrence of postdecision dissonance is related to the concept of cognitive dissonance. This theory states that there is often a lack of consistency or harmony among an individual's various cognitions, or attitudes and beliefs, after a decision has been made—that is, the individual has doubts and second thoughts about the choice made. Further, it is more likely that the intensity of the anxiety will be greater when any of the following conditions exist:

1. The decision is an important one psychologically or financially, or both.
2. There are a number of forgone alternatives.
3. The forgone alternatives have many favorable features.

These factors can relate to many buying decisions. For example, postpurchase dissonance might be expected to be present among many purchasers of such products as automobiles, major appliances, and homes. In these cases, the decision to purchase is usually an important one both financially and psychologically, and there are usually a number of favorable alternatives available.

When dissonance occurs after a decision has been made, the individual may attempt to reduce it by one or more of the following methods:

1. By seeking information that supports the wisdom of the decision.
2. By perceiving information in a way to support the decision.
3. By changing attitudes to a less favorable view of the forgone alternatives.
4. By avoiding the importance of the negative aspects of the decision and enhancing the positive elements.

Dissonance could, of course, be reduced by admitting that a mistake had been made. However, most individuals are reluctant to admit that a wrong decision has been made. Thus, it is more likely that a person will seek out supportive information to reduce dissonance.

---

[5]For further discussion of consumer satisfaction, see Richard L. Oliver and John E. Swan, "Consumer Perceptions of Interpersonal Equity and Satisfaction in Transactions: A Field Survey Approach," *Journal of Marketing,* April 1989, pp. 21–35; Richard L. Oliver and John E. Swan, "Equity and Disconfirmation Perceptions as Influences on Merchant and Product Satisfaction," *Journal of Consumer Research,* December 1989, pp. 372–83; Robert A. Westbrook and Richard L. Oliver, "The Dimensionality of Consumption Emotion patterns and Consumer Satisfaction," *Journal of Consumer Research,* June 1991, pp. 84–91.

These findings have much relevance for the marketer. In a buying situation, when a purchaser becomes dissonant it is reasonable to predict such a person would be highly receptive to advertising and sales promotion that supports the purchase decision. Such communication presents favorable aspects of the product and can be useful in reinforcing the buyer's wish to believe that a wise purchase decision was made. For example, purchasers of major appliances or automobiles might be given a phone call or sent a letter reassuring them that they have made a wise purchase.[6]

GROUP INFLUENCES ON CONSUMER BEHAVIOR

Behavioral scientists have become increasingly aware of the powerful effects of the social environment and personal interactions on human behavior. In terms of consumer behavior, culture, social class, and reference group influences have been related to purchase and consumption decisions. It should be noted that these influences can have both direct and indirect effects on the buying process. By direct effects we mean direct communication between the individual and other members of society concerning a particular decision. By indirect effects we mean the influence of society on an individual's basic values and attitudes as well as the important role that groups play in structuring an individual's personality.

Cultural and Subcultural Influences

Culture is one of the most basic influences on an individual's needs, wants, and behavior, since all facets of life are carried out against the background of the society in which an individual lives. Cultural antecedents affect everyday behavior, and there is empirical support for the notion that culture is a determinant of certain aspects of consumer behavior.

Cultural values are transmitted through three basic organizations: the family, religious organizations, and educational institutions, and, in today's society, educational institutions are playing an increasingly greater role in this regard. Marketing managers should adapt the marketing mix to cultural values and constantly monitor value changes and differences in both domestic and international markets. To illustrate, one of the changing values in America is the increasing emphasis on achievement and career success. This change in values has been recognized by many business firms that have expanded their emphasis on time-saving, convenience-oriented products.

---

[6]For additional discussion of postpurchase feelings and behavior, see Mary C. Gilly and Betsy D. Gelb, "Post-Purchase Consumer Processes and the Complaining Consumer," *Journal of Consumer Research,* December 1982, pp. 323–28; Jagdip Singh, "Consumer Complaint Intentions and Behavior: Definitional and Taxonomical Issues," *Journal of Marketing,* January 1988, pp. 93–107.

HIGHLIGHT 3–3

A Summary of American Cultural Values

It is important for marketers to understand cultural values and to create and adapt products to the values held by consumers. Below is a description of American cultural values and their relevance to marketing.

Value	General Features	Relevance to Marketing
Achievement and success	Hard work is good; success flows from hard work	Acts as a justification for acquisition of goods ("You deserve it")
Activity	Keeping busy is healthy and natural	Stimulates interest in products that are time-savers and enhance leisure-time activities
Efficiency and practicality	Admiration of things that solve problems (e.g., save time and effort)	Stimulates purchase of products that function well and save time
Progress	People can improve themselves; tomorrow should be better	Stimulates desire for new products that fulfill unsatisfied needs; acceptance of products that claim to be "new" or "improved"
Material comfort	"The good life"	Fosters acceptance of convenience and luxury products that make life more enjoyable

Source: Leon G. Schiffman and Leslie Lazar Kanuck, *Consumer Behavior,* 4th ed. 1991, p. 424. Reprinted by permission of Prentice Hall, Inc., Englewood Cliffs, N.J.

In a nation as large as the United States the population is bound to lose a significant amount of its homogeneity, and thus subcultures arise. In other words, there are subcultures in the American culture where people have more frequent interactions than with the population at large and thus tend to think and act alike in some respects. Subcultures are based on such things as geographic areas, religions, nationalities, ethnic groups, and age. Many subcultural barriers are decreasing because of mass communication, mass transit, and a decline in the influence of religious values. However, age groups, such as the teen market, baby boomers, and the mature market, have become increasingly important for marketing strategy. For example, since baby boomers (those born between 1946 and 1962) make up about a third of the U.S. population

Value	General Features	Relevance to Marketing
Individualism	Being one's self (e.g., self-reliance, self-interest, and self-esteem)	Stimulates acceptance of customized or unique products that enable a person to "express his or her own personality"
Freedom	Freedom of choice	Fosters interest in wide product lines and differentiated products
External conformity	Uniformity of observable behavior; desire to be accepted	Stimulates interest in products that are used or owned by others in the same social group
Humanitarianism	Caring for others, particularly the underdog	Stimulates patronage of firms that compete with market leaders
Youthfulness	A state of mind that stresses being young at heart or appearing young	Stimulates acceptance of products that provide the illusion of maintaining or fostering youth
Fitness and health	Caring about one's body, including the desire to be physically fit and healthy	Stimulates acceptance of food products, activities, and equipment perceived to maintain or increase physical fitness

and soon will account for about half of discretionary spending, many marketers are repositioning products to serve them. Snickers candy bars, for instance, used to be promoted to children as a treat but are now promoted to adults as a wholesome, between-meals snack.

Social Class

While one likes to think of America as a land of equality, a class structure can be observed. Social classes develop on the basis of such things as wealth, skill, and power. The single best indicator of social class is occupation. However, interest at this point is in the influence of social class on the individual's

Figure 3–2   *Social Class Groups for Marketing Analysis*

Upper Americans (14 percent of population). This group consists of the upper-upper, lower-upper, and upper-middle classes. They have common goals and are differentiated mainly by income. This group has many different lifestyles, which might be labeled postpreppy, conventional, intellectual, and political, among others. The class remains the segment of our society in which quality merchandise is most prized, special attention is paid to prestige brands, and the self-image ideal is "spending with good taste." Self-expression is more prized than in previous generations, and neighborhood remains important. Depending on income and priorities, theater, books, investment in art, European travel, household help, club memberships for tennis, golf, and swimming, and prestige schooling for children remain high consumption priorities.

Middle class (32 percent of population). These consumers definitely want to "do the right thing" and buy "what's popular." They have always been concerned with fashion and following recommendations of "experts" in print media. Increased earnings result in better living, which means a "nicer neighborhood on the better side of town with good schools." It also means spending more on "worthwhile experiences" for children, including winter ski trips, college educations, and shopping for better brands of clothes at more expensive stores. Appearance of home is important, because guests may visit and pass judgment. This group emulates upper Americans, which distinguishes it from the working class. It also enjoys trips to Las Vegas and physical activity. Deferred gratification may still be an ideal, but it is not often practiced.

Working class (38 percent of population). Working-class Americans are "family folk" depending heavily on relatives for economic and emotional support (e.g., tips on job opportunities, advice on purchases, help in times of trouble). The emphasis on family ties is only one sign of how much more limited and different working-class horizons are socially, psychologically, and geographically compared to those of the middle class. In almost every respect, a parochial view characterizes this blue-collar world. This group has changed little in values and behaviors in spite of rising incomes in some cases. For them, "keeping up with the times" focuses on the mechanical and recreational, and thus, ease of labor and leisure is what they continue to pursue.

Lower Americans (16 percent of population). The men and women of lower America are no exception to the rule that diversities and uniformities in values and consumption goals are to be found at each social level. Some members of this world, as has been publicized, are prone to every form of instant gratification known to humankind when the money is available. But others are dedicated to resisting worldly temptations as they struggle toward what some believe will be a "heavenly reward" for their earthly sacrifices.

Source: Excerpted from Richard P. Coleman, "The Continuing Significance of Social Class to Marketing," *Journal of Consumer Research*, December 1983, pp. 265–80.

behavior. What is important here is that different social classes tend to have different attitudinal configurations and values, which influence the behavior of individual members. Figure 3–2 presents a social class hierarchy developed specifically for marketing analysis and describes some of these important differences in attitudes and values.

For the marketing manager, social class offers some insights into consumer behavior and is potentially useful as a market segmentation variable. However, there is considerable controversy as to whether social class is superior to income for the purpose of market segmentation.

Reference Groups

Groups that an individual looks to (uses as a reference) when forming attitudes and opinions are described as reference groups.[7] Primary reference groups include family and close friends, while secondary reference groups include fraternal organizations and professional associations. A buyer may also consult a single individual about decisions, and this individual would be considered a reference individual.

A person normally has several reference groups or reference individuals for various subjects or different decisions. For example, a woman may consult one reference group when she is purchasing a car and a different reference group for lingerie. In other words, the nature of the product and the role the individual is playing during the purchasing process influence which reference group will be consulted. Reference group influence is generally considered to be stronger for products that are "public" or conspicuous—that is, products that other people see the individual using such as clothes or automobiles.

As noted, the family is generally recognized to be an important reference group, and it has been suggested that the household, rather than the individual, is the relevant unit for studying consumer behavior.[8] This is because within a household the purchaser of goods and services is not always the user of these goods and services. Thus, it is important for marketing managers to determine not only who makes the actual purchase but also who makes the decision to purchase. In addition, it has been recognized that the needs, income, assets, debts, and expenditure patterns change over the course of what is called the *family life cycle*. Basic stages in the family life cycle include:

1. Bachelor stage: young, single people not living at home.
2. Newly married couples: young, no children.
3. Full nest I: young married couples with youngest child under six.
4. Full nest II: young married couples with youngest child six or over.
5. Full nest III: older married couples with dependent children.
6. Empty nest I: older married couples, no children living with them, household head(s) in labor force.
7. Empty nest II: older married couples, no children living at home, household head(s) retired.
8. Solitary survivor in labor force.
9. Solitary survivor, retired.

---

[7]See William O. Bearden and Michael J. Etzel, "Reference Group Influence on Product and Brand Purchase Decisions," *Journal of Consumer Research,* September 1982, pp. 183–94; Terry L. Childers and Akshay R. Rao, "The Influence of Familial and Peer-Based Reference Groups on Consumer Decisions," *Journal of Consumer Research,* September 1992, pp. 198–211.

[8]See Rosann L. Spiro, "Persuasion in Family Decision Making," *Journal of Consumer Research,* March 1983, pp. 393–402.

HIGHLIGHT 3–4

Some Common Verbal Tools Used by Reference Groups

Below are a number of verbal tools used by reference groups to influence consumer behavior. If the statements listed below were made to you by a close friend or someone you admired or respected, do you think that they might change your behavior?

Tools	Definitions	Examples
Reporting	Talking about preferences and behaviors.	"All of us drink Budweiser."
Recommendations	Suggesting appropriate behaviors.	"You should get a Schwinn High Sierra."
Invitations	Asking for participation in events.	"Do you want to go to the Michael Jackson concert with us?"
Requests	Asking for behavior performance.	"Would you run down to the corner and get me a newspaper?"
Prompts	Suggesting desired behaviors.	"It sure would be nice if someone would buy us a pizza!"
Commands	Telling someone what to do.	"Get me some Kleenex, and be quick about it!"
Promises	Offering a reward for performing a behavior.	"If you'll go to Penney's with me, I'll take you to lunch later."
Coercion	Threatening to punish for inappropriate behavior.	"If you don't shut up, I'm going to stuff a sock in your mouth!"
Criticism	Saying something negative about a behavior.	"Quit hassling the salesclerk. You're acting like a jerk."
Compliments	Saying something positive about a behavior.	"You really know how to shop. I bet you got every bargain in the store!"
Teasing	Good-natured bantering about behavior or appearance.	"Man, that shirt makes you look like Bozo the clown!"

Because the life cycle combines trends in earning power with demands placed on income, it is a useful way of classifying and segmenting individuals and families.[9]

---

[9]See Janet Wagner and Sherman Hanna, "The Effectiveness of Family Life Cycle Variables in Consumer Expenditure Research," *Journal of Consumer Research*. December 1983, pp. 281–91.

PRODUCT CLASS INFLUENCES

The nature of the product class selected by the consumer to satisfy an aroused need plays an important role in the decision-making process. Basically, the nature of the product class and the brands within it determine (1) the amount of information the consumer will require before making a decision, and, consequently (2) the time it takes to move through the buying process. In general, product classes in which there are many alternatives that are expensive, complex, or new will require the consumer to collect more information and take longer to make a purchase decision. As illustration, buying an automobile is probably one of the most difficult purchase decisions most consumers make. An automobile is expensive, complex, and there are many new styles and models to choose from. Such a decision will usually require extensive information search and time before a decision is made.

A second possibility is referred to as limited decision making. For these purchases a lesser amount of information is collected and less time is devoted to shopping. For example, in purchasing a new pair of jeans the consumer may already have considerable experience, and price and complexity are somewhat limited. However, since there are many alternative styles and brands, some information processing and decision making is generally needed.

Finally, some product classes require what is called "routinized decision making." For these product classes, such as candy bars or other food products, the consumer has faced the decision many times before and has found an acceptable alternative. Thus, little or no information is collected, and the consumer purchases in a habitual, automatic manner.

SITUATIONAL INFLUENCES

Situational influences can be defined as all those factors particular to a time and place of observation which have a demonstrable and systematic effect on current behavior. In terms of purchasing situations, five groups of situational influences have been identified.[10] These influences may be perceived either consciously or subconsciously and may have considerable effect on product and brand choice.

1. *Physical surroundings* are the most readily apparent features of a situation. These features include geographical and institutional location, decor,

---

[10]Russell W. Belk, "Situational Variables and Consumer Behavior," *Journal of Consumer Research,* December 1975, pp. 156–64. Also see Jacob Hornik, "Situational Effects on the Consumption of Time," *Journal of Marketing,* Fall 1982, pp. 44–55; C. Whan Park, Easwar S. Iyer, and Daniel C. Smith, "The Effects of Situational Factors on In-Store Grocery Shopping Behavior: The Role of Store Environment and Time Available for Shopping," *Journal of Consumer Research,* March 1989, pp. 422–33; Mary Jo Bitner, "Servicescapes: The Impact of Physical Surroundings on Customers and Employees," *Journal of Marketing,"* April 1992, pp. 57–71.

sounds, aromas, lighting, weather, and visible configurations of merchandise or other material surrounding the stimulus object.

2. *Social surroundings* provide additional depth to a description of a situation. Other persons present, their characteristics, their apparent roles and interpersonal interactions are potentially relevant examples.

3. *Temporal perspective* is a dimension of situations that may be specified in units ranging from time of day to season of the year. Time also may be measured relative to some past or future event for the situational participant. This allows such conceptions as time since last purchase, time since or until meals or paydays, and time constraints imposed by prior or standing commitments.

4. *Task definition* features of a situation include an intent or requirement to select, shop for, or obtain information about a general or specific purchase. In addition, task may reflect different buyer and user roles anticipated by the individual. For instance, a person shopping for a small appliance as a wedding gift for a friend is in a different situation than when shopping for a small appliance for personal use.

5. *Antecedent states* make up a final feature that characterizes a situation. These are momentary moods (such as acute anxiety, pleasantness, hostility, and excitation) or momentary conditions (such as cash on hand, fatigue, and illness) rather than chronic individual traits. These conditions are further stipulated to be immediately antecedent to the current situation to distinguish the states the individual brings to the situation from states of the individual resulting from the situation. For instance, people may select a certain motion picture because they feel depressed (an antecedent state and a part of the choice situation), but the fact that the movie causes them to feel happier is a response to the consumption situation. This altered state then may become antecedent for behavior in the next choice situation encountered, such as passing a street vendor on the way out of the theater.

CONCLUSION

The purpose of this chapter was to present an overview of consumer behavior in terms of an analysis of the buying process. The buying process is viewed as a series of five stages: need recognition, alternative search, alternative evaluation, purchase decision, and postpurchase feelings. This process is influenced by group, product class, and situational factors. Clearly, marketing managers must understand consumer behavior to formulate effective marketing strategies.

ADDITIONAL READINGS

Assael, Henry. *Consumer Behavior and Marketing Action*. 4th ed. Boston: PWS-Kent Publishing, 1992.

Engel, James F.; Roger D. Blackwell; and Paul W. Miniard. *Consumer Behavior*. 7th ed. Chicago: Dryden Press, 1993.

Hawkins, Del; Kenneth A. Coney; and Roger Best, Jr. *Consumer Behavior: Implications for Marketing Strategy*. 5th ed. Homewood, Ill.: Richard D. Irwin, 1992.

Mowen, John C. *Consumer Behavior*. 3rd ed. New York: Macmillan Publishing, 1993.

Peter, J. Paul, and Jerry C. Olson. *Consumer Behavior and Marketing Strategy*. 3rd ed. Homewood, Ill.: Richard D. Irwin, 1993.

Schiffman, Leon G., and Leslie Kanuck. *Consumer Behavior*. 4th ed. Englewood Cliffs, N.J.: Prentice Hall, 1991.

Solomon, Michael R. *Consumer Behavior*. Boston: Allyn & Bacon, 1992.

Wilkie, William L. *Consumer Behavior*. 2nd ed. New York: John Wiley & Sons, 1990.

Selected Consumer Behavior Data Sources

1. Demographic information:
U.S. Census of Population.
Marketing Information Guide.
A Guide to Consumer Markets.
State and city governments.
Media (newspapers, magazines, television, and radio stations) make demographic data about their readers or audiences available.

2. Consumer Research Findings:
Journal of Consumer Research   *Journal of Advertising Research*
Journal of Marketing   *Journal of Consumer Marketing*
Journal of Marketing Research   *Journal of Applied Psychology*
Journal of Advertising   *Advances in Consumer Research*

3. Marketing Applications:
Advertising Age   *Nation's Business*
Marketing Communications   *Fortune*
Sales Management   *Forbes*
Business Week   Industry and trade magazines

Chapter 4

Organizational Buyer Behavior

Organizational buyers include individuals involved in purchasing products for businesses, government agencies, and other institutions and agencies. Those who purchase for businesses include industrial buyers who purchase goods and services to aid them in producing other goods and services for sale, and resellers who purchase goods and services to resell at a profit. Government agencies purchase products and services to carry out their responsibilities to society, and other institutions and agencies, such as churches and schools, purchase to fulfill their organizational missions.

The purpose of this chapter is to examine the organizational buying process and the factors that influence it. Figure 4–1 provides a model of the organizational buying process that will be used as a framework for discussion in this chapter.

PRODUCT INFLUENCES ON ORGANIZATIONAL BUYING

A major consideration that affects the organizational buying process is the nature of the product itself. Such factors as the price, riskiness, and technical complexity of the product affect the process in three ways. First, they affect how long it will take for the firm to make a purchasing decision. Second, they have an effect on how many individuals will be involved in the purchasing process. Last, these factors may affect whether structural or behavioral influences play the major role in the purchasing process.

Figure 4–1   *A Model of the Organizational Buying Process*

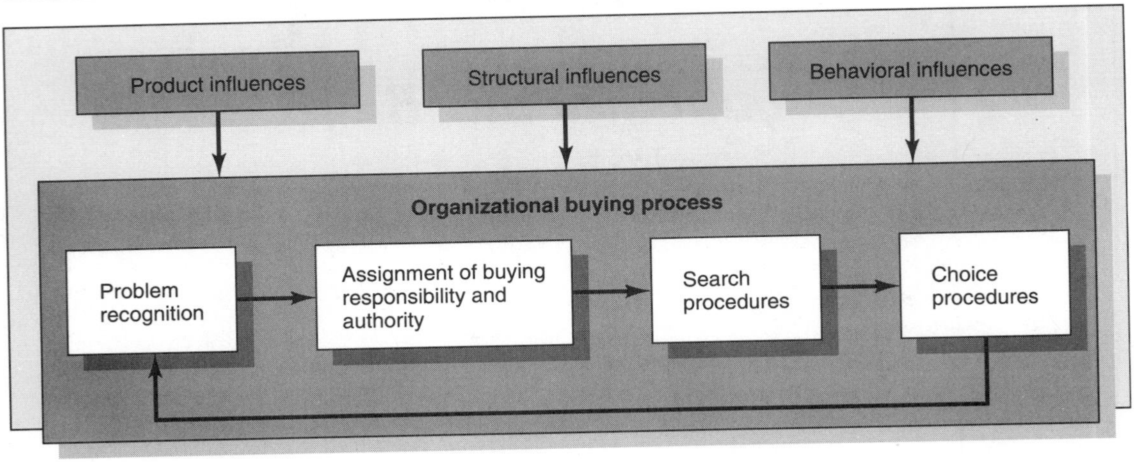

A useful way of examining product class influences is to consider them on the basis of the problems inherent in their adoption.[1] Four basic categories include:

Type I: Routine order products. A Type I product is frequently ordered and used. There is no problem in learning how to use such products, nor is there any question about whether the product will do the job. In short, this type of product is expected to cause no significant problems in use.

Type II: Procedural problem products. For Type II products, the buyer is also confident the product will do the job. However, problems are likely because personnel must be taught how to use the product. A buyer intent on minimizing problems associated with such a product will favor the supplier whose total offering is perceived as likely to reduce to a minimum the time and difficulty required to learn the product's operation.

Type III: Performance problem products. With Type III products, there is doubt whether the product will perform satisfactorily in the application for which it is being considered. Here the problem concerns the technical outcomes of using the product. There is likely to be no firm buying commitment until this problem has been resolved. It is argued that the buyer will favor the supplier who can offer appropriate technical service, provide a free trial period, and who appears flexible enough to adjust to the demands of the buyer's company.

---

[1]Donald R. Lehmann and John O'Shaughnessy, "Difference in Attribute Importance for Different Industrial Products," *Journal of Marketing*, April 1974, pp. 36–42; also see Philip Kotler, *Marketing Management: Analysis, Planning, Implementation, and Control*, 6th ed., Englewood Cliffs, N.J.: Prentice Hall, 1988, chap. 7.

HIGHLIGHT 4-1

Major Differences between Organizational Buyers and Final Consumers

Differences in Purchases

1. Organizational buyers acquire for further production, use in operations, or resale to other consumers. Final consumers acquire only for personal, family, or household use.
2. Organizational buyers commonly purchase installations, raw materials, and semifinished materials. Final consumers rarely purchase these goods.
3. Organizational buyers purchase on the basis of specifications and technical data. Final consumers frequently purchase on the basis of description, fashion, and style.
4. Organizational buyers utilize multiple-buying and team-based decisions more often than final consumers.
5. Organizational buyers are more likely to apply value and vendor analysis.
6. Organizational buyers more commonly lease equipment.
7. Organizational buyers more frequently employ competitive bidding and negotiation.

Source: Adapted from Joel R. Evans and Barry Berman, *Marketing,* 5th ed, New York: Macmillan, 1992, p. 174.

Differences in the Market

1. The demand of organizational buyers is derived from the demand of final consumers.
2. The demand of organizational buyers is more subject to cyclical fluctuations than final-consumer demand.
3. Organizational buyers are fewer in number and more geographically concentrated than final consumers.
4. Organizational buyers often employ buying specialists.
5. The distribution channel for organizational buyers is shorter than for final consumers.
6. Organizational buyers may require special services.
7. Organizational buyers are more likely than final consumers to be able to make goods and services as alternatives to purchasing them.

Type IV: Political problem products. Type IV products give rise to "political" problems, because there is likely to be difficulty in reaching agreement among those affected if the product is adopted. "Political" problems occur when products necessitate large capital outlays, since there are always allocational rivals for funds. More frequently, political problems arise when the product is an input to several departments whose requirements may not be congruent.

There are two important implications of this classification for marketers. First, in a study of purchasing agents, it was found that different product attributes were rated as relatively more important, depending on the type of product. For example, the most important attributes for Type I products were the reliability of delivery and price; for Type II products, the most important attributes were technical service offered, ease of operation or use, and training offered by supplier; for Type III products, the technical service offered, flexibility of supplier, and product reliability were rated as most important; for Type IV products, the price, reputation of supplier, data on product reliability, reliability of delivery, and flexibility of supplier were rated as most important. Thus, marketing strategy for organizational products should be adapted to variations in buyer perceptions of problems in selection, introduction, and performance.

Second, the type of product may influence whether structural or behavioral factors are relatively more important in the purchasing process. For example, behavioral influences may decrease from Type I to Type IV products while structural influences may increase. A routine order product is most probably the sole responsibility of the purchasing agent. Here organizational influences, such as joint decision making, are minimal, and the purchasing agent may well be more strongly influenced by behavioral influences, such as a personal friendship with the supplier. On the other hand, Type IV product decisions may require considerable joint decision making—such as a purchasing committee—and thus be more influenced by structural factors.

STRUCTURAL INFLUENCES ON ORGANIZATIONAL BUYING

The term *structural influences* refers to the design of the organizational environment and how it affects the purchasing process. Two important structural influences on organizational buying are joint decision making and organization-specific factors.

Joint Decision Making

It is common in organizational buying for more than one department and several persons to be involved in the purchasing process. These people may also play a variety of different roles in arriving at a purchase decision. These roles include:

1. *Users* are the people in the organization who actually use the product, for example, a secretary who would use a new word processor.
2. *Influencers* affect the buying decision, usually by helping define the specifications for what is bought. For example, an information systems manager would be a key influencer in the purchase of a new mainframe computer.
3. *Buyers* have the formal authority and responsibility to select the supplier and negotiate the terms of the contract. For example, in the purchase of a mainframe computer, the purchasing manager would likely perform this role.
4. *Deciders* have the formal or informal power to select or approve the supplier that receives the contract. For important technical purchases, deciders may come from R&D, engineering, or quality control.

5. *Gatekeepers* control the flow of information in the buying center. Purchasing personnel, technical experts, and secretaries can all keep marketers and their information from reaching people performing the other four roles.[2]

When several persons are involved in the organizational purchase decision, marketers may need to use a variety of means to reach each individual or group. Fortunately, it is often easy to find which individuals in organizations are involved in a purchase because such information is provided to suppliers. Organizations do this because it makes suppliers more knowledgeable about purchasing practices, thus making the purchasing process more efficient.[3] Also a number of firms have developed closer channel relationships that facilitate these transactions, as discussed in Chapter 10.

Organization-Specific Factors

There are three primary organization-specific factors that influence the purchasing process: orientation, size, and degree of centralization. First, in terms of orientation, the dominant function in an organization may control purchasing decisions. For example, if the organization is technology oriented, it is likely to be dominated by engineering personnel, and buying decisions will be made by them. Similarly, if the organization is production oriented, production personnel may dominate buying decisions.

Second, the size of the organization may influence the purchasing process. If the organization is large, it will likely have a high degree of joint decision making for other than routine order products. Smaller organizations are likely to have more autonomous decision making.

Finally, the degree of centralization of an organization influences whether decisions are made individually or jointly with others. Organizations that are highly centralized are less likely to have joint decision making. Thus, a privately owned, small company with technology or production orientations will tend toward autonomous decision making, while a large-scale, public corporation with considerable decentralization will tend to have greater joint decision making.

BEHAVIORAL INFLUENCES ON ORGANIZATIONAL BUYING

Organizational buyers are influenced by a variety of psychological and social factors. We will discuss two of these, personal motivations and role perceptions.

---

[2]This discussion is based on Eric N. Berkowitz, Roger A. Kerin, Steven W. Hartley, and William Rudelius, *Marketing,* 3rd ed., Homewood, Ill.: Richard D. Irwin, 1992, p. 151.

[3]For research on influence strategies in organizational buying, see Gary L. Frazier and Raymond Rody, "The Use of Influence Strategies in Interfirm Relationships in Industrial Product Channels," *Journal of Marketing,* January 1991, pp. 52–69; Julia M. Bristor, "Influence Strategies in Organizational Buying," *Journal of Business-to-Business Marketing,* no. 1 (1993), pp. 63–98.

HIGHLIGHT 4–2

Functional Areas and Their Key Concerns in Purchasing

Functional Area	Key Concerns in Purchase Decision Making
Design and development engineering	Name reputation of vendor; ability of vendors to meet design specifications
Production	Delivery and reliability of purchases such that interruption of production schedules is minimized
Sales / marketing	Impact of purchased items on marketability of the company's products
Maintenance	Degree to which purchased items are compatible with existing facilities and equipment; maintenance services offered by vendor; installation arrangements offered by vendor
Finance / accounting	Effects of purchases on cash flow, balance sheet, and income statement positions; variances in costs of materials over estimates; feasibility of make-or-buy and lease options to purchasing
Purchasing	Obtaining lowest possible price at acceptable quality levels; maintaining good relations with vendors
Quality control	Assurance that purchased items meet prescribed specifications and tolerances, governmental regulations, and customer requirements

Source: Michael H. Morris, *Industrial and Organizational Marketing* (Columbus, Ohio: Merrill Publishing, 1988), p. 81.

Personal Motivations

Organizational buyers are, of course, subject to the same personal motives or motivational forces as other individuals. Although these buyers may emphasize nonpersonal motives in their buying activities, it has been found that organizational buyers often are influenced by such personal factors as friendship, professional pride, fear and uncertainty (risk), and personal ambitions in their buying activities.

For example, professional pride often expresses itself through efforts to attain status in the firm. One way to achieve this might be to initiate or influence the purchase of goods that will demonstrate a buyer's value to the organization. If new materials, equipment, or components result in cost savings or increased profits, the individuals initiating the changes have demonstrated their value at the same time. Fear and uncertainty are strong motivational forces on organizational buyers, and reduction of risk is often important to them. This can have a strong influence on purchase behavior. Marketers should understand the relative strength of personal gain versus risk-reducing

---

---

motives and emphasize the more important motives when dealing with buyers.

Thus, in examining buyer motivations, it is necessary to consider both personal and nonpersonal motivational forces and to recognize that the relative importance of each is not a fixed quantity. It will vary with the nature of the product, the climate within the organization, and the relative strength of the two forces in the particular buyer.

Role Perception

A final factor that influences organizational buyers is their own perception of their role. The manner in which individuals behave depends on their perception of their role, their commitment to what they believe is expected of their role, the "maturity" of the role type, and the extent to which the institution is committed to the role type.

Different buyers will have different degrees of commitment to their buying role which will cause variations in role behavior from one buyer to the next. By *commitment* we mean willingness to perform their job in the manner expected by the organization. For example, some buyers seek to take charge in their role as buyer and have little commitment to company expectations. The implication for marketers is that such buyers expect, even demand, that they be kept constantly advised of all new developments to enable them to more effectively shape their own role. On the other hand, other buyers may have no interest in prescribing their role activities and accept their role as given to them. Such a buyer is most concerned with merely implementing prescribed company activities and buying policies with sanctioned products. Thus, some buyers will be highly committed to play the role the firm dictates (i.e., the formal organization's perception of their role) while others might be extremely innovative and uncommitted to the expected role performance. Obviously, roles may be heavily influenced by the organizational climate existing in the particular organization.[4]

Organizations can be divided into three groups based on differences in degree of employee commitment. These groups include innovative, adaptive, and lethargic firms. In *innovative* firms, individuals approach their occupational roles with a weak commitment to expected norms of behavior. In an *adaptive* organization, there is a moderate commitment, while in a *lethargic* organization, individuals express a strong commitment to traditionally accepted behavior and behave accordingly. Thus, a buyer in a lethargic firm would probably be less innovative in order to maintain acceptance and status within the organization and would keep conflict within the firm to a minimum.

Buyers' perception of their role may differ from the perception of their role held by others in the organization. This difference can result in variance in perception of the proper and the actual purchase responsibility to be held by the buyer. One study involving purchasing agents revealed that, in every firm included in the study, the purchasing agents believed they had more responsibility and control over certain decisions than the other influential purchase decision makers in the firm perceived them as having. The decisions were (1) design of the product; (2) cost of the product; (3) performance life; (4) naming of the specific supplier; (5) assessing the amount of engineering help available from the supplier; and (6) reduction of rejects. This variance in role perception held true regardless of the size of the firm or the significance of the item purchased to the overall success of the firm. It is important, therefore, that the marketer be aware that such perceptual differences may exist and to determine as accurately as possible the amount of control and responsibility over purchasing decisions held by each purchase decision influencer in the firm.

---

[4]For research on the role of organizational climate in industrial buying, see William J. Qualls and Christopher P. Puto, "Organizational Climate and Decision Framing: An Integrated Approach to Analyzing Industrial Buying Decisions," *Journal of Marketing Research,* May 1989, pp. 179–92.

HIGHLIGHT 4–4

An Operational View of the Organizational Buying Process

Although there is no single format dictating how organizations actually purchase goods and services, a relatively standard process is followed in most cases:

1. A department discovers or anticipates a problem in its operation that it believes can be overcome with the addition of a certain product or service.
2. The department head draws up a requisition form describing the desired specifications he or she believes the product or service must have to solve the problem.
3. The department head sends the requisition form to the firm's purchasing department.
4. Based on the specifications required, the purchasing department conducts a search for qualified sources of supply.
5. Once sources have been located, proposals based on the specifications are solicited, received, and analyzed for price, delivery, service, and so on.

6. Proposals are compared with the cost of producing the product in-house in a make-or-buy decision: if it is decided that the buying firm can produce the product more economically, the buying process for the product in question is terminated; however, if the inverse is true, the process continues.
7. A source or sources of supply is selected from those who have submitted proposals.
8. The order is placed, and copies of the purchase order are sent to the originating department, accounting, credit, and any other interested departments within the company.
9. After the product is shipped, received, and used, a follow-up with the originating department is conducted to determine if the purchased product solved the department's problem.

Although there are many variations of this process in actual operation, this is typical of the process by which organizational goods and services are purchased. It must be understood that in actual practice these steps are combined, not separate.

Source: Adapted from Robert W. Hass, *Business Marketing Management,* 5th ed. PWS-KENT Publishing Company, a division of Wadsworth, Inc., 1992, p. 174.

STAGES IN THE BUYING PROCESS

As with consumer buying, most organizational purchases are made in response to a particular need or problem faced by the firm. Recognition of the need, however, is only the first step in the organizational buying process. The following four stages represent one model of the industrial buying process:

1. Problem recognition.
2. Organizational assignment of buying responsibility and authority.
3. Search procedures for identifying product offerings and for establishing selection criteria.
4. Choice procedures for evaluating and selecting among alternatives.

Problem Recognition

As mentioned previously, most organizational purchases are made in response to a particular need or problem. The product purchased is hopefully the means to solve the particular problem. Buyers must be concerned with budgets and profits since the firm cannot put forth a great amount of financial resources if it does not have sufficient funds, regardless of the benefits that might be derived from the purchase. However, as was mentioned, there is more subjective buying and persuasion in the organizational buying process than some earlier writers indicated.

Assignment of Buying Authority

The influence of individuals on the buying decision will be determined in part by their responsibility as defined by the formal organization. An individual's responsibility in a given buying situation will be a function of (1) the technical complexity of the product; (2) the importance of the product to the firm either in dollar terms or in terms of its relationship with the process or system that will use the product; (3) the product-specific technical knowledge that the individual has; (4) the individual's centrality in the process or system that will use the product.

In some organizations the responsibility for the purchasing decision is assigned to a centralized purchasing unit. When centralization of the buying function occurs, it is usually based on the assumption that knowledge of the market and not knowledge of the physical product itself is the major consideration in the buying decision. Therefore, the purchasing agent will concentrate on such market variables as price, delivery, and seller performance, rather than on the technical aspects of the product.

Search Procedures

This stage involves the search procedures for identifying product offerings and for establishing selection criteria. Basically, buyers perform two key tasks related to the collection and analysis of information. First, the criteria against which to evaluate potential sellers have to be developed. These are usually based on a judgment about what is needed compared to what is available. Second, alternative product candidates must be located in the market. The important point here is that buyers seek sellers just as sellers seek buyers.

Choice Procedures

The final stage in the organizational buying process involves establishing choice procedures for evaluating and selecting among alternatives. Once alternative products and alternative suppliers have been identified, the buyer must choose from among the alternatives. The choice process is guided by the use of decision rules and specific criteria for evaluating the product offering. These decision rules evolve from objectives, policies, and procedures established for buying actions by management. Often some type of rating scheme or value index is used.

The above stages in the organizational buying process have particular significance for marketers in their method of approach to potential buyers. This is not to say that these stages are the only activities organizational buyers go through before making a purchase, or that they are even aware that they are going through them. The stages are presented here only as a convenient way to examine the organizational buying process and the importance of certain activities during particular stages.

CONCLUSION

Organizational buying has long been regarded as the stepchild of marketing in terms of the amount of research effort devoted to its problems. However, considerable recent research has been conducted and in this chapter an overview of the organizational buying process has been presented. Basically, the model viewed organizational buying as a process of problem recognition, assignment of buying authority, search procedures, and choice procedures. Product, structural, and behavioral influences were recognized as playing important roles in terms of the speed and complexity of this process.

ADDITIONAL READINGS

Bingham, Frank G., and Barney T. Raffield III. *Business to Business Marketing Management*. Homewood, Ill.: Richard D. Irwin, 1990.

Corey, E. Raymond. *Industrial Marketing: Cases and Concepts*. 4th ed. Englewood Cliffs, N.J.: Prentice Hall, 1991.

Eckles, Robert W. *Business Marketing Management,* Englewood Cliffs, N.J.: Prentice Hall, 1990.

Perdue, Barbara C., and John O. Summers. "Purchasing Agents' Use of Negotiation Strategies." *Journal of Marketing Research,* May 1991, pp. 175–89.

Sherlock, Paul. *Rethinking Business to Business Marketing*. New York: Free Press, 1991.

Ward, Scott and Frederick E. Webster, Jr. "Organizational Buying Behavior," in T. S. Robertson and H. H. Kassarjian (eds). *Handbook of Consumer Behavior*. Englewood Cliffs, N.J.: Prentice Hall, 1991, pp. 419–58.

Wilson, Elizabeth J.; Gary L. Lilien; and David T. Wilson. "Developing and Testing a Contingency Paradigm of Group Choice in Organizational Buying." *Journal of Marketing Research,* November 1991, pp. 452–66.

Chapter 5

Market Segmentation

Market segmentation is one of the most important concepts in the marketing literature. In fact, a primary reason for studying consumer and organizational buyer behavior is to provide bases for effective segmentation, and a large portion of marketing research is concerned with segmentation. From a marketing management point of view, selection of the appropriate target market is paramount to developing successful marketing programs.

The logic of market segmentation is quite simple and is based on the idea that a single product item can seldom meet the needs and wants of *all* consumers. Typically, consumers vary as to their needs, wants, and preferences for products and services, and successful marketers adapt their marketing programs to fulfill these preference patterns. For example, even a simple product like chewing gum has multiple flavors, package sizes, sugar contents, calories, consistencies (e.g., liquid centers), and colors to meet the preferences of various consumers. While a single product item cannot meet the needs of all consumers, it can almost always serve more than one consumer. Thus, there are usually *groups of consumers* who can be served well by a single item. If a particular group can be served *profitably* by a firm, it is a viable market segment. In other words, the firm should develop a marketing mix to serve the group or market segment.

In this chapter we consider the process of market segmentation. We define *market segmentation* as the process of dividing a market into groups of similar consumers and selecting the most appropriate group(s) for the firm to serve. We break down the process of market segmentation into six steps, as shown in Figure 5–1. While we recognize that the order of these steps may vary,

Figure 5–1   *A Model of the Market Segmentation Process*

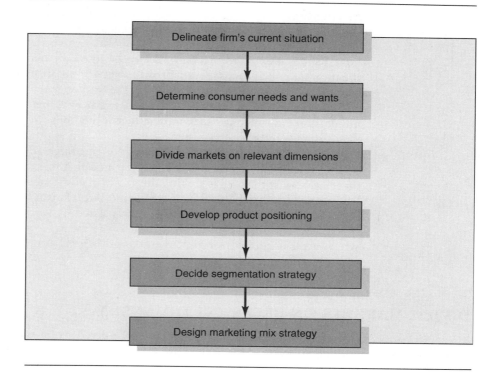

depending on the firm and situation, there are few if any times when market segmentation analysis can be ignored. In fact, even if the final decision is to "mass market" and not segment at all, this decision should be reached only *after* a market segmentation analysis has been conducted. Thus, market segmentation analysis is a cornerstone of sound marketing planning and decision making.

DELINEATE THE FIRM'S CURRENT SITUATION

As emphasized in Chapter 1, a firm must do a complete situational analysis when embarking on a new or modified marketing program. At the marketing planning level, such an analysis aids in determining objectives, opportunities, and constraints to be considered when selecting target markets and developing marketing mixes. In addition, marketing managers must have a clear idea of the amount of financial and other resources that will be available for developing and executing a marketing plan. Thus, the inclusion of this first step in the market segmentation process is intended to be a reminder of tasks to be performed prior to marketing planning.

DETERMINE CONSUMER NEEDS AND WANTS

As emphasized throughout this text, successful marketing strategies depend on discovering and satisfying consumer needs and wants. In some cases, this idea is quite operational. To illustrate, suppose a firm has a good deal of venture capital and is seeking to diversify its interest into new markets. A firm in this situation may seek to discover a broad variety of unsatisfied needs. However, in most situations, the industry in which the firm operates specifies the boundaries of a firm's need satisfaction activities. For example, a firm in the communication industry may seek more efficient methods for serving consumers' long-distance telephone needs.

As a practical matter, new technology often brings about an investigation of consumer needs and wants for new or modified products and services. In these situations, the firm is seeking the group of consumers whose needs could best be satisfied by the new or modified product. Further, at a strategic level, consumer needs and wants usually are translated into more operational concepts. For instance, consumer attitudes, preferences, and benefits sought, which are determined through marketing research, are commonly used for segmentation purposes.

DIVIDE MARKETS ON RELEVANT DIMENSIONS

In a narrow sense, this step is often considered to be the whole of market segmentation (i.e., consumers are grouped on the basis of one or more similarities and treated as a homogeneous segment of a heterogeneous total market). There are three important questions to be considered here:

1. Should the segmentation be a priori or post hoc?
2. How does one determine the relevant dimensions or bases to use for segmentation?
3. What are some bases for segmenting consumer and industrial buyer markets?

A Priori versus Post Hoc Segmentation

Real-world segmentation has followed one of two general patterns. An *a priori segmentation* approach is one in which the marketing manager has decided on the appropriate basis for segmentation in advance of doing any research on a market. For example, a manager may decide that a market should be divided on the basis of whether people are nonusers, light users, or heavy users of a particular product. Segmentation research is then conducted to determine the size of each of these groups and their demographic or psychographic profiles.

HIGHLIGHT 5–1

Hitting Target Markets in the 1990s

By combining data from several sources, a company can have extensive information on its target markets and where they shop. Below are examples of the target market profiles for three products and the stores in the New York area where they are most likely to purchase them. Marketers could design special promotions in these stores to further increase the probability of purchase.

Brand	Heavy User Profile	Lifestyle and Media Profile	Top Stores
Peter Pan peanut butter	Households with kids headed by 18-54 year olds, in suburban and rural areas	Heavy video renters Go to theme parks Below average TV viewers Above average radio listeners	**Foodtown Super Market** Levittown, N.Y. **Pathmark Supermarket** Levittown, N.Y. **King Kullen Market** Bethpage, N.Y.
Stouffers Red Box frozen entrees	Households headed by people 55 and older, and up-scale suburban households headed by 35-54 year olds	Go to gambling casinos Give parties Involved in public activities Travel frequently Heavy newspaper readers Above average TV viewers	**Dan's Supreme Super Market** Flushing, N.Y. **Food Emporium** New York City **Waldbaum Super Market** Flushing, N.Y.
Coors Light beer	Head of household, 21-34, middle to upper income, suburban and urban	Belong to a health club Buy rock music Travel by plane Give parties, cookouts Rent videos Heavy TV sports viewers	**Food Emporium** New York City **Gristades Supermarket** New York City

Source: Michael J. McCarthy, "Marketers Zero in on Their Customers," *The Wall Street Journal*, March 18, 1991, p. B1.

Post hoc segmentation is an approach in which people are grouped into segments on the basis of research findings. For example, people interviewed concerning their attitudes or benefits sought in a particular product category are grouped according to their responses. The size of each of these groups and their demographic and psychographic profiles are then determined.

Both of these approaches are valuable, and the question of which to use depends in part on how well the firm knows the market for a particular product class. If through previous research and experience a marketing manager has successfully isolated a number of key market dimensions, then an a priori approach based on them may provide more useful information. In the case of segmentation for entirely new products, a post hoc approach may be useful for determining key market dimensions. However, even when using a post hoc approach, some consideration must be given to the variables to be included in the research design. Thus, some consideration must be given to the relevant segmentation dimensions regardless of which approach is used.

Relevance of Segmentation Dimensions

Unfortunately, there is no simple solution for determining the relevant dimensions for segmenting markets. Certainly, managerial expertise and experience are needed for selecting the appropriate dimensions or bases on which to segment particular markets. In most cases, however, at least some initial dimensions can be determined from previous research, purchase trends, and managerial judgment. For instance, suppose we wish to segment the market for all-terrain vehicles. Clearly, several dimensions come to mind for initial consideration including sex (male), age (18 to 35 years), lifestyle (outdoorsman), and income level (perhaps $15,000 to $25,000). At a minimum, these variables should be included in subsequent segmentation research. Of course, the most market-oriented approach to segmentation is on the basis of what benefits the potential consumer is seeking. Thus, consideration and research of sought benefits is a strongly recommended approach in the marketing literature. This approach will be considered in some detail in the following section.

Bases for Segmentation

A number of useful bases for segmenting consumer and organizational markets are presented in Figure 5–2. This is by no means a complete list of possible segmentation variables but represents some useful bases and categories. Two commonly used approaches for segmenting markets include benefit segmentation and psychographic segmentation. We will discuss these two in some detail.

Benefit segmentation

The belief underlying this segmentation approach is that the benefits people are seeking in consuming a given product are the basic reasons for the existence of true market segments.[1] Thus, this approach attempts to measure consumer value systems and consumer perceptions of various brands in a product class. To illustrate, the classic example of a benefit segmentation was provided by

---

[1]Russell I. Haley, "Benefit Segmentation: A Decision-Oriented Research Tool," *Journal of Marketing,* July 1968, pp. 30–35; Russell I. Haley, "Benefit Segmentation—20 Years Later," *Journal of Consumer Marketing,* no. 2 (1983), pp. 5–13; Russell I. Haley, "Benefit Segments: Backwards and Forwards," *Journal of Advertising Research,* February–March 1984, pp. 19–25.

Figure 5–2   *Useful Segmentation Bases for Consumer and Organizational Buyer Markets*

	Consumer Markets
Segmentation Base	**Examples of Base Categories**
Geographic:	
Region	Pacific, Mountain, West North Central, West South Central, East North Central, East South Central, South Atlantic, Middle Atlantic, New England.
City, county, or SMSA size	Under 5,000; 5,000–19,999; 20,000–49,999; 50,000–99,999; 100,000–249,999; 250,000–499,999; 500,000–999,999; 1,000,000–3,999,999; 4,000,000 or over.
Population density	Urban, suburban, rural.
Climate	Warm, cold.
Demographic:	
Age	Under 6; 6–12; 13–19; 20–29; 30–39; 40–49; 50–59; 60+.
Sex	Male, female.
Family size	1–2; 3–4; 5+.
Family life cycle	Young, single; young, married, no children; young, married, youngest child under 6; young, married, youngest child 6 or over; older, married, with children; older, married, no children under 18; older, single; other.
Income	Under $10,000; $10,000–$14,999; $15,000–$24,999; $25,000–$34,999; $35,000 or over.
Occupation	Professional and technical; managers, officials, and proprietors; clerical, sales; craftsmen, foremen; operatives; farmers; retired; students; housewives, unemployed.
Education	Grade school or less; some high school; graduated high school; some college; graduated college; some graduate work; graduate degree.
Religion	Catholic, Protestant, Jewish, other.
Race	White, black, oriental, other.
Nationality	American, British, German, Italian, Japanese, other.
Psychographic:	
Social class	Upper Americans, middle class, working class, lower Americans.
Lifestyle	Traditionalist, sophisticate, swinger.
Personality	Compliant, aggressive, detached.
Cognitive and behavioral:	
Attitudes	Positive, neutral, negative.
Benefits sought	Convenience, economy, prestige.
Readiness stage	Unaware, aware, informed, interested, desirous, intention to purchase.
Perceived risk	High, moderate, low.
Innovativeness	Innovator, early adopter, early majority, late majority, laggard.
Involvement	Low, high.
Loyalty status	None, some, total.
Usage rate	None, light, medium, heavy.
User status	Nonuser, ex-user, potential user, current user.

Figure 5–2 *(concluded)*

	Organizational Buyer Markets
Segmentation Base	**Examples of Base Categories**
Source loyalty	Purchase from one, two, three, four, or more suppliers.
Size of company	Small, medium, large relative to industry.
Average size of purchase	Small, medium, large.
Usage rate	Light, medium, heavy.
Product application	Maintenance, production, final product component, administration.
Type of organization	Manufacturer, wholesaler, retailer; government agency.
Location	North, East, South, West sales territories.
Purchase status	New customer, occasional purchaser, frequent purchaser, nonpurchaser.
Attribute importance	Reliability of supply, price, service, durability, convenience, reputation of supplier.

Russell Haley and concerned the toothpaste market. Haley identified five basic segments, which are presented in Figure 5–3. Haley argued that this segmentation could be very useful for selecting advertising copy, media, commercial length, packaging, and new product design. For example, colorful packages might be appropriate for the Sensory Segment, perhaps aqua (to indicate fluoride) for the Worrier Group, and gleaming white for the Social Segment because of this segment's interest in white teeth.

Calantone and Sawyer also used a benefit segmentation approach to segment the market for bank services.[2] Their research was concerned with the question of whether benefit segments remain stable across time. While they found some stability in segments, there were some differences in attribute importance, size, and demographics at different times. Thus, they argue for ongoing benefit segmentation research to keep track of any changes in a market that might affect marketing strategy.

Benefit segmentation is clearly a market-oriented approach to segmentation that seeks to identify consumer needs and wants and to satisfy them by providing products and services with the desired benefits. It is clearly very consistent with the approach to marketing suggested by the marketing concept.

---

[2]Roger J. Calantone and Alan G. Sawyer, "The Stability of Benefit Segments," *Journal of Marketing Research,* August 1978, pp. 395–404; also see James R. Merrill and William A. Weeks, "Predicting and Identifying Benefit Segments in the Elderly Market," in *AMA Educator's Proceedings,* ed. Patrick Murphy et al. (Chicago: American Marketing Association, 1983), pp. 399–403; Wagner A. Kamakura, "A Least Squares Procedure for Benefit Segmentation with Conjoint Experiments," *Journal of Marketing Research,* May 1988, pp. 157–67; Michel Wedel and Jan-Benedict E. M. Steenkamp "A Clusterwise Regression Method for Simultaneous Fuzzy Market Structuring and Benefit Segmentation," *Journal of Marketing Research,* November 1991, pp. 385–96.

HIGHLIGHT 5–2

Market Segmentation at Campbell Soup Company

Campbell Soup Company cooked up its own version of market segmentation, which it calls "regionalization." Basically, the company divided the United States into 22 regions, each with its own marketing and sales force. Each regional staff studies marketing strategies and media buying and has its own ad and trade-promotion budget.

Regional staffs came up with a number of innovative methods to sell Campbell's products, including:

— In Texas and California, where consumers like their food with a bit of a kick, Campbell's nacho cheese soup is spicier than in other parts of the country.

— In New York, when the Giants were bound for the Super Bowl, a local sales manager used part of her ad budget to arrange a football-related radio promotion for Swanson Frozen dinners.

— In Nevada, Campbell treats skiers at Ski Incline resort to hot samples of its soup of the day.

— In the South, Campbell has experimented with a Creole soup and a red-bean soup for the Hispanic market.

Figure 5–3   Toothpaste Market Benefit Segments

	Sensory Segment	Sociable Segment	Worrier Segment	Independent Segment
Principal benefit sought	Flavor and product appearance.	Brightness of teeth.	Decay prevention.	Price.
Demographic strengths	Children.	Teens, young people.	Large families.	Men.
Special behavioral characteristics	Users of spearmint-flavored toothpaste.	Smokers.	Heavy users.	Heavy users.
Brands disproportionately favored	Colgate.	Macleans, Ultra Brite.	Crest.	Cheapest brand.
Lifestyle characteristics	Hedonistic.	Active.	Conservative.	Value-oriented.

Source: Adapted from Russell I. Haley, "Benefit Segmentation: A Decision-Oriented Research Tool," *Journal of Marketing,* July 1968, pp. 30–35.

HIGHLIGHT 5–3

Examples of Items Used in Psychographic Segmentation Research

1. I often watch the newspaper advertisements for announcements of department store sales.
2. I like to watch or listen to baseball or football games.
3. I often try new stores before my friends and neighbors do.
4. I like to work on community projects.
5. My children are the most important thing in my life.

6. I will probably have more money to spend next year than I have now.
7. I often seek out the advice of my friends regarding which store to buy from.
8. I think I have more self-confidence than most people.
9. I enjoy going to symphony concerts.
10. It is good to have charge accounts.

(These items are scored on a "agree strongly" to "disagree strongly" scale.)

Psychographic segmentation

Whereas benefit segmentation focuses on the benefits sought by the consumer, psychographic segmentation focuses on the personal attributes of the consumer. The psychographic or lifestyle approach typically follows a post hoc model of segmentation. Generally, a large number of questions are asked concerning consumer's activities, interests, and opinions, and then consumers are grouped together empirically based on their responses. Although questions have been raised about the validity of this segmentation approach, it provides much useful information about markets.[3]

A well-known psychographic segmentation was developed at SRI International in California. The original segmentation divided consumers in the United States into nine groups and was called VALS,™ which stands for "values and lifestyles." However, while this segmentation was commercially successful, it tended to place the majority of consumers into only one or two groups, and SRI felt it needed to be updated to reflect changes in society. Thus, SRI developed a new typology called VALS 2.™[4]

VALS 2 is based on two national surveys of 2,500 consumers who responded to 43 lifestyle questions. The first survey developed the segmentation, and the second validated it and linked it to buying and media behavior. The ques-

---

[3]John L. Lastovicka, John P. Murry Jr., and Eric Joachimsthaler, "Evaluating the Measurement Validity of Lifestyle Typologies with Qualitative Measures and Multiplicative Factoring," *Journal of Marketing Research*, February 1990, pp. 11–23.

[4]This discussion is taken from J. Paul Peter and Jerry C. Olson, *Consumer Behavior and Marketing Strategy*, 3rd ed. (Homewood, Ill.: Richard D. Irwin, 1993), pp. 557–58.

Figure 5–4   VALS 2™ Eight American Lifestyles

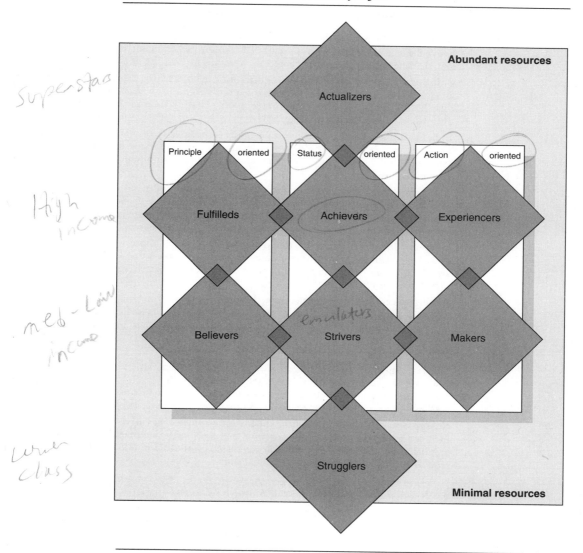

tionnaire asked consumers to respond to whether they agreed or disagreed with statements such as "My idea of fun at a national park would be to stay at an expensive lodge and dress up for dinner" and "I could stand to skin a dead animal." Consumers were then clustered into the eight groups shown and described in Figure 5–4.

The VALS 2 groups are arranged in a rectangle and are based on two dimensions. The vertical dimension represents resources, which include

Figure 5-4   *(concluded)*

Actualizers. These consumers have the highest incomes and such high self-esteem and abundant resources that they can indulge in any or all self-orientations. They are located above the rectangle. Image is important to them as an expression of their taste, independence, and character. Their consumer choices are directed toward the finer things in life.

Fulfilleds. These consumers are the high-resource group of those who are principle-oriented. They are mature, responsible, well-educated professionals. Their leisure activities center on their homes, but they are well-informed about what goes on in the world, and they are open to new ideas and social change. They have high incomes but are practical consumers.

Believers. These consumers are the low-resource group of those who are principle-oriented. They are conservative and predictable consumers who favor American products and established brands. Their lives are centered on family, church, community, and the nation. They have modest incomes.

Achievers. These consumers are the high-resource group of those who are status-oriented. They are successful, work-oriented people who get their satisfaction from their jobs and families. They are politically conservative and respect authority and the status quo. They favor established products and services that show off their success to their peers.

Strivers. These consumers are the low-resource group of those who are status-oriented. They have values very similar to Achievers but have fewer economic, social, and psychological resources. Style is extremely important to them as they strive to emulate people they admire and wish to be like.

Experiencers. These consumers are the high-resource group of those who are action-oriented. They are the youngest of all the segments with a median age of 25. They have a lot of energy, which they pour into physical exercise and social activities. They are avid consumers, spending heavily on clothing, fast foods, music, and other youthful favorites—with particular emphasis on new products and services.

Makers. These consumers are the low-resource group of those who are action-oriented. They are practical people who value self-sufficiency. They are focused on the familiar—family, work, and physical recreation—and have little interest in the broader world. As consumers, they appreciate practical and functional products.

Strugglers. These consumers have the lowest incomes. They have too few resources to be included in any consumer self-orientation and are thus located below the rectangle. They are the oldest of all the segments with a median age of 61. Within their limited means, they tend to be brand-loyal consumers.

Source: Martha Farnsworth Riche, "Psychographics for the 1990s," *American Demographics,* July 1989, pp. 24–26ff. Adapted with permission © American Demographics.

income, education, self-confidence, health, eagerness to buy, intelligence, and energy level. The horizontal dimension represents self-orientations, and includes three different types. *Principle-oriented consumers* are guided by their views of how the world is or should be; *status-oriented consumers* by the action and opinions of others; and *action-oriented consumers* by a desire for social or physical activity, variety, and risk taking.

Each of the VALS 2 groups represents from 9 to 17 percent of the U.S. adult population. Marketers can buy VALS 2 information for a variety of products and can have it tied to a number of other consumer databases.

DEVELOP PRODUCT POSITIONING

By this time the firm should have a good idea of the basic segments of the market that could potentially be satisfied with its product. The current step is concerned with positioning the product in the minds of consumers relative to competing products. Undoubtedly, the classic example of positioning is the 7UP "Uncola" campaign. Prior to this campaign, 7UP had difficulty convincing consumers that the product could be enjoyed as a soft drink and not just as a mixer. Consumers believed that colas were soft drinks but apparently did not perceive 7UP in this way. However, by positioning 7UP as the "Uncola" the company was capable of positioning the product (1) as a soft drink that could be consumed in the same situations as colas and (2) as an alternative to colas. This positioning was very successful.

In determining the appropriate positioning of the product, the firm must consider its offering relative to competition. Some experts argue that different positioning strategies should be used depending on whether the firm is the market leader or a follower, and that followers usually should not attempt positioning directly against the industry leader.[5] While there are many sophisticated research tools available for investigating positioning, they are beyond the scope of this text. The main point here is that, in segmenting markets, some segments otherwise appearing to be approachable might be forgone, since competitive products may already dominate that segment in sales and in the minds of consumers. Product positioning studies are useful for giving the marketing manager a clearer idea of consumer perceptions of market offerings and for selecting appropriate attributes for positioning products or stores.

DECIDE SEGMENTATION STRATEGY

The firm is now ready to select its segmentation strategy. There are four basic alternatives. First, the firm may decide not to enter the market. For example, analysis to this stage may reveal there is no viable market niche for the firm's offering. Second, the firm may decide not to segment but to be a mass marketer. There are at least three situations when this may be the appropriate decision for the firm:

1. The market is so small that marketing to a portion of it is not profitable.
2. Heavy users make up such a large proportion of the sales volume that they are the only relevant target.
3. The brand is the dominant brand in the market, and targeting to a few segments would not benefit sales and profits.

---

[5]See Al Ries and Jack Trout, *Positioning: The Battle for Your Mind* (New York: Warner Books, 1981); Al Ries and Jack Trout, *Marketing Warfare* (New York: McGraw-Hill, 1986).

Target Markets for Three Chrysler Corporation Cars

Marketers often use a variety of segmentation dimensions to understand and describe their target markets. Below is a description of a profile of the most likely buyers Chrysler Corporation found for three of its models, the Chrysler Concorde, Eagle Vision, and Dodge Intrepid. The Concorde is the most expensive model and the Intrepid is the least expensive.

Targets for the Concorde

Family status: Married, two children between the ages of 20 and 25.

Education: Four-year college.

Income and occupation: $52,000 (median). He is a commodities broker who has worked 25 years for the same firm. She is a homemaker.

. . . For the Vision

Family status: Married, two children under the age of 10.

Education: Graduate school.

Income and occupation: $50,000 (median). He sells commercial real estate. She develops computer software.

. . . For the Intrepid

Family status: Married, up to three kids ranging in age from 6 to 16.

Education: 2 to 4 years of college.

Income and occupation: $35,000 to $75,000 range. He installs computer systems. She is a nurse, paralegal, or homemaker.

Media habits: Lots of prime-time TV. Read *House and Garden*, *TV Guide*. Got VCR two years ago, but still can't program it.

First important car:
His: '57 Chevy; **Hers:** '60 Impala

Vacation habits: Winter at Florida time-share, summer at friends' home on the lake.

Habitat: Colonial home in a suburban subdivision outside Philadelphia.

Leisure time: He has a wood shop; she gardens. They dance to oldies or big band music at least once a month.

Media habits: Critical of most TV. Read *Vanity Fair*. Car radio pre-selects are jazz, classical, public radio.

First important car:
His: BMW 2002; **Hers:** Alfa Romeo Spider

Vacation habits: Three annually, one at family resort; one with-out kids at a semi-obscure location; third at home catching up on projects.

Habitat: Renovated 1930s home in northern Chicago suburb.

Leisure time: Work out twice a week at health club, rent videos, collect Art Deco objects and furniture.

Media habits: Moderate TV, family shows and sports. Read how-to, investing and magazines and about participant sports like golf or fishing.

First important car:
His and Hers: Mustangs.

Vacation habits: Two family-centered vacations, one to destinations like Disney World or big cities, the other for camping and backpacking.

Habitat: Split-level home in newer suburbs around the country.

Leisure time: Split between participant sports like softball, and family activities like Boy or Girl Scouts.

Source: Doron P. Levin, "Chrysler's New L/H, as in Last Hope," *The New York Times*, July 12, 1992, p. 6F.

HIGHLIGHT 5–5

Segmentation Bases for Particular Marketing Decision Areas

For general understanding of the market:
Benefits sought.
Product purchase and usage patterns.
Needs.
Brand loyalty and switching patterns.
A hybrid of the variables above.

For positioning studies:
Product usage.
Product preference.
Benefits sought.
A hybrid of the variables above.

For new product concepts (and new product introduction):
Reaction to new concepts (intention to buy, preference over current brand, and so on).
Benefits sought.

For pricing decisions:
Price sensitivity.
Deal proneness.
Price sensitivity by purchase/usage patterns.

For advertising decisions:
Benefits sought.
Media usage.
Psychographic/lifestyle.
A hybrid (of the variables above or purchase/ usage pattern, or both).

For distribution decisions:
Store loyalty and patronage.
Benefits sought in store selection.

Source: Yoram Wind, "Issues and Advances in Segmentation Research," *Journal of Marketing Research,* August 1978, p. 320.

Third, the firm may decide to market to one segment. And fourth, the firm may decide to market to more than one segment and design a separate marketing mix for each. In any case, the firm must have some criteria on which to base its segmentation strategy decisions. Three important criteria on which to base such decisions are that a viable segment must be (1) measurable, (2) meaningful, and (3) marketable.

1. *Measurable.* For a segment to be selected, the firm must be capable of measuring its size and characteristics. For instance, one of the difficulties with segmenting on the basis of social class is that the concept and its divisions are not clearly defined and measured. Alternatively, income is a much easier concept to measure.
2. *Meaningful.* A meaningful segment is one that is large enough to have sufficient sales potential and growth potential to offer long-run profits for the firm.
3. *Marketable.* A marketable segment is one that can be reached and served by the firm in an efficient manner.

HIGHLIGHT 5–6

Differences in Marketing Strategy for Three Segmentation Alternatives

Strategy Elements	Mass Marketing	Single Market Segmentation	Multiple Market Segmentation
Market definition	Broad range of consumers.	One well-defined consumer group.	Two or more well-defined consumer groups.
Product strategy	Limited number of products under one brand for many types of consumers.	One brand tailored to one consumer group.	Distinct brand for each consumer group.
Pricing strategy	One "popular" price range.	One price range tailored to the consumer group.	Distinct price range for each consumer group.
Distribution strategy	All possible outlets.	All suitable outlets.	All suitable outlets—differs by segment.
Promotion strategy	Mass media.	All suitable media.	All suitable media—differs by segment.
Strategy emphasis	Appeal to various types of consumers through a uniform, broad-based marketing program.	Appeal to one specific consumer group through a highly specialized, but uniform, marketing program.	Appeal to two or more distinct market segments through different marketing plans catering to each segment.

Source: Adapted from Joel R. Evans and Barry Berman, *Marketing,* 5th ed., New York: Macmillan, 1992, p. 219.

Segments that meet these criteria are viable markets for the firm's offering. The firm must now give further attention to completing its marketing mix offering.

DESIGN MARKETING MIX STRATEGY

The firm is now in a position to complete its marketing plan by finalizing the marketing mix or mixes to be used for each segment. Clearly, selection of the target market and designing the marketing mix go hand in hand, and thus many marketing mix decisions should have already been carefully considered.

To illustrate, the target market selected may be price sensitive, so some consideration has already been given to price levels, and clearly product positioning has many implications for promotion and channel decisions. Thus, while we place marketing mix design at the end of the model, many of these decisions are clearly made in *conjunction* with target market selection. In the next six chapters of this text, marketing mix decisions will be discussed in detail.

CONCLUSION

The purpose of this chapter was to provide an overview of market segmentation. Market segmentation was defined as the process of dividing a market into groups of similar consumers and selecting the most appropriate group(s) for the firm to serve. Market segmentation was analyzed as a six-stage process: (1) to delineate the firm's current situation; (2) to determine consumer needs and wants; (3) to divide the market on relevant dimensions; (4) to develop product positioning; (5) to decide segmentation strategy; (6) to design marketing mix strategy.

ADDITIONAL READINGS

Anderson, Eugene W., and Steven M. Shugan. "Repositioning for Changing Preferences: The Case of Beef versus Poultry." *Journal of Consumer Research*, September 1991, pp. 219–32.

Dickson, Peter R., and James L. Ginter. "Market Segmentation, Product Differentiation, and Marketing Strategy." *Journal of Marketing*, April 1987, pp. 1–10.

Green, Paul E., and Abba M. Krieger. "Segmenting Markets with Conjoint Analysis." *Journal of Marketing*, October 1991, pp. 20–31.

Kamakura, Wagner A., and Thomas P. Kovak. "Value-System Segmentation: Exploring the Meaning of LOV." *Journal of Consumer Research*, June 1992, pp. 119–32.

Novak, Thomas P.; Jan de Leeuw; and Bruce MacEvoy. "Richness Curves for Evaluating Market Segmentation." *Journal of Marketing Research*, May 1992, pp. 254–67.

Pechmann, Cornelia, and S. Ratneshwar. "The Use of Comparative Advertising for Brand Positioning: Association versus Differentiation." *Journal of Consumer Research*, September 1991, pp. 145–60.

Rangan, V. Kasturi; Rowland T. Moriarty; and Gordon S. Swartz. "Segmenting Customers in Mature Industrial Markets." *Journal of Marketing*, October 1992, pp. 72–82.

The Marketing Mix

Chapter 6

Product Strategy

Product strategy is a critical element of marketing and business strategy, since it is through the sale of products and services that companies survive and grow. This chapter discusses four important areas of concern in developing product strategies. First, some basic issues are discussed, including product definition, product classification, product mix and product line, packaging, and branding and brand equity. Second, the product life cycle and its implications for product strategy are explained. Third, the product audit is reviewed, and finally, five ways to organize for product management are overviewed. These include the marketing manager system, product (brand) manager system, product planning committee, new product manager system, and venture team approaches.

BASIC ISSUES IN PRODUCT MANAGEMENT

Successful marketing depends on understanding the nature of products and basic decision areas in product management. In this section, we discuss the definition and classification of products and the nature of a product mix and product lines. Also considered is the role of packaging and branding.

Product Definition

The way in which the product variable is defined can have important implications for the survival, profitability, and long-run growth of the firm. For example, the same product can be viewed at least three different ways. First, it can be viewed in terms of the tangible product—the physical entity or service that is offered to the buyer. Second, it can be viewed in terms of the

---

HIGHLIGHT 6–1

Elements of Product Strategy

1. *An audit of the firm's actual and potential resources.*
   a. Financial strength.
   b. Access to raw materials.
   c. Plant and equipment.
   d. Operating personnel.
   e. Management.
   f. Engineering and technical skills.
   g. Patents and licenses.
2. *Approaches to current markets.*
   a. More of the same products.
   b. Variations of present products in terms of grades, sizes, and packages.
   c. New products to replace or supplement current lines.
   d. Product deletions.
3. *Approaches to new or potential markets.*
   a. Geographical expansion of domestic sales.
   b. New socioeconomic or ethnic groups.
   c. Overseas markets.
   d. New uses of present products.
   e. Complementary goods.
   f. Mergers and acquisitions.
4. *State of competition.*
   a. New entries into the industry.
   b. Product imitation.
   c. Competitive mergers or acquisitions.

---

extended product—the tangible product along with the whole cluster of services that accompany it. For example, a manufacturer of computer software may offer a 24-hour hotline to answer questions users may have, free or reduced–cost software updates, free replacement of damaged software, and a subscription to a newsletter that documents new applications of the software. Third, it can be viewed in terms of the generic product—the essential benefits the buyer expects to receive from the product. For example, many personal care products bring to the purchaser feelings of self-enhancement and security in addition to the tangible benefits they offer.

From the standpoint of the marketing manager, to define the product solely in terms of the tangible product is to fall into the error of "marketing myopia." Executives who are guilty of committing this error define their company's product too narrowly, since overemphasis is placed on the physical object itself. The classic example of this mistake can be found in railroad passenger service. Although no amount of product improvement could have staved off its decline, if the industry had defined itself as being in the transportation business, rather than the railroad business, it might still be profitable today. On the positive side, toothpaste manufacturers have been willing to exercise flexibility in defining their product. For years toothpaste was an oral hygiene product where emphasis was placed solely on fighting tooth decay and bad breath (e.g., Crest with fluoride). More recently, many manufacturers have recognized the need to market toothpaste as a cosmetic item (to clean teeth of stains), as a defense against gum disease (to reduce the buildup of tartar above the gumline), as an aid for denture wearers, and as a breath freshener. As a result, special purpose brands have been designed to serve these particular needs, such as Ultra Brite, Close-Up, Aqua-Fresh, Aim, Dental Care, and the wide variety of baking soda, tartar-control formula, and gel toothpastes offered under existing brand names.

In line with the marketing concept philosophy, a reasonable definition of product is that it is *the sum of the physical, psychological, and sociological satisfactions the buyer derives from purchase, ownership, and consumption.* From this standpoint, products are consumer-satisfying objects that include such things as accessories, packaging, and service.

Product Classification

A product classification scheme can be useful to the marketing manager as an analytical device to assist in planning marketing strategy and programs. A basic assumption underlying such classifications is that products with common attributes can be marketed in a similar fashion. In general, products are classed according to two basic criteria: (1) end use or market; and (2) degree of processing or physical transformation.

1. *Agricultural products and raw materials.* These are goods grown or extracted from the land or sea, such as iron ore, wheat, sand. In general these products are fairly homogenous, sold in large volume, and have low value per unit or bulk weight.
2. *Industrial goods.* Such products are purchased by business firms for the purpose of producing other goods or for running the business. This category includes the following:
   a. Raw materials and semifinished goods.
   b. Major and minor equipment, such as basic machinery, tools, and other processing facilities.
   c. Parts or components, which become an integral element of some other finished good.
   d. Supplies or items used to operate the business but that do not become part of the final product.
3. *Consumer goods.* Consumer goods can be divided into three classes:
   a. Convenience goods, such as food, which are purchased frequently with minimum effort. Impulse goods would also fall into this category.
   b. Shopping goods, such as appliances, which are purchased after some time and energy are spent comparing the various offerings.
   c. Specialty goods, which are unique in some way so the consumer will make a special purchase effort to obtain them.

In general, the buying motive, buying habits, and character of the market are different for industrial goods vis-à-vis consumer goods. A primary purchasing motive for industrial goods is, of course, profit. As mentioned in a previous chapter, industrial goods are usually purchased as means to an end, and not as an end in themselves. This is another way of saying that the demand

HIGHLIGHT 6–2

A. Classes of Consumer Goods — Some Characteristics and Marketing Considerations

Characteristics and Marketing Considerations	Type of Product		
	Convenience	Shopping	Specialty
Characteristics:			
Time and effort devoted by consumer to shopping	Very little	Considerable	Cannot generalize; consumer may go to nearby store and buy with minimum effort or may have to go to distant store and spend much time and effort
Time spent planning the purchase	Very little	Considerable	Considerable
How soon want is satisfied after it arises	Immediately	Relatively long time	Relatively long time
Are price and quality compared?	No	Yes	No
Price	Usually low	High	High
Frequency of purchase	Usually frequent	Infrequent	Infrequent
Importance	Unimportant	Often very important	Cannot generalize
Marketing considerations:			
Length of channel	Long	Short	Short to very short
Importance of retailer	Any single store is relatively unimportant	Important	Very important
Number of outlets	As many as possible	Few	Few; often only one in a market
Stock turnover	High	Lower	Lower
Gross margin	Low	High	High
Responsibility for advertising	Producer's	Retailer's	Joint responsibility
Importance of point-of-purchase display	Very important	Less important	Less important
Brand or store name important	Brand name	Store name	Both
Importance of packaging	Very important	Less important	Less important

Source: William J. Stanton, Michael J. Etzel, and Bruce J. Walker, *Fundamentals of Marketing,* 9th ed. (New York: McGraw-Hill, 1991), pp. 171, 174.

B. Classes of Industrial Products — Some Characteristics and Marketing Considerations

Characteristics and Marketing Considerations	Type of Product				
	Raw Materials	Fabricating Parts and Materials	Installations	Accessory Equipment	Operating Supplies
Example:	Iron ore	Engine blocks	Blast furnaces	Storage racks	Paper clips
Characteristics:					
Unit price	Very low	Low	Very high	Medium	Low
Length of life	Very short	Depends on final product	Very long	Long	Short
Quantities purchased	Large	Large	Very small	Small	Small
Frequency of purchase	Frequent delivery; long-term purchase contract	Infrequent purchase, but frequent delivery	Very infrequent	Medium frequency	Frequent
Standardization of competitive products	Very much; grading is important	Very much	Very little; custom-made	Little	Much
Quantity of supply	Limited; supply can be increased slowly or not at all	Usually no problem	No problem	Usually no problem	Usually no problem
Marketing considerations:					
Nature of channel	Short; no middlemen	Short; middlemen for small buyers	Short; no middlemen	Middlemen used	Middlemen used
Negotiation period	Hard to generalize	Medium	Long	Medium	Short
Price competition	Important	Important	Not important	Not main factor	Important
Presale/postsale service	Not important	Important	Very important	Important	Very little
Promotional activity	Very little	Moderate	Sales people very important	Important	Not too important
Brand preference	None	Generally low	High	High	Low
Advance buying contract	Important; long-term contracts used	Important; long-term contracts used	Not usually used	Not usually used	Not usually used

for industrial goods is a derived demand. Industrial goods are often purchased directly from the original source with few middlemen, because many of these goods can be bought in large quantities; they have high unit value; technical advice on installation and use is required; and the product is ordered according to the user's specifications. Many industrial goods are subject to multiple-purchase influence and a long period of negotiation is often required.

The market for industrial goods has certain attributes that distinguish it from the consumer goods market. Much of the market is concentrated geographically, as in the case of steel, auto, or shoe manufacturing. For certain products there are a limited number of buyers; this is known as a *vertical market,* which means that *(a)* it is narrow, because customers are restricted to a few industries; and *(b)* it is deep, in that a large percentage of the producers in the market use the product. Some products, such as office supplies, have a *horizontal market,* which means that the goods are purchased by all types of firms in many different industries. In general, buyers of industrial goods are reasonably well informed. As noted previously, heavy reliance is often placed on price, quality control, and reliability of supply source.

In terms of consumer products, many marketing scholars have found the convenience, shopping, and specialty classification inadequate and have attempted to either refine it or to derive an entirely new typology. None of these attempts appear to have met with complete success.[1] Perhaps there is no "best" way to deal with this problem. From the standpoint of the marketing manager, product classification is useful to the extent that it assists in providing guidelines for developing an appropriate marketing mix. For example, convenience goods generally require broadcast promotion and long channels of distribution as opposed to shopping goods, which generally require more targeted promotion and somewhat shorter channels of distribution.

Product Mix and Product Line

The *product mix* is the composite products offered for sale by the firm; *product line* refers to a group of products that are closely related, either because they satisfy a class of need, are used together, are sold to the same customer groups, are marketed through the same types of outlets, or fall within given price ranges. There are three primary dimensions of a firm's product mix: (1) width of the product mix, which refers to the number of product lines the firm handles; (2) depth of the product mix, which refers to the average number of products in each line; (3) consistency of the product mix, which refers to the similarity of product lines. Thus, McDonald's hamburgers represent a product item in its line of sandwiches, whereas hotcakes or Egg McMuffins represent items in a different line, namely, breakfast foods.

---

[1]For a review and suggestions for product classification, see Patrick E. Murphy and Ben M. Enis, "Classifying Products Strategically," *Journal of Marketing,* July 1986, pp. 24–42.

Development of a plan for the existing product line has been called the most critical element of a company's product planning activity.[2] In designing such plans, management needs accurate information on the current and anticipated performance of its products, which should encompass:

1. Consumer evaluation of the company's products, particularly their strengths and weaknesses vis-à-vis competition (i.e., product positioning by market segment information).
2. Objective information on actual and anticipated product performance on relevant criteria, such as sales, profits, and market share.[3]

An integral component of product line planning revolves around the question of how many product variants should be included in the line.[4] Manufacturing costs are usually minimized through large-volume production runs and distribution costs tend to be lower if only one product is sold, stocked, and serviced. At a given level of sales, profits will usually be highest if those sales have been achieved with a single product. However, many product variants are offered by many firms.

There are three reasons as to why organizations offer varying products within a given product line. First, potential customers rarely agree on a single set of specifications regarding their "ideal product," differing greatly in the importance and value they place on specific attributes. For example, in the laundry detergent market, there is a marked split between preferences for powder versus liquid detergent. Second, customers prefer variety. For example, a person may like Italian food, but does not want to only eat spaghetti. Therefore, an Italian restaurant will offer the customer a wide variety of Italian dishes to choose from. Third, the dynamics of competition lead to multiproduct lines. As competitors seek to increase market share, they find it advantageous to introduce new products that subsegment an existing market segment by offering benefits more precisely tailored to the specific needs of a portion of that segment. For example, Procter & Gamble offers Jif peanut butter in a low salt version to target a specific subsegment of the peanut butter market.

Packaging

Distinctive or unique packaging is one method of differentiating a relatively homogeneous product. To illustrate, shelf-stable microwave dinners, pumps rather than tubes of toothpaste or bars of soap, and different sizes and designs

---

[2] Yoram Wind and Henry J. Claycamp, "Planning Product Line Strategy: A Matrix Approach," *Journal of Marketing,* January 1976, p. 2.

[3] Ibid.

[4] The material for this section comes from Glenn L. Urban and Steven H. Star, *Advanced Marketing Strategy* (Englewood Cliffs, N.J.: Prentice Hall, 1991), chap. 16.

of tissue packages are attempts to differentiate a product through packaging and to satisfy consumer needs at the same time.

In some cases, companies have begun utilizing packaging strategies as a means to reposition their products. For example, Procter & Gamble saw its leading position in the bar soap category disappear following Lever Bros.' successful introduction of its Lever 2000 soap.[5] Rather than incur the costs and risks associated with developing and launching a new bar soap, Procter & Gamble decided to battle Lever by repositioning its Safeguard brand. Traditionally a soap targeted at male users, Procter & Gamble crafted a new image for Safeguard as a family soap, relying almost entirely on package changes. The old Safeguard box featured a colored chevron, stretched to cover most of the box. Safeguard's new design has a decidedly less mannish look, shrinking the chevron and sporting contemporary colors on a white metallic wrap. The product description was also changed. Safeguard "deodorant soap" is now touted as "anti-bacterial deodorant soap." And the repositioning theme, "mild enough for the whole family," is also on the package.

In other cases, packaging changes have succeeded in creating new attributes of value in a brand. For example, the R.J. Reynolds Co. used a simple packaging idea to push tobacco's marketing wars in a new direction. Instead of attempting to update the ambiguous image of its flagship Winston brand, Reynolds introduced the Wrap.[6] The Wrap, an aluminized polyester film, addresses a concern that few smokers had ever mentioned: cigarette freshness. Reynolds copied the idea from snack food manufacturers who used similar films for potato chips and candy bars. The Wrap keeps cigarettes fresher longer by reducing moisture and air that reach the product. In reality, the Wrap is simply an update of an idea that worked for the company before. More than 60 years ago, Reynolds' Camel brand introduced the clear wrap that is the industry standard today.

Marketing managers must consider both the consumer and costs in making packaging decisions. On one hand, the package must be capable of protecting the product through the channel of distribution to the consumer. In addition, it is desirable for packages to be convenient size and easy to open for the consumer. For example, single-serving soups and zip-lock packaging in cereal boxes are attempts by manufacturers to serve consumers better. Hopefully, the package is also attractive and informative, capable of being used as a competitive weapon to project a product's image. However, maximizing these objectives may increase the cost of the product to such an extent that consumers are no longer willing to purchase it. Thus, the marketing manager must determine the optimal protection, convenience, positioning, and promotional strengths of packages, subject to cost constraints.

---

[5]F. Warner, "Safeguard's Risky Mission," *Adweek's Marketing Week,* March 16, 1992, pp. 36–37.

[6]F. Warner, "RJR's Wrap Attack," *Adweek's Marketing Week,* February 17, 1992, p. 36.

HIGHLIGHT 6–3

Tips for Developing Effective Packages

1. Ultimate authority and responsibility must lie in the marketing department.
2. A team or systems approach should be utilized including personnel from other areas such as production and engineering.
3. A sequential approach should be followed.
4. Work on new product packages should begin early in the product development process.
5. Needs of both consumers and dealers should be considered.
6. The final package should take into consid-

eration the packages of competitors and any legal or regulatory requirements.
7. The most important objective should be profitability.
8. Packages should not be changed for the sake of change.
9. Consumers and dealers should provide input during the development process.
10. The package should be test-marketed.
11. Package changes should be introduced all at once, not gradually.

Source: Adapted from Richard T. Hise and James U. McNeal, "Effective Package Management," *Business Horizons,* January–February 1988 and reported in Steven J. Skinner, *Marketing* (Boston: Houghton Mifflin Co, 1990), p. 262.

Branding and Brand Equity

Many companies use branding strategies in order to increase the strength of the product image. Factors that serve to increase the brand image strength include:[7] (1) product quality when products do what they do very well (e.g., Windex and Easy-off); (2) consistent advertising and other marketing communications in which brands tell their story often and well (e.g., McDonald's and Pepsi); and (3) brand personality where the brand stands for something (e.g., Disney and Marlboro). The brand name is perhaps the single most important element on the package, serving as a unique identifier. Specifically, a brand is a name, term, symbol, sign, design, or combination thereof which serves to identify and differentiate the products marketed by one or several companies from those of its competitors.[8] A good brand name can evoke feelings of trust, confidence, security, strength, and many other desirable characteristics.[9] To illustrate, consider the case of Bayer Aspirin. Bayer can be sold at up to two times the price of generic aspirin due to the strength of its brand image.

---

[7]James Lowry, "Survey Finds Most Powerful Brands," *Advertising Age,* July 11, 1988, p. 31.

[8]Phillip H. Kotler, *Marketing Management: Analysis, Planning, and Control,* 8th ed. (Englewood Cliffs, N.J.: Prentice Hall, 1991), p. 491.

[9]Terance Shimp, *Promotion Management and Marketing Communications,* 2nd ed. (Hinsdale, Ill.: Dryden Press, 1990), p. 67.

Many companies make use of branding in carrying out market and product development strategies. Line extension is an approach whereby a brand name is used to facilitate entry into a new market segment (e.g., Diet Coke and Liquid Tide). An alternative to line extension is brand extension. In brand extension, a current brand name is used to enter a completely different product class (e.g., Jello pudding pops, Ivory shampoo).[10] A final form of branding commonly used is franchise extension whereby a company attaches the corporate name to a product either to enter a new market segment or different product class (e.g., Honda lawnmower, Toyota Lexus). Each of the above three approaches is an attempt by companies to gain a competitive advantage by making use of an established reputation.

Companies may also choose to assign different or multiple brand names to related products. By doing so, the firm has made a conscious decision to allow the products to succeed or fail on their own merits. Major advantages of using multiple brand names are that: 1) the firm can distance products from other offerings it markets; 2) the image of one product (or set of products) is not associated with other products the company markets; 3) the product(s) can be targeted at a specific market segment; and 4) should the product(s) fail, the probability of failure impacting on other company products is minimized. For example, many consumers are unaware that Dreft, Tide, Oxydol, Bold, Cheer, and Dash laundry detergents are all marketed by Procter & Gamble. The major disadvantage of this strategy is that because new names are assigned, there is no consumer brand awareness and significant amounts of money must be spent familiarizing customers with new brands.

Increasingly, companies are finding that brand names are one of the most valuable assets they possess. Successful extensions of an existing brand can lead to additional loyalty and associated profits. Conversely, a wrong extension can cause damaging associations, as perceptions linked to the brand name are transferred back from one product to the other.[11] Brand equity can be viewed as the set of assets (or liabilities) linked to the brand that add (or subtract) value.[12] The value of these assets is dependent upon the consequences or results of the marketplace's relationship with a brand. Brand equity is determined by the consumer and is the culmination of the consumer's assessment of the product, the company which manufactures and markets the product, and all other variables which impact on the product between manufacturer and consumer consumption.

---

[10]David A. Aaker and Kevin Lane Keller, "Consumer Evaluations of Brand Extensions," *Journal of Marketing,* January 1990, pp. 27–41.

[11]Ibid.

[12]For a detailed discussion of brand equity, see David Aaker, *Managing Brand Equity* (New York and London: The Free Press, 1991).

As a related product branding strategy, many retail firms produce and/or market their products under a so-called private label.[13] For example, KMart has phased in its own store-brand products to compete with the national brands. There's Nature's Classics, a line of fancy snacks and cookies; Oral Pure, a line of dental care products; Prevail house cleaners; B.E., a Gap-style line of weekend wear; and Benchmark, a line of "made in the U.S.A." tools. Such a strategy is highly important in industries where the middleman has gained control over distribution to the consumer. The growth of the large discount and specialty stores, such as KMart, Wal-Mart, Target, The Gap, Limited, and others has accelerated the development of private brands. If a manufacturer refuses to supply certain middlemen with private branded merchandise, the alternative is for these middlemen to go into the manufacturing business, as in the case of Kroger supermarkets.

Private label products differ markedly from so-called generic products that sport labels such as "beer," "cigarettes," and "potato chips." Today's house brands are packaged in distinctively upscale containers. The quality of the products utilized as house brands equals and sometimes exceeds those offered by name brands. While generic products were positioned as a means for consumers to struggle through recessionary times, private label products are being marketed as value brands. Private brands are rapidly growing in popularity. Supermarket sales of store brands exceed $26 billion and are increasing each year. Wal-Mart, which rolled out the Sam's American Choice brand in 1990, has quickly built up a hefty business, expecting sales to reach $2.6 billion by 1995.

As a general rule, private brands are lower priced than national brands because there are some cost savings involved, and this has been the strongest appeal of private brand merchandisers. If a manufacturer is selling its national branded products to middlemen under a private label, then the Robinson-Patman Act requires that any price differential reflect (a) genuine differences in grade and quality; or (b) cost savings in manufacturing or distribution. One of the reasons why manufacturers will supply resellers with private branded merchandise is to utilize their production capacity more fully. Similarly, generic brands use excess capacity and offer manufacturers an alternative for selling their products.

PRODUCT LIFE CYCLE

A firm's product strategy must take into account the fact that products have a life cycle. Figure 6–1 illustrates this life-cycle concept. Products are introduced, grow, mature, and decline. This cycle varies according to industry,

---

[13]For a more detailed discussion, see Elaine Underwood, "Something for Everyone," *Brandweek,* September 7, 1992, pp. 18–24.

Figure 6–1   *The Product Life Cycle*

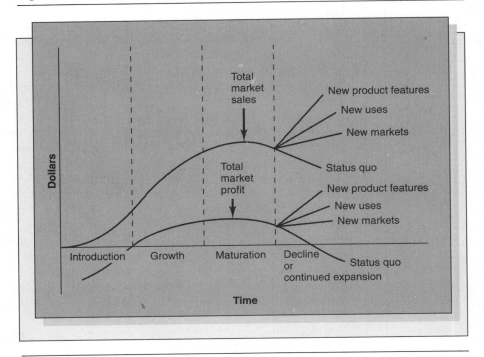

product, technology, and market. Marketing executives need to be aware of the life-cycle concept because it can be a valuable aid in developing marketing strategies.

During the introduction phase of the cycle, there are usually high production and marketing costs, and, since sales are only beginning to materialize, profits are low or nonexistent. Profits increase and are positively correlated with sales during the growth stage as the market begins trying and adopting the product. As the product matures, profits for the initiating firm do not keep pace with sales because of competition. Here the seller may be forced to "remarket" the product, which may involve making price concessions, increasing product quality, or expanding outlays on advertising and sales promotion just to maintain market share. At some time sales decline, and the seller must decide whether to *(a)* drop the product; *(b)* alter the product; *(c)* seek new uses for the product; *(d)* seek new markets; or *(e)* continue with more of the same.[14]

---

[14]Note that the labeling of the new product features, new uses, and new markets curves is arbitrary. In other words, any of the three may result in the highest sales and profits depending on the product and situation.

The usefulness of the product life-cycle concept is primarily that it forces management to take a long-range view of marketing planning. In doing so, it should become clear that shifts in phases of the life cycle correspond to changes in the market situation, competition, and demand. Thus, the astute marketing manager should recognize the necessity of altering the marketing mix to meet these changing conditions. It is possible for managers to undertake strategies which, in effect, can lead to a revitalized product life cycle. For example, past advancements in technology led to the replacement of rotary dial telephones by touch-tone, push-button phones. Today, newer technology is allowing the cordless and cellular phone to replace the traditional touch-tone, push-button phone. When applied with sound judgment, the life-cycle concept can aid in forecasting, pricing, advertising, product planning, and other aspects of marketing management.[15] However, the marketing manager must also recognize that the life cycle is purely a tool for assisting in strategy development and not let the life cycle dictate strategy development.[16]

THE PRODUCT AUDIT

The product audit is a marketing management technique whereby the company's current product offerings are reviewed to ascertain whether each product should be continued as is, improved, or modified, or be deleted. The audit is a task that should be carried out at regular intervals as a matter of policy. Product audits are the responsibility of the product manager unless specifically delegated to someone else.

Deletions

It can be argued that the major purpose of the product audit is to detect "sick" products and then bury them. Criteria must be developed for deciding whether a product is a candidate for deletion. Some of the more obvious factors to be considered are:

— *Sales trends*. How have sales moved over time? What has happened to market share? Why have sales declined? What changes in sales have occurred in competitive products both in our line and in those of other manufacturers?

---

[15]For an overview of issues concerning the product life cycle, see George Day, "The Product Life Cycle: Analysis and Application Issues," *Journal of Marketing,* Fall 1981, pp. 60–67. This is the introductory article to a special section dealing with the product life cycle.

[16]For a discussion of problems related to this issue, see Geoffrey L. Gordon, Roger J. Calantone, and C. Anthony di Benedetto, "Mature Markets and Revitalization Strategies: An American Fable," *Business Horizons,* May-June 1991, pp. 39–50.

HIGHLIGHT 6–4

Top 10 Brands in Eight of the Fastest Growing Supermarket Categories

Canned Soup	Market Share	Beer	Market Share
1. Campbell's	75.3	1. Budweiser	16.9
2. Progresso	8.1	2. Miller Lite	8.7
3. Private Label	5.8	3. Coors Light	7.3
4. Swanson	3.0	4. Bud Light	6.8
5. College Inn	1.9	5. Miller Genuine Draft	4.4
6. Healthy Choice	1.8	6. Busch	4.0
7. Snow's	.5	7. Milwaukee's Best	3.0
8. Healthy Valley	.4	8. Natural Light	3.0
9. Pritikin	.3	9. Bud Dry	2.2
10. Sweet Sue	.3	10. Miller High Life	2.2

Cereal		Disposable Diapers	
1. Private Label	4.8	1. Huggies	30.1
2. Gen. Mill's Cheerios	4.7	2. Pampers	29.2
3. Kellogg's Frosted Flakes	4.3	3. Luvs	20.4
4. Kellogg's Corn Flakes	3.3	4. Private Labels	12.6
5. Gen. Mill's Honey Cheerios	3.3	5. Fitti	1.5
6. Kellogg's Rice Krispies	3.2	6. Cozies	1.4
7. Kellogg's Raisin Bran	2.9	7. Drypers	1.3
8. Kellogg's Frosted Mini-Wheat	2.6	8. Baby's Choice	1.1
9. Kellogg's Froot Loops	2.3	9. Cuddles	.5
10. Gen. Mill's Lucky Charms	2.0	10. Snuggems	.5

Source: "Brand Scorecard," *Advertising Age*, July 20, 1992, p. 20.

— *Profit contribution.* What has been the profit contribution of this product to the company? If profits have declined, how are these tied to price? Have selling, promotion, and distribution costs risen out of proportion to sales? Does the product require excessive management time and effort?

— *Product life cycle.* Has the product reached a level of maturity and saturation in the market? Has new technology been developed that poses a threat to the product? Are there more effective substitutes on the market? Has the product outgrown its usefulness? Can the resources used on this product be put to better use?

Peanut Butter	Market Share	Shelf Stable Drink	Market Share
1. Jif	31.3	1. Ocean Spray	22.4
2. Skippy	20.1	2. Gatorade	17.9
3. Private Label	18.1	3. Hi-C	9.8
4. Peter Pan	14.8	4. Tropicana	7.8
5. Simply Jif	3.9	5. Private Labels	6.6
6. Smuckers	2.8	6. Hawaiian Punch	4.9
7. Reese's	1.9	7. Kool-Aid	4.4
8. Adams	1.4	8. Capri Sun	4.4
9. Laura Scudder's	1.4	9. Squeezit	2.7
10. Generic	.7	10. Welch's	1.6

Packaged Detergents		Frozen Pizza	
1. Tide	23.2	1. Tombstone	17.3
2. Tide With Bleach	14.2	2. Tony's	12.3
3. Cheer	8.5	3. Red Baron	10.6
4. Surf	7.1	4. Totino's	10.2
5. Arm & Hammer	5.5	5. Stouffer's	8.7
6. Wisk Power Scoop	5.0	6. Private Labels	6.4
7. Gain	4.6	7. Celeste	4.6
8. Bold	4.1	8. Jacks	4.2
9. Fab	3.6	9. McCain Ellio's	4.1
10. Oxydol With Bleach	3.3	10. Jeno's	3.1

The above factors should be used as guidelines for making the final decision to delete a product. Deletion decisions are very difficult to make because of their potential impact on customers and the firm. For example, eliminating a product may force a company to lay off some employees. There are other factors to consider, such as keeping consumers supplied with replacement parts and repair service and maintaining the good will of distributors who have an inventory of the product. The deletion plan should provide for the clearing out of stock in question.[17]

---

[17]For further discussion of product deletion decisions, see George J. Avlonitis, "Product Elimination Decision Making: Does Formality Matter?" *Journal of Marketing,* Winter 1985, pp. 41–52.

HIGHLIGHT 6–5

Marketing Strategy Implications of the Product Life Cycle

Stages of the Product Life Cycle

Effects/Responses	Introduction	Growth	Maturity	Decline
Competition	None of importance.	Some emulators.	Many rivals competing for a small piece of the pie.	Few in number, with a rapid shakeout of weak members.
Overall strategy	Market establishment; persuade early adopters to try the product.	Market penetration; persuade mass market to prefer the brand.	Defense of brand position; check the inroads of competition.	Preparations for removal; milk the brand dry of all possible benefits.
Profits	Negligible because of high production and marketing costs.	Reach peak levels as a result of high prices and growing demand.	Increasing competition cuts into profit margins and ultimately into total profits.	Declining volume pushes costs up to levels that eliminate profits entirely.
Retail prices	High, to recover some of the excessive costs of launching.	High, to take advantage of heavy consumer demand.	What the traffic will bear; need to avoid price wars.	Low enough to permit quick liquidation of inventory.

Distribution	Selective, as distribution is slowly built up.	Intensive; employ small trade discounts since dealers are eager to store.	Intensive; heavy trade allowances to retain shelf space.	Selective; unprofitable outlets slowly phased out.
Advertising strategy	Aim at the needs of early adopters.	Make the mass market aware of brand benefits.	Use advertising as a vehicle for differentiation among otherwise similar brands.	Emphasize low price to reduce stock.
Advertising emphasis	High, to generate awareness and interest among early adopters and persuade dealers to stock the brand.	Moderate, to let sales rise on the sheer momentum of word-of-mouth recommendations.	Moderate, since most buyers are aware of brand characteristics.	Minimum expenditures required to phase out the product.
Consumer sales and promotion expenditures	Heavy, to entice target groups with samples, coupons, and other inducements to try the brand.	Moderate, to create brand preference (advertising is better suited to do this job).	Heavy, to encourage brand switching, hopping to convert some buyers into loyal users.	Minimal, to let the brand coast by itself.

Source: William Zikmund and Michael D'Amico, *Marketing,* 3rd ed. (New York: John Wiley & Sons, 1989), p. 243.

HIGHLIGHT 6–6

Ten Ways to Dream Up New Products and Revitalize Older Ones

Originally, some of these ideas were intended to stimulate new-product development and others were for revitalizing older products. Whatever the case may be, they can create additional sales for a company.

1. *Take something out of the product.* Removing caffeine and sugar from soft drinks and some of the sodium from various processed foods resulted in new products.
2. *Add something to the product.* Extra-large chocolate chips boosted sales of Keebler's Chips Deluxe. Periodically, soap and detergent makers add something new to a basic product—bleach, softener, lemon scent, or an antistatic agent.
3. *Listen to consumers' complaints.* "The smell of my antiperspirant clashes with my perfume." "Why is the fruit in my yogurt always at the bottom?" Listening to these gripes resulted in an odorless antiperspirant and a yogurt with fruit dispersed throughout.
4. *Transfer success from one product category to another.* Pump dispensers proved popular with mustard, ketchup, and skin lotion, so this form of packaging was used for toothpaste.
5. *Make the task easier.* Combining shampoo with hair conditioner eliminates one task.

And microwaving is a lot easier than traditional methods of cooking many foods, and the results are just as tasty.

6. *Dream up new uses.* Chex cereals are the key ingredient in a line of party snacks. Sales of Arm & Hammer baking soda increased considerably after the product was advertised as a refrigerator deodorant.
7. *Add new distribution channels.* Woolite, a soap for woolen items, for years was sold only in department stores. When the company made this product available in supermarkets, sales tripled the first year.
8. *Add a dramatic guarantee.* Spray 'n Wash sales were declining as competitive products were introduced. The company then made this guarantee: "If Spray 'n Wash doesn't remove a stain from a shirt—any shirt—we'll buy you a new shirt." This guarantee boosted sales considerably, and only a few people requested a new shirt.
9. *Don't stymie creativity.* A Sony executive walking through a laboratory saw a miniature tape recorder project and a headphone project. Creative thinking combined the two projects, resulting in the Walkman.
10. *Look overseas for inspiration.* Europe gave us mineral water, hair mousse, aseptic packaging, and soft-batch cookies.

Source: Adapted from Calvin L. Hodock, "Nine Surefire Ways to Cook Up New Ideas," *Sales & Marketing Management,* August 1988, p. 40; and Gerald Schoenfeld, "Treat Old Products Like New," *Marketing News,* July 31, 1989, p. 15.

Product Improvement

One of the other important objectives of the audit is to ascertain whether to alter the product in some way or to leave things as they are. Altering the product means changing one or more of the product's attributes or marketing dimensions. Attributes refer mainly to product features, design, package, and so forth. Marketing dimensions refer to such things as price, promotion strategy, and channels of distribution.

It is possible to look at the product audit as a management device for controlling the product strategy. Here, control means feedback on product performance and corrective action in the form of product improvement. Product improvement is a top-level management decision, but the information needed to make the improvement decision may come from the consumer or the middlemen. Suggestions are often made by advertising agencies or consultants. Reports by the sales force should be structured in a way to provide management with certain types of product information; in fact, these reports can be the firm's most valuable product improvement tool. Implementing a product improvement decision will often require the coordinated efforts of several specialists, plus some research. For example, product design improvement decisions involve engineering, manufacturing, accounting, and marketing. When a firm becomes aware that a product's design can be improved, it is not always clear as to how consumers will react to the various alterations. To illustrate, in blind taste tests, the Coca-Cola Company found that consumers overwhelmingly preferred the taste of a reformulated sweeter new Coke over old Coke. However, when placed on the market in labeled containers, new Coke turned out to be a failure due to consumers' emotional attachments to the classic Coke. Consequently, it is advisable to conduct some market tests in realistic settings.

ORGANIZING FOR PRODUCT MANAGEMENT

A firm can organize for managing its products in a variety of ways.[18] Figure 6–2 describes five methods and the types of companies for which they are most useful. Under a *marketing-manager system,* all the functional areas of marketing report to one manager. These include sales, advertising, sales promotion, and product planning. Such companies as PepsiCo, Purex, Eastman Kodak, and Levi Strauss use some form of the marketing-manager system.

With the *product (brand) manager system* there is a middle manager in the organization who focuses on a single product or a small group of new or existing products. Typically, this manager is responsible for everything from marketing research to package design to advertising. This method of organizing is sometimes criticized because product managers often do not have authority commensurate with their responsibilities. However, such companies as General Mills, Pillsbury, and Procter & Gamble have successfully used this method.

A *product-planning committee* is staffed by executives from functional areas, including marketing, production, engineering, finance, and R&D. The

---

[18]This section is based on Joel R. Evans and Barry Berman, *Marketing,* 5th ed. (New York: Macmillan, 1992), pp. 254–58.

Figure 6-2 *Five Methods of Organizing for Product Management*

Organization	Characteristics		
	Staffing	**Ideal Use**	**Permanency**
Marketing-manager system	Key functional areas of marketing report to a manager with considerable authority.	A company makes one product line, has a dominant line, or uses broad category marketing managers.	The system is ongoing.
Product (brand) manager system	Each middle manager focuses on a single product or group of products.	A company makes many distinct products, each requiring expertise.	The system is ongoing.
Product-planning committee	Senior executives from various functional areas participate.	The committee should supplement another product organization.	The committee meets irregularly.
New-product manager system	Separate middle managers focus on new products and existing products.	A company makes several existing products; substantial time, resources, and expertise are needed for new products.	The system is ongoing, but new products are shifted to product managers after introduction.
Venture team	An independent group of company specialists guides all phases of a new product's development.	A company wants to create vastly different products than those currently offered and needs an autonomous structure to aid development.	The team disbands after a new product is introduced, turning responsibility over to a product manager.

Source: Reprinted by permission of Macmillan Publishing Company from *Marketing,* 5th ed., p. 257 by Joel R. Evans and Barry Berman. Copyright 1992 by Macmillan Publishing Company.

committee handles product approval, evaluation, and development on a part-time basis and typically disbands after a product is introduced. The product then becomes the responsibility of a product manager.

A *new product manager system* uses separate managers for new and existing products. After a new product is introduced, the new product manager turns it over to a product manager. This system can be expensive and can cause discontinuity when the product is introduced. However, such firms as General Foods, NCR, and General Electric have used this system successfully.

A *venture team* is a small, independent department consisting of a broad range of specialists who manage a new product's entire development process. The team disbands when the product is introduced. While it can be an expensive method, Xerox, IBM, and Westinghouse use a venture team approach.

Which method to use depends on the diversity of a firm's offerings, the number of new products introduced, the level of innovation, company resources, and management expertise. A combination of product management methods also can be used and many firms find this desirable.

CONCLUSION

This chapter has been concerned with a central element of marketing management—product strategy. The first part of the chapter discussed some basic issues in product strategy, including product definition and classification, product mix and product lines, packaging, and branding and brand equity. The product life cycle was discussed as well as the product audit. Finally, five methods of organizing for product management were presented. Although product considerations are extremely important, remember that the product is only one element of the marketing mix. Focusing on product decisions alone, without consideration of the other marketing mix variables, would be an ineffective approach to marketing strategy.

ADDITIONAL READINGS

Aaker, David. "Brand Extensions: The Good, the Bad, and the Ugly." *Sloan Management Review,* Spring 1990, pp. 47–56.

Brown, Rick. "Making the Product Portfolio a Basis for Action." *Long Range Planning,* 24, no. 1 (1991), pp. 102–10.

Crittendon, Victoria L. "Close the Marketing/Manufacturing Gap." *Sloan Management Review,* Spring 1992, pp. 41–52.

Doyle, Peter. "Building Successful Brands: The Strategic Options." *The Journal of Consumer Marketing,* Spring 1990, pp. 5–20.

Farquhar, Peter H.; Julia Y. Han; and Yuji Ijiri. "Measuring Brand Momentum." *Marketing Management,* Spring 1992, pp. 24–30.

Gatignon, Hubert; Barton Weitz; and Pradeep Bansal. "Brand Introduction Strategies and Competitive Environments." *Journal of Marketing Research,* November 1990, pp. 390–401.

Karel, Jan Willem Karel. "Brand Strategy Positions Products Worldwide." *The Journal of Business Strategy,* May/June 1991, pp. 16–19.

Michell, Paul C. N.; Peter Quinn; and Edward Percival. "Marketing Strategies for Mature Industrial Products." *Industrial Marketing Management,* August 1991, pp. 201–6.

Murphy, John. "Assessing the Value of Brands." *Long Range Planning,* 23, no. 3 (1990), pp. 23–29.

Quelch, John A.; Paul W. Farris; and James Olver. "The Product Management Audit." *The Journal of Product & Brand Management,* Spring 1992, pp. 5–18.

South, John B., and John E. Oliver. "A Value-Added Approach to Product Mix Decisions." *Industrial Marketing Management,* April 1992, pp. 167–71.

St. John, Caron H., and Ernest H. Hall, Jr. "The Interdependency Between Marketing and Manufacturing." *Industrial Marketing Management,* August 1991, pp. 223–28.

Tindall, James R. "Marketing Established Brands." *The Journal of Consumer Marketing,* Fall 1991, pp. 5–11.

Chapter 7

New Product Planning and Development

New products are a vital part of a firm's competitive growth strategy. Most manufacturers cannot live without new products. It is commonplace for major companies to have 50 percent or more of their current sales in products introduced within the past 10 years. For example, the 3M Corporation insists that 25 percent of each division's annual sales come from products developed within the past five years.[1] At Rubbermaid, the product development process has evolved to a point where, on average, one new product is introduced per day.[2]

Some additional facts about new products are:

1. Many new products are failures. Estimates of new product failures range from 33 percent to 90 percent, depending on the industry.
2. Almost one half the resources that firms spend on product innovation are spent on commercial failures.[3]
3. Companies vary widely in the effectiveness of their new product programs.
4. Common elements tend to appear in the management practices that generally distinguish the relative degree of efficiency and success between companies.[4]

---

[1]For a discussion of 3M's new product processes, see Ronald A. Mitsch, "Three Roads to Innovation," *The Journal of Business Strategy,* September/October 1991, pp. 18–21.

[2]Rahul Jacob, "Thriving in a Lame Economy," *Fortune,* October 5, 1992, pp. 44–54.

[3]Robert G. Cooper and Elko J. Kleinschmidt, "New Product Processes at Leading Industrial Firms," *Industrial Marketing Management,* May 1991, pp. 137–41.

[4]Also see E. J. Kleinschmidt and R. G. Cooper, "The Impact of Product Innovativeness on Performance," *The Journal of Product Innovation Management,* December 1991, pp. 240–51.

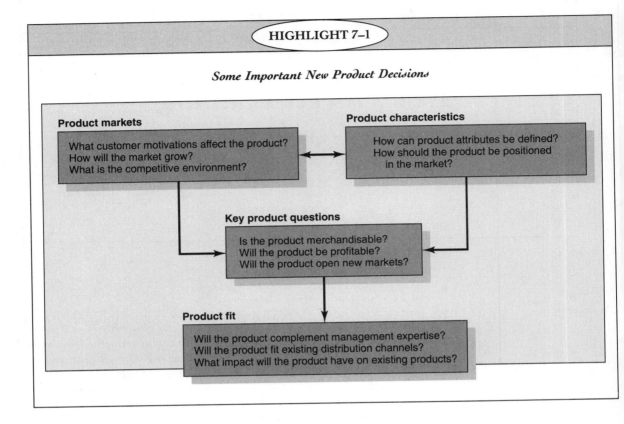

HIGHLIGHT 7–1

Some Important New Product Decisions

Product markets

What customer motivations affect the product?
How will the market grow?
What is the competitive environment?

Product characteristics

How can product attributes be defined?
How should the product be positioned
  in the market?

Key product questions

Is the product merchandisable?
Will the product be profitable?
Will the product open new markets?

Product fit

Will the product complement management expertise?
Will the product fit existing distribution channels?
What impact will the product have on existing products?

In one recent year, almost 10,000 supermarket items were introduced into the market. Less than 20 percent met sales goals. The cost of introducing a new brand in some consumer markets has been estimated to range from $50 million to the hundreds of millions of dollars.[5] To illustrate, Alpo Petfoods spent over $70 million on advertising and promotion alone in launching their new line of cat food. The Gillette Co. spent over $310 million on R&D and promotion costs in introducing the men's Sensor razor.[6] In addition to the outlay cost of new product failures, there are also opportunity costs. These opportunity costs refer not only to the alternative uses of funds spent on product failures, but also to the time spent in unprofitable product develop-

---

[5]Paul Brown, "New? Improved?" *Business Week,* October 21, 1985, pp. 108-12 and Edward M. Tauber, "Brand Leverage: Strategy for Growth in a Cost-Controlled World," *Journal of Advertising Research,* August/September 1988, pp. 26-30.

[6]Mark Maremont and Paula Dwyer, "How Gillette is Honing Its Edge," *Business Week,* September 28, 1992, pp. 60–65.

Ten Steps in the Development of a New Product Policy

1. Prepare a long-range industry forecast for existing product lines.
2. Prepare a long-range profit plan for the company, using existing product lines.
3. Review the long-range profit plan.
4. Determine what role new products will play in the company's future.
5. Prepare an inventory of company capabilities.
6. Determine market areas for new products.
7. Prepare a statement of new product objectives.
8. Prepare a long-range profit plan, incorporating new products.
9. Assign new product responsibility.
10. Provide for evaluation of new product performance.

---

ment. Product development can take many years. For example, Hills Brothers spent 22 years in developing its instant coffee, while it took General Foods 10 years to develop Maxim, its concentrated instant coffee. However, the success of one new product can pave the way for additional and successful, low-cost brand extensions. For example, in the case of Gillette's Sensor razor, the cost to develop and launch the Sensor razor for women was less than $25 million dollars.

Good management, with heavy emphasis on planning, organization, and interaction among the various functional units (e.g, marketing, manufacturing, engineering, R&D), seems to be the key factor contributing to a firm's success in launching new products. The primary reason found for new product failure is an inability on the part of the selling company to match up its offerings to the needs of the customer. This inability to satisfy customer needs can be attributed to three main sources: inadequacy of upfront intelligence efforts, failure on the part of the company to stick close to what the company does best, and the inability to provide better value than competing products and technologies.

NEW PRODUCT POLICY

In developing new product policies, the first question a marketing manager must ask is: "In how many ways can a product be new?" There are at least nine different ways:

1. A product performing an entirely *new function,* such as television, which for the first time permitted the transmission of audiovisual signals.
2. A product that offers *improved performance of an existing function,* such as a wristwatch whose balance wheel has been replaced by a tuning fork.

3. A product that is a *new application of an existing product*. For example, the cable used to provide phone service to homes can now also be used to transmit television signals and to allow for pay-per-view movie screening.

4. A product that offers *additional functions*. The cordless telephone, for instance, does what the earlier telephone did, plus more.

5. An existing product offered to a *new market*. This may be done, for example, by repositioning or by taking a regional brand into other regions. For example, Coors Beer used to be sold only in the states surrounding Colorado.

6. A product that through *lower cost* is able to reach more buyers. Hand calculators and personal computers are an example.

7. An upgraded product defined as an *existing product integrated into another existing product*. The clock-radio is an example.

8. A *downgraded product*. For example, a manufacturer switches from buying a component to producing a cheaper component in-house and marketing it.

9. A *restyled product*. Annual auto and clothing changes are examples.[7]

Another approach to the *new* product question has been developed by H. Igor Ansoff in the form of *growth vectors*.[8] This is the matrix first introduced in Chapter 1 that indicates the direction in which the organization is moving with respect to its current products and markets. It is shown again in Figure 7–1.

Market penetration denotes a growth direction through the increase in market share for present product markets. *Product development* refers to creating new products to replace existing ones. Firms utilizing either market penetration or product development strategies are attempting to capitalize on existing markets and combat competitive entry and/or further market incursions.[9] *Market development* refers to finding new customers for existing products. *Diversification* refers to developing new products and cultivating new markets. Firms utilizing market development and diversification strategies are seeking to establish footholds in new markets and/or preempt competition in emerging market segments.

As shown in Figure 7–1, market penetration and market development strategies utilize present products. A goal of these types of strategies is to either increase frequency of consumption or increase the number of customers utilizing the firm's product(s). A strategic focus is placed on altering the breadth and depth of the firm's existing product lines. Product development and di-

---

[7]C. Merle Crawford, *New Product Management,* 2nd ed. (Homewood, Ill.: Richard D. Irwin, 1987), p. 18.

[8]H. Igor Ansoff, *Corporate Strategy* (New York: McGraw-Hill, 1965), pp. 109-10.

[9]For a discussion of firm objectives in developing new products, see Vijay Mahajan and Jerry Wind, "New Product Models: Practice, Shortcomings and Desired Improvements," *The Journal of Product Innovation Management,* June 1992, pp. 128–39.

Figure 7–1   *Growth Vector Components*

Markets	Products	
	Present	New
Present	Market penetration	Product development
New	Market development	Diversification

versification can be characterized as product mix strategies. New products, as defined in the growth vector matrix, usually require the firm to make significant investments in research and development and may require major changes in its organizational structure.

It has already been stated that new products are the lifeblood of successful business firms. Thus, the critical product policy question is not whether to develop new products but in what direction to move. One way of dealing with this problem is to formulate standards or norms that new products must meet if they are to be considered candidates for launching. In other words, as part of its new product policy, management must ask itself the basic question: "What is the potential contribution of each anticipated new product to the company?"

Each company must answer this question in accordance with its long-term goals, corporate mission, resources, and so forth. Unfortunately, some of the reasons commonly given to justify the launching of new products are so general that they become meaningless. Phrases such as *additional profits, increased growth,* or *cyclical stability* must be translated into more specific objectives. For example, one objective may be to reduce manufacturing overhead costs by utilizing plant capacity better. This may be accomplished by using the new product as an offseason filler. Naturally, the new product proposal would also have to include production and accounting data to back up this cost argument.

In every new product proposal some attention must be given to the ultimate economic contribution of each new product candidate. If the argument is that a certain type of product is needed to "keep up with competition" or "to establish leadership in the market," it is fair to ask, "Why?" To put the question another way, top management can ask: "What will be the effect on the firm's long-run profit picture if we do not develop and launch this or that new product?" Policymaking criteria on new products should specify *(a)* a working definition of the profit concept acceptable to top management; *(b)* a minimum level or floor of profits; *(c)* the availability and cost of capital to develop a new product; and *(d)* a specified time period in which the new product must recoup its operating costs and begin contributing to profits.

It is critical that firms not become solely preoccupied with a short-term focus on earnings associated with new products. Indeed, an advantage Japanese firms possess is that their management is free from the pressure of steady improvement in earnings per share that plagues American managers who emphasize only short-term profits.[10] Japanese managers believe that market share will lead to customer loyalty which, in turn, will lead to profits generated from repeat purchases. Through a continual introduction of new products, firms will succeed in building share. This share growth will then ultimately result in earnings growth and profitability which will be supported by the stock market in terms of higher share prices over the long term.

NEW PRODUCT PLANNING AND DEVELOPMENT PROCESS

Ideally, products that generate a maximum dollar profit with a minimum amount of risk should be developed and marketed. However, it is very difficult for planners to implement this idea because of the number and nature of the variables involved. What is needed is a systematic, formalized process for new product planning. Although such a process does not provide management with any magic answers, it can increase the probability of new product success. Initially, the firm must establish some new product policy guidelines that include: the product fields of primary interest, organizational responsibilities for managing the various stages in new product development, and criteria for making go-ahead decisions. After these guidelines are established, a process such as the one shown in Figure 7–2 should be useful in new product development.

Idea Generation

Every product starts as an idea. But all new product ideas do not have equal merit or potential for economic or commercial success. Some estimates indicate that as many as 60 or 70 ideas are necessary to yield one successful product. This is an average figure, but it serves to illustrate the fact that new product ideas have a high mortality rate. In terms of money, almost three fourths of all the dollars of new product expense go to unsuccessful products.

The problem at this stage is to ensure that all new product ideas available to the company at least have a chance to be heard and evaluated. Ideas are the raw materials for product development, and the whole planning process depends on the quality of the idea generation and screening process.[11] Since idea generation is the least costly stage in the new product development process

---

[10]For a discussion of Japanese product development practices, see R. B. Kennard, "From Experience: Japanese Product Development Processes," *The Journal of Product Innovation Management,* September 1991, pp. 184–88.

[11]For a detailed discussion of the idea generation and screening process, see Linda Rochford, "Generating and Screening New Product Ideas," *Industrial Marketing Management,* November 1991, pp. 287–96.

Figure 7–2   *The New Product Development Process*

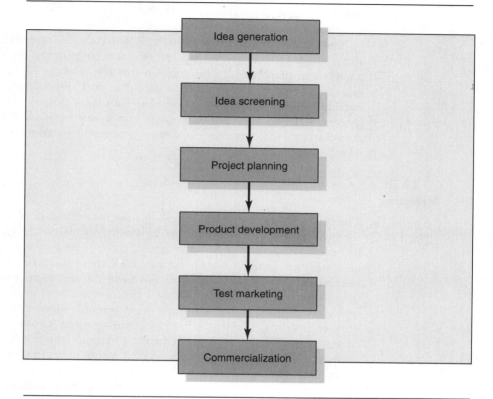

(in terms of investment in funds, time, personnel, and escalation of commit-ment), it makes sense that an emphasis be placed first on recognizing available sources of new product ideas and then on funneling these ideas to appropriate decision makers for screening.

Top management support is critical to providing an atmosphere that stim-ulates new product activity. A top management structure that is unwilling to take risks will avoid new product and other innovation activities and instead concentrate on minor areas of product improvement such as simple style changes. In order to facilitate top management support, it is essential that new product development be focused on meeting market needs.

Both technology push and market pull research activities play an important role in new product ideas and development. By taking a broad view of cus-tomer wants and needs, basic research can lead to ideas that will yield profits to the firm. Marketing, on the other hand, is more responsible for gathering and disseminating information gained from customer and competitor contact. This information relates mainly to specific features and functions of the product that can be improved upon or market needs that current products are not satisfying. Both approaches are essential to the generation of new product ideas and should not be considered mutually exclusive.

Some firms use mechanisms such as "out-rotation," outsider involvement, and rewards for boundary-spanning to foster cooperation between design engineers and marketers.[12] Out-rotation involves placing employees into positions that require direct contact with customers, competitors, and other key outside groups. For example, Hewlett-Packard regularly rotates design engineers to retail sales positions on a temporary basis. Other organizations actively involve "outsiders" in planning or reward engineers for making external customer contacts.

Idea Screening

The primary function of the screening stage is twofold: first, to eliminate ideas for new products that could not be profitably marketed by the firm and, second, to expand viable ideas into a full product concept. New product ideas may be eliminated either because they are outside the fields of the firm's interest or because the firm does not have the necessary resources or technology to produce the product at a profit. However, organizations should not act too hastily in discounting new product ideas due solely to a lack of resources or expertise. Instead, firms should consider forming joint or strategic alliances with other firms. Potential benefits to be gained from alliances include: (1) increased access to technology, funding, and information; (2) market expansion and greater penetration of current markets; and (3) de-escalated competitive rivalries. Motorola is a company that has prospered by forming numerous joint ventures with both American and foreign companies.[13]

Ideas that appear to have adequate profit potential and offer the firm a competitive advantage in the market should be accepted for further study.

---

[12]This section is based on Daryl McKee, "An Organizational Learning Approach to Product Innovation," *The Journal of Product Innovation Management*, September 1992, pp. 232–45.

[13]For a more complete discussion on the advantages and disadvantages of strategic alliances, see Richard N. Cardozo, Shannon H. Shipp, and Kenneth J. Roering, "Proactive Strategic Partnerships: A New Business Markets Strategy," *The Journal of Business and Industrial Marketing,* Winter 1992, pp. 51–63; Frank K. Sonnenberg, "Partnering: Entering the Age of Cooperation," *Journal of Business Strategy,* May/June 1992, pp. 49–52; Godfrey Devlin and Mark Bleackley, "Strategic Alliances—Guidelines for Success," *Long Range Planning* 21, no. 5, (1988) pp. 18–23; Charles W. Joiner, "Harvesting American Technology—Lessons from the Japanese Garden," *Sloan Management Review,* Summer 1989, pp. 61–68; Richard P. Neilson, "Cooperative Strategies in Marketing," *Harvard Business Review,* July–August 1987, pp. 61–68; and Pedro Nueno and Jan Oosterveld, "Managing Technology Alliances," *Long Range Planning* 21, no. 3, (1988), pp. 11–17.

HIGHLIGHT 7–3

Some Sources of New Product Ideas

1. *Sales force.*
   a. Knowledge of customers' needs.
   b. Inquiries from customers or prospects.
   c. Knowledge of the industry and competition.
2. *Research and engineering.*
   a. Application of basic research.
   b. Original or creative thinking.
   c. Testing existing products and performance records.
   d. Accidental discoveries.
3. *Other company sources.*
   a. Suggestions from employees.
   b. Utilization of by-products or scrap.
   c. Specific market surveys.
4. *Outside sources.*
   a. Inventors.
   b. Stockholders.
   c. Suppliers or vendors.
   d. Middlemen.
   e. Ad agencies.
   f. Customer suggestions.

Project Planning

This stage of the process involves several steps. It is here that the product proposal is evaluated further and responsibility for the project is assigned to a project team. The proposal is analyzed in terms of production, marketing, financial, and competitive factors. A development budget is established, and some preliminary marketing and technical research is undertaken. The product is actually designed in a rough form. Alternative product features and component specifications are outlined. Finally, a project plan is written up, which includes estimates of future development, production, and marketing costs along with capital requirements and manpower needs. A schedule or timetable is also included. Finally, the project proposal is given to top management for a go or no-go decision.

Various alternatives exist for creating and managing the project teams. Two of the better-known methods are the establishment of a skunkworks whereby a project team can work in relative privacy away from the rest of the organization and a rugby or relay approach whereby groups in different areas of the company are simultaneously working on the project.[14] The common tie that binds these and other successful approaches together is the degree of interaction that develops between the marketing, engineering, production, and other research staff. The earlier in the process that interactive, cooperative

---

[14]James Quinn, "Managing Innovation: Controlled Chaos," *Harvard Business Review,* May–June 1985, pp. 73–84 and Hirotaka Takeuchi and Ikujiro Nonaka, "The New New Product Development Game," *Harvard Business Review,* January–February 1986, pp. 137–46.

HIGHLIGHT 7–4

How Much Should You Spend on New Product Development?

Based on a study of 203 new products (123 successes and 80 failures), the researchers concluded that the successful companies:

1. Spend twice as much money and three times as much time for preliminary market assessment.
2. Spend twice as much money for marketing research.

Source: Based on research conducted by R. G. Cooper and E. J. Kleinschmidt, "Resources Allocation in the New Product Process," *Industrial Marketing Management*, August 1988, pp. 249–62.

3. Spend twice as much time and twice as much money on preliminary technical assessment.
4. Spend 50 percent more money and 35 percent more time on product development.
5. Spend twice as much money and 50 percent more time on in-house tests.

---

efforts begin, the higher the likelihood is that development efforts will be successful. A key component, contributing to the success of many Japanese companies' product development efforts, relates to the emphasis placed on creating cross-functional teams early on in the development process. Members from many different departments come together to jointly establish new product development goals and priorities and to also generate new product development schedules.[15]

Product Development

At this juncture the product idea has been evaluated from the standpoint of engineering, manufacturing, finance, and marketing. If it has met all expectations, it is considered a candidate for further research and testing. In the laboratory, the product is converted into a finished good and tested. A development report to management is prepared that spells out in fine detail: *(a)* the results of the studies by the engineering department; *(b)* required plan design; *(c)* production facilities design; *(d)* tooling requirements; *(e)* marketing test plan; *(f)* financial program survey; and *(g)* an estimated release date.

---

[15]For a discussion of the R&D-Marketing interface in Japanese firms, see X. Michael Song and Mark E. Parry, "The R&D-Marketing Interface in Japanese High-Technology Firms," *The Journal of Product Innovation Management*, June 1992, pp. 91–112.

HIGHLIGHT 7–5

Nine Underlying Factors Associated With New Product Success

1. *Product superiority/quality.* The competitive advantage the product has by virtue of features, benefits, quality, uniqueness, and so on.
2. *Economic advantage to user.* The product's value for money for the customer.
3. *Overall company/project fit.* The product's synergy with the company—marketing, managerial, business fit.
4. *Technological compatibility.* The product's technological synergy with the company—R&D, engineering, production fit.
5. *Familiarity to the company.* How familiar or "close to home" the product is to the company's current products and markets (as opposed to being targeted at new customers or markets).
6. *Market need, growth, and size.* The magnitude of the market opportunity.
7. *Competitive situation.* How easy the market is to penetrate from a competitive standpoint.
8. *Defined opportunity.* Whether the product has a well-defined category and established market to enter.
9. *Project/product definition.* How well-defined the development process and product are.

Source: Based on research conducted by Robert G. Cooper, "The NewProd System: The Industry Experience," *The Journal of Product Innovation Management,* June 1992, pp. 113–27.

Test Marketing

Up until now the product has been a company secret. Now management goes outside the company and submits the product candidate for customer approval. Test market programs are conducted in lines with the general plans for launching the product. Several of the more commonly utilized forms of test marketing are:[16]

1. *Pseudo sales.*   Potential buyers are asked to answer survey questions or pick items off a shelf in a make-believe store. The key factor is that no spending or risk for the consumer takes place.
2. *Cash sales.*   Here, the buyer must actually make a purchase. The test may be informal, controlled, or in a full-scale test market. However, it is still research, and no release of the product has been made.

---

[16]The material on test marketing was excerpted from C. Merle Crawford, *New Products Management,* 2nd ed. (Homewood, Ill.: Richard D. Irwin, 1987), pp. 284–98.

3. *Limited marketing.*   In this case, the firm decides to market the product gradually. This method allows for continual learning before the product reaches national availability.
4. *National launch.*   Here the firm just launches the product on a national scale and makes adjustments as needed.

The main goal of a test market is to evaluate and adjust, as necessary, the general marketing strategy to be used and the appropriate marketing mix. Additionally, producers can utilize the early interaction with buyers, occurring in test markets, to begin exploration of issues related to the next generation of product development.[17] Especially in cases where new technologies and markets are emerging, firms can benefit greatly from knowledge gained in test markets. Throughout the test market process, findings are being analyzed and forecasts of volume developed. Upon completion of a successful test market phase, the marketing plan can be finalized and the product prepared for launch.

Commercialization

This is the launching step. During this stage, heavy emphasis is placed on the organization structure and management talent needed to implement the marketing strategy. Emphasis is also given to following up such things as bugs in the design, production costs, quality control, and inventory requirements, Procedures and responsibility for evaluating the success of the new product by comparison with projections are also finalized.

The Importance of Time

During the 1990s, companies will place an increasing emphasis on shortening their products' "time-to-market."[18] *Time-to-market* can be defined as the elapsed time between product definition and product availability. A company that can bring out new products faster than its competitors enjoys a huge advantage.[19] Today in many industries, Japanese manufacturers are successfully following such a strategy. In projection television, Japanese producers can develop a new television in one third the time required by U.S. manufac-

---

[17]Patricia W. Meyers and Gerald A. Athaide, "Strategic Mutual Learning Between Producing and Buying Firms During Product Innovation," *The Journal of Product Innovation Management,* September 1991, pp. 155–69.

[18]Joseph T. Vesey, "Time-to-Market: Put Speed in Product Development," *Industrial Marketing Management,* April 1992, pp. 151–58.

[19]George Stalk, Jr., "Time—The Next Source of Competitive Advantage," *Harvard Business Review,* July–August 1988, pp. 41–51.

turers. Successful time-based innovation can be attributed to the use of short production runs whereby products are improved upon on an incremental basis, the use of cross-functional project teams, decentralized work scheduling and monitoring, and a responsive system for gathering and analyzing customer feedback.

Several U.S. companies, including Procter & Gamble, have taken steps to speed up the new product development cycle by giving managers, at the product class and brand family level, more decision-making power. Increasingly, companies are bypassing time-consuming regional test markets in favor of national launches. It is becoming, more than ever, important that firms do a successful job of developing the new product right the first time.[20]

CAUSES OF NEW PRODUCT FAILURE

Many new products with satisfactory potential have failed to make the grade. Many of the reasons for new product failure relate to execution and control problems. Below is a brief list of some of the more important causes of new product failures after they have been carefully screened, developed, and marketed.[21]

1. Faulty estimates of market potential.
2. Unexpected reactions from competitors.
3. Poor timing in the introduction of the product.
4. Rapid change in the market (economy) after the product was approved.
5. Inadequate quality control.
6. Faulty estimates in production costs.
7. Inadequate expenditures on initial promotion.
8. Faulty market testing.
9. Improper channel of distribution.

---

[20]For a complete discussion of issues related to accelerating the new product development process, see C. Merle Crawford, "The Hidden Costs of Accelerated Product Development," *The Journal of Product Innovation Management*, September 1992, pp. 188–99; Murray R. Millson, S. P. Raj, and David Wilemon, "A Survey of Major Approaches for Accelerating New Product Development," *The Journal of Product Innovation Management*, March 1992, pp. 53–69; Rene Cordero, "Managing Time Efficiently to Avoid Product Obsolescence: A Survey of Techniques," *The Journal of Product Innovation Management*, December 1991, pp. 283–94; and Edward F. McDonough III and Gloria Barczak, "Speeding Up New Product Development: The Effects of Leadership Style and Source of Technology," *The Journal of Product Innovation Management*, September 1991, pp. 203–11.

[21]For a more complete list, including factors affecting Japanese and British firms, see Scott Edgett, David Shipley, and Giles Forbes, "Japanese and British Companies Compared: Contributing Factors to Success and Failure in NPD," *The Journal of Product Innovation Management*, March 1992, pp. 3–10.

HIGHLIGHT 7–6

Examples of Misfires in Test Marketing

1. Example: Procter & Gamble claims that competitors stole its patented process for Duncan Hines chocolate chip cookies when they saw how successful the product was in test market.

2. Example: When Campbell Soup first test marketed Prego Spaghetti Sauce, Campbell marketers say they noticed a flurry of new Ragu ads and cents-off deals that they feel were designed to induce shoppers to load up on Ragu and to skew Prego's test results. They also claim that Ragu copied Prego when it developed Ragu Homestyle spaghetti sauce, which was thick, red, flecked with oregano and basil, and which Ragu moved into national distribution before Prego.

3. Example: A health and beauty aids firm developed a deodorant containing baking soda. A competitor spotted the product in a test market, rolled out its own version of the deodorant nationally before the first firm completed its testing, and later successfully sued the product originator for copyright infringement when it launched its deodorant nationally.

4. Example: Campbell Soup spent 18 months developing a blended fruit juice called Juiceworks. By the time the product reached the market, three competing brands were already on store shelves. Campbell dropped its product.

5. Example: Spurred by its incredible success with Fruit 'N' Juice Bars, Dole worked hard to create a new fruity ice cream novelty product with the same type of appeal. Company officials expected that the product that resulted from this development activity, Fruit and Cream Bars, which it test marketed in Orlando, Florida, would do slightly less well because it was more of an indulgence-type product. However, the test market results were so positive that Dole became the number-one brand in the market within three months. The company consequently shortened the test market to six months. When it rolled out the product, though, the company unhappily found four unexpected entrants in the ice cream novelty category. Due to the intense competition, Fruit and Cream sales fell short of expectations.

Source: G. Churchill, *Basic Marketing Research,* 2nd ed. Hinsdale, Ill.: Dryden Press, 1992, p. 150.

Some of the above problems are beyond the control of management; but it is clear that successful new product planning requires large amounts of reliable information in diverse areas. Each department assigned functional responsibility for product development automatically becomes an input to the information system needed by the new product decision maker. For example, when a firm is developing a new product, it is wise for both engineers and marketers to consider both the kind of market to be entered (e.g., consumer, industrial, defense, or export) and specific target segments. These decisions will be of paramount influence on the design and cost of the finished good, which will, of course, directly influence price, sales, and profits.

Need for Research

In many respects it can be argued that the keystone activity of any new product planning system is research—not just marketing research, but technical research as well. Regardless of the way in which the new product planning function is organized in the company, new product development decisions by top management require data that provide a base for making more intelligent choices. New product project reports ought to be more than a collection of "expert" opinions. Top management has a responsibility to ask certain questions, and the new product planning team has an obligation to generate answers to these questions based on research that provides marketing, economic, engineering, and production information. This need will be more clearly understood if some of the specific questions commonly raised in evaluating product ideas are examined:

1. What is the anticipated market demand over time? Are the potential applications for the product restricted?
2. Can the item be patented? Are there any antitrust problems?
3. Can the product be sold through present channels and sales force? What will be the number of new salespersons needed? What additional sales training will be required?
4. At different volume levels, what will be the unit manufacturing costs?
5. What is the most appropriate package to use in terms of color, material, design, and so forth?
6. What is the estimated return on investment?
7. What is the appropriate pricing strategy?

While this list is not intended to be exhaustive, it serves to illustrate the serious need for reliable information. Note, also, that some of the essential facts required to answer these questions can only be obtained through time-consuming and expensive marketing research studies. Other data can be generated in the engineering laboratories or pulled from accounting records. Certain types of information must be based on assumptions, which may or may not hold true, and on expectations about what will happen in the future, as in the case of "anticipated competitive reaction" or the projected level of sales.

Another complication is that many different types of information must be gathered and formulated into a meaningful program for decision making. To illustrate, in trying to answer questions about return on investment of a particular project, the analyst must know something about (1) the pricing strategy to be used and (2) the investment outlay. Regardless of the formula used to measure the investment worth of a new product, different types of information are required. Using one of the simplest approaches—the payback method (the ratio of investment outlay to annual cash flow)—one needs to estimate the magnitude of the product investment outlay and the annual cash flow. The investment outlay requires estimates of such things as production equipment, R&D costs, and nonrecurring introductory marketing expenditures; the annual cash flow requires a forecast of unit demand and price. These data must be collected or generated from many different departments and processed into a form that will be meaningful to the decision maker.

CONCLUSION

This chapter has focused on the nature of new product planning and development. Attention has been given to the management process required to have an effective program for new product development. It should be obvious to the reader that this is one of the most important and difficult aspects of marketing management. The problem is so complex that, unless management develops a plan for dealing with the problem, it is likely to operate at a severe competitive disadvantage in the marketplace.

ADDITIONAL READINGS

Clark, Allen M. "Trends That Will Impact New Products." *The Journal of Consumer Marketing,* Winter 1991, pp. 35–40.

Frey, Don. "Learning the Ropes: My Life as a Product Champion." *Harvard Business Review,* September–October 1991, pp. 46–56.

Harris, Robert G., and David C. Mowery. "Strategies for Innovation: An Overview." *California Management Review,* Spring 1990, pp. 7–16.

Hodick, Calvin L. "Strategies Behind the Winners and Losers." *The Journal of Business Strategy,* September/October 1990, pp. 4–7.

Kuczmarski, Thomas D. *Managing New Products: The Power of Innovation,* 2nd ed. Englewood Cliffs, N.J.: Prentice Hall, 1992.

Mabert, Vincent A.; John F. Muth; and Roger W. Schmenner. "Collapsing New Product Development Times: Six Case Studies." *The Journal of Product Innovation Management,* September 1992, pp. 200–12.

Peters, Tom. "Get Innovative or Get Dead." *California Management Review,* Winter 1991, pp. 9–23.

Sarin, Sharad, and Gour M. Kapur. "Lessons From New Product Failures: Five Case Studies." *Industrial Marketing Management,* November 1990, pp. 301–13.

Chapter 8

Promotion Strategy: Advertising and Sales Promotion

To simplify the discussion of the general subject of promotion, the topic has been divided into two basic categories, personal selling and nonpersonal selling. Personal selling will be discussed in detail in the next chapter, and this chapter will be devoted to nonpersonal selling.

Nonpersonal selling includes all demand creation and demand maintenance activities of the firm other than personal selling. It is mass selling. In more specific terms, nonpersonal selling includes *(a)* advertising, *(b)* sales promotion, and *(c)* publicity. For purposes of this text, primary emphasis will be placed on advertising and sales promotion. Publicity is a special form of promotion that amounts to "free advertising," such as a writeup about the firm's products in a newspaper article. It will not be dealt with in detail in this text.

THE PROMOTION MIX

The promotion mix concept refers to *the combination and types of promotional effort the firm puts forth during a specified time period.* Most business concerns make use of more than one form of promotion, but some firms rely on a single technique. An example of a company using only one promotional device would be a manufacturer of novelties who markets its products exclusively by means of mail order.

In devising its promotion mix, the firm should take into account three basic factors: (1) the role of promotion in the overall marketing mix; (2) the nature of the product; and (3) the nature of the market. Also, it must be recognized

---

HIGHLIGHT 8–1

Some Advantages and Disadvantages of Major Promotion Methods

Advertising

Advantages	Disadvantages
Can reach many consumers simultaneously.	Many consumers reached are not potential buyers (waste of promotion dollars).
Relatively low cost per exposure.	
Excellent for creating brand images.	High visibility makes advertising a major target of marketing critics.
High degree of flexibility and variety of media to choose from; can accomplish many different types of promotion objectives.	Advertisement exposure time is usually brief.
	Advertisements are often quickly and easily screened out by consumers.

Personal Selling

Advantages	Disadvantages
Can be the most persuasive promotion tool; salespeople can directly influence purchase behaviors.	High cost per contact.
	Sales training and motivation can be expensive and difficult.
Allows two-way communication.	Personal selling often has a poor image, making salesforce recruitment difficult.
Often necessary for technically complex products.	Poorly done sales presentations can hurt sales as well as company, product, and brand images.
Allows direct one-on-one targeting of promotional effort.	

Sales Promotion

Advantages	Disadvantages
Excellent approach for short-term price reductions for stimulating demand.	May influence primarily brand-loyal customers to stock up at lower price but attract few new customers.
A large variety of sales promotion tools to choose from.	May have only short-term impact.
Can be effective for changing a variety of consumer behaviors.	Overuse of price-related sales promotion tools may hurt brand image and profits.
Can be easily tied in with other promotion tools.	Effective sales promotions are easily copied by competitors.

Source: J. Paul Peter and Jerry C. Olson, *Consumer Behavior and Marketing Strategy,* 2nd ed. (Homewood, Ill.: Richard D. Irwin, 1990), p. 459.

---

that a firm's promotion mix is likely to change over time to reflect changes in the market, competition, the product's life cycle, and the adoption of new strategies. The following example illustrates how one firm developed its promotion mix along these lines.

Figure 8-1   *An Example of the Role of Various Promotion Tools in the Selling Process*

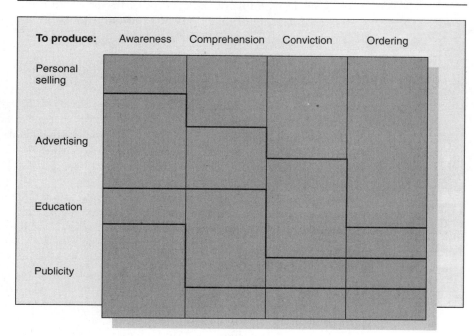

When IBM began to market its magnetic character sensing equipment for banks, the company defined the 500 largest banks as its likeliest market and a research firm was commissioned to study the marketing problems. They selected a representative sample of 185 banks and interviewed the officer designated by each bank as the person who would be most influential in deciding whether or not to purchase the equipment. Researchers sought to establish which of the following stages each banker had reached in the sales process: (1) *awareness* of the new product; (2) *comprehension* of what it offered; (3) *conviction* that it would be a good investment; or (4) the *ordering* stage. They also tried to isolate the promotional factors that had brought the bankers to each stage. IBM's promotional mix consisted of personal selling, advertising, education (IBM schools and in-bank seminars), and publicity (through news releases). Figure 8-1 illustrates the process.

The findings were a revelation to IBM. In the marketing of such equipment IBM had consistently taken the position that advertising had a very minor role to play, that nothing could replace the sales call. IBM found it could cut back on personal selling in the early stages of the selling process, thereby freeing salespeople to concentrate on the vital phase of the process—the actual closing of the sale. While these results may not hold true for all products, they are an excellent example of the concept of the promotion mix and the effectiveness of different combinations of promotion tools for achieving various objectives.

ADVERTISING: PLANNING AND STRATEGY

Advertising seeks to promote the seller's product by means of printed and electronic media. This is justified on the grounds that messages can reach large numbers of people and inform, persuade, and remind them about the firm's offerings. The traditional way of defining advertising is as follows: It is any paid form of nonpersonal presentation of ideas, goods, or services by an identified sponsor.[1]

From a management viewpoint, advertising is a strategic device for gaining or maintaining a competitive advantage in the marketplace. For example, in 1991, Procter & Gamble spent over $2 billion advertising their products. In order to be ranked among the top 100 advertisers in 1991, it was necessary for a firm (Monsanto Co.) to spend over $100 million.[2] Based on past growth patterns, it is expected that advertising expenditures will reach $159 billion by 1996. For manufacturers and resellers alike, advertising budgets represent a large and growing element in the cost of marketing goods and services. For example, in 1992, Chrysler Corp. spent over $40 million solely promoting the redesigned Jeep Cherokee.[3] As part of the seller's promotion mix, advertising dollars must be appropriated and budgeted according to a marketing plan that takes into account such factors as:

1. Nature of the product, including life cycle.
2. Competition.
3. Government regulations.
4. Nature and scope of the market.
5. Channels of distribution.
6. Pricing strategy.
7. Availability of media.
8. Availability of funds.
9. Outlays for other forms of promotion.

---

[1] Peter D. Bennett, ed. *Dictionary of Marketing Terms* (Chicago: American Marketing Association, 1988), p. 4.

[2] For a complete description of ad spending by the top 100 advertisers, see *Advertising Age,* "100 Leading National Advertisers Special Issue," September 23, 1992.

[3] John P. Cortez, "New Jeep Gets $40M Burst," *Advertising Age,* January 20, 1992, p. 6.

| HIGHLIGHT 8-2 |

The 10 Leading U.S. Advertisers, 1991

Rank	Company	Total U.S. Advertising (Millions)	Total U.S. Sales (Millions)	Advertising as a Percentage of Sales
1	Procter & Gamble	$2,149	$15,276	14.1%
2	Philip Morris	2,046	37,890	5.4
3	General Motors	1,442	83,973	1.7
4	Sears	1,179	57,242★	2.1
5	PepsiCo	903	15,168	6.0
6	Grand Metropolitan	745	7,878	9.5
7	Johnson & Johnson	733	6,248	11.7
8	McDonald's	695	3,710	18.7
9	Ford Motor Co.	677	61,149	1.1
10	Eastman Kodak Co.	661	10,882	6.1

★Worldwide sales—U.S. sales not available.

Source: Adapted from *Advertising Age,* "100 Leading National Advertisers Special Issue," September 23, 1992.

Objectives of Advertising

In the long run, and often in the short run, advertising is justified on the basis of the revenues it produces. Revenues in this case may refer either to sales or profits. Economic theory assumes that firms are profit maximizers, and that advertising outlays should be increased in every market and medium up to the point where the additional cost of getting more business just equals the incremental profits. Since most business firms do not have the data required to use the marginal analysis of economic theory, they usually employ a less sophisticated decision-making model. There is also evidence to show that many executives advertise to maximize sales on the assumption that higher sales mean more profits (which may or may not be true).

The point to be made here is that the ultimate goal of the business advertiser is sales and profits. To achieve this goal, an approach to advertising is needed that provides guidelines for intelligent decision making. This approach must recognize the need for measuring the results of advertising, and these measurements must be as valid and reliable as possible. Marketing managers must also be aware of the fact that advertising not only complements other forms

---

HIGHLIGHT 8–3

Preparing the Advertising Campaign: The Eight-M Formula

Effective advertising should follow a plan. There is no one best way to go about planning an advertising campaign, but, in general, marketers should have good answers to the following eight questions:

1. *The management question:* Who will manage the advertising program?
2. *The money question:* How much should be spent on advertising as opposed to other forms of selling?
3. *The market question:* To whom should the advertising be directed?
4. *The message question:* What should the ads say about the product?

5. *The media question:* What types and combinations of media should be used?
6. *The macroscheduling question:* How long should the advertising campaign be in effect before changing ads or themes?
7. *The microscheduling question:* At what times and dates would it be best for ads to appear during the course of the campaign?
8. *The measurement question:* How will the effectiveness of the advertising campaign be measured and how will the campaign be evaluated and controlled?

---

of selling but is subject to the law of diminishing returns. This means that for any advertised product it can be assumed a point is eventually reached at which additional advertising produces little or no additional sales.

Specific Tasks of Advertising

In attempting to evaluate the contribution of advertising to the economic health of the firm, there are at least three different viewpoints on the subject. The generalist viewpoint is primarily concerned with sales, profits, return on investment, and so forth. At the other extreme, the specialist viewpoint is represented by advertising experts who are primarily concerned with measuring the effects of specific ads or campaigns; here primary attention is given to such matters as the Nielsen Index, Starch Reports, Arbitron Index, Simmons Reports, copy appeal, and so forth. A middle view, one that might be classified as more of a marketing management approach, understands and appreciates the other two viewpoints but, in addition, views advertising as a competitive weapon. Emphasis in this approach is given to the strategic aspects of the advertising problem. Following are some of the marketing tasks generally assigned to the advertising function as part of the overall marketing mix:

1. Maintaining dealer cooperation.
2. Familiarizing the consumer with the use of the product.

3. Emphasizing a trademark or brand.
4. Obtaining a list of prospects.
5. Creating goodwill for the product, brand, or company.
6. Stressing unique features of the product.
7. Introducing new products.
8. Generating store traffic.
9. Informing customers of sales prices.
10. Building customer or brand loyalty.
11. Establishing a relationship between the producer and distributor.

The above list is representative but not exhaustive, and it should be noted that some of the points pertain more to middlemen than to producers. For example, the first point is a "channel task," where advertising and other forms of sales promotion are employed to facilitate the flow of the producer's goods through distributors to the ultimate consumer; "cooperative advertising" programs are specifically designed to meet this objective. This is where a channel member, such as a retailer, will receive a certain percentage of gross sales as an advertising allowance. Some manufacturers also provide advertising copy, illustrations, and so forth.

ADVERTISING DECISIONS

In line with what has just been said, the marketing manager must make two key decisions. The first decision deals with determining the size of the advertising budget, and the second deals with how the advertising budget should be allocated. Although these decisions are highly interrelated, we deal with them separately to achieve a better understanding of the problems involved. Today's most successful brands of consumer goods were built by heavy advertising and marketing investment long ago.[4] Recently, many marketers have lost sight of the connection between advertising spending and market share. They practice the art of discounting: cutting ad budgets to fund price promotions or fatten quarterly earnings. Companies employing these tactics may benefit in the short term but will be at a severe competitive disadvantage in the long term.

Marketers at some companies however, remember that brand value and consumer preference for brands drive market share. Most important, they understand the balance of advertising and promotion expenditures needed to build brands and gain share, market by market, regardless of growth trends in the product categories where they compete. For example, Procter & Gamble has built its Jif and Folger's brands from single-digit shares to being among

---

[4]Much of the material for this section is based on John Phillip Jones, "Ad Spending: Maintaining Market Share," *Harvard Business Review,* January-February 1990, pp. 38–42; and James C. Schroer, "Ad Spending: Growing Market Share," *Harvard Business Review,* January-February 1990, pp. 44–48.

HIGHLIGHT 8–4

An Advertising Process Model

Consumer Psychosocial State	Marketing Situation
1. Ignorance	Consumer has no knowledge of the product.
2. Indifference	Consumer is conscious of product's existence by means of advertising.
3. Awareness	Advertising messages generate an awareness of a need for the product or reinforce a need once generated.
4. Interest	Consumer begins seeking more product-brand information by paying closer attention to various ads.
5. Comprehension	Consumer knows main features of product and various brands after intense ad exposure.
6. Conviction	Consumer is receptive to purchase and ready to act.
7. Action	Consumer shops for the product often as a result of the "act now" advertisements or special sales.

category leaders. In peanut butter and coffee, P&G invests more in advertising and less in discounting than its major competitors. What P&G and other smart marketers such as Kellogg, General Mills, Coke, and Pepsico hold in common is an awareness of a key factor in advertising: consistent investment spending. They do not raid their budgets to increase earnings for a few quarters, nor do they view advertising as a discretionary cost.

The Expenditure Question

Most firms determine how much to spend on advertising by one of the following methods:

Percent of sales. This is one of the most popular rule-of-thumb methods, and its appeal is found in its simplicity. The firm simply takes a percentage figure and applies it to either past or future sales. For example, suppose next year's sales are estimated to be $1 million. Using a 2-percent-of-sales criterion, the ad budget would be $20,000. This approach is usually justified by its advocates in terms of the following argument: (a) advertising is needed to generate sales; (b) a number of cents, that is, the percentage used, out of each dollar of sales should be devoted to advertising in order to generate needed sales; and (c) the percentage is easily adjusted and can be readily understood by other executives. The percent-of-sales approach is popular in retailing.

Per-unit expenditure. Closely related to the above technique is one in which a fixed monetary amount is spent on advertising for each unit of the product expected to be sold. This method is popular with higher priced merchandise, such as automobiles or appliances. For instance, if a company is marketing color televisions priced at $500, it may decide that it should spend $30 per set on advertising. Since this $30 is a fixed amount for each unit, this method amounts to the same thing as the percent-of-sales method. The big difference is in the rationale used to justify each of the methods. The per-unit expenditure method attempts to determine the retail price by using production costs as a base. Here the seller realizes that a reasonably competitive price must be established for the product in question and attempts to cost out the gross margin. All this means is that, if the suggested retail price is to be $500 and manufacturing costs are $250, there is a gross margin of $250 available to cover certain expenses, such as transportation, personal selling, advertising, and dealer profit. Some of these expense items are flexible, such as advertising, while others are nearly fixed, as in the case of transportation. The basic problem with this method and the percentage-of-sales method is that they view advertising as a function of sales, rather than sales as a function of advertising.

All you can afford. Here the advertising budget is established as a predetermined share of profits or financial resources. The availability of current revenues sets the upper limit of the ad budget. The only advantage to this approach is that it sets reasonable limits on the expenditures for advertising. However, from the standpoint of sound marketing practice, this method is undesirable because there is no necessary connection between liquidity and advertising opportunity. Any firm that limits its advertising outlays to the amount of available funds will probably miss opportunities for increasing sales and profits.

Competitive parity. This approach is often used in conjunction with other approaches, such as the percent-of-sales method. The basic philosophy underlying this approach is that advertising is defensive. Advertising budgets are based on those of competitors or other members of the industry. From a strategy standpoint, this is a "followership" technique and assumes that the other firms in the industry know what they are doing and have similar goals. Competitive parity is not a preferred method, although some executives feel it is a "safe" approach. This may or may not be true depending in part on the relative market share of competing firms and their growth objectives.

The research approach. Here the advertising budget is argued for and presented on the basis of research findings. Advertising media are studied in terms of their productivity by the use of media reports (such as the Starch Reports) and research studies. Costs are also estimated and compared with study results. A typical experiment is one in which three or more test markets are selected. The first test market is used as a control, either with no advertising or with normal levels of advertising. Advertising with various levels of intensity are used in the other markets, and comparisons are made to see what effect different levels of intensity have. The advertising manager then evaluates the costs and benefits of the different approaches and intensity levels to determine the overall budget. Although the research approach is generally more expensive than some other models, it is a more rational approach to the expenditure decision.

The task approach. Well-planned advertising programs usually make use of the task approach, which initially formulates the advertising goals and defines the tasks to accomplish these goals. Once this is done, management determines how much it will cost to accomplish each task and adds up the total. This approach is often used in conjunction with the research approach. A variation of the task approach is referred to as the *marketing-program approach*. Here all promotional or selling programs are budgeted in relation to each other, and, given a set of objectives, the goal is to find the optimum promotional mix. It should be clear that, in the task or marketing-program approach, the expenditure and allocation decisions are inseparable.

The Allocation Question

This question deals with the problem of deciding on the most effective way of spending advertising dollars. A general answer to the question is that management's choice of strategies and objectives determines the media and appeals to be used. In other words, the firm's or product division's overall marketing plan will function as a general guideline for answering the allocation question.

From a practical standpoint, however, the allocation question can be framed in terms of message and media decisions. A successful ad campaign has two related tasks: (1) say the right things in the ads themselves and (2) use the appropriate media in the right amounts at the right time to reach the target market.

Message strategy. The advertising process involves creating messages with words, ideas, sounds, and other forms of audiovisual stimuli that are designed to affect consumer (or distributor) behavior. It follows that much of advertising is a communication process. To be effective, the advertising message should meet two general criteria: (1) it should take into account the basic principles of communication, and (2) it should be predicated upon a good theory of consumer motivation and behavior.[5]

The basic communication process involves three elements: (1) the sender or source of the communication; (2) the communication or message; and (3) the receiver or audience. Advertising agencies are considered experts in the communications field and are employed by most large firms to create meaningful messages and assist in their dissemination. Translating the product idea or marketing message into an effective ad is termed *encoding*. In advertising, the goal of encoding is to generate ads that are understood by the audience.

---

[5]For a complete discussion of message strategy, see Courtland L. Bovee and William F. Arens, *Contemporary Advertising,* 4th ed. (Homewood, Ill.: Richard D. Irwin, 1992).

HIGHLIGHT 8–5

Some Relative Merits of Major Advertising Media

Newspapers

Advantages
1. Flexible and timely.
2. Intense coverge of local markets.
3. Broad acceptance and use.
4. High believability of printed word.

Disadvantages
1. Short life.
2. Read hastily.
3. Small "pass-along" audience.

Radio

Advantages
1. Mass use (over 25 million radios sold annually).
2. Audience selectivity via station format.
3. Low cost (per unit of time.)
4. Geographic flexibility.

Disadvantages
1. Audio presentation only.
2. Less attention than TV.
3. Chaotic buying (nonstandardized rate structures).
4. Short life.

Outdoor

Advantages
1. Flexible.
2. Relative absence of competing advertisements.
3. Repeat exposure.
4. Relatively inexpensive.

Disadvantages
1. Creative limitations.
2. Many distractions for viewer.
3. Public attack (ecological implications).
4. No selectivity of audience.

Television

Advantages
1. Combination of sight, sound, and motion.
2. Appeals to senses.
3. Mass audience coverage.
4. Psychology of attention.

Disadvantages
1. Nonselectivity of audience.
2. Fleeting impressions.
3. Short life.
4. Expensive.

Magazines

Advantages
1. High geographic and demographic selectivity.
2. Psychology of attention.
3. Quality of reproduction.
4. Pass-along readership.

Disadvantages
1. Long closing periods (6 to 8 weeks prior to publication).
2. Some waste circulation.
3. No guarantee of position (unless premium is paid).

Direct Mail

Advantages
1. Audience selectivity.
2. Flexible.
3. No competition from competing advertisements.
4. Personalized.

Disadvantages
1. Relatively high cost.
2. Consumers often pay little attention and throw it away.

For this to occur, the audience must be able to decode the message in the ad so that the perceived content of the message is the same as the intended content of the message. From a practical standpoint, all this means is that advertising messages must be sent to consumers in an understandable and meaningful way.

Advertising messages, of course, must be transmitted and carried by particular communication channels commonly known as advertising media. These media or channels vary in efficiency, selectivity, and cost. Some channels are preferred to others because they have less "noise," and thus messages are more easily received and understood. For example, a particular newspaper ad must compete with other ads, pictures, or stories on the same page. In the case of radio or TV, while only one firm's message is usually broadcast at a time, there are other distractions (noise) that can hamper clear communications, such as driving while listening to the radio.

The relationship between advertising and consumer behavior is quite obvious. For many products and services, advertising is an influence that may affect the consumer's decision to purchase a particular product or brand. It is clear that consumers are subjected to many selling influences, and the question arises about how important advertising is or can be. Here is where the advertising expert must operate on some theory of consumer behavior. The reader will recall from the discussion of consumer behavior that the buyer was viewed as progressing through various stages from an unsatisfied need through and beyond a purchase decision. The end goal of an advertisement and its associated campaign is to make the consumer feel that, "Hey, this product is right for me."[6] By doing so, the advertisement will have succeeded in moving the consumer to the trial and repeat purchase stage of the consumer behavior process, which is the end goal of advertising strategy.

The planning of an advertising campaign and the creation of persuasive messages requires a mixture of marketing skill and creative know-how. Relative to the dimension of marketing skills, there are some important pieces of marketing information needed before launching an ad campaign. Most of this information must be generated by the firm and kept up to date. Listed below are some of the critical types of information an advertiser should have:

1. *Who* the firms' customers and potential customers are; their demographic, economic, and psychological characteristics; and any other factors affecting their likelihood of buying.
2. *How many* such customers there are.
3. *How much* of the firm's type and brand of product they are currently buying and can reasonably be expected to buy in the short-term and long-term future.

---

[6]For a discussion of developing effective advertising, see Jeffrey F. Durgee, "Qualitative Methods for Developing Advertising That Makes Consumers Feel, 'Hey, That's Right For Me,'" *The Journal of Consumer Marketing,* Winter 1990, pp. 15–21.

4. *Which* individuals, other than customers and potential customers, *influence* purchasing decisions.
5. *Where* they *buy* the firm's brand of product.
6. *When* they buy, and frequency of purchase.
7. *Which* competitive brands they buy and frequency of purchase.
8. *How* they *use* the product.
9. *Why* they buy particular *types* and *brands* of products.

Media mix. Media selection is no easy task. To start with, there are numerous types and combinations of media to choose from. Below is a general outline of some of the more common advertising media.

A. *Printed media.*
   1. National.
      a. Magazines.
      b. Newspapers.
      c. Direct mail.
   2. Local.
      a. Newspapers.
      b. Magazines.
      c. Direct mail.
      d. Handbills or flyers.
      e. Yellow Pages.
B. *Electronic media.*
   1. National (network).
      a. Radio.
      b. Television.
   2. Local.
      a. Radio (AM–FM).
      b. Television.
   3. Individual.
      a. Videocassette.
      b. Floppy disk.
C. *Other.*
   1. Outdoor (example: billboards).
   2. Transit.
   3. Specialty (giveaways).
   4. Point-of-purchase.
   5. Telemarketing (telephone selling).

Of course, each of the above media categories can be further refined. For example, magazines can be broken down into more detailed classes, such as mass monthlies *(Reader's Digest),* news weeklies *(Time),* men's magazines *(Playboy),* women's fashion magazines *(Vogue),* sports magazines *(Sports Il-lustrated),* business magazines *(Forbes),* and so forth. Clearly, one dimension of this advertising management problem involves having an overabundance of media to select from. With only four media to choose from, there are 16 possible go or no-go decisions. With 10 media, there would be approximately 1,000 combinations.

Although the number of media and media combinations available for advertising is overwhelming at first glance, four interrelated factors limit the number of practical alternatives. First, *the nature of the product* limits the number of practical and efficient alternatives. For instance, a radically new and highly complex product could not be properly promoted using billboard advertisements. Instead, the company may choose to develop an *infomercial,* a program-length ad that mixes information and entertainment with sales pitches.[7] Infomercials can either be carried on broadcast media or put on videotapes which are then mailed to targeted customers. Indeed, much of the advertising for one of the candidates in the 1992 presidential election (Ross Perot) was presented in the form of infomercials broadcast prior to the networks' prime time telecasts. Second, the nature and size of the target market also limits appropriate advertising media. For example, it is generally inefficient to advertise industrial goods in mass media publications. Third, *the advertising budget* may restrict the use of expensive media, such as television. And fourth, *the availability* of some media may be limited in particular geographic areas. Although these factors reduce media alternatives to a more manageable number, specific media must still be selected. A primary consideration at this point is media effectiveness or efficiency.

In the advertising industry, a common measure of efficiency or productivity is "cost per thousand" or CPMs. This figure generally refers to the dollar cost of reaching 1,000 prospects, and its chief advantage lies in its simplicity and allowance for a common base of comparison between differing media types. The major disadvantage of the use of CPMs also relates to its simplicity. For example, the same commercial placed in two different television programs, having the same viewership and the same audience profile, may very well generate different responses depending on the level of viewer involvement. This "positive effects" theory states that the more viewers are involved in a television program, the stronger they will respond to commercials.[8] In essence, involving programs produce engaged respondents who demonstrate more favorable responses to advertising messages.

Generally, such measures as circulation, audience size, and sets in use per commercial minute are used in the calculation. Of course, different relative rankings of media can occur, depending on the measure used. A related prob-

---

[7]For a discussion of the growing use of infomercials, see Mark Landler, "The Infomercial Inches Toward Respectability," *Business Week,* May 4, 1992, p. 175.

[8]Kevin J. Clancy, "CPMs Must Bow to Involvement Measurement," *Advertising Age,* January 20, 1992, p. 26.

Procedures for Evaluating Advertising Programs and Some Services
Using the Procedures

Procedures for Evaluating Specific Advertisements

1. *Recognition tests:* Estimate the percentage of people claiming to have read a magazine who recognize the ad when it is shown to them (e.g., Starch Message Report Service).
2. *Recall tests:* Estimate the percentage of people claiming to have read a magazine who can (unaided) recall the ad and its contents (e.g., Gallup and Robinson Impact Service, various services for TV ads as well).
3. *Opinion tests:* Potential audience members are asked to rank alternative advertisements as most interesting, most believable, best liked.
4. *Theater tests:* Theater audience is asked for brand preferences before and after an ad is shown in context of a TV show (e.g., Schwerin TV Testing Service).

Joseph Guiltinan and Gordon Paul, *Marketing Management,* 4th ed. (New York: McGraw-Hill, 1991) p. 278.

Procedures for Evaluating Specific Advertising Objectives

1. *Awareness:* Potential buyers are asked to indicate brands that come to mind in a product category. A message used in an ad campaign is given and buyers are asked to identify the brand that was advertised using that message.
2. *Attitude:* Potential buyers are asked to rate competing or individual brands on determinant attributes, benefits, characterizations using rating scales.

Procedures for Evaluating Motivational Impact

1. *Intention to buy:* Potential buyers are asked to indicate the likelihood they will buy a brand (on a scale from "definitely will not" to "definitely will").
2. *Market test:* Sales changes in different markets are monitored to compare the effects of different messages, budget levels.

---

lem deals with what is meant by "reaching" the prospect, and at least five levels of reaching are possible:

1. *Distribution.* This level refers to circulation or physical distribution of the vehicle into households or other decision-making units. In only some of these households or decision-making units are there genuine prospects for the product.
2. *Exposure.* This level refers to actual exposure of prospects to the message. If the TV set is on, distribution is taking place; but only if the program is being watched can exposure occur.
3. *Awareness.* This level refers to the prospect becoming alert to the message in the sense of being conscious of the ad. Actual information processing starts at this point.

4. *Communication*. This level goes one step beyond awareness—to the point where the prospect becomes affected by the message. Here the effect is to generate some sort of change in the prospect's knowledge, attitude, or desire concerning the product. Two major factors can affect the communication effectiveness of an advertisment. On a macro level, the greater the advertising clutter, the less the prospect is able to be affected by any one message. Advertising clutter refers to the amount of commercials placed on one show (television), one page (newspapers), or in one issue (magazines).[9] For example, the NBC television show "Seinfeld" was found to have the equivalent of 16 minutes, 24 seconds of commercial time per programming hour. On a micro level, recent studies have found that the more a prospect likes an individual commercial, the greater will be the likelihood that a positive response will occur.[10]

5. *Response*. This level represents the overt action that results because of the ad. Response can mean many things, such as a simple telephone or mail inquiry, a shopping trip, or a purchase.

The advertiser has to decide at what level to evaluate the performance of a medium, and this is a particularly difficult problem. Ideally, the advertiser would like to know exactly how many dollars of sales are generated by ads in a particular medium. However, this is very difficult to measure since so many other factors are simultaneously at work that could be producing sales. On the other hand, the distribution of a medium is much easier to measure but distribution figures are much less meaningful. For example, a newspaper may have a distribution (circulation) of 100,000 people, yet none of these people may be prospects for the particular product being advertised. Thus, if this media were evaluated in terms of distribution, it might be viewed as quite effective even though it may be totally ineffective in terms of producing sales. This problem further illustrates the importance of insuring that the media selected are those used by the target market.

From what has been said so far, it should be clear that advertising decisions involve a great deal of complexity and a myriad of variables. For many executives, until recently, believing in the effectiveness of advertising may have been a matter of faith.[11] Marketing departments might have collected voluminous statistics on television and other media ratings and carefully compared the costs of marketing with total sales. But none of this data

---

[9]For a discussion of the negative effects of advertising clutter, see Joe Mandese, "TV Clutter: Who has the Most, Who's Hurt the Worst," *Advertising Age,* May 4, 1992, p. 18 and Joe Mandese, "Advertisers Talk Tough on Clutter, Vow to Hold Back Dollars From Nets," *Advertising Age,* May 11, 1992, pp. S6–S10.

[10]Cyndee Miller, "New Study Downplays 'Likability' as Major Factor in Ad Success," *Marketing News,* April 4, 1992, pp. 2–3.

[11]The discussion of single-source data is based on Magid M. Abraham and Leonard M. Lodish, "Getting the Most Out of Advertising and Promotion," *Harvard Business Review,* May-June 1990, pp. 50–60.

measured what was really important: the incremental sales of a product over and above those that would have happened without advertising. Thanks to a new kind of marketing data, this situation is changing. Single-source marketing data correlates information from actual consumer purchases (available from universal-product-code scanners used in supermarkets and drugstores) with information on the kind of television and other advertising that consumers see or hear. Armed with the results of such analyses, managers can make sound decisions regarding advertising effectiveness.[12]

In addition to the use of single-source data, application of quantitative techniques has become quite popular in the area of advertising planning. Linear programming, dynamic programming, heuristic programming, and simulation have been applied to the problem of selecting media schedules, and more comprehensive models of advertising decisions have also been developed. These sophisticated types of applications have enabled advertisers to overcome past problems associated with the use of such simplistic planning tools as GRPs (Gross Rating Points), which fail to differentiate between the importance of reach and frequency.[13] However, although these models represent a vast improvement over earlier ones, they must be viewed as an aid in advertising decision making, and not as a replacement for sound managerial decisions and judgment.

SALES PROMOTION

In marketing, the word *promotion* is used in many ways. For instance, it is sometimes used to refer to a specific activity, such as advertising or publicity. In the general sense, promotion has been defined as "any identifiable effort on the part of the seller to persuade buyers to accept the seller's information and store it in retrievable form." However, the term *sales promotion* has a more restricted and technical meaning and has been defined by the American Marketing Association as follows:

> Media and nonmedia marketing pressure applied for a predetermined, limited period of time at the level of consumer, retailer, or wholesaler in order to stimulate trial, increase consumer demand, or improve product availability.[14]

---

[12]For a discussion of other means to judge advertising effectiveness, see Anthony J. Adams and Margaret H. Blair, "Persuasive Advertising and Sales Accountability: Past Experience and Forward Validation," *Journal of Advertising Research,* March/April 1992, pp. 20–25 and Brian Wansik and Michael L. Ray, "Estimating an Advertisement's Impact on One's Consumption of a Brand," *Journal of Advertising Research,* May/June 1992, pp. 9–16.

[13]For a discussion of problems inherent in the use of GRPs, see Peter R. Dickson, "GRP: A Case of a Mistaken Identity," *Journal of Advertising Research,* February/March 1991, pp. 55–59.

[14]Peter D. Bennett, ed. *Dictionary of Marketing Terms* (Chicago: American Marketing Association, 1988), p. 179.

HIGHLIGHT 8–7

Some Objectives of Sales Promotion

When directed at consumers:

1. To obtain the trial of a product.
2. To introduce a new or improved product.
3. To encourage repeat or greater usage by current users.
4. To bring more customers into retail stores.
5. To increase the total number of users of an established product.

Source: Adapted from Steven J. Skinner, *Marketing* (Boston: Houghton Mifflin Co., 1990), p. 542.

When directed at salespersons:

1. To motivate the sales force.
2. To educate the sales force about product improvements.
3. To stabilize a fluctuating sales pattern.

When directed at resellers:

1. To increase reseller inventories.
2. To obtain displays and other support for products.
3. To improve product distribution.
4. To obtain more and better shelf space.

The popularity of sales and other promotions has been increasing. In the four-year period between 1987 and 1991, the promotion-to-advertising expenditure ratio increased from a 64 percent to 46 percent split to a 75 percent to 25 percent level.[15] Dollars spent on trade promotions accounted for almost two thirds of all promotional dollars spent. Reasons for this growth of sales promotion include a shifting emphasis from pull to push marketing strategies by many firms, a widening of the focus of advertising agencies to include promotional services to firms, an emphasis on the part of management towards short-term results, and the emergence of new technology. For example, supermarket cash registers can now be equipped with a device that will dispense coupons to a customer at the point of purchase. The type, variety, and cash amount of the coupon will vary from customer to customer based on their purchases. In essence, it is now possible for the Coca-Cola Company to dispense coupons to only those customers who purchase Pepsi, thus avoiding wasting promotional dollars on already loyal Coke drinkers.

Push versus Pull Marketing

Push and pull marketing strategies comprise the two options available to firms interested in getting their product into customers' hands. *Push strategies* include all activities aimed at getting products into the dealer pipeline and accelerating

---

[15]Scott Humes, "Trade Promos Devour Half of All Marketing $," *Advertising Age*, April 13, 1992, pp. 3–4.

sales by offering inducements to dealers, retailers, and salespeople. Inducements might include introductory price allowances, distribution allowances, and advertising-dollar allowances.[16] A *pull strategy*, on the other hand, is one whereby a manufacturer relies mainly on product advertising or consumer sales promotions. These activities are aimed at motivating the consumer to pull the product through the channel.

Several forces and developments have contributed to the increasing use of push marketing strategies by many manufacturers.[17]

1. *Changes in the balance of power between manufacturers and retailers.* Due to the decreasing importance of network television and the increasing use of optical scanning equipment, retailers no longer have to depend on manufacturers for facts. This leads to more power on the part of retailers.

2. *Growth and consolidation of retail package goods businesses.* The growth of regional and national grocery chains such as Safeway and Kroger have led to increasing clout for the retailer. For example, many supermarkets now charge manufacturers a slotting allowance on new products. A slotting allowance is a fee manufacturers pay retailers to allocate shelf space to new products.

3. *Low growth rate of the U.S. population.* The U.S. population is growing at only .8% annually, and growth in per-capita consumption of most mature products is modest. This situation, coupled with excess production capacity, has aggravated competition for market share and the use of price promotions to secure it.[18]

4. *Time constraints of the consumer.* Today's consumer is less interested in shopping, more likely to hold a job, under greater time pressure, and less inclined to prepare a shopping list ahead of a store visit. Hence, today's consumer is more susceptible to prominent displays in the store.[19]

5. *Reduced product differentiation and brand loyalty.* Due to the similarity of many brands and the growing use of sales promotions, consumers are no longer as brand loyal as they once were. Therefore, more and more sales promotions are needed as an incentive to get the consumer to buy a particular brand. To illustrate, consider the case of domestic car manufacturers. Advertising can no longer be used as a stand-alone

---

[16]Definition of push marketing and its activities is from Courtland L. Bovee and William F. Arens, *Contemporary Advertising,* 4th ed. (Homewood, Ill.: Richard D. Irwin, 1992), p. G-17.

[17]For a fuller explanation of the rise in push marketing strategies, see Terence A. Shimp, *Promotion Management and Marketing Communications,* 2nd ed. (Chicago, Ill.: Dryden Press, 1990), pp. 517–20 and Alvin Achenbaum and F. Kent Mitchel, "Pulling Away from Push Marketing," *Harvard Business Review,* May–June 1987, pp. 38–40.

[18]Robert D. Buzzell, John A. Quelch, and Walter J. Salmon, "The Costly Bargain of Trade Promotion," *Harvard Business Review,* March-April 1990, pp. 141–48.

[19]Ibid.

promotional strategy to induce consumer automobile purchases. Instead, the manufacturer must also offer additional incentives to the consumer through the dealer including rebates, special option packages, and extended warranties.

Trade Sales Promotions

Trade promotions are those promotions aimed at distributors and retailers of products who make up the distribution channel. The major objectives of trade promotions are to: (1) convince retailers to carry the manufacturer's products; (2) reduce the manufacturer's and increase the distributor's or retailer's inventories; (3) support advertising and consumer sales promotions; (4) encourage retailers to either give the product more favorable shelf space or place more emphasis on selling the product; and (5) serve as a reward for past sales efforts.

Types of dealer sales promotions vary. The most common types are:

1. Point-of-purchase displays including special racks, banners, signs, price cards, and other mechanical product dispensers. For example, an end-of-the-aisle display for Chips Ahoy cookies would be provided to the retailer by Nabisco.
2. Contests in which organizations and individual sales people are rewarded for sales efforts.
3. Trade shows that are regularly scheduled events where manufacturers provide information and display products.
4. Sales meetings at which information and support materials are presented to dealers.
5. Push money, which is a form of extra payment given to resellers for meeting specified sales goals.
6. Dealer loaders, which are premiums in the form of merchandise, gifts, or displays given to the reseller for purchasing large quantities of the product.
7. Trade deals, which are price discounts given for meeting certain purchase requirements.
8. Advertising allowances whereby the manufacturer helps to support retailer advertising efforts in which the manufacturer's product is displayed.

Promotions built around price discounts and advertising/other allowances are likely to have higher distributor/retailer participation levels than other type promotions because there is a direct economic incentive attached to the promotion.[20] The importance attached to individual types of promotions may vary by the size of distributor/retailer. For example, small retailers do not consider contests, sweepstakes, and sales quotas as being

---

[20]This discussion is based on Donald R. Glover, "Distributor Attitudes Toward Manufacturer-Sponsored Promotions," *Industrial Marketing Management*, August 1991, pp. 241–49.

important to their decision to participate in promotions; getting the full benefit of such promotions is difficult due to their size. Marketers must keep in mind that not all distributors or retailers will have the same reaction to promotions offered. Differences in attitudes need to be carefully considered by the manufacturer when designing and implementing trade promotion programs.

Consumer Promotions

Consumer promotions can fulfill several distinct objectives for the manufacturer. Some of the more commonly sought-after objectives include: (1) inducing the consumer to try the product; (2) rewarding the consumer for brand loyalty; (3) encouraging the consumer to trade up or purchase larger sizes of a product; (4) stimulating the consumer to make repeat purchases of the product; (5) reacting to competitor efforts; and (6) reinforcing and serving as a complement to advertising and personal selling efforts.

Listed below are brief descriptions of some of the most commonly utilized forms of consumer promotion activities.

1. *Sampling.* Consumers are offered regular or trial sizes of the product either free or at a nominal price. For example, Hershey Foods Corp. handed out 750,000 candy bars on 170 college campuses as a means of gaining trial.[21]
2. *Price deals.* Consumers are given discounts from the product's regular price. For example, Coke and Pepsi are frequently available at discounted prices.
3. *Bonus packs.* Bonus packs consist of additional amounts of the product that a company gives to buyers of the product. For example, manufacturers of disposable razors frequently add additional razors to their packages at no additional charge.
4. *Rebates and refunds.* Consumers, either on the spot or through the mail, are given cash reimbursements for purchasing products. For example, consumers are offered a $3 mail-in rebate for purchasing a Norelco coffee maker.
5. *Sweepstakes and contests.* Consumers can win cash and/or prizes either through chance selection or games of skill. For example, Marriott Hotels teamed up with Hertz Rent-A-Car in a scratch card sweepstakes that offered over $90 million in prizes.
6. *Premiums.* A premium is a reward or gift that comes from purchasing a product. For example, Coca-Cola gave away an estimated 20 million pairs of 3-D glasses to enable Super Bowl watchers to see their 3-D commercial. AT&T gave away fax and voice-paging machines to purchasers of their small business systems.
7. *Coupons.* Probably the most familiar and widely used of all consumer promotions, coupons are cents-off or added value incentives. A recent study found that coupon users need to see an average increase of 42 percent in

---

[21]*Advertising Age,* September 27, 1989, p. 3.

the value of a coupon to try a brand they don't usually buy.[22] That means if a consumer redeems a 50 cents coupon for a frequently used product, it would require at least a 70 cents coupon to entice that consumer to try another brand. Due to the high incidence of coupon fraud, manufacturers, including Royal Crown Cola and General Mills, are now experimenting with the use of personalized checks as an alternative to coupons. An added advantage of this alternative is a quicker redemption for retailers. As mentioned previously, point-of-purchase coupons are becoming an increasingly efficient way for marketers to target their promotional efforts at specific consumers.

What Sales Promotion Can and Can't Do

Advocates of sales promotion often point to its growing popularity as a justification for the argument that we don't need advertising; sales promotion itself will suffice. Marketers should bear in mind that sales promotion is only one part of a well-constructed overall promotional plan. While proven to be extremely effective in achieving the objectives listed in the previous sections, there are several compelling reasons why sales promotion should not be utilized as the sole promotional tool. These reasons include sales promotion's inability to: (1) generate long-term buyer commitment to a brand; (2) change, except on a temporary basis, declining sales of a product; (3) convince buyers to purchase an otherwise unacceptable product; and (4) make up for a lack of advertising or sales support for a product. In addition, promotions can often fuel the flames of competitive retaliation far more than other marketing activities.[23] When the competition gets drawn into the promotion war, the effect can be a significant muting of the sharp sales increases predicted by the initiator of the promotion. Worse yet, promotions can often devalue the image of the promoted brand in the consumer's eyes. To illustrate, General Foods cut back the yearly advertising expenditures on Maxwell House coffee by $60 million in the mid 80s and reallocated the funds to sales promotion activities. Within a year, Folger's coffee dislodged Maxwell House as the largest selling brand. It took three years for Maxwell House to finally regain the top spot. In the process, General Foods ended up restoring the advertising budget to an even higher level than it was prior to Maxwell House's fall from grace.

Some consumer products firms are instituting new pricing policies to try to cut back on the amount of sales promotions used. For example, Procter & Gamble has instituted an everyday low-price strategy for many of its products,

---

[22]"Coupons-At Right Price Can Torpedo Brand Loyalty," *Advertising Age,* May 18, 1992, p. 52.

[23]For a further discussion of the dangers involved in using sales promotions, see John P. Jones, "The Double Jeopardy of Sales Promotions," *Harvard Business Review,* September-October 1990.

including Cascade dish, Era liquid laundry, and Oxydol powder laundry detergents.[24] The intent of the policy is to give retailers a lower list price in exchange for the cutting of trade allowances. While the net cost of the product to retailers remains unchanged, retailers are losing promotional dollars that they, not Procter & Gamble, controlled. In many situations, although trade allowances are supposed to be used for retail sales, it is not uncommon to see retailers put as much as 30 percent of trade allowance money into their own bottom lines. The rationale behind companies', such as Procter & Gamble's, efforts to cut back on trade and other promotions is to: (1) not force brand-loyal customers to pay unusually high prices when a product isn't on special; (2) allow consumers to benefit from a lower average shelf price since retailers will no longer have discretion over the use of allowance dollars; and (3) improve efficiencies in manufacturing and distribution systems because retailers will lose the incentive to do heavy forward buying of discounted items.

CONCLUSION

This chapter has been concerned with nonpersonal selling. Remember that advertising and sales promotion are only two of the ways by which sellers can affect the demand for their product. Advertising and sales promotion are only part of the firm's promotion mix, and, in turn, the promotion mix is only part of the overall marketing mix. Thus, advertising and sales promotion begin with the marketing plan and not with the advertising and sales promotion plans. Ignoring this point can produce ineffective and expensive promotional programs because of a lack of coordination with other elements of the marketing mix.

ADDITONAL READINGS

Balasubramanian, Siva K., and V. Kumar. "Analyzing Variations in Advertising and Promotional Expenditures." *Journal of Marketing,* April 1990, pp. 57–68.

Bello, Daniel C., and Gloria J. Barczak. "Using Industrial Trade Shows to Improve New Product Development." *The Journal of Business and Industrial Marketing,* Summer/Fall 1990, pp. 43–56.

Campbell, Leland, and William D. Diamond. "Framing and Sales Promotions: The Characteristics of a Good Deal." *The Journal of Consumer Marketing,* Fall 1990, pp. 25–31.

Davies, Gary. "Marketing to Retailers: A Battle for Distribution?" *Long Range Planning* 23, no. 6, 1990, pp. 101–8.

---

[24]For a discussion of this topic, see Zachary Schiller, "Not Everyone Loves a Supermarket Special," *Business Week,* February 17, 1992, pp. 64–68 and Jenifer Lawrence and Judann Dagnoli, "P&G's Low-Price Strategy Cuts Trade Fees, Irks Retailers," *Advertising Age,* December 21, 1991, pp. 3,28.

Fader, Peter S., and Leonard M. Lodish. "A Cross-Category Analysis of Category Structure and Promotional Activity for Grocery Products." *Journal of Marketing,* October 1990, pp. 52–65.

Gotlieb, Jerry B., and Dan Sarel. "Comparative Advertising Effectiveness: The Role of Involvement and Source Credibility." *Journal of Advertising* 20, no. 1, pp. 38–46.

Higie, Robin A., and Murphy A. Sewall. "Using Recall and Brand Preference to Evaluate Advertising Effectiveness." *Journal of Advertising Research,* April/May 1991, pp. 56–63.

Krishna, Aradhna; Imran S. Currim; and Robert W. Shoemaker. "Consumer Perceptions of Promotional Activity." *Journal of Marketing,* April 1991, pp. 4–16.

Lammers, H. Bruce. "The Effect of Free Samples on Immediate Consumer Purchase." *The Journal of ConsumerMarketing,* Spring 1991, pp. 31–37.

Parsons, Andrew J. "Focus and Squeeze: Consumer Marketing in the '90s." *Marketing Management,* Winter 1992, pp. 51–55.

Pechmann, Cornelia, and David W. Stewart. "How Direct Comparative Ads and Market Share Affect Brand Choice." *Journal of Advertising Research,* December 1991, pp. 47–55.

Strutton, David H., and James R. Lumpkin. "Information Sources Used By Elderly Health Care Product Adoptors." *Journal of Advertising Research,* July/August 1992, pp. 20–30.

Swandby, Richard K. "Selecting the Right Show." *Sales and Marketing Management,* July 1992, pp. 50–56.

Walker, Mary; Lynn Langmeyer; and David Langmeyer. "Celebrity Endorsers: Do You Get What You Pay For." *The Journal of Consumer Marketing,* Spring 1992, pp. 69–76.

Walters, Rockney G. "Assessing the Impact of Retail Price Promotions on Product Substitution, Complementary Purchase, and Interstore Sales Displacement." *Journal of Marketing,* April 1991, pp. 17–28.

Woodside, Arch G., and Praveen K. Soni. "Direct-Response Advertising Information." *Journal of Advertising,* December 1991, pp. 26–36.

Major Federal Agencies Involved in Control of Advertising

Agency	Function
Federal Trade Commission	Regulates commerce between states; controls unfair business practices; takes action on false and deceptive advertising; most important agency in regulation of advertising and promotion.
Food and Drug Administration	Regulatory division of the Department of Health, Education, and Welfare; controls marketing of food, drugs, cosmetics, medical devices, and potentially hazardous consumer products.
Federal Communications Commission	Regulates advertising indirectly, primarily through the power to grant or withdraw broadcasting licenses.
Postal Service	Regulates material that goes through the mails, primarily in areas of obscenity, lottery, and fraud.
Alcohol and Tobacco Tax Division	Part of the Treasury Department; has broad powers to regulate deceptive and misleading advertising of liquor and tobacco.
Grain Division	Unit of the Department of Agriculture responsible for policing seed advertising.
Securities and Exchange Commission	Regulates advertising of securities.

Information Source	Description
Patent Office	Regulates registration of trademarks.
Library of Congress	Controls protection of copyrights.
Department of Justice	Enforces all federal laws through prosecuting cases referred to it by other government agencies.

Chapter 9

Promotion Strategy: Personal Selling

Personal selling, unlike advertising or sales promotion, involves direct face-to-face relationships between the seller and the prospect or customer. The behavioral scientist would probably characterize personal selling as a type of personal influence. Operationally, it is a complex communication process, one not completely understood by marketing scholars.

IMPORTANCE OF PERSONAL SELLING

Most business firms find it impossible to market their products without some form of personal selling. To illustrate, some years ago vending machines became quite popular. The question may be raised about whether or not these machines replaced the salesperson. The answer is both yes and no. In a narrow sense of the word, the vending machine has replaced some retail sales clerks who, for most convenience goods, merely dispensed the product and collected money. On the other hand, vending machines and their contents must be "sold" to the vending machine operators, and personal selling effort must be exerted to secure profitable locations for the machines.

The policies of self-service and self-selection have done much to eliminate the need for personal selling in some types of retail stores. However, the successful deployment of these policies have required manufacturers to do two things: *(a)* presell the consumer by means of larger advertising and sales promotion outlays; and *(b)* design packages for their products that would "sell" themselves, so to speak.

The importance of the personal selling function depends partially on the nature of the product. As a general rule, goods that are new, technically complex, and/or expensive require more personal selling effort. The sales-

---

HIGHLIGHT 9–1

The Typical American Salesperson

—Age: 33.
—Male: 70 percent.
—Female: 30 percent.
—Some college or degree: 82 percent.
—Graduate degree: 92 percent.
—Most likely to leave after: 4.3 years.
—Average length of service: 6.3 years.
—Usual pay: salary, 20 percent; commission, 30 percent; combination, 50 percent.
—Earnings per years: trainee, $25,000; experienced salesperson, $40,000.
—Cost to train: $18,000.

—Length of training: 3 months.
—Cost per sales call: $95 to $350.
—Sales calls per day: 6.5.
—Number of calls to close: 5.
—Cost of field expenses: $20,000.
—Value of benefits: $14,000.
—Average sales volume: $1 million.
—Hours per week in selling activities within the territory: 41.
—Hours per week in nonselling activities, such as paperwork and planning sales calls: 10.
—Turnover rate: 20 percent.

Source: Charles Futrell, *Fundamentals of Selling,* 3rd ed. (Homewood, Ill.: Richard D. Irwin, 1990), p. 8.

---

person plays a key role in providing the consumer with information about such products to reduce the risks involved in purchase and use. Insurance, for example, is a complex and technical product that often needs significant amounts of personal selling. In addition, many industrial goods cannot be presold, and the salesperson has a key role to play in finalizing the sale. Due to the increasing complexity and technical nature of today's products and services, more and more companies are adopting team selling approaches.[1] In these cases, salespeople are coupled with technical experts in order to forge strong customer partnerships and add value to the company's product offerings. However, most national branded convenience goods are purchased by the consumer without any significant assistance from retail store personnel.

The importance of personal selling also is determined to a large extent by the needs of the consumer. In the case of pure competition (a large number of small buyers with complete market knowledge of a homogeneous product), there is little need for personal selling. A close approximation to this situation is found at auctions for agricultural products, such as tobacco or wheat. At the other extreme, when a product is highly differentiated, such as housing, and marketed to consumers with imperfect knowledge of product offerings, then personal selling becomes a key factor in the promotion mix. In fact, in

---

[1]Cathy Hyatt Hills, "Making the Team," *Sales & Marketing Management,* February 1992, pp. 54–57.

some cases, the consumer may not even be seeking the product; for instance, life insurance is often categorized as an unsought good. Finally, sellers who differentiate their products at the point of sale will usually make heavy use of personal selling in their promotion mix. For example, automobile buyers are given the opportunity to purchase various extras or options at the time of purchase.

It is important to remember that, for many companies, the salesperson represents the customer's main link to the firm. In fact, to some, the salesperson is the company. Therefore, it is imperative that the company take advantage of this unique link. Through the efforts of the successful salesperson, a company can build relationships with customers that continue long beyond the initial sale. It is the salesperson who serves as the conduit through which information regarding product flaws, improvements, applications, and / or new uses can pass from the customer to the marketing department. To illustrate the importance of using salespeople as an information resource, consider this fact. In some industries, customer information serves as the source for up to 90 percent of new product and process ideas.[2] Along with techniques described in the previous chapter, personal selling provides the push needed to get middlemen to carry new products, increase their amount of purchasing, and devote more effort in merchandising a product or brand.[3]

The classic relationship between marketing and sales has often entailed confusion and poor communication.[4] Disgruntled salespeople grumble about marketing programs they see as ineffective, while the marketing staff claims mediocre sales are the result of poor execution on the part of the sales force. Salespeople continually complain that they are being asked to serve as the marketing research arm of the organization, being charged with gathering customer information which detracts from their selling efforts. Meanwhile, the marketing staff asserts that rarely, if ever, does the sales staff contribute meaningful information. Regardless of who's right, the results are all too often the same; sales are down and valuable information is lost. It is of critical importance that a synergistic relationship be built between the marketing and the sales function. Toward this end, each function must understand the benefits derived from such an alliance. These benefits include: (1) better targeted marketing programs; (2) more diverse and accurate marketplace information flows; (3) quicker response times; (4) stronger customer relationships; and above all (5) improved financial results.

---

[2]Eric von Hipple, "The Sources of Innovation," *The McKinsey Quarterly,* Winter 1988, pp. 72–79.

[3]Terance A. Shimp, *Promotion Management and Marketing Communication,* 2nd ed. (Chicago, Ill.: Dryden Press, 1990), p. 602.

[4]This section is based on Phillip Carpenter, "Bridging the Gap Between Marketing and Sales," *Sales & Marketing Management,* March 1992, pp. 28–31

THE SALES PROCESS

Personal selling is as much an art as it is a science. The word *art* is used to describe that portion of the selling process that is highly creative in nature and difficult to explain. This does not mean there is little control over the personal selling element in the promotion mix. It does imply that, all other things equal, the trained salesperson can outsell the untrained one.

Before management selects and trains salespeople, it should have an understanding of the sales process. Obviously, the sales process will differ according to the size of the company, the nature of the product, the market, and so forth, but there are some elements common to almost all selling situations that should be understood. For the purposes of this text, the term *sales process* refers to two basic factors: (1) the sequence of stages or steps the salesperson should follow in trying to sell goods and services; and (2) a set of basic principles that, if adhered to, will increase the likelihood of a sale being made.

The traditional approach to personal selling involves a formula or step-by-step procedure. It is known as the AIDAS formula and has five steps: (1) get the prospect's *attention;* (2) arouse the prospect's *interest;* (3) stimulate the prospect's *desire* for the product; (4) get buying *action;* and (5) build *satisfaction* into the transaction. This approach to selling implies two things. First, the prospect or potential buyer goes through these five steps. Second, the salesperson can influence the behavior of the prospect if this process is managed skillfully. Although this model represents a logical approach to explaining the sales process, it emphasizes a how-to approach to selling, rather than attempting to explain why sales are made, or conversely, why purchases are made.

An explanation of the selling process in terms of why individuals purchase would require a full understanding of consumer behavior. Obviously, as we saw in Chapter 3, this is a difficult task, because so many variables are difficult to measure or control. However, a useful framework for a better understanding of the selling process is illustrated in Figure 9–1.

This approach views the selling process as an input-output system: the inputs are marketing stimuli, such as price, quality, service, and style. Personal selling is viewed as one of the channels by which knowledge about these marketing stimuli are transmitted to the buyer. In this model, the buyer's mind is a processor of the various stimuli, and, since the workings of the mind are only partially understood, it can be considered a "black box." The explanation of what goes on in this black box depends on which approach or theory of behavior is employed.[5] The outputs for the model represent purchasing responses, such as brand choice, dealer choice, and the like. Here the sales process is viewed as a social situation involving two persons. The interaction of the

---

[5]For a review, see J. Paul Peter and Jerry C. Olson, *Consumer Behavior and Marketing Strategy,* 2nd ed. (Homewood, Ill.: Richard D. Irwin, 1990).

Figure 9–1   *A Model of the Selling Process*

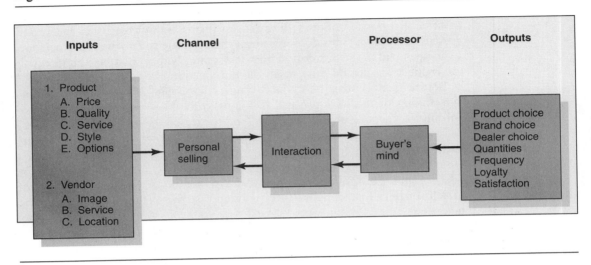

two persons depends on the economic, social, physical, and personality characteristics of both the seller and the buyer.[6] A successful sale is situationally determined by these factors and can be considered social behavior as well as individual behavior. The prospect's perception of the salesperson is a key factor in determining the salesperson's effectiveness and role expectations.[7] The salesperson's confidence and ability to "play the role" of a salesperson is crucial in determining behavior and is influenced by personality, knowledge, training, and previous experience.[8] Hiring and training a good salesperson is one of the most important tasks a manager faces. There are few decisions more essential and directly related to the continued financial and other successes of a company than deciding: (1) who is chosen to represent the company's products and services; and (2) how these products and services are to be represented.[9]

[6]Kaylene C. Williams and Rosann L. Spiro, "Communication Style in the Salesperson-Customer Dyad," *Journal of Marketing Research,* November 1985, pp. 434–43.

[7]Barton A. Weitz, Harish Sujen, and Mita Sujen, "Knowledge, Motivation, and Adaptive Behavior: A Framework for Improving Selling Effectiveness," *Journal of Marketing,* October 1986, pp. 174–91.

[8]Alan J. Dubinsky, Roy D. Howell, Thomas N. Ingram, and Danny N. Bellinger, "Salesforce Socialization," *Journal of Marketing,* October 1986, pp. 192–207.

[9]Robert G. Head, "Systemizing Salesperson Selection," *Sales & Marketing Management,* February 1992, pp. 65–68.

HIGHLIGHT 9–2

Six Steps to a More Effective Selling Effort

As more and more companies refocus their entire organizations, from manufacturing to finance, on sales and customer service, the following ingredients are necessary to make it happen.

1. *Rethink training.* Salespeople now require new skills. They must be taught to be advocates of their customers with detailed knowledge of their customers' businesses to enable them to target sales opportunities as well as service problems. High-pressure selling tactics and one-time slam dunk sales will not be effective.

2. *Total involvement.* Effective salespeople no longer act alone. The efforts of product designers, plant managers, and financial officers must be a part of selling and serving customers.

3. *Top management support.* CEOs and other top managers must be visibly and frequently involved in any change effort. This often includes regularly making sales calls and leading sales training meetings.

4. *Relating objectives to motivation.* Discourage incentives which encourage quick hit sales. Include measures of long-term customer satisfaction in compensation plans.

5. *Use technology.* Increase responsiveness with marketing and distribution technology. Technology can be used to track customer relationships, to insure the right products get to the right place at the right time, and to simplify order-taking.

6. *Stay close to the customer.* Pay attention to customers. Call them often or send notes to frequent shoppers. Assign an employee to good customers.

Source: Adapted from "Smart Selling," *Business Week,* August 3, 1992, pp. 46–47; "America's Best Sales Forces," *Sales & Marketing Management,* September, 1992, pp. 46–52.

Selling Fundamentals

From what has been said so far, the only reasonable conclusion that can be drawn is that there is no one clear-cut theory of personal selling nor one single technique that can be applied universally. Most sales training programs attempt to provide the trainee with the fundamentals of selling, placing emphasis on the "how" and "what" and leaving the "why" questions to the theorists.

A primary objective of any sales training program is to impart knowledge and techniques to the participants. Organizations have come to realize that, in today's competitive environment, the success of a sales presentation depends on actions and decisions made well before the salesperson walks into the

---

HIGHLIGHT 9–3

A Partial List of Secondary Sources of Prospect Information

—*Middle Market Directory* (Dun & Bradstreet). Lists 14,000 firms worth between $500,000 and $1 million.

—*Million Dollar Directory* (Dun & Bradstreet). Lists names, addresses, and business lines of firms worth more than $1 million.

—*Thomas Register of American Manufacturers* (Thomas). Annual that lists manufacturers by product classifications, company profits, and specific product information.

—*Encyclopedia of Associations* (Gale). Lists 21,500 national associations, more than 4,000 international organizations, and more than 50,000 regional, state, and local organizations.

—*Standard & Poor's Register of Corporations, Directors, and Executives* (Standard & Poor's). Annual publication listing names, titles, and addresses of over 50,000 firms.

—*Directory of Corporate Affiliations* (Macmillan Directory Division). Lists 4,000 U.S. firms as well as their over-40,000 divisions, subsidiaries, and so on.

—*Moody's Industrial Directory* (Moody's). Annual that lists names, type of business, and a brief financial statement for over 10,000 publicly held corporations.

—*U.S. Industrial Directory* (Time). Annual that lists sales, employees, and financial statistics for the 500 largest industrial firms and 50 largest diversified service firms.

—*Trade Shows and Professional Exhibits Directory* (Gale). Lists more than 3,200 trade shows, including location, timing, attendance expected, and so on.

—*World Scope: Industrial Company Profiles* (Wright Investor's Service). Extensive coverage of 5,000 companies from 25 countries, within 27 major industry groupings.

—*National Trade and Professional Associations* (Columbia Books). Lists over 6,200 trade and professional associations, along with pertinent information about each.

—*The International Corporate 1000* (Graham & Trotman). Profiles the 1,000 largest companies in the world—650 from Europe, South America, the Middle East, and the Pacific Basin and 350 from the United States and Canada.

Source: Barton A. Weitz, Stephen B. Castleberry, and John F. Tanner, *Selling: Building Partnerships,* (Homewood, Ill.: Richard D. Irwin, 1992), p. 182.

---

prospect's office.[10] An analysis of numerous training manuals reveals subjects or topics common to many programs. Following are brief descriptions of some fundamentals well-trained salespeople should know.

---

[10]Alan Rosenthal, "How to Improve Presentations," *Business Marketing,* June 1992, pp. 40–41.

1. They should have thorough knowledge of the company they represent, including its past history. This includes the philosophy of management as well as the firm's basic operating policies.
2. They should have thorough technical and commercial knowledge of their products or product lines. This is particularly true when selling industrial goods. When selling very technical products, many firms require their salespeople to have training as engineers.
3. They should have good working knowledge of competitors' products. This is a vital requirement because the successful salesperson will have to know the strengths and weaknesses of those products that are in competition for market share.
4. They should have in-depth knowledge of the market for their merchandise. *The market* here refers not only to a particular sales territory but also to the general market, including the economic factors that affect the demand for their goods.
5. They should have a thorough understanding of the importance of prospecting and the methods used to effectively locate and qualify prospects (the decision-making unit). General issues to be evaluated are the prospective buyer's needs, financial resources, and willingness to be approached. Salespeople must realize that not everyone (company or individual) is a valid prospect. A concerted effort must be placed on determining and prioritizing genuine prospects, for the cost (in terms of dollars and human resources) of trying to sell to all can be prohibitive.[11]
6. They should have accurate knowledge of the buyer or the prospect to whom they are selling. Under the marketing concept, knowledge of the customer is a vital requirement. Salespeople can't get close to their customers unless they know what the customers are all about.[12] One of the best ways to seal a relationship is to help a customer solve his/her problems— but first, one has to know what those problems are. Areas of desirable knowledge salespeople should possess include customer applications of the product and customer requirements as they relate to product quality, durability, cost, design, and service. Knowledgeable salespeople should be able to quantify, as well as describe, product benefits to the buyer. Effective selling requires salespeople to understand the unique characteristics of each account, including how the customer will make his/her decision.[13]

---

[11]John R. Graham, "Customer-Centered Selling," *The American Salesman,* August 1992, pp. 16–19.

[12]For a discussion of relationship selling, see Barry J. Farber and Joyce Wycoff, "Relationships: Six Steps to Success," *Sales & Marketing Management,* April 1992, pp. 50–58.

[13]John P. Kirwin, Jr., "The Precision Selling Payoff," *Sales & Marketing Management,* January 1992, pp. 59–61.

Reimer Express Lines is one example of a company that goes out of its way to get to know a customer.[14] When Kodak Canada first hired Reimer as its transportation supplier, a Reimer person spent every Friday morning at the Kodak warehouse to act as a loading advisor for the shippers at Kodak to better understand their needs and special requirements. As a result of Reimer's efforts, Kodak has greatly increased the scope of their relationship. Avco Financial Services is another example where knowledge of the customer serves as a driving force. Avco branches have been redesigned to reflect the personality of customers, who will then be more "at home" doing business with Avco. This means hiring and retaining employees from the local areas, having employees dress in the style of their customers, and getting to know customers on a first-name basis.

There are no magic secrets of successful selling. The difference between good salespeople and mediocre ones is often the result of training plus experience. Training is no substitute for experience; the two complement each other. The difficulty with trying to discuss the selling job in terms of basic principles is that experienced, successful salespeople will always be able to find exceptions to these principles. Often successful selling seems to defy logic and, sometimes, common sense. Trying to program salespeople to follow definite rules or principles in every situation can stifle their originality and creativity.[15] However, six significant factors have been found to contribute most to salesperson failure.[16] These include: (1) poor listening skills; (2) failure to concentrate on top priorities; (3) a lack of sufficient effort; (4) inability to determine customer needs; (5) lack of planning for sales presentatons; and (6) inadequate product/service knowledge. What can be gleaned from these factors is an appreciation of the complex interrelationships existing between company and individual efforts as a prerequisite for sales success.

MANAGING THE SALES PROCESS

Every personal sale can be divided into two parts: the part done by the salespeople and the part done for the salespeople by the company. For example, from the standpoint of the product, the company should provide the salesperson with a product skillfully designed, thoroughly tested, attrac-

---

[14]This section is based on "Customers Write Our Ever-Changing Script," *The American Salesman,* March 1992, pp. 9–10.

[15]For a review of research findings regarding factors that are predictive of salespeople's performance, see Gilbert A. Churchill, Jr., Neil M. Ford, Steven W. Hartley, and Orville C. Walker, Jr., "The Determinants of Salesperson Performance: A Meta-Analysis," *Journal of Marketing Research,* May 1985, pp. 87–93.

[16]For a detailed descussion of this topic, see Thomas N. Ingram, Charles H. Schwepker, Jr., and Don Hutson, "Why Salespeople Fail," *Industrial Marketing Management,* August 1992, pp. 225–30; and Thomas N. Ingram and Keun S. Lee, "Sales Force Commitment and Turnover," *Industrial Marketing Management,* May 1990, pp. 149–54.

tively packaged, adequately advertised, and priced to compare favorably with competitive products. Salespeople have the responsibility of being thoroughly acquainted with the product, its selling features, points of superiority, and a sincere belief in the value of the product. From a sales management standpoint, the company's part of the sale involves the following:

1. Efficient and effective sales tools, including continuous sales training, promotional literature, samples, trade shows, product information, and adequate advertising.
2. An efficient delivery and reorder system to ensure that customers will receive the merchandise as promised.
3. An equitable compensation plan that rewards performance, motivates the salesperson, and promotes company loyalty. It should also reimburse the salesperson for all reasonable expenses incurred while doing the job.
4. Adequate supervision and evaluation of performance as a means of helping salespeople do a better job, not only for the company but for themselves as well.

Being a successful sales manager is much different from being a successful salesperson.[17] Reports, budgets, meetings and other tasks take on new importance as the focus changes from getting the order to running an entire department or division. Indeed, the role of the sales manager can be likened to that of a good athletic coach.[18] The sales manager must continually remind the sales force of the fundamentals, constantly encourage peak efforts, and consistently praise effective performance. Simultaneously, the sales manager is charged with developing an effective overall game plan so that organizational goals can be realized. An important key to maximizing sales productivity and end performance is the ability of the sales manager to give good coaching to the many and not to rely on the individual efforts of a few.

The Sales Management Task

Since the advent of the marketing concept, a clear-cut distinction has been made between marketing management and sales management. Marketing management refers to all activities in the firm that have to do with satisfying demand. Sales management is a narrower concept dealing with those functions directly related to personal selling. Generally speaking, sales managers are in middle management and report directly to the vice president of marketing.

---

[17]Bill Kelley, "From Salesperson to Manager: Transition and Travail," *Sales & Marketing Management,* February 1992, pp. 32–36.

[18]For a discussion of this topic, see Saul W. Gellerman, "The Tests of a Good Salesperson," *Harvard Business Review,* May-June 1990, pp. 64–69

Figure 9-2 *An Example of a Sales Organization*

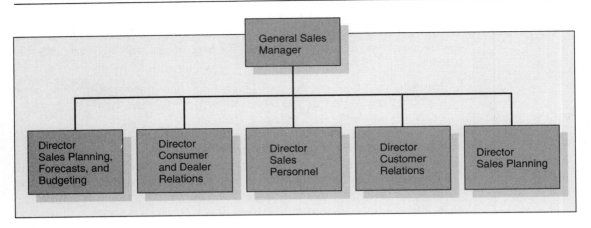

Their basic responsibilities can be broken down into at least seven major areas: (1) developing an effective sales organization for the company; (2) formulating short-range and long-range sales programs; (3) recruiting, training, and supervising the sales force; (4) formulating sales budgets and controlling selling expenses, (5) coordinating the personal selling effort with other forms of promotional activities; (6) maintaining lines of communication between the sales force, customers, and other relevant parts of the business, such as advertising, production, and logistics; and in some firms, (7) developing sales forecasts and other types of relevant marketing studies to be used in sales planning and control.

Sales managers are line officers whose primary responsibility is establishing and maintaining an active sales organization. In terms of authority, they usually have equivalent rank to that of other marketing executives who manage aspects of the marketing program, such as advertising, product planning, or physical distribution. The sales organization may have separate departments and department heads to perform specialized tasks, such as training, personnel, promotion, and forecasting. Figure 9-2 is an example of such a sales organization.

In other cases, a general marketing manager may have product managers or directors reporting to them. This is common in cases where the firm sells numerous products and each product or product line is handled by a separate manager. Another common arrangement is to have sales managers assigned to specific geographic regions or customer groups. This type of specialization enables the sales force to operate more efficiently by avoiding overlaps. Regardless of the method used, the sales force should be structured to meet the unique needs of the consumer, the company, and its management.

Controlling the Sales Force

There are two obvious reasons why it is critical that the sales force be properly controlled. First, personal selling can be the largest marketing expense component in the final price of the product. Second, unless the sales force is somehow directed, motivated, and audited on a continual basis, it is likely to be less efficient than it is capable of being. Controlling the sales force involves four key functions: (1) forecasting sales; (2) establishing sales territories and quotas; (3) analyzing expenses; and (4) motivating and compensating performance.

Forecasting sales. Sales planning begins with a forecast of sales for some future period or periods. From a practical standpoint, these forecasts are made on a short-term basis of a year or less, although long-range forecasts of one to five years are made for purposes other than managing the sales force, such as financing, production, and development. Generally speaking, forecasting is the marketing manager's responsibility. In large firms, because of the complexity of the task, it is usually delegated to a specialized unit, such as the marketing research department. Forecast data should be integrated into the firm's marketing decision support system for use by sales managers and other corporate executives. For many companies, the sales forecast is the key instrument in the planning and control of operations.[19]

The sales forecast is an estimate of how much of the company's output, either in dollars or in units, can be sold during a specified future period under a proposed marketing plan and under an assumed set of economic conditions. A sales forecast has several important uses: (1) it is used to establish sales quotas; (2) it is used to plan personal selling efforts as well as other types of promotional activities in the marketing mix; (3) it is used to budget selling expenses; and (4) it is used to plan and coordinate production, physical distribution, inventories, personnel, and so forth.

Sales forecasting has become very sophisticated in recent years, especially with the increased availability of computer hardware and software. It should be mentioned, however, that a forecast is never a substitute for sound business judgment. At the present time there is no single method of sales forecasting known that gives uniformly accurate results with infallible precision. Outlined below are some commonly used sales forecasting methods.[20]

---

[19]For additional discussion on the use of sales force automation and other technological systems in sales management, see "Productivity Gains Are Up Another Notch," *Sales & Marketing Management,* September 1992, pp. 110–12; Thayer C. Taylor, "The Future," *Sales & Marketing Management,* June 1992, pp. 47–55; "Software Directory Update, " *Sales & Marketing Management,* June 1992, pp. 58–60; "Sales Automation Faces Hard Times," *Sales & Marketing Management,* April 1992, p. 115; and "The Simple ABCs of SFA: The Customer Comes First," *Sales & Marketing Management,* March 1992, pp. 84–85.

[20]Based on a survey by the National Industrial Conference Board: "Forecasting Sales," *Studies in Business Policy,* No. 106.

1. *Jury of executive opinion method.* This combines and averages the views of top management representing marketing, production, finance, purchasing, and administration.
2. *Sales force composite method.* This is similar to the first method in that it obtains the combined views of the sales force about the future outlook for sales. In some companies all salespeople, or district managers, submit estimates of the future sales in their territory or district.
3. *Customer expectations method.* This approach involves asking customers or product users about the quantity they expect to purchase.
4. *Time series analyses.* This approach involves analyzing past sales data and the impact of factors that influence sales (long-term growth trends, cyclical fluctuations, seasonal variations).
5. *Correlation analysis.* This involves measuring the relationship between the dependent variable, sales, and one or more independent variables that can explain increases or decreases in sales volumes.
6. *Other quantitative techniques.* Numerous statistical and mathematical techniques can be used to predict or estimate future sales. Two of the more important techniques are *(a)* growth functions, which are mathematical expressions specifying the relationship between demand and time; and *(b)* simulation models, where a statistical model of the industry is developed and programmed to develop values for the key parameters of the model.

Establishing sales territories and quotas. The establishment of sales territories and sales quotas represents management's need to match personal selling effort with sales potential (or opportunity). Sales territories are usually specified geographic areas assigned to individual salespeople. These areas represent an attempt to make the selling task more efficient.[21] The underlying rationale is that the control of sales operations will be facilitated by breaking down the total market into smaller and more manageable units. Implied here is the notion that there are some distinct economic advantages to dividing the total market into smaller segments. These segments should represent clusters of customers, or prospects, within some degree of physical proximity. Of course, there are criteria other than geography for establishing territories. One important criterion is that of product specialization. In this case, salespeople are specialists relative to particular product or customer situations.

From a marketing management point of view, there are many advantages to establishing sales territories. First, it facilitates the process of sales planning by making it easier to coordinate personal selling, transportation, storage, and other forms of promotion. Second, it promotes better customer relations

---

[21]For a complete discussion of establishing territories and quotas, see William J. Stanton and Richard H. Buskirk, *Management of the Sales Force,* 7th ed. (Homewood, Ill.: Richard D. Irwin, 1987).

HIGHLIGHT 9–4

Ten Organizations That Lead the Way in Selling

1. *DuPont*. A pioneer in team selling. Groups of sales representatives, technicians, and plant managers work together to solve customer problems, and to create and sell new products.
2. *Merck*. Leads the way in converting salespeople into pharmaceutical experts. It trains its sales representatives over 12 months in pharmaceuticals and trust-building sales techniques. Continuing refresher courses are mandatory.
3. *Reynolds Metals*. A leading innovator who has developed team selling to educate customers such as automobile manufacturers on new uses of aluminum.
4. *Wal-Mart Stores*. Has nurtured customer confidence by selling the basics: everyday low pricing, items always in stock, cashiers always available. Has also demanded simplified selling from suppliers in the form of data linkups and coordinated inventory management.
5. *Nordstrom*. Has proven that department stores can survive. Its intense, personalized attention to the customer has resulted in great customer loyalty, and steady growth.

6. *Home Depot*. The CEO and founder Bernard Marcus is also the chief salesperson. Continually follows up with intense training.
7. *Dell Computer*. Utilizes advanced technology to keep track of customers and intense training to successfully sell a complex product by telephone and mail.
8. *Toyota Motors*. Their luxury car line Lexus utilizes customer satisfaction as a key measure for setting dealer compensation. Lexus showrooms are now the new standard for U.S. auto dealerships.
9. *General Electric*. Refocusing their selling efforts in several areas: training salespeople to work long-term with customers, experimenting with team-based compensation, assigning staff full-time to customers' factories, and nurturing deep relationships with their own suppliers.
10. *Vanguard Group*. A marketer of mutual funds which has perfected the low-key sell. It utilizes reliable customer service, easy-to-understand products, and low fees to appeal to investors who shy away from hard-sell, high-commission brokers.

Source: Adapted from "Smart Selling," *Business Week,* August 3, 1992, p. 48; "Is Your Net Working?" *Sales & Marketing Management,* October, 1992, p. 67–69; "The First 90 Days," *Sales & Marketing Management,* September, 1992, p. 66–71.

because salespeople will be more familiar with the accounts they service. Third, it is an effective way of making sure that each market is well covered. Fourth, it aids management in the evaluation and control of selling costs. And fifth, it helps in the evaluation of performance.[22]

---

[22]For additional discussion, consult Andris Zoltners and P. Sinha, "Sales Territory Alignment: A Review and Model," *Management Science,* November 1983, pp. 1237–56.

The question of managing sales territories cannot be discussed meaningfully without saying something about quotas. *Sales quotas* represent specific sales goals assigned to each territory or sales unit over a designated time period. Quotas are primarily a planning and control device because they provide management with measurable, quantitative standards of performance. The most common method of establishing quotas for territories is to relate sales to forecasted sales potential. For example, if the Ajax Drug Company's territory M has an estimated industry sales potential for a particular product of $400,000 for the year, the quota might be set at 25 percent of that potential, or $100,000. The 25 percent figure represents the market share Ajax estimates to be a reasonable target. This $100,000 quota may represent an increase of $20,000 in sales over last year (assuming constant prices) that is expected from new business.

In establishing sales quotas for its individual territories or sales personnel, management needs to take into account three key factors. First, all territories will not have equal potential and, therefore, compensation must be adjusted accordingly. Second, all salespeople will not have equal ability, and assignments may have to be made accordingly. Some companies adjust quotas up or down depending upon the specific salesperson's: (1) years of experienc with the company; (2) past sales performance; and (3) need for organizational resources to support his/her efforts.[23] Third, the sales task in each territory may differ from time period to time period. For instance, the nature of some territories may require that salespeople spend more time seeking new accounts, rather than servicing established accounts, especially in the case of so-called new territories. The point to be made here is that quotas can vary, not only by territory but also by assigned tasks. The effective sales manager should assign quotas not only for dollar sales but also for each major selling function. Figure 9–3 is an example of how this is done for the Ajax Drug Company, where each activity is assigned a quota and a weight reflecting its relative importance.

Analyzing expenses. Sales forecasts should include a sales expense budget. In some companies, sales expense budgets are developed from the bottom up. Each territorial or district manager submits estimates of expenses and forecasted sales quotas. These estimates are usually prepared for a period of a year and then broken down into quarters and months. The chief sales executive then reviews the budget requests from the field offices and from staff departments. Expenses may be classified as fixed, semivariable or variable, and direct or indirect. Certain items, such as rent or administrative salaries, are fixed. In field offices, employee compensation is the principal expense, and it may be fixed or semivariable, depending on the plan. Other items, such as travel, samples, or other promotional material, are variable in nature. Some expenses are directly traceable to the sale of specific products, such as samples or displays, while other expenses are indirect, as in the case of administrative salaries and rent. Sales commissions and shipping expenses tend to vary in direct proportion

---

[23]For additional discussion, see David J. Good and Robert W. Stone, "How Sales Quotas Are Developed," *Industrial Marketing Management,* February 1991, pp. 51–55.

Figure 9–3 *Ajax Drug Company Sales Activity Evaluation*

Territory: M
Salesperson: Smith

Functions	(1) Quota	(2) Actual	(3) Percent (2 ÷ 1)	(4) Weight	(5) Score (3 × 4)
Sales volume:					
A. Old business	$380,000	$300,000	79	0.7	55.7
B. New business	$ 20,000	$ 20,000	100	0.5	50.0
Calls on prospects:					
A. Doctors	20	15	75	0.2	15.0
B. Druggists	80	60	75	0.2	15.0
C. Wholesalers	15	15	100	0.2	20.0
D. Hospitals	10	10	100	0.2	20.0
				2.0	175.7

Performance Index = 175.7

to sales, while travel expense and entertainment may not be tied to sales volume in any direct proportion.

It should be understood that selling costs are budgeted much in the same way as manufacturing costs. Selling costs are usually broken down by product lines, sales region, customers, salespersons, or some other unit. Proper budgeting requires a reasonable cost accounting system. From a budgeting standpoint, the firm should use its accounting system to analyze marketing costs as a means of control.

Motivating and compensating performance. The sales manager's personnel function includes more than motivating and compensating the sales force; but from the vantage point of sales force productivity, these two tasks are of paramount importance. Operationally, it means that the sales manager has the responsibility of keeping the morale and efforts of the sales force at high levels through supervision and motivation. These closely related tasks are accomplished through interaction with the sales force by: (1) spending time in the field visiting customers; (2) communicating on a frequent basis via letters, telephone, or in-person meetings; (3) giving credit and praise for work well done; (4) providing performance feedback on a regular basis; and (5) developing incentive schemes through which greater opportunity for earnings (as in sales contests) or job promotion can be achieved.[24]

[24]For a complete discussion of the skills and policies utilized by sucessful sales leaders in motivating salespeople, see David W. Cravens, Thomas N. Ingram, Raymond W. LaForge, and Clifford E. Young, "Hallmarks of Effective Sales Organizations," *Marketing Management,* Winter 1992, pp. 57–66; Thomas R. Wortruba, John S. Macfie, and Jerome A Colletti, "Effective Sales Force Recognition Programs," *Industrial Marketing Management,* February 1991, pp. 9–15; and Dr. Ken Blanchard, "Reward Salespeople Creatively," *Personal Selling Power,* March 1992, p. 24.

HIGHLIGHT 9–5

Effort- and Results-Oriented Measures for Evaluating Salespeople

Effort-Oriented Measures

1. Number of sales calls made.
2. Number of MRO calls made.
3. Number of complaints handled.
4. Number of checks on reseller stocks.
5. Uncontrollable lost job time.
6. Number of inquiries followed up.
7. Number of demonstrations completed.

Results-Oriented Measures

1. Sales volume (total or by product or model).
2. Sales volume as a percentage of quota.
3. Sales profitability (dollar gross margin or contribution).
4. Number of new accounts.
5. Number of stockouts.
6. Number of distributors participating in programs.
7. Number of lost accounts.
8. Percentage volume increase in key accounts.
9. Number of customer complaints.
10. Distributor sales-inventory ratios.

Source: Joseph P. Guiltinan and Gordon W. Paul, *Marketing Management,* 3rd ed. (New York: McGraw-Hill, 1991), p. 358.

Compensation is a principal method by which firms are able to recruit, motivate, and retain their sales forces.[25] Devising a compensation plan for a company is a technical matter, but there are some general guidelines in formulating such a plan. First, a firm should be mindful of any modifications necessary to meet its particular needs when adopting another company's compensation plan. Second, the plan should make sense (i.e., should have a logical rationale) to both management and the sales force. Third, the plan should not be so overly complex that it cannot be understood by the average salesperson. Fourth, as suggested in the section on quotas, the plan should be fair and equitable to avoid penalizing the sales force because of factors beyond their control; conversely, the plan should ensure rewards for performance in proportion to results. Fifth, the plan should allow the sales force to earn salaries that permit them to maintain an acceptable standard of living. Sixth, the plan should attempt to minimize attrition by

---

[25]For a discussion of this and other means by which companies can recruit, motivate, and retain salespeople, see Jeffrey K. Sager, "Recruiting and Retaining Committed Salespeople," *Industrial Marketing Management,* May 1991, pp. 99–103; and Jeffrey K. Sager, "How to Retain Salespeople," *Industrial Marketing Management,* May 1990, pp. 155–66.

HIGHLIGHT 9–6

Characteristics Related to Sales Performance in Different Types of Sales Jobs

Type of Sales Job	Characteristics That Are Relatively Important	Characteristics That Are Relatively Less Important
Trade selling	Age, maturity, empathy, knowledge of customer needs and business methods.	Aggressiveness, technical ability, product knowledge, persuasiveness.
Missionary selling	Youth, high energy and stamina, verbal skill, persuasiveness.	Empathy, knowledge of customers, maturity, previous sales experience.
Technical selling	Education, product and customer knowledge—usually gained through training, intelligence.	Empathy, persuasiveness, aggressiveness, age.
New business selling	Experience, age and maturity, aggressiveness, persuasiveness, persistence.	Customer knowledge, product knowledge, education, empathy.

Source: Gilbert A. Churchill, Jr., Neil M. Ford; and Orville C. Walker, Jr., *Sales Force Management,* 4th ed. (Homewood, Ill.: Richard D. Irwin, 1993), p. 450.

---

giving the sales force some incentive, such as a vested retirement plan, for staying with the company. Finally, and perhaps most important, the individual compensation plan must be tied to the overall sales and marketing plans.[26]

There are two basic types of compensation: salary and commission. *Salary* usually refers to a specific amount of monetary compensation at an agreed rate for definite time periods. *Commission* is usually monetary compensation provided for each unit of sales and expressed as a percentage of sales. The base on which commissions are computed may be: volume of sales in units of product, gross sales in dollars, net sales after returns, sales volume in excess of a quota, and net profits. Very often, several compensation approaches are combined. For example, a salesperson might be paid a base salary, a commission on sales exceeding a volume figure, and a percentage share of the company's profits for that year.

---

[26]Robert G. Head, "Restoring Balance to Sales Compensation," *Sales & Marketing Management,* August 1992, pp. 48–53.

HIGHLIGHT 9–7

Sales Activities and Performance Outcomes That Can Be Encouraged by Compensation and Incentive Programs

—Sell a greater overall dollar volume.
—Increase sales of more profitable products.
—Push new products.
—Push selected items at designated seasons.
—Achieve a higher degree of market penetration by products, kinds of customers, or territories.

—Secure large average orders.
—Secure new customers.
—Service and maintain existing business.
—Reduce turnover of customers.
—Achieve full-line (balanced) selling.
—Reduce direct selling costs.
—Increase the number of calls made.
—Submit reports and other data promptly.

Source: Gilbert A. Churchill, Jr., Neil M. Ford, and Orville C. Walker, Jr., *Sales Force Management*, 4th ed. (Homewood, Ill.: Richard D. Irwin, 1993), p. 575.

Some other important elements of sales compensation plans are:

1. *Drawing account.* Periodic money advances at an agreed rate. Repayment is deducted from total earnings computed on a commission or other basis, or is repaid from other assets of the salesperson if earnings are insufficient to cover the advance (except in the case of a guaranteed drawing account).

2. *Special payments for sales operations.* Payments in the nature of piece rates on operations, rather than commissions on results. Flat payments per call or payments per new customer secured can be included in this category. To the extent that these payments are estimated by size of customers' purchases, they resemble commissions and are sometimes so labeled. Other bases for special payments are demonstrations, putting up counter or window displays, and special promotional work.

3. *Bonus payments.* Usually these are lump-sum payments, over and above contractual earnings, for extra effort or merit or for results beyond normal expectation.

4. *Special prizes.* Monetary amounts or valuable merchandise to reward the winners of sales contests and other competitions. Practices vary from firms that never use this device to firms where there is continuous use and almost every member of the sales force expects to get some compensation from this source during the year, in which case prizes amount to a form of incentive payment. For example, Nissan Motor Corporation, U.S.A.

employs a mystery shopper who visits Nissan dealerships and acts as a prospective car buyer.[27] This person awards $200 American Express Gift Cheques to dealer salespeople who take the time to explain all the features of a particular model automobile to the buyer.

5. *Profit sharing.* A share of the profits of the business as a whole, figured on the basis of earnings, retail sales, profits in an area, or other factors. Sometimes profit sharing is intended to build up a retirement fund.

6. *Expense allowances.* Provision for travel and other business expenses, which becomes an important part of any compensation plan. No agreement for outside sales work is complete without an understanding about whether the company or the salesperson is to pay travel and other business expenses incurred in connection with work; and, if the company is responsible, just what the arrangements should be. Automobile, hotel, entertainment, and many other items of expense may be included in the agreement.

7. *Maximum earnings or cutoff point.* A limitation on earnings. This figure may be employed for limiting maximum earnings when it is impossible to predict the range of earnings under commission or other types of incentive plans.

8. *Fringe benefits.* Pensions, group insurance, health insurance, and so forth. These are commonly given to sales forces as a matter of policy and become a definite part of the compensation plan.[28]

CONCLUSION

This chapter has attempted to outline and explain the personal selling aspect of the promotion mix. Before ending the discussion, a brief comment might be made concerning the overall value of personal selling. Personal selling in a growing economy must always play an important part in the marketing of goods and services. As long as production continues to expand through the development of new and highly technical products, personal selling will occupy a key role in our marketing system.

ADDITIONAL READINGS

Chonko, Lawrence B.; John F. Tanner, Jr.; and William A. Weeks. "Selling and Sales Management in Action: Reward Preferences of Salespeople." *The Journal of Personal Selling & Sales Management,* Summer 1992, pp. 67–78.

---

[27]Michael Dodson, "Flexible Incentives," *The American Salesman,* April 1992, pp. 11–12.

[28]For an excellent review of recruiting, selecting, and motivating sales personnel, see James M. Comer and Alan J. Dubinsky, *Managing the Successful Sales Force* (Lexington, Mass.: D. C. Heath, 1985).

Cravens, David W.; Thomas N. Ingram; and Raymond W. LaForge. "Evaluating Multiple Sales Channel Strategies." *The Journal of Business and Industrial Marketing,* Summer/Fall 1991, pp. 37–48.

De Rose, Louis J. "How Industrial Markets Buy Value Selling: A Strategy for Dealing With Changes" *The Journal of Business and Industrial Marketing,* Winter 1992, pp. 65–69.

Erffmeyer, Robert C.; K. Randall Russ; and Joseph F. Hair, Jr. "Traditional and High-Tech Sales Training Methods." *Industrial Marketing Management,* May 1992, pp. 125–31.

Gilsan, George B., and Jon Hawes. "Selecting Creative People for Sales Positions." *Industrial Marketing Management,* November 1990, pp. 331–37.

Kennedy, Ellen J., and Leigh Lawton. "Men and Women in Industrial Sales; Satisfaction and Outcomes." *Industrial Marketing Management,* February 1992, pp. 5–14.

Lambert, Douglas M.; Howard Marmorstein; and Arun Sharma. "Industrial Salespeople as a Source of Market Information." *Industrial Marketing Management,* May 1990, pp. 141–48.

Moriarty, Rowland T., and Ursula Moran. "Managing Hybrid Marketing Systems." *Harvard Business Review,* November-December 1990, pp. 146–55.

Rodgers, George. "Strategic Planning and Sales Teams." *The Journal of Business and Industrial Marketing,* Summer/Fall 1991, pp. 25–30.

Sager, J. K. "Reducing Sales Manager Job Stress." *The Journal of Consumer Marketing,* Fall 1990, pp. 5–14.

Sager, J. K. "A Longitudinal Assessment of Change in Sales Force Turnover." *Journal of the Academy of Marketing Science* 19, no. 1, pp. 25–36.

Schul, Patrick L., and Brent M. Wren. "The Emerging Role of Women in Industrial Selling: A Decade of Change." *Journal of Marketing,* July 1992, pp. 38–54.

Singhapakdi, Anusorn, and Scott J. Vitell. "Marketing Ethics: Sales Professionals Versus Other Marketing Professionals." *The Journal of Personal Selling & Sales Management,* pp. 27–38.

Viswanathan, Madhubalan, and Eric M. Olson. "The Implementation of Business Strategies: Implications for the Sales Function." *The Journal of Personal Selling & Sales Management,* Winter 1992, pp. 45–58.

Wotruba, Thomas R., and Pradeep K. Tyagi. "Met Expectations and Turnover in Direct Selling." *Journal of Marketing,* July 1991, pp. 24–35.

Chapter 10

Distribution Strategy

Channel of distribution decisions involve numerous interrelated variables that must be integrated into the total marketing mix. Because of the time and money required to set up an efficient channel, and since channels are often hard to change once they are set up, these decisions are critical to the success of the firm.

This chapter is concerned with the development and management of channels of distribution and the process of goods distribution in an extremely complex, highly productive, and specialized economy. It should be noted at the outset that channels of distribution provide the ultimate consumer or industrial user with time, place, and possession utility. Thus, an efficient channel is one that delivers the product when and where it is wanted at a minimum total cost.

THE NEED FOR MARKETING INTERMEDIARIES

A channel of distribution is the combination of institutions through which a seller markets products to the user or ultimate consumer. The need for other institutions or intermediaries in the delivery of goods is sometimes questioned, particularly since the profits they make are viewed as adding to the cost of the product. However, this reasoning is generally fallacious, since producers use marketing intermediaries because the intermediary can perform functions *more cheaply and more efficiently* than the producer can. This notion of efficiency is critical when the characteristics of our economy are considered.

For example, our economy is characterized by heterogeneity in terms of both supply and demand. In terms of numbers alone, there are nearly 6 million establishments comprising the supply segment of our economy, and there are

---

HIGHLIGHT 10–1

What Intermediaries Add to the Cost of a Compact Disc

Production of disc	.74
Packaging (tuck box, etc.)	1.72
American Federation of Musicians dues	.27
Songwriters royalties	.39
Recording artist's royalties	1.01
Freight to·wholesaler	.36
Manufacturer's advertising and selling expenses	1.74
Manufacturer's administrative expenses	1.76
Manufacturer's cost	$7.99
Manufacturer's profit margin	1.10
Manufacturer's price to wholesaler	$9.09
Freight to retailer	.38
Wholesaler's advertising, selling, and administrative expense	.47
Wholesaler's cost	$9.94
Wholesaler's profit margin	.80
Wholesaler's price to retailer	$10.74 $6.90
Retailer's advertising, selling, and administrative expenses	1.76
Retailer's profit margin	3.49
Retailer's price to consumer	$15.99

Source: From *Principles of Marketing,* 3rd. ed., p. 339 by Thomas C. Kinnear and Kenneth L. Bernhardt. Copyright © 1990, 1986 by Scott, Foresman and Company. Reprinted by permission of Harper Collins, Publishers.

---

close to 90 million households making up the demand side. Clearly, if each of these units had to deal on a one-to-one basis to obtain needed goods and services, and there were no intermediaries to collect and disperse assortments of goods, the system would be totally inefficient. Thus, the primary role of intermediaries is to bring supply and demand together in an efficient and orderly fashion.

CLASSIFICATION OF MARKETING INTERMEDIARIES AND FUNCTIONS

There are a great many types of marketing intermediaries, many of which are so specialized by function and industry that they need not be discussed here. Figure 10–1 presents the major types of marketing intermediaries common to many industries. Although there is some overlap in this classification, these categories are based on the marketing functions performed. That is, various

Figure 10–1 *Major Types of Marketing Intermediaries*

Middleman—an independent business concern that operates as a link between producers and ultimate consumers or industrial buyers.

Merchant middleman—an intermediary who buys the goods outright and necessarily takes title to them.

Agent—a business unit that negotiates purchases, sales, or both but does not take title to the goods in which it deals.

Wholesaler—merchant establishment operated by a concern that is primarily engaged in buying, taking title to, usually storing and physically handling goods in large quantities, and reselling the goods (usually in smaller quantities) to retailers or to industrial or business users.

Retailer—merchant middleman who is engaged primarily in selling to ultimate consumers.

Broker—an intermediary who serves as a go-between for the buyer or seller; assumes no title risks, does not usually have physical custody of products, and is not looked upon as a permanent representative of either the buyer or the seller.

Sales agent—an independent channel member, either an individual or company, who is responsible for the sale of a firm's products or services but does not take title to the goods sold.

Distributor—a wholesale intermediary, especially in lines where selective or exclusive distribution is common at the wholesale level in which the manufacturer expects strong promotional support; often a synonym for wholesaler.

Jobber—an intermediary who buys from manufacturers and sells to retailers; a wholesaler.

Facilitating agent—a business firm that assists in the performance of distribution tasks other than buying, selling, and transferring title (i.e., transportation companies, warehouses, etc.)

Source: Based on Peter D. Bennett, ed., *Dictionary of Marketing Terms,* (Chicago: American Marketing Association, 1988).

intermediaries perform different marketing functions and to different degrees. Figure 10–2 is a listing of the more common marketing functions performed in the channel.

It should be remembered that whether or not a manufacturer utilizes intermediaries to perform these functions, the functions have to be performed by someone. In other words, the managerial question is not whether to perform the functions but who will perform them and to what degree.

CHANNELS OF DISTRIBUTION

As previously noted, a channel of distribution is the combination of institutions through which a seller markets products to the user or ultimate consumer. Some of these links assume the risks of ownership; others do not. Some perform marketing functions while others perform nonmarketing or facilitating functions, such as transportation. The conventional channel of distribution patterns for consumer goods markets are shown in Figure 10–3.

Some manufacturers use a direct channel, selling directly to the ultimate consumer (e.g., Avon Cosmetics). In other cases, one or more intermediaries may be used. For example, a manufacturer of paper cartons may sell to retailers,

Figure 10–2   *Marketing Functions Performed in Channels of Distribution*

Buying—purchasing products from sellers for use or for resale.

Selling—promoting the sale of products to ultimate consumers or industrial buyers.

Sorting—a function performed by intermediaries in order to bridge the discrepancy between the assortment of goods and services generated by the producer and the assortment demanded by the consumer. This function includes four distinct processes: sorting out, accumulation, allocation and assorting.

Sorting out—a sorting process that breaks down a heterogeneous supply into separate stocks that are relatively homogeneous.

Accumulation—a sorting process that brings similar stocks from a number of sources together into a larger homogeneous supply.

Allocation—a sorting process that consists of breaking a homogeneous supply down into smaller and smaller lots.

Assorting—a sorting process that consists of building an assortment of products for use in association with each other.

Concentration—the process of bringing goods from various places together in one place.

Financing—providing credit or funds to facilitate a transaction.

Storage—maintaining inventories and protecting products to provide better customer service.

Grading—classifying products into different categories on the basis of quality.

Transportation—physically moving products from where they are made to where they are purchased and used.

Risk-taking—taking on business risks involved in transporting and owning products.

Marketing research—collecting information concerning such things as market conditions, expected sales, consumer trends, and competitive forces.

Source: Based on Peter D. Bennett, ed., *Dictionary of Marketing Terms*, (Chicago: American Marketing Association, 1988).

---

or a manufacturer of small appliances may sell to retailers under a private brand. The most common channel in the consumer market is the one in which the manufacturer sells through wholesalers to retailers. For instance, a cold remedy manufacturer may sell to drug wholesalers who, in turn, sell a vast array of drug products to various retail outlets. Small manufacturers may also use agents, since they do not have sufficient capital for their own sales forces. Agents are commonly used intermediaries in the jewelry industry. The final channel in Figure 10–3 is used primarily when small wholesalers and retailers are involved. Channels with one or more intermediaries are referred to as indirect channels.

In contrast to consumer products, the direct channel is often used in the distribution of organizational goods. The reason for this stems from the structure of most organizational markets, which often have relatively few but extremely large customers. Also, many organizational products, such as computers, need a great deal of presale and postsale service. Distributors are used in organizational markets when the number of buyers is large and the size of the buying firm is small. As in the consumer market, agents are used in organizational markets in cases where manufacturers do not wish to have their own sales forces. Such an arrangement may be used by small manufacturers

Figure 10–3   *Conventional Channels of Distribution for Consumer Goods*

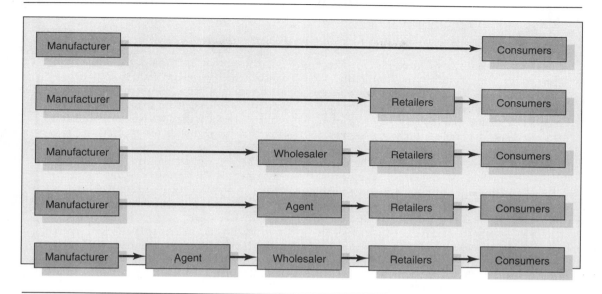

Figure 10–4   *Conventional Channels of Distribution for Organizational Goods*

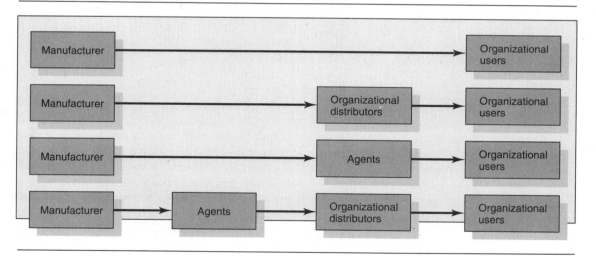

or when the market is geographically dispersed. The final channel arrangement in Figure 10–4 may also be used by a small manufacturer or when the market consists of many small customers. Under such conditions, it may not be economical for sellers to have their own sales organization.

HIGHLIGHT 10–2

"Are Channels of Distribution What the Textbooks Say?"

The middleman is not a hired link in a chain forged by the manufacturer, but rather an independent market, the focus of a large group of customers for whom he buys. Subsequent to some market analysis of his own, he selects products and suppliers, thereby setting at least one link in the channel.

After some experimentation, he settles upon a method of operation, performing those functions he deems inescapable in the light of his own objectives, forming policies for himself wherever he has freedom to do so. Perhaps these methods and policies conform closely to those of a Census category of middleman, but perhaps they do not.

Source: Phillip McVey, "Are Channels of Distribution What the Textbooks Say?" *Journal of Marketing,* January 1960, pp. 61–65. This article can be considered a classic in the field of marketing.

It is true that his choices are in many instances tentative proposals. He is subject to much influence from competitors, from aggressive suppliers, from inadequate finances and faulty information, as well as from habit. Nonetheless, many of his choices are independent.

As he grows and builds a following, he may find that his prestige in his market is greater than that of the suppliers whose goods he sells. In some instances his local strength is so great that a manufacturer is virtually unable to tap that market, except through him. In such a case the manufacturer can have no channel policy with respect to that market.

SELECTING CHANNELS OF DISTRIBUTION

General Considerations

Given the numerous types of channel intermediaries and functions that must be performed, the task of selecting and designing a channel of distribution may at first appear to be overwhelming. However, in many industries, channels of distribution have developed over many years and have become somewhat traditional. In such cases, the producer may be limited to this type of channel to operate in the industry. This is not to say that a traditional channel is always the most efficient and that there are no opportunities for innovation, but the fact that such a channel is widely accepted in the industry suggests it is highly efficient. A primary constraint in these cases and in cases where no traditional channel exists is that of *availability* of the various types of middlemen. All too often in the early stages of channel design, executives map out elaborate channel networks only to find out later that no such independent intermediaries exist for the firm's product in selected geographic areas. Even if they do exist, they may not be willing to accept the seller's products. In general, there are six basic considerations in the initial development of channel strategy. These are outlined in Figure 10–5.

Figure 10-5   *Considerations in Channel Planning*

1. *Customer characteristics.*
   a. Number.
   b. Geographical dispersion.
   c. Purchasing patterns.
   d. Susceptibilities to different selling methods.
2. *Product characteristics.*
   a. Perishability.
   b. Bulkiness.
   c. Degree of standardization.
   d. Installation and maintenance services required.
   e. Unit value.
3. *Intermediary characteristics.*
   a. Availability.
   b. Willingness to accept product or product line.
   c. Strengths.
   d. Weaknesses.
4. *Competitive characteristics.*
   a. Geographic proximity.
   b. Proximity in outlet.
5. *Company characteristics.*
   a. Financial strength.
   b. Product mix.
   c. Past channel experience.
   d. Present company marketing policies.
6. *Environmental characteristics.*
   a. Economic conditions.
   b. Legal regulations and restrictions.

It should be noted that for a particular product any one of these characteristics may greatly influence choice of channels. To illustrate, highly perishable products generally require direct channels, or a firm with little financial strength may require middlemen to perform almost all of the marketing functions.

Specific Considerations

The above characteristics play an important part in framing the channel selection decision. Based on them, the choice of channels can be further refined in terms of (1) distribution coverage required; (2) degree of control desired; (3) total distribution cost; and (4) channel flexibility.

Distribution coverage required. Because of the characteristics of the product, the environment needed to sell the product, and the needs and expectations of the potential buyer, products will vary in the intensity of distribution coverage they require. Distribution coverage can be viewed along a continuum ranging from intensive to selective to exclusive distribution.

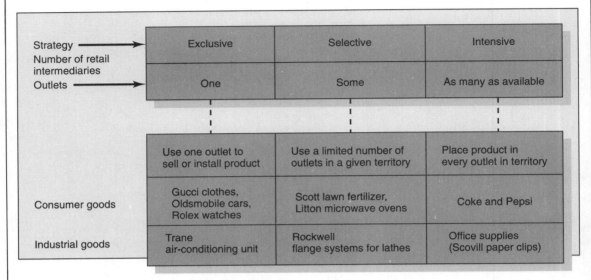

HIGHLIGHT 10–3

Intensive, Selective, and Exclusive Distibution: Market Coverage

Source: Reprinted from *Principles of Marketing,* 3rd ed., p. 355 by Thomas C. Kinnear and Kenneth L. Bernhardt. Copyright © 1990, 1986 by Scott, Foresman and Company. Reprinted by permission of Harper Collins, Publishers.

Intensive distribution. Here the manufacturer attempts to gain exposure through as many wholesalers and retailers as possible. Most convenience goods require intensive distribution based on the characteristics of the product (low unit value) and the needs and expectations of the buyer (high frequency of purchase and convenience).

Selective distribution. Here the manufacturer limits the use of intermediaries to the ones believed to be the best available. This may be based on the service organization available, the sales organization, or the reputation of the intermediary. Thus, appliances, home furnishings, and better clothing are usually distributed selectively. For appliances, the intermediary's service organization could be a key factor, while for better clothing and home furnishings, the intermediary's reputation would be an important consideration.

Exclusive distribution. Here the manufacturer severely limits distribution, and intermediaries are provided exclusive rights within a particular territory. The characteristics of the product are a determining factor here. Where the product requires certain specialized selling effort and/or investment in unique facilities or large inventories, this arrangement is usually selected. Retail paint stores are an example of such a distribution arrangement.

Degree of control desired. In selecting channels of distribution, the seller must make decisions concerning the degree of control desired over the marketing of the firm's products. Some manufacturers prefer to keep as much control over the policies surrounding their product as possible. Ordinarily, the degree of control achieved by the seller is proportionate to the directness of the channel. One Eastern brewery, for instance, owns its own fleet of trucks and operates a wholly owned delivery system direct to grocery and liquor stores. Its market is very concentrated geographically, with many small buyers, so such a system is economically feasible. However, all other brewers in the area sell through wholesalers or distributors.

When more indirect channels are used, the manufacturer must surrender some control over the marketing of the firm's product. However, attempts are commonly made to maintain a degree of control through some other indirect means, such as sharing promotional expenditures, providing sales training, or other operational aids, such as accounting systems, inventory systems, or marketing research data on the dealer's trading area.[1]

Total distribution cost. The total distribution cost concept has developed out of the more general topic of systems theory. The concept suggests that a channel of distribution should be viewed as a total system composed of interdependent subsystems, and that the objective of the system (channel) manager should be to optimize total system performance. In terms of distribution costs, it generally is assumed that the total system should be designed to minimize costs, other things being equal. The following is a representative list of the major distribution costs to be minimized.

1. Transportation.
2. Order processing.
3. Cost of lost business (an "opportunity" cost due to inability to meet customer demand).
4. Inventory carrying costs, including:
   a. Storage-space charges.
   b. Cost of capital invested.
   c. Taxes.
   d. Insurance.
   e. Obsolescence and deterioration.
5. Packaging.
6. Materials handling.

---

[1]For further discussion, see John Gaski, "The Theory of Power and Conflict in Channels of Distribution," *Journal of Marketing,* Summer 1984, pp. 9–29; Gul Butaney and Lawrence H. Wortzel, "Distributor Power versus Manufacturer Power: The Customer Role," *Journal of Marketing,* January 1988, pp. 52–63.

The important qualification to the total cost concept is the statement "other things being equal." The purpose of the total cost concept is to emphasize total system performance to avoid suboptimization. However, other important factors must be considered, not the least of which are level of customer service, sales, profits, and interface with the total marketing mix.

Channel flexibility. A final consideration relates to the ability of the manufacturer to adapt to changing conditions. To illustrate, in recent years much of the population has moved from inner cities to suburbs and thus make most of their purchases in shopping centers and malls. If a manufacturer had long-term, exclusive dealership with retailers in the inner city, the ability to adapt to this population shift could have been severely limited. In general, the less certain the future seems to be, the less favorable are channel alternatives involving long commitments.

MANAGING A CHANNEL OF DISTRIBUTION

Once the seller has decided on the type of channel structure to use and selected the individual members, the entire coalition should operate as a total system. From a behavioral perspective, the system can be viewed as a social system since each member interacts with the others, each member plays a role vis-à-vis the others, and each has certain expectations of the other.[2] Thus, the behavioral perspective views a channel of distribution as more than a series of markets or participants extending from production to consumption.

A Channel Leader

If a channel of distribution is viewed as a social system comprised of interacting firms with a common set of objectives, then integration among them seems desirable. This is because the channel, as a system, can be conceived as a competitive unit in and of itself; in other words, any success that the product has is determined largely by the effectiveness and efficiency with which human, material, and monetary resources have been mobilized throughout the entire interfirm network.

If the above view is taken, the question arises about who should exert primary leadership in the channel—that is, becomes the "channel captain" or "channel commander." There is little agreement about the answer. Some marketers believe the manufacturer or the owner of the brand name should be the

---

[2]F. Robert Dwyer and M. Ann Welsh, "Environmental Relationships of the Internal Political Economy of Marketing Channels," *Journal of Marketing Research,* November 1985, pp. 397–414; John F. Gaski and John R. Nevin, "The Differential Effects of Exercised and Unexercised Power Sources in a Marketing Channel," *Journal of Marketing Research,* May 1985, pp. 130–42; James C. Anderson and James A. Narus, "A Model of Distributor Firm and Manufacturing Firm Working Partnerships," *Journal of Marketing,* January 1990, pp. 42–58.

HIGHLIGHT 10–4

Manufacturers and Intermediaries: A Perfect Working Relationship

The Perfect Intermediary

1. Has access to the market that the manufacturer wants to reach.
2. Carries adequate stocks of the manufacturer's products and a satisfactory assortment of other products.
3. Has an effective promotional program—advertising, personal selling, and product displays. Promotional demands placed on the manufacturer are in line with what the manufacturer intends to do.
4. Provides services to customers—credit, delivery, installation, and product repair—and honors the product warranty conditions.
5. Pays its bills on time and has capable management.

Source: Adapted from William J. Stanton, Michael J. Etzel and Bruce J. Walker, *Fundamentals of Marketing,* 9th ed., New York: McGraw-Hill, 1991, p.305.

The Perfect Manufacturer

1. Provides a desirable assortment of products—well designed, properly priced, attractively packaged, and delivered on time and in adequate quantities.
2. Builds product demand for these products by advertising them.
3. Furnishes promotional assistance to its middlemen.
4. Provides managerial assistance for its middlemen.
5. Honors product warranties and provides repair and installation service.

The Perfect Combination

1. Probably doesn't exist.

---

channel captain. The argument here is that the manufacturer or brand name owner (1) has the most to lose if the system malfunctions or fails; (2) has the most technical expertise; and (3) in many cases has greater resources than other channel members. Others believe the retailer should be the channel captain, since the retailer is the closest link to the consumer and, therefore, can judge better the consumer needs and wants. Still others argue the wholesaler should seek to gain channel control, or that the locus of control should be at the level where competition is greatest.

Vertical Marketing Systems

To this point in the chapter the discussion has focused primarily on conventional channels of distribution. In conventional channels, each firm is relatively independent of the other members in the channel. However, one of the important developments in channel management in recent years is the increasing use of vertical marketing systems.

HIGHLIGHT 10–5

Pushing or Pulling through the Channel System

A producer has a special challenge with respect to channel systems: How to ensure that the product reaches the end of the channel. Intermediaries—especially retailers—don't have this problem, since they already control that end of the channel.

The two basic methods of recruiting middlemen are *pushing* and *pulling*.

Pushing a product through the channels means using normal promotion effort—personal selling and advertising—to help sell the whole marketing mix to possible channel members. This method is common—since these sales transactions are usually between rational, presumably profit-oriented buyers and sellers. The approach emphasizes the importance of building a channel—and securing the wholehearted cooperation of channel members. The producer—in effect—tries to develop a team that will work well together to get the product to the user.

By contrast, pulling means getting consumers to ask intermediaries for the product. This usually involves highly aggressive promotion to final consumers or users—perhaps using coupons or samples—and temporary bypassing of intermediaries. If the promotion works, the intermediaries are forced to carry the product—to satisfy their customers.

Source: Adapted with permission from E. Jerome McCarthy and William D. Perreault, Jr., *Basic Marketing: A Managerial Approach,* 11th ed. (Homewood, Ill.: Richard D. Irwin, 1993), pp. 428–30.

Vertical marketing systems are channels in which members are more dependent on one another and develop long-term working relationships in order to improve the efficiency and effectiveness of the system. Figure 10–6 shows the major types of vertical marketing systems, which include administered, contractual, and corporate systems.[3]

Administered systems

Administered vertical marketing systems are the most similar to conventional channels. However, in these systems there is a higher degree of interorganizational planning and management than in a conventional channel. The dependence in these systems can result from the existence

---

[3]This section is based on Donald J. Bowersox and M. Bixby Cooper, *Strategic Marketing Channel Management* (New York: McGraw-Hill, 1992), 104–7; Bert Rosenbloom, *Marketing Channels: A Management View,* 4th ed. (Hinsdale, Ill.: Dryden Press), pp. 440–65; Eric N. Berkowitz, Roger A. Kerin, Steven W. Hartley, and William Rudelius, *Marketing,* 3rd ed. (Homewood, Ill.: Richard D. Irwin, 1992), pp. 387–90.

Figure 10–6 *Major Types of Vertical Marketing Systems*

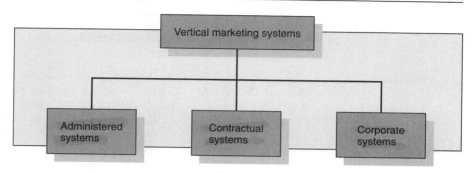

of a strong channel leader such that other channel members work closely with this company in order to maintain a long-term relationship. While any level of channel member may be the leader of an administered system, Wal-Mart, KMart, and Sears are excellent examples of retailers who have established administered systems with many of their suppliers.

Contractual systems

Contractual vertical marketing systems involve independent production and distribution companies entering into formal contracts to perform designated marketing functions. Three major types of contractual vertical marketing systems are the retail cooperative organization, wholesaler-sponsored voluntary chain, and various franchising programs.

In a retail cooperative organization, a group of independent retailers unite and agree to pool buying and managerial resources to improve competitive position. In a wholesaler-sponsored voluntary chain, a wholesaler contracts with a number of retailers and performs channel functions for them. Usually, retailers agree to concentrate a major portion of their purchasing with the sponsoring wholesaler and to sell advertised products at the same price. The most visible type of contractual vertical marketing systems involve a variety of franchise programs. Franchises involve a parent company (the franchisor) and an independent firm (the franchisee) entering into a contractual relationship to set up and operate a business in a particular way. Many products and services reach consumers through franchise systems, including automobiles (Ford), gasoline (Mobil), hotels and motels (Holiday Inn), restaurants (McDonald's), car rentals (Avis), and soft drinks (Pepsi). In fact, some analysts predict that within the next ten years, franchises will account for 50 percent of all retail sales.

HIGHLIGHT 10–6

Franchising: An Alternative to Conventional Channels of Distribution

A franchise is a means by which a producer of products or services achieves a direct channel of distribution without wholly owning or managing the physical facilities in the market. In effect, the franchisor provides the franchisee with the franchisor's knowledge, manufacturing, and marketing techniques for a financial return.

Ingredients of a Franchised Business

Six key ingredients should be included within a well-balanced franchise offered to a franchisee. These are given in order of importance:

— *Technical knowledge* in its practical form is supplied through an intensive course of study.
— *Managerial techniques* based on proven and time-tested programs are imparted to the franchisee on a continuing basis, even after the business has been started or taken over by the franchisee.
— *Commercial knowledge* involving prescribed methods of buying and selling is explained and codified. Most products to be obtained, processed, and sold to the franchisee are supplied by the franchisor.
— *Financial instruction* on managing funds and accounts is given to the franchisee during the indoctrination period.
— *Accounting controls* are set up by the franchisor for the franchisee.

— *Protective safeguards* are included in the intensive training of the franchisee for employees and customers, including the quality of the product, as well as the safeguards for assets through adequate insurance controls.

Elements of an Ideal Franchise Program

— **High gross margin.** In order for the franchisee to be able to afford a high franchise fee (which the franchisor needs), it is necessary to operate on a high gross margin percentage. This explains the widespread application of franchising in the food and service industries.
— **In-store value added.** Franchising works best in those product categories where the product is at least partially processed in the store. Such environments require constant on-site supervision—a chronic problem for company-owned stores using a hired manager. Owners simply are willing to work harder over longer hours.
— **Secret processes.** Concepts, formulas, or products that the franchisee can't duplicate without joining the franchise program.
— **Real estate profits.** The franchisor uses income from ownership of property as a significant revenue source.
— **Simplicity.** The most successful franchises have been those that operate on automatic pilot: All the key decisions have been thought through, and the owner merely implements the decisions.

Source: Partially adapted from Philip D. White and Albert D. Bates, "Franchising Will Remain Retailing Fixture, but Its Salad Days Have Long Since Gone," *Marketing News,* February 17, 1984, p. 14.

Corporate systems

Corporate vertical marketing systems involve single ownership of two or more levels of a channel. When a manufacturer purchases wholesalers or retailers, it is called *forward integration*. When wholesalers or retailers purchase channel members above them, it is called *backward integration*. Firms may choose to develop corporate vertical marketing systems in order to compete more effectively with other marketing systems, to obtain scale economies and to increase channel cooperation and avoid channel conflict.

CONCLUSION

The purpose of this chapter has been to introduce the reader to the process of distribution of goods in an extremely complex, highly productive, and highly specialized economy. It is important that the reader understand the vital need for marketing intermediaries in such an economy to bring about exchanges between buyers and sellers in a reasonably efficient manner. If the reader appreciates this concept, the major objective of this chapter has been achieved. The chapter also examined conventional channels of distribution for both consumer and organizational goods, and the various types of marketing intermediaries available to a seller. Finally, the selection and management of channels of distribution were discussed.

ADDITIONAL READINGS

Anderson, Erin, and Barton Weitz. "The Use of Pledges to Build and Sustain Commitment in Distribution Channels." *Journal of Marketing Research,* February 1992, pp. 18–34.

Bowersox, Donald J., and M. Bixby Cooper. *Strategic Marketing Channel Management.* New York: McGraw-Hill, Inc., 1992.

Boyle, Brett; R. Robert Dwyer; Robert A. Robicheaux; and James T. Simpson. "Influence Strategies in Marketing Channels: Measures and Uses in Different Relationship Structures." *Journal of Marketing Research,* November 1992, pp. 462–73.

Dant, Rajiv and Patrick L. Schul. "Conflict Resolution Processes in Contractual Channels of Distribution." *Journal of Marketing,* January 1992, pp. 38–54.

Justis, Robert, and Richard Judd. *Franchising.* Cincinatti, Ohio: South-Western Publishing, 1989.

Rosenbloom, Bert, *Marketing Channels: A Managerial View.* 4th ed. Chicago: Dryden Press, 1991.

Stern, Louis W.; Adel I. El-Ansary; and James R. Brown. *Management in Marketing Channels.* Englewood Cliffs, N.J.: Prentice Hall, 1989.

Stern, Louis W., and Adel I. El-Ansary. *Marketing Channels.* 4th ed. Englewood Cliffs, N.J.: Prentice Hall, 1992.

Chapter 11

Pricing Strategy

One of the most important and complex decisions a firm has to make relates to pricing its products or services. If consumers or organizational buyers perceive a price to be too high, they may purchase competitive brands or substitute products, leading to a loss of sales and profits for the firm. If the price is too low, sales might increase, but profitability may suffer. Thus, pricing decisions must be given careful consideration when a firm is introducing a new product or planning a short- or long-term price change.

This chapter discusses demand, supply, and environmental influences that affect pricing decisions and emphasizes that all three must be considered for effective pricing. However, as will be discussed in the chapter, many firms price their products without explicitly considering all of these influences.

DEMAND INFLUENCES ON PRICING DECISIONS

Demand influences on pricing decisions concern primarily the nature of the target market and expected reactions of consumers to a given price or change in price. There are three primary considerations here: demographic factors, psychological factors, and price elasticity.

△ **Demographic factors.** In the initial selection of the target market that a firm intends to serve, a number of demographic factors are usually considered. Demographic factors that are particularly important for pricing decisions include the following:

1. Number of potential buyers.
2. Location of potential buyers.

HIGHLIGHT 11–1

The Meaning of Price

Alternative Terms	What Is Given in Return
Price	Most physical merchandise.
Tuition	College courses, education.
Rent	A place to live or the use of equipment for a specific time period.
Interest	Use of money.
Fee	Professional services of lawyers, doctors, consultants.
Fare	Transportation: air, taxi, bus.
Toll	Use of road or bridge, or long-distance phone rate.
Salary	Work of managers.
Wage	Work of hourly workers.
Bribe	Illegal actions.
Commission	Sales effort.

Source: From *Principles of Marketing,* 3rd ed., p. 576, by Thomas C. Kinnear and Kenneth L. Bernhardt. Copyright © 1990, 1986 by Scott Foresman and Company. Reprinted by permission of Harper Collins, Publishers.

3. Position of potential buyers (resellers or final consumers).
4. Expected consumption rates of potential buyers.
5. Economic strength of potential buyers.

These factors help determine market potential and are useful for estimating expected sales at various price levels.

△ *Psychological factors.* Psychological factors related to pricing concern primarily how consumers will perceive various prices or price changes. For example, marketing managers should be concerned with such questions as:

1. Will potential buyers use price as an indicator of product quality?
2. Will potential buyers be favorably attracted by odd pricing?
3. Will potential buyers perceive the price as too high relative to the service the product gives them?
4. Are potential buyers prestige oriented and therefore willing to pay higher prices to fulfill this need?
5. How much will potential buyers be willing to pay for the product?

While psychological factors have a significant effect on the success of a pricing strategy and ultimately on marketing strategy, answers to the above questions may require considerable marketing research. In fact, a review of buyers' subjective perceptions of price concluded that very little is known about how price affects buyers' perceptions of alternative purchase offers and how these perceptions affect purchase response.[1] However, some tentative generalizations about how buyers perceive price have been formulated. For example, research has found that persons who choose high-priced items usually perceive large quality variations within product categories and see the consequences of a poor choice as being undesirable. They believe that quality is related to price and see themselves as good judges of product quality. In general, the reverse is true for persons who select low-priced items in the same product categories. Thus, although information on psychological factors involved in purchasing may be difficult to obtain, marketing managers must at least consider the effects of such factors on their desired target market and marketing strategy.[2]

Price elasticity. Both demographic and psychological factors affect price elasticity. Price elasticity is a measure of consumers' price sensitivity, which is estimated by dividing relative changes in the quantity sold by the relative changes in price:

$$e = \frac{\% \text{ change in quantity demanded}}{\% \text{ change in price}}$$

Although difficult to measure, there are two basic methods commonly used to estimate price elasticity. First, price elasticity can be estimated from historical data or from price/quantity data across different sales districts. Second, price elasticity can be estimated by sampling a group of consumers from the target market and polling them concerning various price/quantity relationships. While both of these approaches provide estimates of price elasticity, the former approach is limited to the consideration of price changes, while the latter approach is often expensive and there is some question as to the validity of subjects' responses. However, even a crude estimate of price elasticity is a useful input to pricing decisions.

SUPPLY INFLUENCES ON PRICING DECISIONS

For the purpose of this text, supply influences on pricing decisions can be discussed in terms of three basic factors. These factors relate to the objectives, costs, and nature of the product.

---

[1] Kent B. Monroe, "Buyers' Subjective Perceptions of Price," *Journal of Marketing Research,* February 1973, pp. 70–80; also see Donald R. Lichtenstein and Scot Burton, "The Relationship between Perceived and Objective Price-Quality," *Journal of Marketing Research,* November 1989, pp. 429–43.

[2] For research concerning the effects of price and several other marketing variables on perceived product quality, see Akshay R. Rao and Kent B. Monroe, "The Effect of Price, Brand Name, and Store Name on Buyers' Perceptions of Product Quality: An Integrative Review," *Journal of Marketing Research,* August 1989, pp. 351–57; William B. Dodds, Kent B. Monroe, and Dhruv Grewal, "Effects of Price, Brand, and Store Evaluations on Buyers' Product Evaluations," *Journal of Marketing Research,* August 1991, pp. 307–19.

HIGHLIGHT 11–2

Increasing Consumer Prices

Marketers can increase consumer prices in a number of ways. Prices can be increased for the same quantity and quality or maintained for less quantity, less quality, or fewer auxiliary services. Price deals could be reduced or eliminated or interest rates and charges could be increased. Recently, a number of marketers have focused their pricing strategies on the second option, maintaining the same price but offering less quantity. Below are several examples of the use of this strategy.

Brand	Product	It Looks Like	You Pay	But You Get
Knorr	Leek soup and recipe mix	More: Box is 1/2″ deeper	The same	Less: Makes three 8-oz. servings, reduced from four
StarKist	Canned tuna	A bit less: Can is 1/16″ less tall	The same	Less: Weight of tuna reduced by 3/8 oz., or 5.8 percent
Lipton	Instant lemon-flavored tea	The same	The same	Less: Weight reduced by 7.5 percent; company claims it contains same number of servings as before
Brim	Decaffeinated coffee	The same	The same	Less: Weight reduced by 4.2 percent; company claims it contains same number of servings as before

Source: David E. Kalish, "Prices Stable, but Products Are Less Filling," *Wisconsin State Journal,* January 6, 1991, p. 1D.

Pricing Objectives

Pricing objectives should be derived from overall marketing objectives, which in turn should be derived from corporate objectives. Since it is traditionally assumed that business firms operate to maximize profits in the long run, it is often thought that the basic pricing objective is solely concerned with long-run profits. However, the profit maximization norm does not provide the operating marketing manager with a single, unequivocal guideline for selecting prices. In addition, the marketing manager does not have perfect cost, revenue, and market information to be able to evaluate whether or not this objective is being reached. In practice, then, many other objectives are employed as guidelines for pricing decisions. In some cases, these objectives may be considered as operational approaches to achieve long-run profit maximization.

Research has found that the most common pricing objectives are (1) pricing to achieve a target return on investment; (2) stabilization of price and margin; (3) pricing to achieve a target market share; and (4) pricing to meet or prevent competition.

Cost Considerations in Pricing

The price of a product usually must cover costs of production, promotion, and distribution, plus a profit for the offering to be of value to the firm. In addition, when products are priced on the basis of costs plus a fair profit, there is an implicit assumption that this sum represents the economic value of the product in the marketplace.

Cost-oriented pricing is the most common approach in practice, and there are at least three basic variations: *markup pricing, cost-plus pricing,* and *rate-of-return pricing*. Markup pricing is commonly used in retailing, where a percentage is added to the retailer's invoice price to determine the final selling price. Closely related to markup pricing is cost-plus pricing, where the costs of producing a product or completing a project are totalled and a profit amount or percentage is added on. Cost-plus pricing is most often used to describe the pricing of jobs that are nonroutine and difficult to "cost" in advance, such as construction and military weapon development.

Rate-of-return or *target pricing* is commonly used by manufacturers. In this method, price is determined by adding a desired rate of return on investment to total costs. Generally, a break-even analysis is performed for expected production and sales levels and a rate of return is added on. For example, suppose a firm estimated production and sales to be 75,000 units at a total cost of $300,000. If the firm desired a before-tax return of 20 percent, the selling price would be $(300,000 + 0.20 \times 300,000) \div 75,000 = \$4.80$.

Cost-oriented approaches to pricing have the advantage of simplicity, and many practitioners believe that they generally yield a good price decision. However, such approaches have been criticized for two basic reasons. First, cost approaches give little or no consideration to demand factors. For example, the price determined by markup or cost-plus methods has no necessary relationship to what people will be willing to pay for the product. In the case of rate-of-return pricing, little emphasis is placed on estimating sales volume. Even if it were, rate-of-return pricing involves circular reasoning, since unit cost depends on sales volume but sales volume depends on selling price. Second, cost approaches fail to reflect competition adequately. Only in industries where all firms use this approach and have similar costs and markups can this approach yield similar prices and minimize price competition. Thus, in many industries, cost-oriented pricing could lead to severe price competition, which could eliminate smaller firms. Therefore, although costs are a highly important consideration in price decisions, numerous other factors need to be examined.

HIGHLIGHT 11–3

Basic Break-Even Formulas

The following formulas are used to calculate break-even points in units and in dollars:

$$BEP_{(in\ units)} = \frac{FC}{(SP - VC)}$$

$$BEP_{(in\ dollars)} = \frac{FC}{1 - (VC/SP)}$$

where

FC = Fixed cost
VC = Variable cost
SP = Selling price

If, as is generally the case, a firm wants to know how many units or sales dollars are necessary to generate a given amount of profit, profit (P) is simply added to fixed costs in the above formulas. In addition, if the firm has estimates of expected sales and fixed and variable costs, the selling price can be solved for. (A more detailed discussion of break-even analysis is provided in Section III of this book.)

Product Consideration in Pricing

Although numerous product characteristics can affect pricing, three of the most important are (1) perishability, (2) distinctiveness, and (3) stage in the product life cycle.

Perishability. Goods that are very perishable in a physical sense must be priced to promote sales without costly delays. Foodstuffs and certain types of raw materials tend to be in this category. Products can be considered perishable in two other senses. High fashion, fad, and seasonal products are perishable not in the sense that the product deteriorates but in the sense that demand for the product is confined to a specific time period. Perishability also relates to consumption rate, which means that some products are consumed very slowly, as in the case of consumer durables. Two important pricing considerations here are that (1) such goods tend to be expensive because large amounts of service are purchased at one time; and (2) the consumer has a certain amount of discretionary time available in making replacement purchase decisions.

Distinctiveness. Products can be classified in terms of how distinctive they are. Homogeneous goods are perfect substitutes for each other, as in the case of bulk wheat or whole milk, while most manufactured goods can be differentiated on the basis of certain features, such as package, trademark, engineering design, and chemical features. Thus, few consumer goods are perfectly homogeneous, and one of the primary marketing objectives of any firm is to make its product distinctive in the minds of buyers. Large sums of money are often invested to accomplish this task, and one of the payoffs for such investments is the seller's ability to charge higher prices for distinctive products.

Life cycle. The stage of the life cycle that a product is in can have important pricing implications. With regard to the life cycle, two approaches to pricing are skimming and penetration price policies. A *skimming* policy is one in which the seller charges a relatively high price on a new product. Generally, this policy is used when the firm has a temporary monopoly and in cases where demand for the product is price inelastic. In later stages of the life cycle, as competition moves in and other market factors change, the price may then be lowered. Digital watches and calculators are examples of this. A *penetration* policy is one in which the seller charges a relatively low price on a new product. Generally, this policy is used when the firm expects competition to move in rapidly and where demand for the product is, at least in the short run, price elastic. This policy is also used to obtain large economies of scale and as a major instrument for rapid creation of a mass market. A low price and profit margin may also discourage competition. In later stages of the life cycle, the price may have to be altered to meet changes in the market.

ENVIRONMENTAL INFLUENCES ON PRICING DECISIONS

Environmental influences on pricing include variables that are uncontrollable by the marketing manager. Two of the most important of these are competition and government regulation.

Competition

In setting or changing prices, the firm must consider its competition and how competition will react to the price of the product. Initially, consideration must be given to such factors as:

1. Number of competitors.
2. Size of competitors.
3. Location of competitors.
4. Conditions of entry into the industry.
5. Degree of vertical integration of competitors.
6. Number of products sold by competitors.
7. Cost structure of competitors.
8. Historical reaction of competitors to price changes.

These factors help determine whether the firm's selling price should be at, below, or above competition. Pricing a product at competition (i.e., the average price charged by the industry) is called "going rate pricing" and is popular for homogeneous products, since this approach represents the collective wisdom of the industry and is not disruptive of industry harmony. An example of pricing below competition can be found in sealed-bid pricing, where the firm is bidding directly against competition for project contracts. Although cost and profits are initially calculated, the firm attempts to bid below competitors to obtain the job contract. A firm may price above competition because it has a superior product or because the firm is the price leader in the industry.

Government Regulations

Prices of certain goods and services are regulated by state and federal governments. Public utilities are examples of state regulation of prices. However, for most marketing managers, federal laws that make certain pricing practices illegal are of primary consideration in pricing decisions. The list below is a summary of some of the more important legal constraints on pricing. Of course, since most marketing managers are not trained as lawyers, they usually seek legal counsel when developing pricing strategies to ensure conformity to state and federal legislation.

1. Price-fixing is illegal per se. Sellers must not make any agreements with *(a)* competitors, or *(b)* distributors concerning the final price of the goods. The Sherman Antitrust Act is the primary device used to outlaw horizontal price fixing. Section 5 of the Federal Trade Commission Act has been used to outlaw price fixing as an "unfair" business practice.
2. Deceptive pricing practices are outlawed under Section 5 of the Federal Trade Commission Act. An example of deceptive pricing would be to mark merchandise with an exceptionally high price and then claim that the lower selling price actually used represents a legitimate price reduction.
3. Price discrimination that lessens competition or is deemed injurious to it is outlawed by the Robinson-Patman Act (which amends Section 2 of the Clayton Act). Price discrimination is not illegal per se, but sellers cannot charge competing buyers different prices for essentially the same products if the effect of such sales is injurious to competition. Price differentials can be legally justified on certain grounds, especially if the price differences reflect cost differences. This is particularly true of quantity discounts.
4. Promotional pricing, such as cooperative advertising, and price deals are not illegal per se; but if a seller grants advertising allowances, merchandising service, free goods, or special promotional discounts to customers, it must do so on proportionately equal terms. Sections 2(d) and 2(e) of the Robinson-Patman Act are designed to regulate such practices so that price reductions cannot be granted to some customers under the guise of promotional allowances.[3]

---

[3]For further discussion of legal issues involved in pricing, see Louis W. Stern and Thomas L. Eovaldi, *Legal Aspects of Marketing Strategy* (Englewood Cliffs, N.J.: Prentice Hall, 1984), chap. 5.

A GENERAL PRICING DECISION MODEL

From what has been discussed thus far, it should be clear that effective pricing decisions involve the consideration of many factors and, depending on the situation, any of these factors can be the primary consideration in setting price. In addition, it is difficult to formulate an exact sequencing of when each factor should be considered. However, several general pricing decision models have been advanced with the clearly stated warning that all pricing decisions will not fit the framework. Below is one such model, which views pricing decisions as a nine-step sequence.

1. *Define market targets.* All marketing decision making should begin with a definition of segmentation strategy and the identification of potential customers.
2. *Estimate market potential.* The maximum size of the available market determines what is possible and helps define competitive opportunities.
3. *Develop product positioning.* The brand image and the desired niche in the competitive marketplace provide important constraints on the pricing decision as the firm attempts to obtain a unique competitive advantage by differentiating its product offering from that of competitors.
4. *Design the marketing mix.* Design of the marketing mix defines the role to be played by pricing in relation to and in support of other marketing variables, especially distribution and promotional policies.
5. *Estimate price elasticity of demand.* The sensitivity of the level of demand to differences in price can be estimated either from past experience or through market tests.
6. *Estimate all relevant costs.* While straight cost-plus pricing is to be avoided because it is insensitive to demand, pricing decisions must take into account necessary plant investment, investment in R&D, and investment in market development, as well as variable costs of production and marketing.
7. *Analyze environmental factors.* Pricing decisions are further constrained by industry practices, likely competitive response to alternative pricing strategies, and legal requirements.
8. *Set pricing objectives.* Pricing decisions must be guided by a clear statement of objectives that recognizes environmental constraints and defines the role of pricing in the marketing strategy while at the same time relating pricing to the firm's financial objectives.
9. *Develop the price structure.* The price structure for a given product can now be determined and will define selling prices for the product (perhaps in a variety of styles and sizes) and the discounts from list price to be offered to various kinds of intermediaries and various types of buyers.[4]

---

[4]Frederick E. Webster, *Marketing for Managers* (New York: Harper & Row, 1974), pp. 178–79; also see Thomas T. Nagle, *The Strategy and Tactics of Pricing* (Englewood Cliffs, N.J.: Prentice Hall, 1987), Kent B. Monroe, *Pricing: Making Profitable Decisions,* 2nd ed. (New York: McGraw-Hill), 1990.

HIGHLIGHT 11–4

Some Short-Term Price Reduction Tactics

1. Cents-off deals: "Package price is 20¢ off."
2. Special offers: "Buy one, get one free"; "Buy three tires and get the fourth free."
3. Coupons: Store or manufacturer coupons in newspaper, magazines, flyers, and packages.
4. Rebates: Mail in proof-of-purchase seals for cash or merchandise.
5. Increase quantity for same price: "2 extra ounces of coffee free."
6. Free installation or service for a limited time period.
7. Reduce or eliminate interest charges for a limited time: "90 days same as cash."
8. Special sales: "25 percent off all merchandise marked with a red tag."

While all pricing decisions cannot be made strictly on the basis of this model, such an approach has three advantages for the marketing manager. First, it breaks the pricing decision into nine manageable steps. Second, it recognizes that pricing decisions must be fully integrated into overall marketing strategy. Third, it aids the decision maker by recognizing the importance of both qualitative and quantitative factors in pricing decisions.

CONCLUSION

Pricing decisions that integrate the firm's costs with marketing strategy, business conditions, competition, consumer demand, product variables, channels of distribution, and general resources can determine the success or failure of a business. This places a very heavy burden on the price maker. Modern-day marketing managers cannot ignore the complexity or the importance of price management. Pricing policies must be continually reviewed and must take into account the fact that the firm is a dynamic entity operating in a very competitive environment. There are many ways for money to flow out of a firm in the form of costs, but often there is only one way to bring revenues in and that is by the price-product mechanism.

ADDITIONAL READINGS

Biswas, Abhijit, and Edward A. Blair. "Contextual Effects of Reference Prices in Retail Advertisements." *Journal of Marketing,* July 1991, pp. 1–12.

Kalwani, Manohar U., and Chi Kin Yim. "Consumer Price and Promotion Expectations: An Experimental Study." *Journal of Marketing Research,* February 1992, pp. 90–100.

Mayhew, Glenn E., and Russell S. Winer. "An Empirical Analysis of Internal and External Reference Prices Using Scanner Data." *Journal of Consumer Research,* June 1992, pp. 62–70.

Monroe, Kent B. *Pricing: Making Profitable Decisions,* 2nd ed., New York: McGraw-Hill, 1990.

Nagle, Thomas T. *The Strategy and Tactics of Pricing,* Englewood Cliffs, N.J.: Prentice Hall, 1987.

Parker, Philip M. "Price Elaticity Dynamics Over the Adoption Life Cycle." *Journal of Marketing Research,* August 1992, pp. 358–67.

Rao, Akshay R. and Mark E. Bergen. "Price Premium Variations as a Consequence of Buyers' Lack of Information." *Journal of Consumer Research,* December 1992, pp. 412–23.

Seymour, Daniel T., ed. *Pricing Decisions.* Chicago: Probus Publishing, 1989.

Urbany, Joel E., and Peter R. Dickson. "Consumer Normal Price Estimation: Market versus Personal Standards." *Journal of Consumer Research,* June 1991, pp. 45–51.

Walters, Rockney G. "Assessing the Impact of Retail Price Promotions on Product Substitution, Complementary Purchase, and Interstore Sales Displacement." *Journal of Marketing,* April 1991, pp. 17–28.

Marketing in Special Fields

Chapter 12
The Marketing of Services

Chapter 13
International Marketing

The Marketing of Services

For many years, the fastest growing segment of the American economy has not been the production of tangibles but the performance of services. Spending on services has increased to such an extent that today it captures about 50 cents of the consumer's dollar. Meanwhile, the service sector has also grown steadily in its contribution to the U.S. gross national product and now accounts for approximately 71 percent of the country's GNP and 80 percent of its employment.[1] However, for the most part, the area of services marketing remains ill-defined and misunderstood.[2]

Contrary to conventional wisdom, service sector workers are not a vast army of hamburger flippers, baggage handlers, nurse's aides, baby-sitters, travel agents, or customer service representatives.[3] This statement is not meant to downplay the important role these people play in delivering quality services. Rather, it is meant to drive home the point that the composition of the service work force is quite varied. About two thirds of its job holders can be classified as white-collar workers. Of these, about 43 percent are "knowledge workers"—managers, executives, and a variety of professionals ranging from

---

[1]Ron Zemke, "The Emerging Art of Service Management," *Training,* January 1992, pp. 36–42; and James Brian Quinn, Jordan J. Baruch, and Penny C. Paquette, "Exploiting the Manufacturing-Services Interface," *Sloan Management Review,* Summer 1988, pp. 45–56.

[2]Valerie A. Zeithaml, A. Parasuraman, and L. L. Berry, "Problems and Strategies in Services Marketing," *Journal of Marketing,* Spring 1985, pp. 33–46.

[3]Material related to the diversity of the service sector was taken from Stephen S. Roach, "Services Under Siege—The Restructuring Imperative," *Harvard Business Review,* September-October 1991, pp. 82–91.

scientists to lawyers to entertainers. Needless to say, these workers are generally well-educated and have career tracks and earning potential that compare favorably with any occupation group in manufacturing.

Unfortunately, some marketing textbooks still devote little, if any, attention to program development for the marketing of services. Rather, they tend to soley concentrate on differentiating between characteristics of services and products. This omission is usually based on the assumption that the marketing of goods and the marketing of services are the same, and, therefore, the techniques discussed under goods apply as well to the marketing of services. Basically, this assumption is true. Whether selling products or services, the marketer must be concerned with developing a marketing strategy centered around the four controllable decision variables that comprise the marketing mix: the product (or service), the price, the distribution system, and promotion. In addition, the use of marketing research is as valuable to the marketer of services as it is to the marketer of goods.

However, because services possess certain distinguishing characteristics, the task of determining the marketing mix ingredients for a service marketing strategy may present different and more difficult problems than may appear at first glance. The purpose of this chapter is threefold. First, the reader will become acquainted with the special characteristics of service marketing. Second, obstacles will be described which, in the past, impeded development of service marketing. Third, current trends and strategies of innovation in service marketing will be explored. Using this approach, the material in the other chapters of the book can be integrated into a better understanding of the marketing of services.

Before proceeding, some attention must be given to what the authors refer to when using the term *services*. Probably the most frustrating aspect of the available literature on services is that the definition of what constitutes a service remains unclear. The fact is that no common definition and boundaries have been developed to delimit the field of services. The American Marketing Association has defined services as follows:

1. *Service products,* such as a bank loan or home security that are intangible, or at least substantially so. If totally intangible, they are exchanged directly from producer to user, cannot be transported or stored, and are almost instantly perishable. Service products are often difficult to identify, since they come into existence at the same time they are bought and consumed. They are comprised of intangible elements that are inseparable, they usually involve customer participation in some important way, cannot be sold in the sense of ownership transfer, and have no title. Today, however, most products are partly tangible and partly intangible, and the dominant form is used to classify them as either goods or services (all are products). These common, hybrid forms, whatever they are called, may or may not have the attributes just given for totally intangible services.

2. *Services,* as a term, is also used to describe activities performed by sellers and others which accompany the sale of a product, and aid in its exchange or its utilization (e.g., shoe fitting, financing, an 800 number). Such services are either presale or postsale and supplement the product but do not comprise it. If performed during sale, they are considered to be intangible parts of the product.[4]

The first definition includes such services as insurance, entertainment, banking, airlines, health care, telecommunications, and hotels; and the second definition includes services such as wrapping and delivery because these services exist in connection with the sale of a product or another service. This suggests that marketers of goods are also marketers of services. For example, one could argue that McDonalds is not in the hamburger business. Its hamburgers are actually not very different from those of the competition. McDonalds is in the service business: ". . . you deserve a break today, . . . we do it all for you . . . "[5] In fact, a recent study found that the quality of a company's service can cause it to gain or lose as much as 10 percent in sales revenue.[6] Services, which accompany products, can affect sales in two ways: (1) directly, by enhancing the reliability of product availability; and (2) indirectly, by increasing a buyer's preference for and loyalty to a supplier that provides reliable service with fewer problems.[7] Honda, Apple, and Merck are prime examples of companies which build their strategies not around products but around deep knowledge of highly developed core service strategies, such as: (1) stressing senior management involvement with customers; (2) going all out to resolve customer complaints; and (3) placing an emphasis on retaining current customers.[8]

More and more manufacturers are also exploiting their service capabilities as a stand-alone revenue producer.[9] For example, General Motors, Ford, and Chrysler all offer financing services. General Electric has extended its financial service offerings to include a MasterCard, which offers discounts at major

---

[4]Peter D. Bennett, ed. *Dictionary of Marketing Terms* (Chicago: American Marketing Association, 1988), p. 21.

[5]Carolyn R. Fryer, "What's Different About Services Marketing," *Journal of Services Marketing,* Fall 1991, pp. 53–58.

[6]Harry N. Shycon, "Improved Customer Service: Measuring the Payoff," *The Journal of Business Strategy,* January/February 1992, pp. 13–17.

[7]Ibid.

[8]For a discussion of customer service in product companies, see A. Lynn Daniel, "Overcome the Barriers to Superior Customer Service," *The Journal of Business Strategy,* January/February 1992, pp. 18–24; and James Brian Quinn, Thomas L. Doorley, and Penny C. Paquette, "Beyond Products: Services-Based Strategies," *Harvard Business Review,* March-April 1990, pp. 58–67.

[9]James Brian Quinn, Jordan J. Baruch, and Penny C. Paquette, "Exploiting the Manufacturing-Service Interface," *Sloan Management Review,* Summer 1988, pp. 45–56.

retailers and service companies, along with rebates for purchasing GE appliances.[10] Likewise, Sears introduced the Discover Card, which was not positioned as a direct competitor to Visa and MasterCard.

IMPORTANT CHARACTERISTICS OF SERVICES

Services possess several unique characteristics that often have a significant impact on marketing program development. These special features of services may cause unique problems and often result in marketing mix decisions that are substantially different from those found in connection with the marketing of goods. Some of the more important of these characteristics are intangibility, inseparability, perishability and fluctuating demand, highly differentiated marketing systems, and a client relationship.

Intangibility

The obvious basic difference between goods and services is the intangibility of services, and many of the problems encountered in the marketing of services are due to the intangibility. To illustrate, how does an airline make tangible a trip from Philadelphia to San Francisco? These problems are unique to service marketing.

The fact that many services cannot appeal to a buyer's sense of touch, taste, smell, sight, or hearing before purchase places a burden on the marketing organization. For example, hotels that promise a good night's sleep to their customers cannot actually show this service in a tangible way. Obviously, this burden is most heavily felt in a firm's promotional program, but, as will be discussed later, it may affect other areas. Depending on the type of service, the intangibility factor may dictate use of distribution channels because of the need for personal contact between the buyer and seller. Since a service firm is actually selling an idea or experience, not a product, it must tell the buyer what the service will do because it is often difficult to illustrate, demonstrate, or display the service in use. For example, the hotel must somehow describe to the consumer how a stay at the hotel will leave the customer feeling well rested and ready to begin a new day. NYNEX, one of the Bell Operating Companies, recently ran a television advertising campaign, called "How it Works," that focused on making kids and adults more at ease with technology.[11] As these consumers' comfort level with technology rises and they understand how, for example, cellular phones can benefit their lives, NYNEX expects their willingness to adopt emerging technologies to also increase.

---

[10]Gary Levin, "GE Will Tap Riney for Card's Media Launch," *Advertising Age,* September 7, 1992, p. 37.

[11]Terry Lefton, "NYNEX Tries to Explain Itself," *Adweeks's Marketing Week,* April 27, 1992, p. 8.

HIGHLIGHT 12–1

Seven of the Most Critical Differences Between Products and Services

Products	**Services**
1. The customer owns an object.	**1.** The customer owns a memory. The experience cannot be sold or passed on to a third party.
2. The goal of product producing is uniformity—all widgets are alike.	**2.** The goal of service is uniqueness; each customer and each contact is "special."
3. A product can be put into inventory; a sample can be sent in advance for the customer to review.	**3.** A service happens in the moment. It cannot be stockpiled.
4. The customer is an end user who is not involved in the production process.	**4.** The customer is a coproducer who is a partner in creating the service.
5. One conducts quality control by comparing output to specifications.	**5.** Customers conduct quality control by comparing expectations to experience.
6. If improperly produced, the product can be pulled off the line or "recalled."	**6.** If improperly performed, apologies and reparations are the only means of recourse.
7. The morale of production employees is important.	**7.** The morale of service employees is critical.

Source: Ron Zemke, "The Emerging Art of Service Management," *Training,* January 1992, pp. 36–42.

Inseparability

In many cases, a service cannot be separated from the person of the seller. In other words, the service must often be created and marketed simultaneously. Because of the simultaneous production and marketing of most services, the main concern of the marketer is usually the creation of time and place utility. For example, the barber produces the service of a haircut and markets it at the same time. Many services, therefore, are "tailored" and nonmass-produced. Because a company's employees are "the company" at the point of customer contact, they must be given wide latitude in determining how best to tailor a specific service to meet a particular customer's needs.[12]

The implications of inseparability on issues dealing with the selection of channels of distribution and service quality are quite important. Inseparable services cannot be inventoried, and thus direct sale is the only feasible channel of distribution. Service quality is unable to be completely standardized due to

---

[12]Craig Cina, "Five Steps to Service Excellence," *The Journal of Services Marketing,* Spring 1990, pp. 39–47.

HIGHLIGHT 12–2

Expectations of Service Customers in Selected Industries

Type of Service	Type of Customer	Principal Expectations
Automobile repair	Consumers	*Be competent.* "Fix it right the first time." *Explain things.* "Explain why you need the suggested repairs—provide an itemized list." *Be respectful.* "Don't treat me as a dumb female."
Automobile insurance	Consumers	*Keep me informed.* "I shouldn't have to learn about insurance law changes from the newspaper." *Be on my side.* "I don't want them to treat me like I am a criminal just because I have a claim." *Play fair.* "Don't drop me when something goes wrong." *Protect me from catastrophe.* "Make sure my estate is covered in the event of a major accident." *Provide prompt service.* "I want fast settlement of my claims."
Hotel	Consumers	*Provide a clean room.* "Don't have a deep-pile carpet that can't be completely cleaned. . . . You can literally see germs down there." *Provide a secure room.* "Good bolts and peephole on door." *Treat me like a guest.* "It is almost like they're looking you over to decide whether or not they're going to let you have a room." *Keep your promise.* "They said the room would be ready, but it wasn't at the promised time."

Source: A. Parasuraman, Leonard L. Berry, and Valarie A. Zeithaml, "Understanding Customer Expectations of Service," *Sloan Management Review,* Spring 1991, pp. 39–48.

---

the inability to mechanize the service encounter. In fact, until recently most service firms did not differentiate between the production and marketing of services and, in many cases, viewed the two as equivalent.

Some industries have been able to modify the inseparability characteristics. In some industries, there may be a tangible representation of the service, such as a contract, by someone other than the producer. In other words, if tangible representations of the service are transferrable, various intermediaries, like agents, can be utilized. The reader is probably familiar with this practice in the marketing of insurance. The service itself remains inseparable from the seller, but the buyer has a tangible representation of the service in the form of a policy. This enables the use of intermediaries in the marketing of insurance.

Type of Service	Type of Customer	Principal Expectations
Property and casualty insurance	Business customers	*Fulfill obligations.* "Pay up." *Learn my business and work with me.* "I expect them to know me and my company." *Protect me from catastrophe.* "They should cover your risk exposure so there is no single big loss." *Provide prompt service.* "Fast claim service."
Equipment repair	Business customers	*Share my sense of urgency.* "Speed of response. One time I had to buy a second piece of equipment because of the huge downtime with the first piece." *Be competent.* "Sometimes you are quoting stuff from their instruction manuals to their own people and they don't even know what it means." *Be prepared.* "Have all the parts ready."
Truck and tractor rental/ leasing	Business customers	*Keep the equipment running.* "Need to have equipment working all the time—that is the key." *Be flexible.* "The leasing company should have the flexibility to rent us equipment when we need it." *Provide full service.* "Get rid of all the paperwork and headaches."

Another example would be in the use of a credit card, whereby the card itself is a tangible representation of a service that is being produced and consumed each time the card is used.

Technology has also aided service companies by allowing for separability between the production and delivery of services. To illustrate, a well-designed voice mail system allows companies and callers to cut down on missed phone calls, eliminate long waits on hold, deliver clear, consistent messages, and answer routine calls automatically. In essence, the service delivery, the passing of the message to the appropriate party, has been separated from the production, creation, and storage of the message. More will be said about the distribution of services later in the chapter.

Perishability and Fluctuating Demand

Services are perishable, and markets for most services fluctuate either by season (tourism), days (airlines), or time of day (movie theaters). Unused telephone capacity and electrical power; vacant seats on planes, trains, busses and in stadiums; and time spent by bank tellers waiting for customers to use their window represent business that is lost forever.

The combination of perishability and fluctuating demand has created many problems for marketers of services. Specifically, in the area of distribution, channels must be found to have the services available for peak periods, and new channels and strategies must be developed to make use of the service during slack periods. Many firms are attempting to cope with these problems, and several innovations in the distribution of services have occurred in recent years. For example, many electric utilities no longer build to a capacity that will meet peak electrical demand. Instead, they rely on an intricate system of buying unused power from other utilities in other regions of the country. Likewise, to stimulate demand for unused capacity, many downtown hotels offer significant discounts to travelers who stay over on weekends.

Highly Differentiated Marketing Systems

Although the marketer of a tangible product is not compelled to use an established marketing system, such systems often are available and may be the most efficient. If an established system is not available, the marketer can at least obtain guidelines from the systems used for similar products. In the case of services, however, there may be little similarity between the marketing systems needed and those used for other services. To illustrate, the marketing of banking and other financial services bears little resemblance to the marketing of computer services, airlines, or telecommunications. The entire area of service marketing, therefore, demands greater creativity and ingenuity on the part of marketing management. For example, J.B. Hunt Transport Services, a trucking company, made an arrangement with Santa Fe Railway to combine forces on some routes. This enabled J.B. Hunt's customers to take advantage of the cheaper fuel and labor associated with rail transport, coupled with the faster, more reliable service offered by trucks.[13] Likewise, Bank One laid out its financial center near Columbus, Ohio, like a shopping mall, complete with rock music and neon signs.[14] To reach the tellers, customers walk past minishops selling such offerings as real estate, travel services, and discount stockbrokerage services.

---

[13]Sally Solo, "Every Problem is an Opportunity," *Fortune,* November 16, 1992, p. 93.

[14]Terence P. Pare, "Banks Discover the Consumer," *Fortune,* February 12, 1990, pp. 96–104.

Client Relationship

In the marketing of a great many services, a client relationship exists between the buyer and the seller, as opposed to a customer relationship. Examples of this type of relationship are the physician-patient and the financial institution-investor relationships. The buyer abides by the suggestions or advice provided by the seller, and these relationships may be of an ongoing nature. Also, since many service firms are client-serving organizations, they may approach the marketing function in a more professional manner, as seen in health care, financial, legal, governmental, and educational services. For example, lawyers and physicians do not utilize comparative advertising where one firm's or physician's services are compared against a named competitor. In fact, since 1990, the American Bar Association has barred attorneys from airing television commercials that use dramatizations, testimonials, music, jingles, or multiple voices.[15]

Several recent studies on service marketing by professionals serves to highlight two challenges professional face.[16] First, in many cases, fear or hostility is brought to the purchase because the customer is uncertain about how genuine the professional's concern for his or her satisfaction is. For example, many unpleasant reasons exist for consulting doctors, lawyers, or bankers. These could include surgery, being sued, or having to take out a loan. Second, even high-quality service delivery by the professional can lead to dissatisfied customers. For a physician, the ability to provide quality medical care may be overshadowed by a brusque, unfriendly personality. It is vitally important that the professional service providers strive to build long-term, positive relationships with clients. Highlight 12–3 exhibits one possible means by which such a relationship can be established.

Service Quality

The issue of service quality is one of paramount importance to all service providers. In a recent study, more than 40 percent of all customers surveyed listed poor service as the number one reason for switching to the competition, while only 8 percent listed price as a reason for switching.[17] According to the same study, it is easier and five times cheaper to keep an existing customer

---

[15]Jeffery, D. Zbar, "Fla. Judge Rules for Lawyer Ad Limits," *Advertising Age,* October 12, 1992, p. 38.

[16]For a full discussion of problems faced in marketing professional services, see Christopher W. L. Hart, Leonard A. Schlesinger, and Don Maher, "Guarantees Come to Professional Service Firms," *Sloan Management Review,* Spring 1992, pp. 19–29; Gabriel R. Bitran and Johannes Hoech, "The Humanization of Service: Respect at the Moment of Truth," *Sloan Management Review,* Winter 1990, pp. 89–96; and Betsy D. Gelb, Samuel V. Smith, and Gabriel M. Gelb, "Service Marketing Lessons from the Professionals," *Business Horizons,* September–October 1988, pp. 29–34.

[17]For further details and discussion, see Frank K. Sonnenberg, "Service Quality: Forethought, Not Afterthought," *The Journal of Business Strategy,* September/October 1989, pp. 54–57.

HIGHLIGHT 12–3

Five Circumstances Which Make the Use of Unconditional Guarantees by Professional Service Providers an Effective Marketing Tool

1. *Prices are too high.* Fees for management consulting, legal, advertising, and many other types of professional service firms often run into six figures. By offering compensation for a service failure, the guarantee reduces perceived risk and creates value for clients.
2. *The negative consequences of unsolved problems are high.* Bad service from a restaurant can ruin someone's evening; bad service from a medical center or law firm can ruin someone's life. The greater the client's expected aggravation, expense, and time lost, the greater the guarantee's power.
3. *Services are highly customized.* The professional service firm's past performance with other buyers typically does not provide a reliable indication of how the firm will do with a new project, since different customers are often served in entirely different ways. A guarantee can provide a strong indication of a firm's reliability.
4. *Brand name recognition isn't easily achieved through conventional means.* Marketing opportunities and differentiating characteristics tend to be restricted for professional service firms. An unconditional guarantee can provide such a differentiator, making the firm stand out in potential clients' minds.
5. *Buyer resistance is high.* Clients tend to purchase professional services very cautiously, which sends the firm on long and often fruitless sales efforts. An unconditional guarantee can effectively overcome resistance and close the sale.

Source: Christopher W. L. Hart, Leonard A. Schlessinger, and Dan Maher, "Guarantees Come to Professional Service Firms," *Sloan Management Review,* Spring 1992, pp. 19–29.

than to recruit a new one. Unlike products where quality is often measured against accepted standards, service quality is measured against performance.[18] Since services are frequently produced in the presence of a customer, are labor intensive, and are not able to be stored or objectively examined, the definition and measurement of what constitutes good service quality can be difficult. In

---

[18]The material in this section draws from research performed by Leonard L. Berry, Valerie A. Zeithaml, and A. Parasuraman, "Quality Counts in Services, Too," *Business Horizons,* May–June 1985, pp. 44–52; A. Parasuraman, Valerie A. Zeithaml, and Leonard L. Berry, "A Conceptual Model of Service Quality and Its Implications for Future Research," *Journal of Marketing,* Fall 1985, pp. 41–50; Leonard L. Berry, A. Parasuraman, and Valerie A. Zeithaml, "The Service-Quality Puzzle," *Business Horizons,* September–October 1988, pp. 35–43; Stephen W. Brown and Teresa A. Swartz, "A Gap Analysis of Professional Service Quality," *Journal of Marketing,* April 1989, pp. 92–98; Leonard L. Berry, Valerie A. Zeithmal, and A. Parasuraman, "Five Imperatives for Improving Service Quality," *Sloan Management Review,* Summer 1990, pp. 29–38; and A. Parasuraman, Leonard L. Berry, and Valerie A. Zeithaml, "Understanding Customer Expectations of Service," *Sloan Management Review,* Spring 1991, pp. 39–48.

general, problems in the determination of good service quality are attributable to differences in the expectations, perceptions, and experiences regarding the service encounter between the service provider and user. These gaps can be classified as:

1. The gap between consumer expectations and management perceptions of the consumer's expectations.
2. The gap between management perceptions of consumer expectations and the firm's service quality specifications.
3. The gap between service quality specifications and actual service quality.
4. The gap between actual service delivery and external communications about the service.

In essence, the customer perceives the level of service quality as being a function of the magnitude and direction of the gap between expected service and perceived service. Management of a company may not even realize that they are delivering poor-quality service due to differences in the way managers and consumers view acceptable quality levels. To overcome this problem and to avoid losing customers, firms must be aware of the determinants of service quality. A brief description of these determinants follows.

1. *Reliability* involves consistency of performance and dependability. For example, does a bank always send out accurate customer statements?
2. *Responsiveness* concerns the willingness or readiness of employees to provide service. For example, will a physician see patients on the same day they call in to say they are ill?
3. *Competence* means possession of the necessary skills and knowledge to perform the service. For example, is a bank teller able to give a prospective borrower the name and location of the appropriate loan officer?
4. *Access* involves approachability and ease of contact. For example, banks and other services that have weekend operations are more accessible than those that do not.
5. *Courtesy* involves politeness, respect, consideration, and friendliness of contact personnel.
6. *Communication* means keeping customers informed in language they can understand. It also means listening to customers. For example, a hotel clerk explains in a polite manner why a guest's room is not ready yet.
7. *Credibility* involves trustworthiness, believability, and honesty. For example, a bank's reputation may be built on an ability to always process loans within a promised time period.
8. *Security* is the freedom from danger, risk, or doubt. For example, a telephone company offers 20-minute responses to service calls or a bank offers bounce-proof checking accounts.
9. *Understanding* the customer involves making the effort to understand the customer's needs. For example, flight attendants on a customer's regular route learn what types of beverages the customer drinks.

10. *Tangibles* include the physical evidence of the service. For example, employees are always visible in a hotel lobby dusting, emptying ashtrays, or otherwise cleaning up.

Each of the above determinants plays an important role in how the customer views the service quality of a firm. Turning service quality into a powerful competitive weapon requires continuous striving for service superiority— consistently performing above the adequate service level and capitalizing on opportunities for exceeding the desired service level.[19] Relentless efforts to continually improve service performance may well be rewarded by improvements in customer attitudes toward the firm: from customer frustration to customer preference to intense customer loyalty.[20] What should be obvious is that in order to to be successful, a service firm must have dedicated employees.

The Importance of Internal Marketing

Service quality goes beyond the relationship between a customer and a company. Rather, it is the personal relationship between a customer and the particular employee that the customer happens to be dealing with at the time of the service encounter.[21] The above statement underlies the importance of having customer-oriented, frontline people.[22] If frontline service personnel are unfriendly, unhelpful, uncooperative, or uninterested in the customer, the customer will tend to project that same attitude on the company as a whole. The character and personality of an organization reflects the character and personality of its top management.[23] Management must develop programs that will stimulate employee commitment to customer service. In order to be successful, these programs must contain five critical components:

1. A careful selection process in hiring frontline employees. In order to do this, management has to clearly define the skills the service person must bring to the job.[24] For example, Fairfield Inn often considers as many as 25 candidates for each housekeeping or front desk position.[25]

---

[19]A. Parasuraman, Leonard L. Berry, and Valerie A. Zeithaml, "Understanding Customer Expectations of Service," Spring 1991, pp. 39–48.

[20]Ibid.

[21]William A. Sheldon, "Gaining the Service Quality Advantage," *The Journal of Business Strategy*, March/April 1988, pp. 45–48.

[22]Much of the material for this section was taken from Karl Albrecht and Ron Zemke, *Service America* (Homewood, Ill.: Dow-Jones Irwin, 1985), and Ron Zemke and Dick Schaaf, *The Service Edge 101 Companies That Profit from Customer Care*, (New York: New American Library, 1989).

[23]Charles E. Cox, "18 Ways to Improve Customer Service," *HR Magazine*, March 1992, pp. 69–72.

[24]Chip R. Bell and Kristen Anderson, "Selecting Super Service People," *HR Magazine*, February 1992, pp. 52–54.

[25]James A. Schlesinger and James L. Heskett, "Breaking the Cycle of Failure in Services," *Sloan Management Review*, Spring 1991, pp. 17–28.

2. A clear, concrete message that conveys a particular service strategy that frontline people can begin to act on. People delivering service need to know how their work fits in the broader scheme of business operations.[26] They need to have a cause because servicing others is just too demanding and frustrating to be done well each day without one.[27]

3. Significant modeling by managers, that is, managers demonstrating the behavior that they intend to reward employees for performing. For example, Virgin Atlantic Airways Chairman Richard Branson regularly travels economy class on his airline to talk to customers and solicit ideas for improvement.[28]

4. An energetic follow-through process, in which managers provide the training, support, and incentives necessary to give the employees the capability and willingness to provide quality service. For example, NYNEX offers its employees the Chairman's Award for World Class Service and provides extensive training in process management to help them attain it.[29]

5. An emphasis on teaching employees to have good attitudes. This type of training usually focuses on specific social techniques, such as eye contact, smiling, tone of voice, and standards of dress.

However, organizing and implementing such programs will only lead to temporary results unless managers practice a strategy of internal marketing. The authors define internal marketing as "the continual process by which managers actively encourage, stimulate, and support employee commitment to the company, the company's goods and services, and the company's customers." Emphasis should be placed on the word *continual*. Managers who consistently pitch in to help when needed, constantly provide encouragement and words of praise to employees, strive to help employees understand the benefits of performing their jobs well, and emphasize the importance of employee actions on both company and employee results are practitioners of internal marketing. In service marketing, successful internal marketing efforts, leading to employee commitment to service quality, are the key to prosperity.

Federal Express serves as a prime example of the benefits accruing to a company which successfully practices internal marketing.[30] In 1990, Federal Express became the first service organization to win the Malcom Baldridge

---

[26]Leonard L. Berry and A. Parasuraman, "Services Marketing Starts From Within," *Marketing Management,* Winter 1992, pp. 25–34.

[27]Ibid.

[28]Leonard L. Berry and A. Parasuraman, "Prescriptions for a Service Quality Revolution in America," *Organizational Dynamics,* Spring 1992, pp. 5–15.

[29]Richard B. Chase and Robert H. Hayes, "Beefing Up Operations in Service Firms," *Sloan Management Review,* Fall 1991, pp. 15–26.

[30]This example is from David E. Bowen and Edward E. Lawler III, "The Empowerment of Service Workers: What, Why, How, and When," *Sloan Management Review,* Spring 1992, pp. 31–39.

National Quality Award. The company's motto is "people, service, and profits." Behind its blue, white, and red planes and uniforms are self-managing work teams, gainsharing plans, and empowered employees seemingly consumed with providing flexible and creative services to customers with varying needs. Federal Express is a high-involvement, horizontally coordinated organization which encourages employees to use their judgment above and beyond the rulebook.

OVERCOMING THE OBSTACLES IN SERVICE MARKETING

The factors of intangibility and inseparability, as well as difficulties in coming up with objective definitions of acceptable service quality make comprehension of service marketing extremely difficult. However, in view of the size and importance of services in our economy, considerable innovation and ingenuity are needed to make high-quality services available at convenient locations for consumers as well as business people. In fact, the area of service marketing probably offers more opportunities for imagination and creative innovation than does product marketing.

Unfortunately, in the past most service firms have lagged in the area of creative marketing. Even those service firms that have done a relatively good marketing job have been extremely slow in recognizing opportunities in all aspects of their marketing programs. Five reasons can be given for this past lack of innovative marketing on the part of service industries: (1) a limited view of marketing; (2) a lack of competition; (3) a lack of creative management; (4) no obsolescence; and (5) a lack of innovation in the distribution of services.

Limited View of Marketing

Because of the nature of their service, many firms depended to a great degree on population growth to expand sales. A popular example here is the telephone company, which did not establish a marketing department until 1955. It was then that the company realized it had to be concerned not only with population growth, but also with meeting the needs of a growing population. Increases in educational levels and rises in the standards of living also bring about the need for new and diversified services. A study conducted by *American Demographics* concluded that college-educated householders are much more likely to buy services—from dry cleaning to financial services—than those with less education.[31] As a well-educated, younger generation replaces the less educated, older one, the demand for services will only increase.

---

[31]Judith Waldrop, "Spending by Degree," *American Demographics,* February 1990, pp. 22–26.

Service firms must meet these changing needs by developing new services and new channels, and altering existing channels, to meet the changing composition and needs of the population. For many service industries, growth has come as a result of finding new channels of distribution. For example, some banks and other financial service companies were able to grow and tap into new markets by establishing limited service kiosks in malls and supermarkets. Airlines have successfully brought in a whole new class of travelers by offering advance-purchase discounted fares. Traditionally, users of these fares either drove or utilized other means of transportation in order to reach their destination.

While many service firms have succeeded in adopting a marketing perspective, others have been slow to respond. It was not until deregulation of the telecommunications industry took place in 1984 that the telephone companies began taking a broadened view of marketing. Even today, critics of these companies point to the obsession with inventing new technology versus using current technology in meeting customer needs as a weakness of these companies. To illustrate, many of these companies began marketing a service called an integrated services digital network (ISDN). Two years after this service came on the market, a majority of potential customers still were not aware of what the service could do and whether and how they could use it.

Limited Competition

A second major cause of the lack of innovative marketing in many service industries was due to the lack of competition. Many service industries, like banking, railroads, and public utilities have, throughout most of their histories, faced very little competition; some have even been regulated monopolies. Obviously, in an environment characterized by little competition, there was not likely to be a great deal of innovative marketing. However, two major forces have recently changed this situation. First, in the past two decades the banking, financial services, railroad, cable, airline, and telecommunications industries have all been deregulated in varying degrees. With deregulation has come a need to be able to compete effectively. For example, AT&T was once the sole provider of long-distance telephone service. Now, AT&T has to compete against such companies as MCI and U.S. Sprint, who to a large degree owe their success to the savvy use of marketing skills. Second, service marketing has taken on an international focus. Today, many foreign companies are competing in domestic service markets. Foreign interests own several banks, many hotels (including Holiday Inn), and shares in major airlines (including Northwest). Likewise, American companies are expanding overseas as markets open up. Each of the seven regional Bell Operating Companies has an equity stake in either cellular, cable television, or telephone network systems in Europe. In the 1990s, the amount of competition facing service companies will continue to increase as the world becomes more and more of a global market.

Noncreative Management

For many years, the managements of service industries have been criticized for not being progressive and creative. Railroad management was criticized for many years for being slow to innovate. More recently, however, railroads have become leading innovators in the field of freight transportation, introducing such innovations as piggyback service and containerization and in passenger service, introducing luxury overnight accommodations on trains with exotic names such as the Zephyr. Some other service industries, however, have been slow to develop new services or to innovate in the marketing of their existing services. In fact, as a whole, U.S. firms currently lag behind their Japanese and German competitors not only in collecting customer satisfaction data, but in also designing services which address customer's functional needs.[32]

No Obsolescence

A great advantage for many service industries is the fact that many services, because of their intangibility, are less subject to obsolescence than goods. While this is an obvious advantage, it has also led some service firms to be sluggish in their approach to marketing. Manufacturers of goods may constantly change their marketing plans and seek new and more efficient ways to produce and distribute their products. Since service firms are often not faced with obsolescence, they often failed to recognize the need for change. This failure has led to wholesale changes in many industries as new operators, who possessed marketing skills, revolutionized the manner in which the service is performed and provided. Many a barbershop and hair dresser have gone out of business due to an inability to compete against the new wave of hairstyling salons. Many accountants have lost clients to tax preparation services such as H&R Block that specialize in doing one task well and have used technology, including computerized filing services, to their advantage. Likewise, the old, big, movie house has become a relic of the past as entrepreneurs realized the advantages to be gained from building and operating theater complexes that contain several minitheaters in or near suburban malls.

A Lack of Innovation in the Distribution of Services

As discussed in Chapter 10, the channel of distribution is viewed as the sequence of firms involved in moving a product from the producer to the user. The channel may be direct, as in the case where the manufacturer sells directly to the ultimate consumer, or it may contain one or more institutional interme-

---

[32]Howard Schlossberg, "Study: U.S. Firms Lag in Using Customer Satisfaction Data," *Marketing News,* June 1992, p. 14.

diaries. Some of the intermediaries assume risks of ownership, some perform various marketing functions, such as advertising, while others may perform nonmarketing or facilitating functions, such as transporting and warehousing.[33]

Apparently using this concept as a frame of reference, most marketing writers generalize that, because of the intangible and inseparable nature of services, direct sale is the only possible channel for distributing most services. The only traditional indirect channel used involves one agent intermediaries. This channel is used in the distribution of such services as securities, housing, entertainment, insurance, and labor. In some cases, individuals are trained in the production of the service and franchised to sell it, as in the case of dance studios and employment agencies. It is noted that, because they are intangible, services cannot be stored, transported, or inventoried; and since they cannot be separated from the person of the seller, they must be created and distributed simultaneously. Finally, because there is no physical product, traditional wholesalers and other intermediaries can rarely operate in such markets and retailing cannot be an independent activity. For these reasons, it is generally concluded that the geographic area in which most service marketers can operate is restricted.

All of these generalizations are certainly true, using the concept of "channels of distribution" developed for goods. However, the practice of viewing the distribution of services using the framework developed for goods has severely limited thinking. It has focused attention away from understanding the problem and identifying the means to overcome the handicaps of intangibility and inseparability. Most important, however, it has led to a failure to distinguish conceptually between the production and distribution of services; hence, it supports the idea that services must be created and distributed simultaneously. This had resulted in a lack of attention to channel decisions for producers of services.

THE SERVICE CHALLENGE

Despite traditional thinking and practices on the part of many marketing managers and writers concerning the similarities between the operation of manufacturing and services organizations, the past decade has seen the growth of many innovative ways of meeting the service challenge. The service challenge is the quest to: (1) constantly develop new services that will better meet customer needs; (2) improve upon the quality and variety of existing services;

---

[33]This section of the chapter draws from James H. Donnelly, Jr., "Marketing Intermediaries in Channels of Distribution for Services," *Journal of Marketing,* January 1976, pp. 55–57; and James H. Donnelly, Jr., and Joseph P. Guiltinan, "Selecting Channels of Distribution for Services," in *Handbook of Modern Marketing,* ed. Victor P. Buell (New York: McGraw-Hill, 1986), chap. 24.

and (3) provide and distribute these services in a manner that best serves the customer. This next section illustrates successful examples of innovation in various service industries where companies have met the service challenge.

Banking

The days when banking was considered a dead-end career for marketers are over. Perhaps the area of banking best exemplifies the changes that are taking place as service organizations begin to become practitioners of the "marketing concept." In recent years, the banking industry has been very active in the development of new retail banking services, particularly those using technology or more sophisticated hardware and data processing systems. Direct pay deposit allows employees of businesses and recipients of social security to have their pay deposited directly into their checking accounts. Likewise, direct payment programs allow customers to have payments for such services as Blue Cross and Blue Shield, car loans, and utility bills deducted automatically from their checking accounts.

On another front, Bank of America is developing an expert system that will allow service reps to think like expert problem solvers.[34] Problems that used to take over a month to be solved can be taken care of in two weeks. In many banks, computers allow customers to access account information via their telephone on a 24-hour-a-day basis. Using a telephone's push buttons, customers can get information on account balances, mortgage rates, and other services and also stop payment on checks. Computers also allow for platform automation, enabling bankers in any branch to bring up on a screen all the information the bank has about the customer. Every face-to-face contact with a customer can now mean an opportunity to make a sale and further the relationship with the customer.

Banks have also learned the value of bundling services. For example, NCNB of Charlotte, North Carolina, offers a Financial Connections account that combines checking, savings, credit card, and auto loan features. Benefits to the customer include free ATM transactions, interest-bearing checking accounts, no-fee credit cards, and the convenience of one-stop banking. In addition, the bank offers preapproved auto loans and cash flow statements. Most banks also offer targeted marketing activities towards senior citizens, which may include discount coupons for entertainment, travel newsletters, and lower monthly minimum required balances.

Citicorp was the first bank to create a national marketing unit for its retail bank operations.[35] The goal of such a unit is to create a "brand approach" to banking whereby a consistent product lineup is available nationwide. By con-

---

[34]Much of the material on the marketing activities of banks was taken from Terence P. Pare, "Banks Discover the Consumer," *Fortune*, February 12, 1990, pp. 96–104.

[35]Judith Graham, "Citicorp Bets on McBanking," *Advertising Age*, June 5, 1989, pp. 3, 72.

solidating branch marketing activities, Citicorp is able to enjoy economies of scale, which, until recently, eluded banks, with a presence in many regional markets. Citicorp opted for such an approach after finding that highly satisfied branch banking customers increased their business nearly 50 percent more than less satisfied customers.[36] Banks have also begun extensive promotion campaigns. Numerous banks offer low initial loan rates and run sweepstakes and other seasonal promotions in conjunction with credit card companies that give consumers a chance to win each time they charge a purchase. In addition, many new banks now offer affinity cards, such as the NationsBank USAIR card which allows customers to accumulate frequent flier miles with each purchase made using the card.[37]

Competition in banking will continue to intensify as most states remove barriers to interstate banking. It is estimated that, by the end of the decade, the number of financial institutions will be cut in half as the larger banks expand.[38] The banks that survive will be those who best mastered the skills of service marketing.

Health care

The distribution of health care services is of vital concern. In health care delivery, the inseparability characteristic presents more of a handicap than in other service industries because users (patients) literally place themselves in the hands of the seller. However, although direct personal contact between producer and user is often necessary, new and more efficient channels of distribution appear to be evolving.

While medical care is traditionally associated with the solo practice, fee-for-service system, several alternative delivery systems have been developed. One method is the health maintenance organization (HMO) concept. This type of delivery system stresses the creation of group health care clinics using teams of salaried health practitioners (physicians, pharmacists, technicians, and so forth) that serve a specific enrolled membership on a prepaid basis.

The HMO performs an intermediary role between practitioner and patient. It increases availability and convenience by providing a central location and "one-stop shopping." For example, a member can visit a general practitioner for a particular ailment and undergo treatment by the appropriate specialist in the same visit. The HMO also assumes responsibility for arranging for or providing hospital care, emergency care, and preventive services. In addition,

---

[36] "How Does Service Drive the Service Company." *Harvard Business Review*, November–December 1991, pp. 146–58.

[37] For a discussion of trends in credit cards, see "Pushing Plastic is Still One Juicy Game," *Business Week*, September 21, 1992.

[38] "Consultant Predicts Bank Crisis for this Decade," *Marketing News*, February 5, 1990, p. 8.

the prepaid nature of the program encourages more frequent preventive visits, while the traditional philosophy of medical care is primarily remedial. HMO programs have inspired similar innovations in other phases of health care, such as dentistry.[39]

The health care industry is becoming highly competitive. Due to a large increase in the number of available beds coupled with government tightening of hospital stay and payment policies, many hospitals are plagued by problems of overcapacity. An estimated 440 hospitals are expected to close by 1996.[40] In order to cope with these problems, some hospitals are beginning to implement customer satisfaction programs and are developing innovative marketing programs. For example, the Humana Hospital chain offers a Center of Excellence at each of its member hospitals. Each Center of Excellence specializes in treating a specific type of illness. To illustrate, the Center of Excellence in Humana's hospital in Lexington, Kentucky, specializes in the treatment of diabetes. In this way, Humana reaps the benefits of economies of scale. Other hospitals have begun targeting specific groups of the population including expectant mothers, senior citizens, and those persons with alcohol or other chemical dependency problems. For example, Edmond Regional Medical Center in Edmond, Oklahoma, developed an advertising campaign targeted at expectant mothers which conveyed the benefits of giving birth at a small hospital where the emphasis is on personalized care.[41] Current trends show hospitals and other health providers becoming more and more market oriented as they try to differentiate their offerings from those of the competition.

Insurance

In recent years, the insurance industry has exploded with new product and service offerings. Not too long ago, customers were faced with limited options in choosing life, hospital, or auto insurance. Now, there is a wide array of insurance policies to choose from, including universal life policies, which double as retirement savings, nursing care insurance, reversible mortgages, which allow people to take equity from their house while still living in it, and other offerings aimed at serving an aging population. To illustrate, Prudential Insurance Company offers a program whereby terminally ill policyholders are allowed to withdraw funds against the face value of their policy while still

---

[39]For a discussion of problems associated with and trends affecting HMOs and other forms of managed care, see Lee Smith, "The Right Cure for Health Care," *Fortune,* October 19, 1992, pp. 88–89; Lynn G. Coleman, "Total Quality Management Prescribed as a Cure for Health Care Ailments," *Marketing News,* May 11, 1992, pp. 5, 8. Lynn G. Coleman, "Bottom-Line Focus Considered Fatal in Health Care," *Marketing News,* May 11, 1992, pp. 1, 18.

[40]Michelle Holleran, "Most Hospitals Measure Satisfaction Incorrectly," *Marketing News,* September 14, 1992, p. 4.

[41]Judith Schwartz, "Birth of a Marketing Trend: Consumerism Comes to OB/GYN," *Brandweek,* September 21, 1992, pp. 57–58.

alive. In addition to insurance services, most insurance companies now offer a full range of financial services including auto loans, mortgages, mutual funds, and certificates of deposit.

Distribution of insurance services has also been growing. The vending machines found in airports for aircraft insurance have been finding their way into other areas. Travel auto insurance is now available in many motel chains and through the American Automobile Association. Group insurance written through employers and labor unions also has been extremely successful. In each instance, the insurance industry has used intermediaries to distribute its services.

Travel

The travel industry, most notably the airlines, has been a leader in the use of technology. Computerized reservation systems allow customers to book plane tickets from home or work. Travel agents, who act as intermediaries in the channel of distribution, are conveniently located and easy to access. Technology has also allowed airlines to make strategic pricing decisions through the use of yield management.[42] In yield management, certain seats on aircraft are discounted and certain seats aren't. Through the use of computer programs, managers are able to determine who their customer segments are and who is likely to purchase airline tickets when and to where.

Airlines are also beginning to utilize their technology and reservation systems for promotional purposes. Currently, American Airlines is exploring new ways to offer on-line advertising on its sophisticated Sabre computerized reservation system.[43] Sabre now offers short, copy-only paid ads that appear at the top of the travel agent's screen when the agent signs on. But American is exploring means to offer new ads when the travel agent books a flight. For example, under one scenario, if a traveler wants flight information from New York to San Francisco, the reservation system might automatically display an ad for various tourist attractions in San Francisco. At Northwest Airlines, their *World Traveler* magazine is using fax-on-demand to give customers advertising information.[44] Readers of *World Traveler* simply call an 800 number, enter the product code they desire information on, and their fax number. Information on the desired product is then faxed back to the reader by the advertiser.

Recent experiences in the lodging industry point out potential opportunities and pitfalls in service branding strategies.[45] Marriott, one of the most respected

[42]"What's Ahead for Travel Industry," *Advertising Age,* January 22, 1990, pp. 20–22.

[43]Jennifer Lawrence, "Airlines See Ad $ in Reservation Systems," *Advertising Age,* June 15, 1992, p. 42.

[44]"Northwest's Fax-On-Demand," *Inbound/Outbound Magazine,* June 1992, p. 8.

[45]Material for the discussion on the lodging industry came from Elaine Underwood, "Joined at the Hip," *Adweek's Marketing Week,* June 1, 1992, pp. 22–23; and Sak Onkvisit and John L. Shaw, "Service Marketing: Image, Branding, and Competition," *Business Horizons,* January-February 1989, pp. 13–18.

HIGHLIGHT 12–4

Ten Lessons in Good Services Marketing

1. Customers do not buy your services—they buy solutions to their problems.
2. There are only two conditions under which customers will change their behavior: 1) when it's a matter of life and death (and then not in every case); or 2) if they want to—if they are given a reason to change.
3. The most important parts of employees' contributions to the goals of your organization are being made at their discretion.
4. Management and leadership are exercised outside, not inside the office.
5. Quality service means never having to say "that's not my job."
6. How your employees feel is eventually how your customers will feel.
7. Customers should never be required to re-state their request or complain to several employees before having it resolved.
8. If you establish negative expectations for your customers, you will always meet them.
9. The delivery of quality service is never the customer's job.
10. If you are an underdog: only compete in market segments where you have or can develop strengths; avoid head-to-head competition with dominant competitors; emphasize profits rather than volume; focus on specialization rather than diversification.

Source: Adapted from James H. Donnelly, Jr., *Close To The Customer* (Homewood, Ill.: Business One-Irwin, 1992).

---

names in the lodging industry, is generally regarded as one of the more prestigious hotels. When Marriott decided to enter the lower priced segment of the hotel market, they did so with new brands. By altering the physical appearance and changing the names of their new motels to Courtyard by Marriott, Comfort Inn, and Marriott Resorts, Marriott was able to distinguish between their upscale offerings and those that were moderately priced. Holiday Inn, on the other hand, has experienced difficulty in trying to change from its middle–class image. They created Hampton Inns and Holiday Express for the budget segment, and Crowne Plaza and Embassy Suites for the upscale market. Due to overlapping between segments, Holiday Inn had difficulties in differentiating between the brands, especially in instances when two of the brands were located in the same city. By far, the most confused brand strategy relates to the use of the Ramada name. The Ramada Renaissance is a 16-unit chain of four-star hotels owned and operated in the U.S. by Ramada International Hotels & Resorts. Concurrently, there exists the 600-unit Ramada Hotel and Inn chain, which is owned and operated by Hospitality Franchise Systems, a privately held outfit that also manages the Howard Johnson and

Days Inn franchises. As a result, much confusion reigns in consumers' minds when asked to define what type of hotel the Ramada name brings to mind. The examples point out the necessity of multiple brands for service marketers when practicing market segmentation.

Implications for Service Marketers

The preceding sections emphasized the use of all components of the marketing mix. Many service industries have been criticized for an overdependence on advertising. The overdependence on one or two elements of the marketing mix is one that service marketers cannot afford. The sum total of the marketing mix elements represents the total impact of the firm's marketing strategy. The slack created by severely restricting one element cannot be compensated by heavier emphasis on another, since each element in the marketing mix is designed to address specific problems and achieve specific objectives.

Services must be made available to prospective users, which implies distribution in the marketing sense of the word. The revised concept of the distribution of services points out that service marketers must distinguish conceptually between the production and distribution of services. The problem of making services more efficiently and widely available must not be ignored.

The above sections also pointed out the critical role of new service development. In several of the examples described, indirect distribution of the service was made possible because "products" were developed that included a tangible representation of the service. This development facilitates the use of intermediaries, because the service can now be separated from the producer. In addition, the development of new services paves the way for companies to expand and segment their markets. With the use of varying service bundles, new technology, and alternative means of distributing the service, companies are now able to practice targeted marketing.

Promotional programs, other than advertising, also play a critical role in service marketing. By running sweepstakes in which contestants were eligible to win prizes each time they used their ATM cards, banks were able to make the public more aware of the ease and convenience of using ATMs. Likewise, no-excuse refunds for poor service have enabled such hotels as Holiday Inn to retain a quality reputation.

CONCLUSION

This chapter has dealt with the complex topic of service marketing. While the marketing of services has much in common with the marketing of products, unique problems in the area require highly creative marketing management skills. Many of the problems in the service area can be traced to the intangible and inseparable nature of services and the difficulties involved in providing service quality. However, considerable progress has been made in understanding and reacting to these difficult problems, particularly in the area of distribution. In view of the major role services play in our economy, it is important for marketing practitioners to better understand and appreciate the unique problems of service marketing.

ADDITIONAL READINGS

Babakus, Emin, and Gregory W. Boller. "An Empirical Assessment of the ServQual Scale." *Journal of Business Research,* Vol. 24, 1992, pp. 253–68.

Bitner, Mary Jo. "Evaluating Service Encounters: The Effects of Physical Surroundings and Employee Responses." *Journal of Marketing,* April 1990, pp. 68–82.

Bolton, Ruth N., and James H. Drew. "A Longitudinal Analysis of the Impact of Service Changes on Customer Attitudes." *Journal of Marketing,* January 1991, pp. 1–9.

Bowen, John. "Development of a Taxonomy of Services to Gain Strategic Marketing Insights." *Journal of the Academy of Marketing Sciences,* Winter 1990, pp. 43–49.

Cespedes, Frank V. "Once More: How Do You Improve Customer Service?" *Business Horizons,* March-April 1992, pp. 58–67.

Collier, David A. "New Marketing Mix Stresses Service." *The Journal of Business Strategy,* March/April 1991, pp. 42–45.

Cronin, J. Joseph, Jr., and Steven A. Taylor. "Measuring Service Quality: A Reexamination and Extension." *Journal of Marketing,* July 1992, pp. 55–68.

Gallagher, Katherine, and Charles B. Weinberg. "Coping With Success: New Challenges for NonProfit Marketing." *Sloan Management Review,* Fall 1991, pp. 27–42.

Grove, Stephen J., and Raymond P. Fisk. "Observational Data Collection Methods for Service Marketing: An Overview." *Journal of the Academy Of Marketing Science,* Summer 1992, pp. 217–24.

Magrath, Allan J., and Kenneth G. Hardy. "Manufacturer Services for Distributors." *Industrial Marketing Management,* April 1991, pp. 119–24.

Mayo, Edward J., and Lance P. Jarvis. "Excessive Growth in the Service Firm: A Strategic Marketing Planning Challenge." *The Journal of Services Marketing,* Spring 1992, pp. 5–14.

Peterson, Robert A., and William R. Wilson. "Measuring Customer Satisfaction: Fact and Artifact." *Journal of the Academy of Marketing Science,* Winter 1992, pp. 61–71.

Reichheld, Frederick F., and W. Earl Sasser, Jr. "Zero Defections: Quality Comes to Services." *Harvard Business Review,* September-October 1990, pp. 105–11.

Shapiro, Benson P., V. Kasturi Rangan, and John J. Sviokla, "Staple Yourself to an Order," *Harvard Business Review,* July-August 1992, pp. 113–22.

Sisodia, Rajendra S. "Marketing Information and Decision Support Systems for Services." *The Journal of Services Marketing,* Winter 1992, pp. 51–64.

Stone, Merlin. "Marketing Strategies for Leisure Services." *Long Range Planning* 23, no. 5 (1990), pp. 76–90.

Zeithaml, Valerie A.; A. Parasuraman; and Leonard L. Berry. *Delivering Quality Service: Evaluating Customer Perceptions and Expectations.* New York: Free Press, 1990.

International Marketing

A growing number of U.S. corporations have transversed geographical boundaries and become truly multinational in character. For most other domestic corporations, the question is no longer "Should we go international?" Instead, the questions being asked relate to how and where the companies should enter the international marketplace. The past decade has seen the reality of a truly world market unfold. In today's world, the global economy is now over 50 percent integrated versus 25 percent in 1980 and 10 percent in 1950.[1] Primary reasons for the convergence of previously separated individual markets evolving to a network of interdependent economies include:

1. The growing affluence and economic development of lesser developed countries. From 1985 to 2000, the world workforce is expected to grow by some 600 million people, or 27 percent.[2] The growth will take place unevenly. The vast majority of new workers—570 million of the 600 million workers—will join the work forces of the developing countries. By the year 2000, it is estimated that Third World nations will account for one fourth of the industrial value added in the world (versus one eighth today).[3]
2. The integration of world financial markets. For example, interest rate changes occurring in West Germany greatly influence interest rates in the United States and Japan.

---

[1]David A. Heenan, "The Case for Convergent Capitalism," *The Journal of Business Strategy,* November/December 1988, pp. 54–57.

[2]William B. Johnston, "Global Work Force 2000: The New World Labor Market," *Harvard Business Review,* March–April 1991, pp. 115–27.

[3]David A. Heenan, "The Case for Convergent Capitalism," *The Journal of Business Strategy,* November/December 1988, pp. 54–57.

HIGHLIGHT 13–1

Examples of Various Types of Multinational Companies (MNCs)

American-Owned MNCs

General Motors

IBM

General Electric

F. W. Woolworth

Sears Roebuck

Mobil Oil

ITT

Ford Motor

Pan Am

American Express

Bank America

Eastman Kodak

Procter & Gamble

Gulf & Western

Foreign-Owned MNCs

Unilever

Royal Dutch / Shell

Nestle

Datsun (Nissan)

Honda

Toyota Motors

Sony

Volkswagen

Perrier

Norelco

Nonprofit MNCs

Red Cross (Swiss)

Roman Catholic Church (Italy)

U.S. Army (U.S.)

American Firms Owned by Foreign MNCs

Magnavox

Gimbel's Department Store

Libby, McNeill & Libby

Stouffer Foods

Saks-Fifth Avenue

Bantam Books

Baskin-Robbins

Capitol Records

Kiwi Shoe Polish

Lipton

---

3. Increased efficiencies in transportation networks. To illustrate, consider the case of Western Europe. Airlines are now allowed to schedule flights between two countries other than their home countries.[4]

4. The opening up of new markets. For example, recent political events in Eastern Europe have led to the opening up of a marketplace of over 137 million potential new consumers for U.S. companies.

---

[4]Eric G. Friberg, "1992: Moves Europeans Are Making," *Harvard Business Review*, May–June 1989, pp. 85–89.

Multinational firms invest in foreign countries for the same basic reasons they invest in the domestic United States. These reasons vary from firm to firm, but fall under the categories of achieving offensive or defensive goals. Offensive goals are to: (1) increase long-term growth and profit prospects; (2) maximize total sales revenue; (3) take advantage of economies of scale; and (4) improve overall market position. As many American markets reach saturation, American firms look to foreign markets as outlets for surplus productive capacity and potential sources of larger profit margins and returns on investment. The gross domestic product (GDP) of European countries and Japan is rapidly catching up to that of the United States.[5] Since the GDP provides the ultimate source for living standard improvement, the implication is that the trend may prove to be a potential boom for the sale of American goods and services abroad. For example, while the dog food market in the U.S. is slipping at a rate of 3 percent per year, in Spain it is enjoying a 17 percent annual growth rate.[6] The potential in Eastern Europe and the old Soviet Union is even greater. By the mid-90s, Pepsico expects to sell over 100 million cases of soda bottled at 60 East European plants, while Procter & Gamble expects to distribute as much Crest toothpaste in the former Soviet Union as it does in Canada.[7]

Multinational firms also invest overseas to achieve defensive goals. Chief among these goals are the desire to: (1) compete with foreign competitors on their own turf instead of in the United States; (2) have access to technological innovations that are developed in other countries; (3) take advantage of significant differences in operating costs between countries[8]; (4) preempt competitors' global moves; and (5) not be locked out of future markets by arriving too late. To illustrate, in a recent year, there were 307 foreign acquisitions of U.S. companies.[9] Such well-known companies as Pillsbury, A&P, Shell Oil, CBS Records, and Firestone Tire & Rubber are now owned by foreign interests. Even smaller regional companies, such as the Rolling Rock Brewery, are not immune from foreign take-over.[10] Since 1980, the share of the domestic high-tech market held by foreign producers has grown from less than 8 percent

[5]Aaron Bernstein, "The Good Life Isn't Only in America," *Business Week,* November 2, 1992, p. 34.

[6]"DataWatch," *Advertising Age,* September 28, 1992, p. I-14.

[7]For an in-depth discussion of marketing opportunities in Eastern Europe, see John A. Quelch, Erich Joachimsthaler, and Jose Luis Nueno, "After the Wall: Marketing Guidelines for Eastern Europe," *Sloan Management Review,* Winter 1991, pp. 82–93.

[8]For a discussion of why small and mid-sized companies should go global, see "Gaining a Global Outlook," *Sales & Marketing Management,* January 1992, pp. 52–57.

[9]Kenneth M. Davidson, "Fire Sale on America?" *The Journal of Business Strategy,* September/October 1989, pp. 9–14.

[10]Maria Mallory, "Rolling Rock's Mug Runneth Over," *Business Week,* June 1, 1992, p. 76.

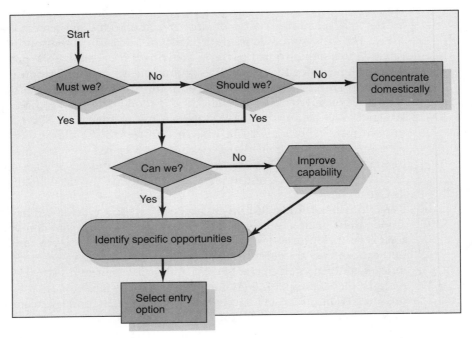

HIGHLIGHT 13–2

The Decision Process Involved in Determining Whether to Compete in International Markets

Source: Betty Jane Punnett and David A. Ricks, *International Business* (Boston: PWS-Kent Publishing Co., 1992), p. 257.

to an amount nearing 20 percent.[11] In such diverse industries as power tools, tractors, television, and banking, U.S. companies have lost the dominant position they once held. By investing solely in domestic operations, U.S. companies are more susceptible to foreign incursions. For example, there are nine times as many Japanese firms trading from abroad as there are foreign firms operating from Japan.[12]

[11]Gene Koretz, "Has High-Tech America Passed Its High-Water Mark?" *Business Week*, February 5, 1990, p. 18.

[12]Peter Enderwick, "The International Competitiveness of Japanese Service Industries: A Cause for Concern?" *California Management Review*, Summer 1990, pp. 22–37.

Basically, marketing abroad is the same as marketing at home. Regardless of which part of the world the firm sells in, the marketing program must still be built around a sound product or service that is properly priced, promoted, and distributed to a carefully analyzed target market. In other words, the marketing manager has the same controllable decision variables in both domestic and nondomestic markets.

Although the development of a marketing program may be the same in either domestic or nondomestic markets, special problems may be involved in the implementation of marketing programs in nondomestic markets. These problems often arise because of the environmental differences that exist among various countries that marketing managers may be unfamiliar with.

In this chapter, marketing management in an international context will be examined. Methods of organizing international versus domestic markets, international market research tasks, methods of entry strategies into international markets, and potential marketing strategies for a multinational firm will be discussed. In examining each of these areas, the reader will find a common thread—knowledge of the local cultural environment—that appears to be a major prerequisite for success in each area.

With the proper adaptations, U.S. companies do have the capabilities and resources needed to compete successfully in the international marketplace. To illustrate, companies as diverse as Amway, General Electric, Eastman Kodak, Mobil, McDonald's, and Coca-Cola each generate over one-half billion dollars in annual sales in Japan alone.[13] Smaller companies can also be successful. System Software Associates Inc. of Chicago, a $62 million company, generates more than half its sales outside the United States.[14]

ORGANIZING FOR INTERNATIONAL MARKETING

When compared with the tasks it faces at home, a firm attempting to establish an international marketing organization faces a much higher degree of risk and uncertainty. In a foreign market, management is often less familiar with the cultural, political, and economic situation. Many of these problems arise as a result of conditions specific to the foreign country. Managers are also faced with many decisions relating to internal organization, operation, and control issues. These problems usually come as a result of deciding whether to take a multidomestic or global approach to managing international operations.

---

[13]Carla Rapport, "You Can Make Money in Japan," *Fortune,* February 12, 1990, pp. 85–92.

[14]For an explanation of how a small company was able to go international, see Edward R. Koepfler, "Strategic Options for Global Market Players," *The Journal of Business Strategy,* July / August, 1989, pp. 46–50.

Problem Conditions: External

While numerous problems could be cited, attention here will focus on those U.S. firms most often face when entering foreign markets.

Cultural misunderstanding. Differences in the cultural environment of foreign countries may be misunderstood or not even recognized because of the tendency for marketing managers to use their own cultural values and priorities as a frame of reference. Some of the most common areas of difference lie in the way dissimilar cultures perceive time, thought patterns, personal space, material possessions, family roles and relationships, personal achievement, competitiveness, individuality, social behavior, and other interrelated subjective issues.[15] Another important source of misunderstandings is in the perceptions of managers about the people with whom they are dealing. Feelings of superiority can lead to changed communication mannerisms.

The tendency to rely on one's own cultural values has been called the major cause of many international marketing problems. For example, the Japanese often say "yes" when they mean "no."[16] They rarely give a direct negative response—even if they want to deny a request or express a negative intent—especially to a foreigner. They are also wary of the common American practice of bringing lawyers to initial meetings. American managers must make the necessary efforts to learn, understand, and adapt to the cultural norms of the managers and customers they deal with in other parts of the world.[17] Failure to do so will result in missed market opportunities. Highlight 13–3 provides further examples of cultural differences that could lead to marketing problems.

On the other hand, companies should not shy away from attempting to enter international markets because conventional wisdom says that products and services will not succeed in some regions purely due to cultural reasons.[18] For example, until the beginning of 1989, the United States could not sell frozen concentrated orange juice in Korea. "The Korean people don't drink it," assured Korean officials. But American producers finally negotiated a small opening into the market. By the end of the first month of sales, the entire year's quota allowed by the Korean government was snapped up by Korean distributors. Likewise, Dunkin' Donuts heard that the Japanese people do not eat sugary donuts and never have. The company still decided to open one test

---

[15]For a full explanation on cultural differences, see Rose Knotts, "Cross-Cultural Management: Transformations and Adaptations," *Business Horizons,* January-February 1989, pp. 29–33.

[16]"In Japan, if Your Prospect Says "Yes," Don't Start Celebrating Yet," *Marketing News,* February 5, 1990, p. 18.

[17]For a further discussion of the influence of foreign culture, see Naoko Oikawa and John F. Tanner, Jr., "The Influence of Japanese Culture on Business Relationships and Negotiations," *The Journal of Services Marketing,* Summer 1992, pp. 67–74; and Sergey Frank, "Global Negotiations," *Sales & Marketing Management,* May 1992, pp. 64–69.

[18]This section is based on material contained in Mike Van Horn, "Market-Entry Approaches for the Pacific Rim," *The Journal of Business Strategy,* March/April 1990, pp. 14–19.

outlet in Japan. Customers were interviewed and the company discovered several things. First, the Japanese people like donuts but donuts that are not so big and sugary. So the company made smaller, less sugary donuts. Second, the decor inside the shop was too garish for Japanese tastes, so the decor was made more subtle. Third, the stools were too high, so they were shortened. As a result of these cultural adaptations, Dunkin' Donuts is now a major presence in Japan.

Political uncertainty. Governments are unstable in many countries, and social unrest and even armed conflict must sometimes be reckoned with. Other nations are newly emerging and anxious to exert their independence. These and similar problems can greatly hinder a firm seeking to establish its position in a foreign market. For example, in China, many companies had to scale back and adapt their marketing efforts after the government there used military force to quell the student uprisings in 1990.

Import restrictions. Tariffs, import quotas, and other types of important restrictions hinder international business. These are usually established to promote national self-sufficiency and can be a huge roadblock for the multinational firm. For example, currently a number of countries, including South Korea, Taiwan, Thailand, and Japan, place import restrictions on a variety of goods produced in America, including telecommunications equipment, satellites, rice, and wood products.[19] In other cases, the government may not impose restrictions that are commonly adhered to in the United States. For example, the Walt Disney Co. pulled out of China for two years to protest the lack of official help in policing unauthorized use of its trademarks.[20] Disney took this move even though its "Mickey & Donald" television show was the highest rated television program in China, drawing an estimated 300 million viewers each Sunday. Fortunately for Walt Disney, a bilateral agreement was reached between the U.S. and China in 1992, thus providing a means of fighting copyright breaches.

Exchange controls. Often a nation will establish limits on the amount of earned and invested funds that can be withdrawn from that nation. These exchange controls are usually established by nations that are experiencing balance-of-payment problems. Nevertheless, these and other types of currency regulations are important considerations in the decision to expand into a foreign market. For example, the Soviet ruble has only been recently convertible to hard currency. For foreign companies dealing with the former Soviet Union, barter is still a primary means to buy and sell goods.[21]

---

[19]Paul Magnusson and Blanca Riemer, "Carla Hills, Trade Warrior," *Business Week,* January 22, 1990, pp. 50–56.

[20]Andrew Geddes, "Disney Will Return to China," *Advertising Age,* April 27, 1992, p. I-12.

[21]For a discussion of American marketers in the former Soviet Union, see "Moscow Meets Madison Avenue," *Advertising Age,* September 28, 1992, pp. 16, 31, 44; and Karl Seppala and Mark Meyer, "Time Ripe for U.S. Firms to Enter Soviet Market," *Marketing News,* February 5, 1990, pp. 6, 9.

Ownership and personnel restrictions. In many nations, governments have a requirement that the majority ownership of a company operating in that nation be held by nationals of the country. Other nations require that the majority of the personnel of a foreign firm be local citizens. Each of these restrictions can act as obstacles to foreign expansion. To illustrate, consider the case of Coca-Cola. In order to comply with foreign ownership requirements, Coca-Cola would have had to share technical knowledge, including the proprietary secret recipe for its soft drink concentrate, with its Indian partners. Coca-Cola refused and instead decided to pull out of India in the late 70s after operating there for over 25 years.[22] Coca-Cola remained out of the Indian market until 1992. At that time, the Indian government decided to loosen its rules on foreign investment. Coca-Cola then reentered the Indian market as a minority partner with Britannia Industries, Ltd., India's largest food processing company.[23]

Problem Conditions: Internal

Given the types of external problems just discussed, the reader can see that the external roadblocks to success in a foreign market are substantial. Unfortunately, several major internal problems may also arise.

The Multidomestic versus the Global Approach

There are two distinct kinds of multinational corporations—the multidomestic corporation and the global corporation.[24] The multidomestic company pursues different strategies in each of its foreign markets. Each overseas subsidiary is autonomous. A company's management tries to operate effectively across a series of worldwide positions with diverse product requirements, growth rates, competitive environments, and political risks. Local managers are given the authority and control to make the necessary decisions; however, they are also held responsible for results. In effect, the company competes on a market-by-market basis. Honeywell and General Foods are examples of two American companies that operated well in this manner.

---

[22]Anant R. Negandi and Peter A. Donhowe, "It's Time to Explore New Global Trade Options," *The Journal of Business Strategy*, January/February 1989, pp. 27–31.

[23]For a more complete discussion of foreign investment in India, see Rahul Jacob, "India is Opening for Business," *Fortune*, November 16, 1992, pp. 128–30; and "Coke Forms Joint Venture to Pursue Indian Market," *Marketing News*, November 25, 1991, p. 2.

[24]This section was taken from James F. Bolt, "Global Competitors: Some Criteria for Success," *Business Horizons*, January–February 1988, pp. 34–41.

HIGHLIGHT 13–3

Examples of Cultural Differences That Could Lead to Marketing Problems

Body Language

— Standing with your hands on your hips is a gesture of defiance in Indonesia.
— Carrying on a conversation with your hands in your pockets makes a poor impression in France, Belgium, Finland, and Sweden.
— When you shake your head from side to side, that means "yes" in Bulgaria and Sri Lanka.
— Crossing your legs to expose the sole of your shoe is really taboo in Muslim countries. In fact, to call a person a "shoe" is a deep insult.

Physical Contact

— Patting a child on the head is a grave offense in Thailand or Singapore, since the head is revered as the location of the soul.
— In an Oriental culture, touching another person is considered an invasion of privacy, while in Southern European and Arabic countries it is a sign of warmth and friendship.

Promptness

— Be on time when invited for dinner in Denmark or in China.

— In Latin countries, your host or business associate would be surprised if you arrived at the appointed hour.

Eating and Cooking

— It is rude to leave anything on your plate when eating in Norway, Malaysia, or Singapore.
— In Egypt, it is rude *not* to leave something.
— In Italy and Spain, cooking is done with oil.
— In Germany and Great Britain, margarine and butter are used.

Other Social Customs

— In Sweden, nudity and sexual permissiveness are quite all right, but drinking is really frowned on.
— In Spain, there is a very negative attitude toward life insurance. By receiving insurance benefits, a wife feels that she is profiting from her husband's death.
— In Western European countries, many consumers still are reluctant to buy anything (other than a house) on credit. Even for an automobile, they will pay cash after having saved for some time.

Source: William J. Stanton; Michael J. Etzel; and Bruce J. Walker, *Fundamentals of Marketing,* 9th ed. (New York: McGraw-Hill, 1991) p. 536.

The global company, on the other hand, pits its entire resources against the competition in an integrated fashion. Foreign subsidiaries and divisions are largely interdependent in both operations and strategy. These "stateless" corporations standardize manufacturing, regularly offer innovative solutions to the market, and seek creative collaborations with other firms to merge complementary skills and gain access to new markets.[25] The global company operates as though the world were one large market, not a series of individual countries. Since there is no one clear-cut way to organize a global company, three alternative structures are normally used: (1) worldwide product divisions, each responsible for selling its own products throughout the world; (2) divisions responsible for all products sold within a geographic area; and (3) a matrix system that combines elements of both these arrangements. Many multinational companies already have structured their organization in a global fashion including IBM, Caterpillar, Timex, General Electric, Siemens, and Mitsubishi. Others are rapidly following.

Most companies are realizing the need to take a global approach to managing their businesses. However, recognizing the need and actually implementing a truly global approach are two distinctly different tasks. For some companies, industry conditions dictate that they take a global perspective. The ability to actually implement a global approach to managing international operations, however, largely depends on factors unique to the company. Globalization, as a competitive strategy, is inherently more vulnerable to risk than a multi-domestic or domestic strategy, due to the permanence of the organizational structure once established.[26] Industry conditions and internal factors dictating that companies pursue a global strategy are explored next.

Industry Conditions Dictating a Global Perspective

In determining whether or not to globalize a particular business, managers should look first to the business's industry.[27] Market, economic, environmental, and competitive factors all influence the potential gains to be realized by following a global strategy. Factors constituting the external environment that are conducive to a global strategy are:

1. *Market factors.* Homogenous market needs, global customers, shortening product life cycles, transferable brands and advertising, and the ability to internationalize distribution channels.

---

[25]For a further discussion on global marketing, see Michael R. Czinkota and Ilkka A. Ronkainen, "Global Marketing 2000: A Marketing Survival Guide," *Marketing Management,* Winter 1992, pp. 37–45.

[26]For a complete discussion of the risks associated with pursuing a global strategy, see Barrie James, "Reducing the Risks of Globalization," *Long Range Planning,* February 1990, pp. 80–88.

[27]This section is based on George S. Yip, Pierre M. Loewe, and Michael Y. Yoshino, "How to Take Your Company to the Global Market," *Columbia Journal of World Business,* Winter 1988, pp. 37–48.

2. *Economic factors.* Worldwide economies of scale in manufacturing and distribution, steep learning curves, worldwide sourcing efficiencies, rising product development costs, and significant differences in host-country costs.

3. *Environmental factors.* Falling transportation costs, improving communications, favorable government policies, and the increasing speed of technological change.

4. *Competitive factors.* Competitive interdependencies among countries, global moves of competitors, and opportunities to preempt a competitor's global moves.[28]

Many of the reasons given in the first part of the chapter as to why a domestic company should become a multinational can also be used to support the argument that a firm should take a global perspective. This is because the integration of markets is forcing companies that wish to remain successful to not only become multinationals but also to take a global perspective in doing so. In the past, companies had the option of remaining domestic or going multinational due to the separation of markets. This is no longer the case.

Internal Factors that Facilitate a Global Strategy

There are several internal factors that can either facilitate or impede a company's efforts to undertake a global approach to marketing strategies. These factors and their underlying dimensions are:

1. *Structure.* The ease of installing a centralized global authority and the absence of rifts between present domestic and international divisions or operating units.

2. *Management processes.* The capabilities and resources available to perform global planning, budgeting, and coordination activities, coupled with the ability to conduct global performance reviews and implement global compensation plans.

3. *Culture.* The ability to project a global versus national identity, a worldwide versus domestic commitment to employees, and a willingness to tolerate interdependence among business units.

4. *People.* The availability of employable foreign nationals and the willingness of current employees to commit to multicountry careers, frequent travel, and having foreign superiors.

Overall, whether a company should undertake a multidomestic or global approach to organizing its international operations will largely depend on the nature of the company and its products, how different the foreign culture is from the domestic market, and the company's ability to implement a global

---

[28]Ibid.

perspective. Indeed, in many cases, firms do not undertake either purely multidomestic or global approaches to marketing. Instead, a hybrid approach is employed. For example, McDonalds' markets its products and services through 12,000 outlets in 59 countries.[29] While the firm maintains standardized specifications for its equipment technology, customer service, cleanliness, value, and operational systems, the menus do vary somewhat from country to country.

The 3M Corporation pursues an even more diverse approach.[30] In Latin America, the company conducts its business on more a national, rather than a regional approach; while in Europe, a centralized regional approach to marketing is followed. Regardless of approach, management and organizational skills which emphasize the need to handle diversity will be the critical factors that determine the long-term success of any company's endeavors in the international marketplace.[31]

PROGRAMMING FOR INTERNATIONAL MARKETING

In this section of the chapter, the major areas in developing an international marketing program will be examined. As was mentioned at the outset, marketing managers must organize the same controllable decision variables that exist in domestic markets. However, many firms that have been extremely successful in marketing in the United States have not been able to duplicate their success in foreign markets.

International Marketing Research

Because the risks and uncertainties are so high, marketing research is equally important (and probably more so) in foreign markets than in domestic markets.[32] In attempting to analyze foreign consumers and industrial markets, at least four important dimensions must be considered.

Population characteristics. Obviously, population is one of the major components of a market, and significant differences exist between and within foreign countries. The marketing manager should be familiar with the total population and with the regional, urban, rural, and inter-urban distribution. Other demographic variables, such as the number and size of families, edu-

---

[29]Saeed Samiee and Kendall Roth, "The Influence of Global Marketing Standardization on Performance," *Journal of Marketing,* April 1992, pp. 1–17.

[30]For a discussion of 3M's approach to international marketing, see Harry Hammerly, "Matching Global Strategies With National Responses," *The Journal of Business Strategy,* March/April 1992, pp. 8–12.

[31]Milton Leontiades, "The Japanese Art of Managing Diversity," *The Journal of Business Strategy,* March/April 1991, pp. 30–36.

[32]S. Tamer Cavusgil, "Guidelines for Export Market Research," *Business Horizons,* November–December 1985, pp. 27–33.

HIGHLIGHT 13–4

One Dozen of the Top Global Companies

Company	Foreign Sales as Percent of Sales	Best-Selling Product Abroad	Biggest Market Abroad
Boeing	46%	Commercial airliners	Western Europe
Caterpillar	50	Earthmoving equipment	Western Europe
Dow	55	Industrial chemicals	Canada
Eastman Kodak	45	Amateur film	Britain
Ford Motor	25	Escort subcompact	Britain
General Electric	22	Aircraft engines	West Germany
Hewlett-Packard	52	Computer workstations	West Germany
Merck	50	Vasotec (blood pressure medicine)	n.a.
Outboard Marine	20	Outboard motors	Canada
Scott Paper	38	Bathroom tissue	Western Europe
Sun Microsystems	42	Computer workstations	Japan
3M	46	Pressure-sensitive tape	West Germany

Source: Charles W. Lamb, Jr., Joseph F. Hair, Jr., and Carl McDaniel, *Principles of Marketing* (Cincinnati: South-Western Publishing, 1992) p. 729.

---

cation, occupation, and religion, are also important. In many markets, these variables can have a significant impact on the success of a firm's marketing program. For example, in the United States, a cosmetics firm can be reasonably sure of the desire to use cosmetics being almost universal among women of all income classes. However, in Latin America the same firm may be forced to segment its market by upper-, middle-, and lower-income groups, as well as by urban and rural areas. This is because upper-income women want high-quality cosmetics promoted in prestige media and sold through exclusive outlets. In some rural and less prosperous areas, the cosmetics must be inexpensive, while in other rural areas women do not accept cosmetics. Even in markets that are small in geographical area, consumers may differ in many of the variables mentioned. Any one or set of such differences may have a strong bearing on consumers' ability and willingness to buy.

Ability to buy. To assess the ability of consumers in a foreign market to buy, four broad measures should be examined: (1) gross national product or per capita national income; (2) distribution of income; (3) rate of growth in buying power; and (4) extent of available financing. Since each of these vary in different areas of the world, the marketing opportunities available must be examined closely.

HIGHLIGHT 13–5

Competitive Advantages of Multinational Companies

Advantage	Description
General Competitive Advantages	
Proprietary technology	Product, process, or management technology held by a firm, which others can obtain only through R&D or contracting with the possessor
Goodwill based on brand or trade name	Reputation for quality, service, etc., developed through experience
Scale economies in production	Large-scale production facilities that lower unit costs of production
Scale economies in purchasing	Lower costs of inputs through purchasing large quantities
Scale economies in financing	Access to funds at a lower cost for larger firms
Scale economies in distribution	Shipments of large quantities of products/inputs to necessary locations, lowering unit shipping costs
Scale economies in advertising	Sales in several markets, allowing somewhat standardized advertising across markets
Government protection	Free or preferential access to a market limited by government fiat
Human resource management	Skill at fostering teamwork among employees and optimizing productivity
Multinational Competitive Advantages	
Multinational marketing capability	Knowledge of and access to markets in several countries
Multinational sourcing capability	Reliable access to raw materials, intermediate goods, etc., in several countries that reduces single-source costs
Multinational diversification	Operations in several countries so that country risk and business risk are reduced
Managerial experience in several countries	Skill for managing multicountry operations gained through experience in different countries (learning curve gains)

Source: Robert Grosse and Duane Kuwaja, *International Business: Theory and Managerial Applications,* 2nd ed. (Homewood, Ill.: Richard D. Irwin, 1992) p. 36.

Willingness to buy. The cultural framework of consumer motives and behavior is integral to the understanding of the foreign consumer. Cultural values and attitudes toward the material culture, social organizations, the supernatural, aesthetics, and language should be analyzed for their possible influence on each of the elements in the firm's marketing program. It is easy to see that such factors as the group's values concerning acquisition of material goods, the role of the family, the positions of men and women in society, as well as the various age groups and social classes will all have an effect on marketing, because each influences consumer behavior, values, and the overall pattern of life.

In some areas there appears to be a convergence of tastes and habits, with different cultures becoming more and more integrated into one homogenous culture, although still separated by national boundaries. This appears to be the case in Western Europe, where consumers are developing into a mass market. This obviously will simplify the task for a marketer in this region. However, cultural differences still prevail among most areas of the world and strongly influence consumer behavior.

Differences in research tasks and processes

In addition to the dimensions mentioned above, the processes and tasks associated with carrying out the market research program will also most likely differ from country to country. Many market researchers count on census data for in-depth demographic information. However, in foreign countries there are a variety of problems the market researcher is likely to encounter in using census data. These include:[33]

1. *Language.* Some nations publish their census reports in English. Other countries offer only their native language.
2. *Data content.* Data contained in a census will vary from country to country and often omit items of interest to researchers. For example, most foreign nations do not include an income question on their census. Others do not include such items as marital status or education levels.
3. *Timeliness.* The United States takes a census every 10 years. Japan and Canada conduct one every five years. However, some northern European nations are abandoning the census as a data collection tool and instead are relying on population registers to account for births, deaths, and changes in marital status or place of residence.
4. *Availability in the United States.* If a researcher requires detailed household demographics on foreign markets, the cost and time required to obtain the data will be significant. For example, to get minimal-quality data on Western Europe and Pacific Rim countries might require trips to over 10 different university libraries, as well as to the U.S. Bureau of the Census and the Library of Congress.

---

[33]Donald B. Pittenger, "Gathering Foreign Demographics Is No Easy Task," *Marketing News,* January 8, 1990, pp. 23, 25.

Problems can also be encountered in carrying out research activities.[34] For example, in most nations there are no large-sample theater tests or on-air, day-after recall studies so common in the United States. Other difficulties arise in gathering purchase data. Foreign retailers lag far behind American retailers in the installation and use of checkout scanning devices. Techniques commonly used in the collection of data also differ. For example, while telephone interviewing is the most commonly used survey method in the United States, it's relatively rare in the United Kingdom, where most research is conducted door-to-door.

To perform effective research in foreign markets, companies must recognize the need to employ researchers well-versed in the buying habits of the particular market. Sometimes, companies will utilize creative means to accomplish this goal. For example, Grassroots Research, a San Francisco-based marketing research company, employs free-lance journalists residing in their native countries to carry out foreign research assignments for U.S. clients. These journalist have in-depth knowledge of their home markets, speak the local native language(s) fluently, and, most important, possess the acumen and skills necessary to provide accurate, unbiased information to their U.S. client companies.

Product Planning for International Markets

Before a firm can market a product, there must be something to sell—a product or service. From this standpoint, product planning is the starting point for the entire marketing program. Once this is accomplished, management can then determine whether there is an adequate market for the product and can decide how the product should be marketed. Most firms would not think of entering a domestic market without extensive product planning. Unfortunately, this is often not the case with foreign markets. Often, firms will enter foreign markets with the same product sold in the United States, or at best, one with only minor changes. In many cases, these firms have encountered serious problems. An example of such a problem occurred when American manufacturers began to export refrigerators to Europe. The firms exported essentially the same models sold in the United States. However, the refrigerators were the wrong size, shape, and temperature range for some areas and had weak appeal in others—thus failing miserably. Although adaptation of the product to local conditions may have eliminated this failure, this adaptation is easier said than done. For example, even in the domestic market, overproliferation of product varieties and options can dilute economies of scale. This dilution results in higher production costs, which may make the price of serving each market segment with an "adapted" product prohibitive. The solution to this problem

---

[34]Jack J. Honomich, "British, U.S. Researchers Ponder Their Differences," *Advertising Age,* August 28, 1989, pp. 42, 49.

is not easy. In some cases, changes can be made rather inexpensively, while in others the sales potential of the particular market may not warrant extensive product changes. In any case, management must examine these problems carefully to avoid foreign marketing failures.[35]

International Distribution Systems

The role of the distribution network in facilitating the transfer of goods and titles and in the demand stimulation process is as important in foreign markets as it is at home. Figure 13–1 illustrates some of the most common channel arrangements in international marketing. The continuum ranges from no control to almost complete control of the distribution system by manufacturers.

The channel arrangement where manufacturers have the least control is shown at the left of Figure 13–1. These are the most indirect channels of distribution. Here manufacturers sell to resident buyers, export agents, or export merchants located in the United States. In reality, these are similar to domestic sales, since all of the marketing functions are assumed by the intermediaries.[36]

Manufacturers become more directly involved and, hence, have greater control over distribution when agents and distributors located in foreign markets are selected. Both perform similar functions, except that agents do not assume title to the manufacturers' products, while distributors do. If manufacturers should assume the functions of foreign agents or distributors and establish their own foreign branch, they greatly increase control over their international distribution system. Manufacturers' effectiveness will then depend on their own administrative organization, rather than on independent intermediaries. If the foreign branch sells to other intermediaries, such as wholesalers and retailers, as is the case with most consumer goods, manufacturers again relinquish some control. However, since the manufacturers are located in the market area, they have greater potential to influence these intermediaries. For example, Coca-Cola recently purchased six antiquated bottling plants located in what was formerly East Germany. Utilizing former technicians, factory hands, and clerks selected from the plants, the Coca-Cola Company began direct sales to retail and institutional establishments in the region. In the first year alone, Coke sold 74 million cases of soda in the new territory, whereas previously they had sold none.[37]

---

[35]See Theodore Levitt, "The Globalization of Markets," *Harvard Business Review*, May–June 1983, pp. 92–102, for an excellent discussion of the extent to which a company can market the same product in different countries.

[36]The manufacturer does have slightly more control over the export agent than the resident buyer or export merchant, since the export agent does not take title to the goods.

[37]Walecia Konrad and Igor Reichlin, "The Real Thing is Thundering Eastward," *Business Week*, April 13, 1992, pp. 96–98.

Figure 13-1 *Common Distribution Channels for International Marketing*

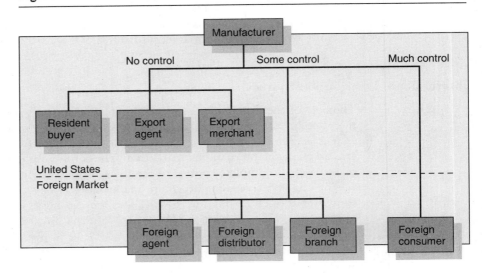

The channel arrangement that enables manufacturers to exercise a great deal of control is shown at the right of Figure 13–1. Here, manufacturers sell directly to industrial users or ultimate consumers. Although this arrangement is most common in the sale of industrial goods, some consumer goods companies have also pursued this arrangement.

Pricing for International Marketing

In domestic markets, pricing is a complex task. The basic approaches used in price determination in foreign markets are the same as those discussed earlier in the chapter on pricing. However, the pricing task is often more complicated in foreign markets because of additional problems associated with tariffs, anti-dumping laws, taxes, inflation, and currency conversion.[38]

Import duties are probably the major constraint for foreign marketers and are encountered in many markets. Management must decide whether import duties will be paid by the firm, by the foreign consumer, or shared by both. This and similar constraints may force the firm to abandon an otherwise desirable pricing strategy or may force the firm out of a market altogether.

---

[38]For a more complete discussion of issues affecting pricing in foreign markets, see James K. Weekly, "Pricing in Foreign Markets: Pitfalls and Opportunities," *Industrial Marketing Management,* April 1992, pp. 173–79.

Another pricing problem arises because of the rigidity in price structures found in many foreign markets. Many foreign intermediaries are not aggressive in their pricing policies. They often prefer to maintain high unit margins at the expense of low sales volume, rather than develop large sales volume by means of lower prices and smaller margins per unit. Many times this rigidity is encouraged by legislation that prevents retailers from cutting prices substantially at their own discretion. These are only a few of the pricing problems encountered by foreign marketers.

However, in some cases foreign pricing policies and customs can give the U.S. marketer a competitive advantage. For example, in Japan, American-style shopping malls with stores such as Toys "Я" Us, Talbots, and Virgin Records are able to compete effectively against center-city stores which still adhere to Japanese pricing policies designed to give the retailer huge margins.[39] In fact, imports of consumer goods into Japan have more than tripled within the last decade. Clearly, the marketer must be aware of both the constraints and the opportunities available in foreign market areas.

International Advertising and Sales Promotion

When expanding their operations into the world marketplace, most firms are aware of the language barriers that exist and realize the importance of translating their messages into the proper idiom. However, there are numerous other issues that must be resolved, such as selecting appropriate media and advertising agencies in foreign markets.

There are many problems in selecting media in foreign markets. Often the media that are traditionally used in the domestic market are not available in foreign markets. For example, it was not until recently that national commercial TV became a reality in the former Soviet Union. If media are available, they may be so on a limited basis only or they may not reach the potential buyers. (For example, one firm was forced to use sound trucks or roving movie vans to reach potential buyers in the Sub-Sahara area of Africa.) In addition to the problem of availability, other difficulties arise from the lack of accurate media information. There is no rate and data service or media directory that covers all the media available throughout the world. Where data are available, the accuracy is often questionable.

Another important promotion decision that must be made is the type of agency used to prepare and place the firm's advertisements. Along with the growth in multinational product companies, advertising agencies are also taking on a multinational look. Among the top 15 advertising agencies, less than half are U.S. owned.[40] Alliances and takeovers have served to stimulate

---

[39]Carla Rapport, "Ready, Set, Sell—Japan Is Buying," *Fortune,* September 11, 1989, pp. 159–64.

[40]Laurel Wentz, "Publicis–FCB Leads Euro-networks," *Advertising Age,* June 12, 1989, p. 36.

HIGHLIGHT 13–6

Checklist of Country Selection Criteria for Companies Considering Investment in Eastern Europe

Overall Economic and Political Conditions

— What is the foreign debt service expense as a percentage of hard currency foreign exchange earnings?

— What is the inflation rate? If hyperinflation exists, are appropriate fiscal and monetary policies being implemented to bring it under control?

— How substantial are raw material reserves that can be converted to hard currency?

— Are state subsidies, cheap credits, and tax concessions for state enterprises being phased out?

— Does the government intend to sell stakes in state enterprises to foreign investors?

— Is there an emerging capital market based on real interest rates?

— What progress is being made toward developing a code of company law?

— Is political decision-making authority centralized or fragmented?

— How rapid and sustainable is continued progress toward democracy and a free market economy? Is there any historical tradition to support such trends?

Climate for Foreign Investment

— What percentage ownership may foreign companies have in joint ventures? Is government approval required and, if so, how long does it take to obtain?

— Is private ownership of property recognized?

— Are intellectual property rights upheld?

— Can foreign investors obtain premises easily? Can they own real estate?

— Can an initial capital investment by a foreign company be held in hard currency?

— Can a foreign investor sell its stake in a joint venture?

— Can hard currency be used to pay for imported raw materials or to repatriate profits?

— What is the tax rate on business enterprise profits?

Market Attractiveness

— What is the sales potential in this country?

— Do the country's geographical location and political relations permit it to serve as a gateway to other East European markets?

— How well developed are the necessary managerial and technical skills?

— How skilled is the labor pool? What are labor costs?

— Can continued supply of the raw materials required for production be assured?

— What is the quality of the transportation and telecommunications infrastructure?

— Will Western executives accept being located in the country?

— To what degree have government officials developed a familiarity with Western business practices?

Source: John A. Quelch, Erich Joachimsthaler, and Jose Luis Nueno, "After the Wall: Marketing Guidelines for Eastern Europe," *Sloan Management Review,* Winter 1991, p. 85.

growth in the formation of global agencies. For the U.S. company, there are two major approaches to choosing an agency. The first is to use a purely local agency in each area where the advertisement is to appear. The rationale for this approach is that a purely local agency employing only local nationals can better adapt the firm's message to the local culture.

The other approach is to use either a U.S.-based multinational agency or a multinational agency with U.S. offices to develop and implement the ad campaign. For example, the Coca-Cola Company uses one agency to create ads for the 80 nations that Diet Coke is marketed in. The use of these so-called super agencies is increasing (annual growth rates averaging over 30 percent in the last decade). By using global advertising agencies, companies are able to take advantage of economies of scale and other efficiencies. However, global agencies are not without their critics. Many managers believe that small, local agencies in emerging markets take a more entrepreneurial and fresher approach to advertising than do the global agencies.[41] Much discussion has developed over which approach is best, and it appears that both approaches can be used successfully by particular firms.[42]

The use of sales promotion can also lead to opportunities and problems for marketers in foreign markets. Sales promotions often contain certain characteristics that are more attractive than other elements of the promotion mix.[43] In less wealthy countries, consumers tend to be even more interested in saving money through price discounts, sampling, or premiums. Sales promotion can also be used as a strategy for bypassing restrictions on advertising placed by some foreign governments. In addition, sales promotion can be an effective means for reaching people who live in rural locations where media support for advertising is virtually nonexistent.

However, laws in some countries place even more restrictions on sales promotion than those found in the United States. Laws may not permit gifts or premiums to be given, and companies may be required to keep detailed records of promotional transactions. For example, in France a limit is placed on the amount of money companies can spend on sales promotion activities. In addition, retailers and wholesalers in foreign countries may either lack: (1) the appropriate facilities necessary to merchandise the promotional materials; or (2) the capability to either understand how a specific promotion works or explain it to their customers.

---

[41]Kathleen Barnes, "Nestle Exec Criticizes Sluggish Global Shops," *Advertising Age,* November 13, 1989.

[42]For a discussion on this topic, see R. Blackwell, R. Ajami, and K. Stephan, "Winning the Global Advertising Race: Planning Globally, Acting Locally," *Journal of International Consumer Marketing* 3, no. 2 (1991), pp. 97–120; and J. H. Holmes, "Toward More Effective International Advertising," *Journal of International Consumer Marketing* 3, no. 1 (1990), pp. 51–65.

[43]The section on sales promotion is based on John Burnett, *Promotion Management* (St. Paul, Minn.: West Publishing Co.), 1988, chap. 21.

STRATEGIES FOR INTERNATIONAL MARKETING

A major decision facing companies that desire to enter the international marketplace relate to the choice of a market entry strategy. The decision on what type of strategy to employ depends upon many factors, including the analysis of market opportunities, company capabilities, and the degree of marketing involvement and commitment the company is willing to make.[44] A company can decide to: (1) make minimal investments of funds and risks by limiting its efforts to exporting; (2) make large initial investments of resources and management effort to try to establish a permanent share of international markets; or (3) take an incremental approach whereby the company starts with the mode of entry which requires the least commitment and gradually increases resource commitment over time.[45] All three approaches can be profitable. In general, there are eight ways by which a company can initially enter the international marketplace:

1. *Exporting.* Exporting occurs when a company produces the product outside the final destination and then ships it there for sale. It is the easiest and most common approach for a company making its first international move.
2. *Licensing.* Companies can grant patent rights, trademark rights, and the rights to use technological processes to foreign companies. It is the favorite strategy for small- and medium-sized companies. Although it may be the least profitable way to enter a market, it also minimizes risks.
3. *Franchising.* Franchising is a form of licensing whereby the franchiser provides a standard package of products, systems, and management services to the franchisee. The foreign franchisee provides market knowledge, capital, and personal involvement in management. Potentially, franchising offers an effective mix of centralized and decentralized decision making.
4. *Joint ventures.* A company may decide to share management with one or more collaborating foreign firms. Advantages of joint ventures include access to a partner's distribution system, access to an otherwise closed market, access to technology, and access to capital or personnel resources.[46] For example, Hercules, Inc., a company which operates in the specialty chemicals, aerospace, and engineered polymers industries, has been involved in joint ventures with companies in Japan, Australia, Italy, and Belgium.[47]

---

[44]The material for this section comes from Phillip R. Cateora, *International Marketing,* 7th ed. (Homewood Ill.: Richard D. Irwin, 1990), chap. 10.

[45]For a discussion on alternative ways to enter foreign markets, see Sam C. Okoroafo, "Modes of Entering Foreign Markets," *Industrial Marketing Management,* November 1991, pp. 341–46.

[46]For a discussion of issues related to joint ventures, see Stratford Sherman, "Are Strategic Alliances Working?" *Fortune,* September 21, 1992, pp. 77–78.

[47]Walter G. Schmid, "Heinz Covers the Globe," *The Journal of Business Strategy,* March/April, 1989, pp. 17–20.

5. *Consortia*. A consortium is similar to a joint venture except for two unique characteristics. Consortia typically involve a large number of participants and usually operate in countries or markets in which none of the participants is currently active.

6. *Manufacturing*. Local manufacturing is used when the demand justifies the investment. Low-cost labor/materials or gaining access to otherwise closed markets may provide the impetus for setting up local manufacturing operations. For example, the only way to avoid high tariffs imposed on outsiders by countries in Europe is to establish manufacturing operations.

7. *Management contract*. In this situation, a management company agrees to manage some or all of the functions of another company's operations in exchange for management fees, a share of the profits, or, sometimes, stock options.

8. *Acquisition*. Some companies prefer to enter markets through the acquisition of other companies. Advantages of acquisition include complete control over operations, obtaining new technology, the inclusion of local managers in the organization, immediate access to new markets, and the instant credibility and gains realized by owning an already established company.[48] For example, acquisition has been a key element in Heinz's strategy.[49] Seventy percent of the company's products offered worldwide do not bear the Heinz label.

Regardless of the choice of method(s) used to gain entry into a foreign marketplace, companies must somehow integrate these operations. The complexities involved in operating on a worldwide basis dictate that firms decide on a choice of operating strategies.

Although the task of international marketing is similar to that at home, there are areas where significant differences arise that can have an important influence on the outcome of a marketing program. These differences must be considered when developing alternative marketing strategies for foreign markets. A critical decision marketing managers must make relates to the extent of adaptation of the marketing mix elements for the foreign country the company operates in. One approach to this strategy involves five alternative strategies for marketing abroad.[50] Each of these strategies is based on the idea of adapting either the product, the communication process, or both to the particular market; or operating on a basis where all of the elements of the

---

[48]Marc C. Particelli, "A Global Arena," *Journal of Consumer Marketing*, Fall 1990, pp. 43–52.

[49]"Building Successful Global Partnerships," *The Journal of Business Strategy*, September/October 1988, pp. 12–15.

[50]This section is based on Warren J. Keegan, "Five Strategies for Multinational Marketing," *European Business*, January 1970, pp. 35–40. Also see Warren J. Keegan, "Multinational Product Planning: Strategic Alternatives," *Journal of Marketing*, January 1969, pp. 58–62.

marketing mix are standardized. In essence, these approaches represent alternatives, ranging from a purely global to a purely multidomestic approach, that companies can pursue in regards to the product and communication elements of the marketing mix.

Strategy One: Same Product, Same Message Worldwide

This approach involves a uniform strategy for each market offering the same product and same advertising appeals. Obviously, this approach has numerous advantages: it is simple, demands on management time are minimal, and it requires no original analysis or data generation. The product is unchanged, so there are opportunities for economies of scale in production as well as marketing. In sum, it is the lowest-cost strategy.

Unfortunately, the uniform strategy does not work for all products, although some firms, such as Pepsi-Cola and Coca-Cola, have been successful using this strategy. For example, in Moscow, Pepsi's ad slogan, "The new generation chooses Pepsi," can be seen everywhere, from television shows to newspaper headlines to outdoor billboards.[51] Other firms, such as Chrysler and some food product manufacturers, have not been successful with the uniform approach. These firms have been forced to adapt their marketing mix. Especially in the case of advertising, standardization opportunities are most likely to occur in less affluent, developing markets because American and other foreign products are often perceived as superior to local products.[52]

Strategy Two: Same Product, Different Communications

This strategy becomes necessary when the product fills a different need or is used differently but under conditions similar to those in the domestic market. Thus, the only adjustment necessary is in marketing communications. Examples of products where this strategy can be used are bicycles and motorcycles. In the United States, they fill a recreation need, while in many parts of the world they serve as basic transportation.

Since the product remains unchanged, this strategy is also a relatively low-cost alternative. Additional costs would be incurred in identifying different product functions and reformulating the advertising and other

---

[51]Genine Babakian, "Arise Comrades, Cast Off Your Chains and Go Get a Coke," *Brandweek,* July 20, 1992, pp. 22–23.

[52]For a discussion of issues related to the standardization of advertising, see William L. James and John S. Hill, "International Advertising Messages: To Adapt or Not to Adapt," *Journal of Advertising Research,* June/July 1991, pp. 65–71.

communications. For example, in Europe, although consumers like and purchase many brands from marketers based in other countries, they prefer commercials produced locally and targeted specifically to their tastes.[53]

Strategy Three: Different Product, Same Communications

This strategy involves a uniform approach to communications with the product being adapted to local conditions. This strategy assumes that the product will serve the same function in the foreign market but under different use conditions. For example, Campbell's Soup initially fared poorly in the English market. The English were not used to condensed soup, so they neglected to add water. Consequently, they thought the soup was too strong and bitter. Realizing this, Campbell's added water to their soups, thus adapting their product to British needs and wants.[54]

Strategy Four: Different Product, Different Communications

This strategy involves adapting both the product and the communications to local conditions. This is necessary because of different market conditions or because the product serves different functions.

Nescafe was forced to use this strategy in England when its instant coffee, which sold well in Europe, did poorly in England. Thus, a special blend was developed for England. When marketing the new blend, it was found that coffee was viewed as a nontraditional drink, since tea was the traditional drink. The firm was forced to develop special advertisements emphasizing that coffee was for the young person looking for something different.

Strategy Five: Product Invention

When customer needs and conditions under which the product is used are in no way similar to the domestic market, this strategy may be necessary. This involves the invention or development of an entirely new product, designed to satisfy specific customer needs at a price within reach of the consumer. While it is often costly to pursue this strategy, it may be a rewarding one for mass markets in less developed nations of the world. Figure 13–2 summarizes the five strategies.

---

[53]Nancy Giges, "Europeans Buy Outside Goods, But Like Local Ads," *Advertising Age,* April 27, 1992, pp. I-1, I-26.

[54]For a discussion of issues related to the adaptation of global products, see James Wills, A. Coskun Samli, and Laurence Jacobs, "Developing Global Products and Marketing Strategies: A Construct and a Research Agenda," *Journal of the Academy of Marketing Science* 19, no. 1, Winter 1991, pp. 1–10.

Figure 13–2 *Multinational Product-Communication Mix: Strategic Alternatives*

Product Strategy	Communications Strategy	Product Examples	Product Function or Need Satisfied	Conditions of Product Use
1. Same	Same.	Soft drinks, automobiles.	Same.	Same.
2. Same	Different.	Bicycles, recreation, transportation.	Different.	Same.
3. Different	Same.	Gasoline, detergents.	Same.	Different.
4. Different	Different.	Clothing, greeting cards.	Different.	Different.
5. Invention	Develop new communications.	Hand-powered washing machine.	Same.	Different.

The choice of a particular strategy, of course, depends on the specific product-market mix. Depending on the area of the world under consideration and the particular product mix, different degrees of standardization / adaptation to the marketing mix elements may take place. As a guideline, standardization of one or more parts of the marketing mix is a function of many factors that individually and collectively affect companies in different decision areas.[55] These factors and their resulting influence are:

1. When markets are economically alike, standardization is more practical.
2. When worldwide customers, not countries, are the basis for segmenting markets, a standardization strategy is more effective.
3. The greater the degree of similarity in the markets in terms of customer behavior and lifestyle, the more effective a standardization strategy is.
4. The higher the cultural compatibility of the product across the host countries, the more appropriate is standardization.
5. When a firm's competitive position is similar in different markets, standardization is more practical.
6. When competing against the same adversaries, with similar share positions, in different countries, standardization is more appropriate than when competing against purely local companies.
7. Industrial and high-technology products are more suitable for standardization than consumer products.
8. The greater the differences in physical, political, and legal environments between home and host countries, the greater will be the necessary degree of adaptation.
9. The more similar the marketing infrastructure in the home and host countries, the more likely is the effectiveness of standardization.

---

[55]Material in this section is based on Subhash C. Jain, "Standardization of International Marketing Strategy: Some Research Hypotheses," *Journal of Marketing,* January 1989, pp. 70–79.

Whatever the case, the decision to adapt or standardize marketing should be made only after a thorough analysis of the product-market mix has been undertaken. The company's end goal is to develop, manufacture, and market the products best suited to the actual and potential needs of the local (wherever that may be) customer and to the social and economic conditions of the marketplace.[56] While it is true that a good product knows no national boundaries, there can be subtle differences, from country to country and from region to region, in the ways a product is used and what customers expect from it.

CONCLUSION

The world is truly becoming a global market. Many companies that seek to avoid operating in the international arena are destined for failure. For those willing to undertake the challenges and risks necessary to become multinational corporations, the sky is the limit. The purpose of this chapter was to introduce the reader to the opportunities, problems, and challenges involved in international marketing.

ADDITIONAL READINGS

Batres, Roberto E. "One Market for the Americas." *The Journal of Business Strategy,* March/April 1992, pp. 13–17.

Baum, Herbert M. "Borderless North America: One Company's Response." *Marketing Management,* Winter 1992, pp. 46–48.

Belle, Pedro. "Globalizing the Rest of the World." *Harvard Business Review,* July–August 1991, pp. 50–55.

Clark, Terry. "International Marketing and National Character: A Review and Proposal for an Integrative Theory." *Journal of Marketing,* October 1990, pp. 66–79.

Clarke, Christopher J., and Kieron Brennan. "Global Mobility—The Concept." *Long Range Planning,* February 1992, pp. 73–80.

Dahringer, Lee D. "Marketing Services Internationally: Barriers and Management Strategies." *The Journal of Services Marketing,* Summer 1991, pp. 5–17.

De Meyer, Arnoud. "Tech Talk: How Managers Are Stimulating Global R&D Communication." *Sloan Management Review,* Spring 1991, pp. 49–58.

Hong, Sung-Tai, and Youjae Yi. "A Cross-National Comparison of Country of Origin Effects on Product Evaluations." *Journal of International Consumer Marketing* 4, no. 4 (1992), pp. 49–71.

Katabe, Masaaki, and Dale F. Duhan. "The Perceived Veracity of PIMS Strategy Principles in Japan: An Empirical Inquiry." *Journal of Marketing,* January 1991, pp. 26–41.

---

[56]This material is taken from Hideo Sugiura, "How Honda Localizes Its Global Strategy," *Sloan Management Review,* Fall 1990, pp. 77–82.

Matejka, Ken, and Dick Dunsing. "Japanese / American Management Myths." *Business Horizons,* November / December 1991, pp. 54–58.

Nonaka, Ikujiro. "Redundant, Overlapping Organization: A Japanese Approach to Managing the Innovation Process." *California Management Review,* Spring 1990, pp. 27–38.

Roth, Martin S. "Depth Versus Breadth Strategies for Global Brand Image Management." *Journal of Advertising,* June 1992, pp. 25–36.

Takada, Hirokazu, and Dipak Jain. "Cross-National Analysis of Diffusion of Consumer Durable Goods in Pacific Rim Countries." *Journal of Marketing,* April 1991, pp. 48–54.

PART E

Marketing Response to a Changing Society

Chapter 14
*Marketing Management: Social
and Ethical Dimensions*

Marketing Management: Social and Ethical Dimensions

The primary concern of this chapter is the role of marketing in society. While we believe that marketing and the free enterprise system offer the best and most effective system of exchange that has been developed, we also believe that marketers have a responsibility to society that goes beyond the profit objectives of an organization.[1]

In the remainder of this chapter we first investigate the relative power and rights of marketers and consumers. Then we discuss four influences that act as checks and balances to control the power of business in general and marketing in particular. These include legal, political, competitive, and ethical influences.

THE RIGHTS OF MARKETERS AND CONSUMERS

Both marketers and consumers are granted certain rights by society, and both have a degree of power. Overall, many people believe that marketers have considerably more power than consumers. Several years ago, Professor Philip Kotler provided the following list of rights granted to marketers (sellers):

1. Sellers have the right to introduce any product in any size, style, color, etc., so long as it meets minimum health and safety requirements.
2. Sellers have the right to price the product as they please so long as they avoid discrimination that is harmful to competition.

---

[1]This chapter is based on J. Paul Peter and Jerry C. Olson, *Consumer Behavior and Marketing Strategy*, 3rd ed. (Homewood, Ill.: Richard D. Irwin, 1993), chap. 20.

3. Sellers have the right to promote the product using any resources, media, or message, in any amount, so long as no deception or fraud is involved.
4. Sellers have the right to introduce any buying schemes they wish, so long as they are not discriminatory.
5. Sellers have the right to alter the product offering at any time.
6. Sellers have the right to distribute the product in any reasonable manner.
7. Sellers have the right to limit the product guarantee or postsale services.[2]

While this list is not exhaustive, it does serve to illustrate that marketers have a good deal of power and latitude in their actions.

Since the Consumer Bill of Rights was issued in the early 1960s, consumers have been granted at least four basic rights. First, consumers are granted the *right to safety* which means the right to be protected against products and services that are hazardous to health and life. Second, consumers are granted the *right to be informed* which is the right to be protected against fraudulent, deceitful, or misleading advertising or other information that could interfere with making an informed choice. Third, consumers are granted the *right to choose*—the right to have access to a variety of competitive products that are priced fairly and are of satisfactory quality. Finally, consumers are granted the *right to be heard* or the right to be ensured that their interests will be fully and fairly considered in the formulation and administration of government policy. While this list may appear to grant the consumer considerable rights and protection, it has an important weakness: most of these rights depend on the assumption that consumers are both capable of being and willing to be highly involved in purchase and consumption. In fact, however, many consumers are neither. Young children, many elderly people, and the uneducated poor often do not have the cognitive abilities to process information well enough to be protected. Further, even those consumers who do have the capacity often are not willing to invest the time, money, cognitive energy, and effort to ensure their rights.

The right to choose is also predicated on the assumption that consumers are rational, autonomous, knowledgeable information processors and decision makers. While we believe that most consumers are capable of being so, evidence suggests that consumers often do not behave this way. Further, the right to choose ignores the power of marketing to influence attitudes, intentions, and behaviors. Consumers' needs, wants, and satisfaction may be developed by marketers, for instance. Thus, the assumption of consumer autonomy is not easily supported.

Finally, no matter how much effort consumers exert to ensure they are choosing a good product, they cannot process information that is not available. For example, consumers cannot be aware of product safety risks that are hidden from them.

---

[2]Phillip Kotler, "What Consumerism Means for Marketers," *Harvard Business Review*, May–June 1972, pp 48–57. Also see Joseph V. Anderson, "Power Marketing: Its Past, Present, and Future," *Journal of Consumer Marketing*, Summer 1987, pp. 5–13.

Figure 14-1 *Major Sources of Consumer Protection*

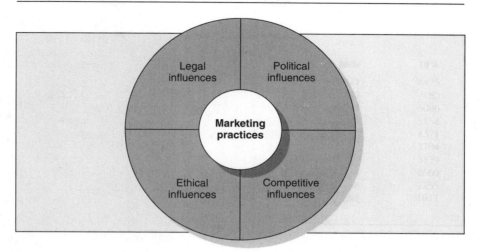

Overall, then, if there were no other forces in society, marketers might well have more rights and power than consumers do. This is not to say that consumers cannot exert countercontrol on marketers or that consumers do not vary in the degree to which they are influenced by marketers. However, as our society and system of government and exchange evolved, a number of constraints or societal influences on marketing activities have also developed. As shown in Figure 14-1, these include legal, political, competitive, and ethical influences.

Before discussing each of these societal influences, three points should be noted. First, as noted earlier, we believe that marketing and the free enterprise system offer the best and most effective system of exchange that has ever been developed. This does not mean that the system could not be improved. For example, there is still a large group of poor, uneducated, hungry people in our society who have little chance of improving their lot.

Second, while marketing usually receives the brunt of society's criticism of business, marketing managers are no more or less guilty of wrongdoing than other business executives. Corporate responsibility to society is a shared responsibility of all business executives, regardless of functional field. In addition, marketing executives are no more or less ethical than most other groups in society. Similarly, while business, particularly big business, is commonly singled out for criticism, there is no question that other fields—including medicine, engineering, and law—also have their share of societal problems. Some consumers could also be criticized for the billions of dollars of merchandise that is shoplifted annually, as well as for other crimes against businesses and society.

Figure 14-2   *Some Problem Areas in Marketing*

Product Issues

Unsafe products
Poor-quality products
Poor service repair/maintenance after sale
Deceptive packaging and labeling practices

Pricing Issues

Deceptive pricing
Fraudulent or misleading credit practices
Warranty refund problems

Promotion Issues

Deceptive advertising
Advertising to children
Bait-and-switch advertising
Anxiety-inducing advertising
Deceptive personal selling tactics

Distribution Issues

Sale of counterfeit products and brands
Pyramid selling
Deceptive in-store selling influences

Third, while some critics of marketing focus on the field in general, many of the problems are confined to a relatively small percentage of firms and practices. Figure 14-2 presents a list of some of the most commonly cited areas of concern, divided into product, promotion, pricing, and distribution issues. Many of these practices are subject to legal influences or constraints.

LEGAL INFLUENCES

Legal influences are federal, state, and local legislation and the agencies and processes by which these laws are upheld. Figure 14-3 presents examples of recent federal legislation designed to protect consumers. Some federal legislation is designed to control practices in specific industries (such as food); others are aimed at controlling functional areas (such as product safety).

A variety of government agencies are involved in enforcing these laws and investigating business practices. In addition to state and local agencies, this includes a number of federal agencies, such as those listed in Chapter 1.

Legal influences and the power of government agencies to regulate business and marketing practices grew dramatically in the 1970s; but the 1980s witnessed a decrease in many areas of regulation. In fact, deregulation of business was the major thrust in this period, and government agencies considerably reduced their involvement in controlling business practices. Thus, while legal constraints are an important form of consumer protection, it appears that this influence, at least at the federal level, has diminished somewhat.[3]

---

[3]For complete discussions of legal influences on marketing, see Louis W. Stern and Thomas L. Eovaldi, *Legal Aspects of Marketing Strategy* (Englewood Cliffs, N.J.: Prentice Hall, 1984); Robert J. Posch, Jr., *The Complete Guide to Marketing and the Law* (Englewood Cliffs, N.J.: Prentice Hall, 1988).

Figure 14–3   *Examples of Consumer-Oriented Legislation*

Year	Legislation	Major Provision of Law
1988	Toxic Substances Control Act Amendment	Provides adequate time for planning and implementation of school asbestos management plans.
1988	Federal Food, Drug and Cosmetic Act Amendment	Bans reimportation of drugs produced in the United States. Places restrictions on distribution of drug samples, bans certain resales of drugs by health care facilities.
1986	Truth in Mileage Act	Amends the Motor Vehicle Information and Cost Savings Act to strengthen, for the protection of consumers, the provisions respecting disclosure of mileage when motor vehicles are transferred.
1986	Petroleum Overcharge Distribution and Restitution Act	Provides for distribution to injured consumers of escrow funds remaining from oil company settlements of alleged price allocation violations under the Emergency Petroleum Allocation Act of 1973.
1986	Superfund Amendments and Reauthorization Act	Extends and amends the Comprehensive Environmental Response Compensation and Liability Act of 1980. Authorizes appropriations for and revises the EPA Hazardous Substance Response Trust Fund program for financing cleanup of uncontrolled hazardous waste sites.
1986	Anti-Drug Abuse Act	Amends the Food, Drug and Cosmetic Act to revise provisions on regulation of infant formula manufacture.
1986	Processed Products Inspection Improvement Act	Amends the Meat Inspection Act to eliminate USDA continuous inspection requirements for meats, poultry, and egg processing plants for a six-year trial period.
1986	Emergency Response Act	Amends the Toxic Substances Control Act to require the EPA to promulgate regulations pertaining to inspections, development of asbestos management plans, and response actions.
1986	Safe Drinking Water Act Amendments	Amends the Safe Drinking Water Act. Authorizes appropriations for and revises EPA safe drinking water programs, including grants to states for drinking water standards enforcement and groundwater protection programs.
1986	Drug Export Amendments Act	Amends the Food, Drug and Cosmetic Act to remove restrictions on export of human and veterinary drugs not yet approved by FDA or USDA for use in the U.S. and establishes conditions governing export of such drugs.
1986	Comprehensive Smokeless Tobacco Health Education Act	Provides for public education concerning the health consequences of using smokeless tobacco products. Prohibits radio and television advertising of smokeless tobacco.
1986	Recreational Boating Safety Act Amendment	Enhances boating safety by requiring a report relating to informational displays on gasoline pumps.

Source: John R. Nevin, "Consumer Protection Legislation: Evolution, Structure and Prognosis," Working paper, University of Wisconsin–Madison, Madison, Wis., August 1989.

Figure 14–4   *Some Political Groups Concerned with Consumerism*

Broad-Based National Groups	**Special-Interest Groups**
Consumer Federation of America	Action for Children's Television
National Wildlife Federation	American Association of Retired Persons
Common Cause	Group against Smoking and Pollution

Smaller Multi-Issue Organizations	**Local Groups**
National Consumer's League	Public-interest research groups
Ralph Nader's Public Citizen	Local consumer protection offices
	Local broadcast and newspaper consumer "action lines"

Source: Adapted from Paul N. Bloom and Stephen A. Greyser, "The Maturing of Consumerism," *Harvard Business Review*, November–December 1981, pp. 130–39.

POLITICAL INFLUENCES

By *political influences,* we mean the pressure exerted to control marketing practices by various consumer groups. These groups use a variety of methods to influence marketing practices, such as lobbying with various government agencies to enact legislation, boycotting companies for unfair practices, or working directly with consumers in redress assistance and education. Figure 14–4 lists some organizations that are designed to serve consumer interests. These are but a few examples; one tally found over 100 national organizations and over 600 state and local groups that are concerned with consumerism.

Bloom and Greyser argue that consumerism has reached the mature stage of its life cycle and that its impact has been fragmented.[4] Yet they believe consumerism will continue to have some impact on business, and they offer three strategies for coping with it. First, businesses can try to accelerate the decline of consumerism by *reducing demand* for it. This could be done by improving product quality, expanding services, lowering prices, and toning down advertising claims. Highlight 14–1 describes one industry's attempt to reduce demand for consumerism.

Second, businesses can *compete* with consumer groups by having active consumer affairs departments that offer redress assistance and consumer education. Alternatively, a business could fund and coordinate activities designed to "sell" deregulation and other probusiness causes.

---

[4]Paul N. Bloom and Stephen A. Greyser, "The Maturing of Consumerism," *Harvard Business Review*, November–December 1981, pp. 130–39; also see Paul N. Bloom and Ruth Belk Smith, *The Future of Consumerism* (Lexington, Mass.: Lexington Books, 1986).

HIGHLIGHT 14–1

Political Influences: TV Network Guidelines for Advertising to Children

Each of the major television networks has its own set of guidelines for children's advertising, although the basics are very similar. A few rules, such as the requirement of a static "island" shot at the end, are written in stone; others, however, occasionally can be negotiated.

Many of the rules below apply specifically to toys. The networks also have special guidelines for kid's food commercials and for kid's commercials that offer premiums.

	ABC	CBS	NBC
Must not overglamorize product	✔	✔	✔
No exhortative language, such as "Ask Mom to buy . . ."	✔	✔	✔
No realistic war settings	✔		✔
Generally no celebrity endorsements	✔	Case-by-case	✔
Can't use "only" or "just" in regard to price	✔	✔	✔
Show only two toys per child or maximum of six per commercial	✔		✔
Five-second "island" showing product against plain background at end of spot	✔	✔	✔ (4 to 5)
Animation restricted to one third of a commercial	✔		✔
Generally no comparative or superiority claims	Case-by-case	Handle w/care	✔
No costumes or props not available with the toy	✔		✔
No child or toy can appear in animated segments	✔		✔
Three-second establishing shot of toy in relation to child	✔	✔ (2.5 to 3)	
No shots under one second in length		✔	
Must show distance a toy can travel before stopping on its own		✔	

Source: Joanne Lipman, "Double Standard for Kids' TV Ads." *The Wall Street Journal*, June 10, 1988, p. 21.

HIGHLIGHT 14–2

Code of Ethics of the American Marketing Association

Members of the American Marketing Association (AMA) are committed to ethical professional conduct. They have joined together in subscribing to this Code of Ethics embracing the following topics:

Responsibilities of the Marketer

Marketers must accept responsibility for the consequence of their activities and make every effort to ensure that their decisions, recommendations, and actions function to identify, serve, and satisfy all relevant publics: customers, organizations, and society. Marketer's professional conduct must be guided by:

1. The basic rule of professional ethics: not knowingly to do harm.
2. The adherence to all applicable laws and regulations.
3. The accurate representation of their education, training, and experience.
4. The active support, practice, and promotion of this Code of Ethics.

Honesty and Fairness

Marketers shall uphold and advance the integrity, honor, and dignity of the marketing profession by:

1. Being honest in serving consumers, clients, employees, suppliers, distributors, and the public.

Source: The American Marketing Association, Chicago.

2. Not knowingly participating in conflict of interest without prior notice to all parties involved.
3. Establishing equitable fee schedules including the payment or receipt of usual, customary, and/or legal compensation or marketing exchanges.

Rights and Duties of Parties in the Marketing Exchange Process

Participants in the marketing exchange process should be able to expect that:

1. Products and services offered are safe and fit for their intended uses.
2. Communications about offered products and services are not deceptive.
3. All parties intend to discharge their obligations, financial and otherwise, in good faith.
4. Appropriate internal methods exist for equitable adjustment and/or redress of grievances concerning purchases.

It is understood that the above would include, *but is not limited to,* the following responsibilities of the marketer:

In the area of product development and management,
—Disclosure of all substantial risks associated with product or service usage.
—Identifications of any product component substitution that might materially change

---

Third, businesses can *cooperate* with consumer groups by providing financial and other support. Overall, most of these strategies would likely further reduce the impact and importance of political influences. However, to the degree that following these strategies leads business firms to increase their social responsibility activities in the long run, the consumer could benefit.

the product or impact on the buyer's purchase decision.

—Identification of extra-cost added features.

In the area of promotions,

—Avoidance of false and misleading advertising.

—Rejection of high pressure manipulation, or misleading sales tactics.

—Avoidance of sales promotions that use deception or manipulation.

In the area of distribution,

—Not manipulating the availability of a product for purpose of exploitation.

—Not using coercion in the marketing channel.

—Not exerting undue influence over the reseller's choice to handle the product.

In the area of pricing,

—Not engaging in price fixing.

—Not practicing predatory pricing.

—Disclosing the full price associated with any purchase.

In the area of marketing research,

—Prohibiting selling or fund raising under the guise of conducting research.

—Maintaining research integrity by avoiding misrepresentation and omission of pertinent research data.

—Treating outside clients and suppliers fairly.

Organizational Relationships

Marketers should be aware of how their behavior may influence or impact on the behavior of others in organizational relationships. They should not demand, encourage, or apply coercion to obtain unethical behavior in their relationships with others, such as employees, suppliers, or customers.

1. Apply confidentiality and anonymity in professional relationships with regard to privileged information.
2. Meet their obligations and responsibilities in contracts and mutual agreements in a timely manner.
3. Avoid taking the work of others, in whole, or in part, and represent this work as their own or directly benefit from it without compensation or consent of the originator or owner.
4. Avoid manipulation to take advantage of situations to maximize personal welfare in a way that unfairly deprives or damages the organization or others.

Any AMA members found to be in violation of any provision of this Code of Ethics may have his or her association membership suspended or revoked.

COMPETITIVE INFLUENCES

Competitive influences refer to actions of competing firms intended to affect each other and consumers. These actions can be taken in many ways. For example, one firm might sue another firm or point out its alleged fraudulent activities to consumers. Johnson & Johnson frequently took competitors to court to protect its Tylenol brand of pain reliever from being shown in comparative ads. Burger King publicly accused McDonald's of overstating the weight of its hamburgers.

Perhaps the most important consumer protection generated by competition is that it reduces the impact of information from any single firm. In other words, in a marketing environment where there are many active competitors, no single firm can dominate the information flow to consumers. In this sense, conflicting competitive claims, images, information, and offers may help consumers from being unduly influenced by a single firm or brand. Conversely, it may also lead to information overload.

Consumers may also benefit from the development and marketing of better products and services brought about by competitive pressure. Current merger trends and the concentration of various industries may lessen these competitive constraints and societal advantages, however.

ETHICAL INFLUENCES

Perhaps the most important constraints on marketing practices are *ethical influences* and involve *self-regulation* by marketers. Many professions have codes of ethics (see Highlight 14–2), and many firms have their own consumer affairs offices that seek to ensure that the consumer is treated fairly. In addition, some companies have developed a more positive image with consumers by emphasizing consumer-oriented marketing tactics such as offering toll-free hot lines for information and complaints, promoting unit pricing, and supporting social causes.

A difficult problem in discussing ethical constraints is that there is no single standard by which actions can be judged. Laczniak summarizes five ethical standards that have been proposed by various marketing writers:

1. *The Golden Rule:* Act in the way you would expect others to act toward you.
2. *The Utilitarian Principle:* Act in a way that results in the greatest good for the greatest number.
3. *Kant's Categorical Imperative:* Act in such a way that the action taken under the circumstances could be a universal law or rule of behavior.
4. *The Professional Ethic:* Take actions that would be viewed as proper by a disinterested panel of professional colleagues.
5. *The TV Test:* A manager should always ask: "Would I feel comfortable explaining to a national TV audience why I took this action?"[5]

---

[5]Gene R. Laczniak, "Framework for Analyzing Marketing Ethics," *Journal of Macromarketing,* Spring 1983, pp. 7–18; also see Donald P. Robin and R. Eric Reidenbach, "Social Responsibility, Ethics, and Marketing Strategy: Closing the Gap between Concept and Application," *Journal of Marketing,* January 1987, pp. 44–58; Jerry R. Godsby and Shelby D. Hunt, "Cognitive Moral Development and Marketing," *Journal of Marketing,* January 1992, pp. 55–68.

Figure 14–5 *Marketing Scenarios that Raise Ethical Questions*

Scenario 1

The Thrifty Supermarket Chain has 12 stores in the city of Gotham, U.S.A. The company's policy is to maintain the same prices for all items at all stores. However, the distribution manager knowingly sends the poorest cuts of meat and the lowest-quality produce to the store located in the low-income section of town. He justifies this action based on the fact that this store has the highest overhead due to factors such as employee turnover, pilferage, and vandalism. *Is the distribution manager's economic rationale sufficient justification for his allocation method?*

Scenario 2

The independent Chevy Dealers of Metropolis, U.S.A., have undertaken an advertising campaign headlined by the slogan: "Is your family's life worth 45 MPG?" The ads admit that while Chevy subcompacts are *not* as fuel efficient as foreign imports and cost more to maintain, they are safer according to government-sponsored crash tests. The ads implicitly ask if responsible parents, when purchasing a car, should trade off fuel efficiency for safety. *Is it ethical for the dealers association to use a fear appeal to offset an economic disadvantage?*

Scenario 3

A few recent studies have linked the presence of the artificial sweetener subsugural to cancer in laboratory rats. While the validity of these findings has been hotly debated by medical experts, the Food and Drug Administration has ordered products containing the ingredient banned from sale in the United States. The Jones Company sends all of its sugar-free J.C. Cola (which contains subsugural) to European supermarkets because the sweetener has not been banned there. *Is it acceptable for the Jones Company to send an arguably unsafe product to another market without waiting for further evidence?*

Scenario 4

The Acme Company sells industrial supplies through its own sales force, which calls on company pur-

chasing agents. Acme has found that providing the purchasing agent with small gifts helps cement a cordial relationship and creates goodwill. Acme follows the policy that the bigger the order, the bigger the gift to the purchasing agent. The gifts range from a pair of tickets to a sports event to outboard motors and snowmobiles. Acme does not give gifts to personnel at companies that they know have an explicit policy prohibiting the acceptance of such gifts. *Assuming no laws are violated, is Acme's policy of providing gifts to purchasing agents morally proper?*

Scenario 5

The Buy American Electronics Company has been selling its highly rated System X Color TV sets (21, 19 and 12 inches) for $700, $500, and $300, respectively. These prices have been relatively uncompetitive in the market. After some study, Buy American substitutes several cheaper components (which engineering says may slightly reduce the quality of performance) and passes on the savings to the consumer in the form of a $100 price reduction on each model. Buy American institutes a price-oriented promotional campaign that neglects to mention that the second-generation System X sets are different from the first. *Is the company's competitive strategy ethical?*

Scenario 6

The Smith & Smith Advertising Agency has been struggling financially. Mr. Smith is approached by the representative of a small South American country that is on good terms with the U.S. Department of State. He wants S & S to create a multimillion dollar advertising and public relations campaign that will bolster the image of the country and increase the likelihood that it will receive U.S. foreign aid assistance and attract investment capital. Smith knows the country is a dictatorship that has been accused of numerous human rights violations. *Is it ethical for the Smith & Smith Agency to undertake the proposed campaign?*

Source: Gene R. Laczinak, "Framework for Analyzing Marketing Ethics," *Journal of Macromarketing*, Spring 1983, p. 8.

Following these standards could result in many different interpretations of ethical marketing practice. If you doubt this, try applying them to the scenarios in Figure 14–5 and then comparing your answers with those of other readers.

Overall, then, what constitutes ethical marketing behavior is a matter of social judgement. Even in the areas such as product safety, what constitutes ethical marketing practices is not always clear. While at first blush it might be argued that all products should either be completely safe or not be allowed on the market, deeper inspection reveals questions such as "How Safe?" and "For whom?" For example, bicycles often head the list of the most hazardous products, yet few consumers or marketers would argue that bicycles should be banned from the market. Much of the problem in determining product safety concerns the question of whether the harm done results from an inherent lack of product safety or unsafe use by the consumer.

CONCLUSION

In this chapter we have discussed some of the important relationships between marketers and consumers that involve questions of social responsibility. Overall, while society offers marketers considerable power and latitude in performing marketing tasks, marketers also have a variety of constraints placed on their behavior. These include legal, political, competitive, and ethical influences.

ADDITIONAL READINGS

Akaah, Ishmael P., and Edward A. Riordan. "Judgments of Marketing Professionals about Ethical Issues in Marketing Research: A Replication and Extension." *Journal of Marketing Research,* February 1989, pp. 112–20.

Bellizzi, Joseph A., and Robert E. Hite. "Supervising Unethical Salesforce Behavior." *Journal of Marketing,* April 1989, pp. 36–47.

Boedecker, Karl A.; Fred W. Morgan; and Jeffrey J. Stoltman. "Legal Dimensions of Salespersons' Statements: A Review and Managerial Suggestions." *Journal of Marketing,* January 1991, pp. 70–80.

Ferrell, O. C., and Steven J. Skinner. "Ethical Behavior and Bureaucratic Structure in Marketing Research Organizations." *Journal of Marketing Research,* February 1988, pp. 103–9.

Hunt, Shelby D.; Van R. Wood; and Lawrence B. Chonko. "Corporate Ethical Values and Organizational Commitment in Marketing." *Journal of Marketing,* July 1989, pp. 79–90.

Laczniak, Gene R., and Patrick E. Murphy. *Ethical Marketing Decisions: The Higher Road.* Boston: Allyn and Bacon, 1993.

Smith, N. Craig, and John A. Quelch. *Ethics in Marketing.* Homewood, Ill.: Richard D. Irwin, 1993.

Analyzing Marketing Problems and Cases

HIGHLIGHT 1

A Case for Case Analysis

Cases assist in bridging the gap between classroom learning and the so-called real world of marketing management. They provide us with an opportunity to develop, sharpen, and test our analytical skills at:

—Assessing situations.
—Sorting out and organizing key information.
—Asking the right questions.
—Defining opportunities and problems.

—Identifying and evaluating alternative courses of action.
—Interpreting data.
—Evaluating the results of past strategies.
—Developing and defending new strategies.
—Interacting with other managers.
—Making decisions under conditions of uncertainty.
—Critically evaluating the work of others.
—Responding to criticism.

Source: David W. Cravens and Charles W. Lamb, Jr., *Strategic Marketing: Cases and Applications,* 4th ed. (Homewood, Ill.: Richard D. Irwin, 1993), p. 95.

The use of business cases was developed by faculty members of the Harvard Graduate School of Business Administration in the 1920s. Case studies have been widely accepted as one effective way of exposing students to the decision-making process.

Basically, cases represent detailed descriptions or reports of business problems. They are usually written by a trained observer who actually had been involved in the firm or organization and had some dealings with the problems under consideration. Cases generally entail both qualitative and quantitative data which the student must analyze to determine appropriate alternatives and solutions.

The primary purpose of the case method is to introduce a measure of realism into management education. Rather than emphasizing the teaching of concepts, the case method focuses on application of concepts and sound logic to real-world business problems. In this way, the student learns to bridge the gap between abstraction and application and to appreciate the value of both.

The primary purpose of this section is to offer a logical format for the analysis of case problems. Although there is no one format that can be successfully applied to all cases, the following framework is intended to be a logical sequence from which to develop sound analyses. This framework is presented for analysis of comprehensive marketing cases; however, the process should also be useful for shorter marketing cases, incidents, and problems.

A CASE ANALYSIS FRAMEWORK

A basic approach to case analysis involves a four-step process. First, the problem is defined. Second, alternative courses of action are formulated to solve the problem. Third, the alternatives are analyzed in terms of their strengths and weaknesses. And fourth, an alternative is accepted, and a course of action is recommended. This basic approach is quite useful for the student well versed in case analysis, particularly for shorter cases or incidents. However, for the newcomer, this framework may well be inadequate and oversimplified. Thus, the following expanded framework and checklists are intended to aid the student in becoming proficient at case and problem analysis.

1. Analyze and Record the Current Situation

Whether the analysis of a firm's problems is done by a manager, student, or paid business consultant, the first step is to analyze the current situation. This does not mean writing up a history of the firm but entails the type of analysis described below. This approach is useful not only for getting a better grip on the situation but also for discovering both real and potential problems—the central concern of any case analysis.

Phase 1: The environment. The first phase in analyzing a marketing problem or case is to consider the environment in which the firm is operating. The environment can be broken down into a number of different components such as the economic, social, political, and legal areas. Any of these may contain threats to a firm's success or opportunities for improving a firm's situation.

Phase 2: The industry. The second phase involves analyzing the industry in which the firm operates. A framework provided by Michael Porter includes five competitive forces which need to be considered to do a complete industry analysis.[1] The framework is shown in Figure 1 and includes rivalry among existing competitors, threat of new entrants, and threat of substitute products. In addition, in this framework, buyers and suppliers are included as competitors since they can threaten the profitability of an industry or firm.

While rivalry among existing competitors is an issue in most cases, analysis and strategies for dealing with the other forces can also be critical. This is particularly so when a firm is considering entering a new industry and wants to forecast its potential success. Each of the five competitive forces is discussed below.

Rivalry among existing competitors. In most cases and business situations a firm needs to consider the current competitors in its industry in order to develop successful strategies. Strategies such as price competition, advertising

---

[1]Michael E. Porter, *Competitive Strategy* (New York: Free Press, 1980). Also see Michael E. Porter, *Competitive Advantage: Creating nad Sustaining Superior Performance* (New York: Free Press, 1985); Michael E. Porter, *The Competitive Advantage of Nations* (New York: Free Press, 1990).

Figure 1.   *Competitive Forces in an Industry*

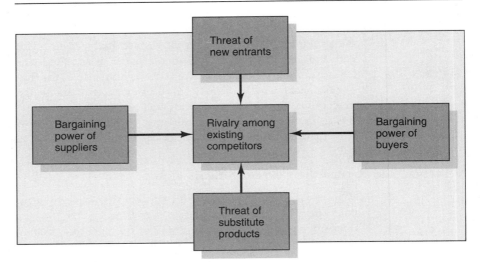

Source: Adapted from Michael E. Porter, "Industry Structure and Competitive Strategy: Keys to Profitability," *Financial Analysts Journal,* July–August 1980, p. 33.

battles, sales promotion offers, new product introductions, and increased customer service are commonly used to attract customers from competitors.

In order to fully analyze existing rivalry, it is important to determine which firms are the major competitors and what are their annual sales, market share, growth profile, and strengths and weaknesses. Also, it is useful to analyze their current and past marketing strategies to try to forecast their likely reactions to a change in a competitive firm's strategy. Finally, it is important to consider any trends or changes in government regulation of an industry or changes in technology that could affect the success of a firm's strategy.

Threat of new entrants. It is always possible for firms in other industries to try to compete in a new industry. New entrants are more likely in industries that have low entry barriers. *Entry barriers* include such things as a need for large financial resources, high brand equity for existing brands in an industry, or economies of scale obtained by existing firms in an industry. Also, existing firms in an industry may benefit from experience curves; that is, their cumulative experience in producing and marketing a product may reduce their per-unit costs below those of inexperienced firms. In general, the higher the entry barriers, the less likely outside firms are to enter an industry. For example, the entry barriers for starting up a new car company are much higher than for starting up a new software company.

Threat of substitute products. In a broad sense, all firms in an industry compete with industries producing substitute products. For example, in cultures where bicycles are the major means of transportation, bicycle manufacturers compete with substitute products such as motor scooters and automobiles. Substitutes limit the potential return in an industry by placing a ceiling on the prices a firm in the industry can profitably charge. The more attractive the price-performance alternative offered by substitutes, the tighter the lid on industry profits. For example, the price of candy, such as Raisinets chocolate-covered raisins, may limit the price Del Monte can charge for "healthy snacks," such as Strawberry Yogurt Raisins.

Bargaining power of suppliers. Suppliers can be a competitive threat in an industry because they can raise the price of raw materials or reduce their quality. Powerful suppliers can reduce the profitability of an industry or firm if companies cannot raise their prices to cover price increases by suppliers. Also, suppliers may be a threat because they may forward integrate into an industry by purchasing a firm that they supply or other firms in the industry.

Bargaining power of buyers. Buyers can compete with an industry by forcing prices down, bargaining for higher quality or more services, and playing competitors off against each other. All of these tactics can lower the profitability of a firm or industry. For example, because Wal-Mart sells such a large percentage of many companies' products, it can negotiate for lower prices than smaller retailers can. Also, buyers may be a threat because they may backward integrate into an industry by purchasing firms that supply them or other firms in the industry.

Phase 3: The firm. The third phase involves analysis of the firm itself not only in comparison with the industry and industry averages but also internally in terms of both quantitative and qualitative data. Key areas of concern at this stage are such factors as objectives, constraints, management philosophy, financial condition, and the organizational structure and culture of the firm.

Phase 4: The marketing strategy. Although there may be internal personnel or structural problems in the marketing department itself that need examination, typically an analysis of the current marketing strategy is the next phase. In this phase, the objectives of the marketing department are analyzed in comparison with those of the firm in terms of agreement, soundness, and attainability. Each element of the marketing mix as well as other areas, like marketing research and decision support systems, is analyzed in terms of whether it is internally consistent, synchronized with the goals of the department and firm, and focused on specific target markets. Although cases often are labeled in terms of their primary emphasis, such as "Pricing" or "Advertising," it is important to analyze the marketing strategy and entire marketing mix, since a change in one element will usually affect the entire marketing program.

In performing the analysis of the current situation, the data should be analyzed carefully to extract the relevant from the superfluous. Many cases contain information that is not relevant to the problem; it is the analyst's job to discard this information to get a clearer picture of the current situation. As the analysis proceeds, a watchful eye must be kept on each phase to determine (1) symptoms of problems; (2) current problems; and (3) potential problems.

HIGHLIGHT 2

What Does Case "Analysis" Mean?

A common criticism of prepared cases goes something like this: "You repeated an awful lot of case material, but you really didn't analyze the case." Yet, at the same time, it is difficult to verbalize exactly what "analysis" means—that is, "I can't explain exactly what it is, but I know it when I see it!"

This is a common problem since the term *analysis* has many definitions and means different things in different contexts. In terms of case analysis, one thing that is clear is that analysis means going beyond simply describing the case information. It includes determining the implications of the case information for developing strategy. This determination may involve careful mathematical analysis of sales and profit data or thoughtful interpretation of the text of the case.

One way of thinking about analysis involves a series of three steps: synthesis, generalizations, and implications. Below is a brief example of this process.

The high growth rate of frozen pizza sales has attracted a number of large food processors, including Pillsbury (Totino's), Quaker Oats (Celeste), American Home Products (Chef Boy-ar-dee), Nestle (Stouffer's), General Mills (Saluto), and H. J. Heinz (La Pizzeria). The major independents are Jeno's, Tony's, and John's. Jeno's and Totino's are the market leaders, with market shares of about 19 percent each. Celeste and Tony's have about 8 to 9 percent each, and the others have about 5 percent or less.   **Case Material**

The frozen pizza market is a highly competitive and highly fragmented market.   **Synthesis**

In markets such as this, attempts to gain market share through lower consumer prices or heavy advertising are likely to be quickly copied by competitors and thus not be very effective.   **Generalizations**

Lowering consumer prices or spending more on advertising are likely to be poor strategies. Perhaps increasing freezer space in retail outlets could be effective (this might be obtained through trade discounts). A superior product, e.g., better-tasting pizza, microwave pizza, or increasing geographic coverage of the market, may be better strategies for obtaining market share.   **Implications**

Note that none of the three analysis steps includes any repetition of the case material. Rather, they involve abstracting a meaning of the information and, by pairing it with marketing principles, coming up with the strategic implications of the information.

Symptoms of problems are indicators of a problem but are not problems in and of themselves. For example, a symptom of a problem may be a decline in sales in a particular sales territory. However, the problem is the root cause of the decline in sales—perhaps the field representative quit making sales calls and is relying on phone orders only.

The following is a checklist of the types of questions that should be asked when performing the analysis of the current situation.

Checklist for Analyzing the Current Situation

Phase 1: The environment.

1. What is the state of the economy and are there any trends that could affect the industry, firm, or marketing strategy?
2. What are current trends in cultural and social values and how do these affect the industry, firm, or marketing strategy?
3. What are current political values and trends and how do they affect the industry, firm, or marketing strategy?
4. Is there any current or pending federal, state, or local legislation that could change the industry, firm, or marketing strategy?
5. Overall, are there any threats or opportunities in the environment that could influence the industry, firm, or marketing strategy?

Phase 2: The industry.

1. What industry is the firm in?
2. Which firms are the major competitors in the industry and what is their annual sales, market share, and growth profile?
3. What strategies have competitors in the industry been using, and what has been their success with them?
4. What are the relative strengths and weaknesses of competitors in the industry?
5. How much threat is there of new competitors coming into the industry, and what are the major entry barriers?
6. Are there any substitute products for this industry, and what are their advantages and disadvantages compared to this industry's products?
7. How much bargaining power do suppliers have in this industry, and what is its impact on the firm and industry profits?
8. How much bargaining power do buyers have in this industry, and what is its impact on the firm and industry profits?

Phase 3: The firm.

1. What are the objectives of the firm? Are they clearly stated? Attainable?
2. What are the strengths of the firm? Managerial expertise? Financial? Copyrights or patents?
3. What are the constraints and weaknesses of the firm?
4. Are there any real or potential sources of dysfunctional conflict in the structure of the firm?
5. How is the marketing department structured in the firm?

Phase 4: The marketing strategy.

1. What are the objectives of the marketing strategy? Are they clearly stated? Are they consistent with the objectives of the firm? Is the entire marketing mix structured to meet these objectives?

2. What marketing concepts are at issue in the current strategy? Is the marketing strategy well planned and laid out? Is the strategy consistent with sound marketing principles? If the strategy takes exception to marketing principles, is there a good reason for it?

3. To what target market is the strategy directed? Is it well defined? Is the market large enough to be profitably served? Does the market have long-run potential?

4. What competitive advantage does the marketing strategy offer? If none, what can be done to gain a competitive advantage in the market place?

5. What products are being sold? What is the width, depth, and consistency of the firm's product lines? Does the firm need new products to fill out its product line? Should any product be deleted? What is the profitability of the various products?

6. What promotion mix is being used? Is promotion consistent with the products and product images? What could be done to improve the promotion mix?

7. What channels of distribution are being used? Do they deliver the product at the right time and right place to meet consumer needs? Are the channels typical of those used in the industry? Could channels be made more efficient?

8. What pricing strategies are being used? How do prices compare with similar products of other firms? How are prices determined?

9. Are marketing research and information systematically integrated into the marketing strategy? Is the overall marketing strategy internally consistent?

The relevant information from this preliminary analysis is now formalized and recorded. At this point the analyst must be mindful of the difference between facts and opinions. Facts are objective statements, such as financial data, whereas opinions are subjective interpretations of facts or situations. The analyst must make certain not to place too much emphasis on opinions and to carefully consider any variables that may bias such opinions.

Regardless of how much information is contained in the case or how much additional information is collected, the analyst usually finds that it is impossible to specify a complete framework for the current situation. At this point, assumptions must be made. Clearly, since each analyst may make different assumptions, it is critical that assumptions be explicitly stated. When presenting a case, the analyst may wish to distribute copies of the assumption list to all class members. In this way, confusion is avoided in terms of how the analyst perceives the current situation, and others can evaluate the reasonableness and necessity of the assumptions.

2. Analyze and Record Problems and Their Core Elements

After careful analysis, problems and their core elements should be explicitly stated and listed in order of importance. Finding and recording problems and their core elements can be difficult. It is not uncommon on reading a case for the first time for the student to view the case as a description of a situation in which there are no problems. However, careful analysis should reveal symptoms, which lead to problem recognition.

HIGHLIGHT 3

Understanding the Current Situation through SWOT Analysis

A useful approach for gaining an understanding of the situation an organization is facing at a particular time is called SWOT analysis. SWOT stands for the organization's *strengths* and *weaknesses* and the *opportunities* and *threats* it faces in the environment. Below are some questions an analyst should ask in performing a SWOT analysis.

Potential Internal Strengths

—Core competences in key areas.
—Adequate financial resources.
—Well thought of by buyers.
—An acknowledged market leader.
—Well-conceived functional area strategies.
—Access to economies of scale.
—Insulated (at least somewhat) from strong competitive pressures.
—Proprietary technology.
—Cost advantages.
—Better advertising campaigns.
—Product innovation skills.
—Proven management.
—Ahead on experience curve.
—Better manufacturing capability.
—Superior technological skills.
—Other?

Potential Internal Weaknesses

—No clear strategic direction.
—Obsolete facilities.
—Subpar profitability because . . . .
—Lack of managerial depth and talent.
—Missing some key skills or competences.
—Poor track record in implementing strategy.
—Plagued with internal operating problems.
—Falling behind in R&D.
—Too narrow a product line.
—Weak market image.
—Weak distribution network.
—Below-average marketing skills.
—Unable to finance needed changes in strategy.
—Higher overall unit costs relative to key competitors.
—Other?

Potential External Opportunities

—Serve additional customer groups.
—Enter new markets or segments.
—Expand product line to meet broader range of customer needs.
—Diversify into related products.
—Vertical integration (forward or backward).
—Falling trade barriers in attractive foreign markets.
—Complacency among rival firms.
—Faster market growth.
—Other?

Potential External Threats

—Entry of lower-cost foreign competitors.
—Rising sales of substitute products.
—Slower market growth.
—Adverse shifts in foreign exchange rates and trade policies of foreign governments.
—Costly regulatory requirements.
—Vulnerability to recession and business cycle.
—Growing bargaining power of customers or suppliers.
—Changing buyer needs and tastes.
—Adverse demographic changes.
—Other?

Source: Adapted from Arthur A. Thompson, Jr., and A. J. Strickland III, *Strategic Management: Concepts and Cases,* 6th ed. (Homewood, Ill.: Richard D Irwin, 1992), p. 88. Reprinted by permission.

Recognizing and recording problems and their core elements is most critical for a meaningful case analysis. Obviously, if the root problems are not explicitly stated and understood, the remainder of the case analysis has little merit, since the true issues are not being dealt with. The following checklist of questions is designed to assist you in performing this step of the analysis.

Checklist for Analyzing Problems and Their Core Elements

1. What is the primary problem in the case? What are the secondary problems?
2. What proof exists that these are the central issues? How much of this proof is based on facts? On opinions? On assumptions?
3. What symptoms are there that suggest these are the real problems in the case?
4. How are the problems, as defined, related? Are they independent, or are they the result of a deeper problem?
5. What are the ramifications of these problems in the short run? In the long run?

3. Formulate, Evaluate, and Record Alternative Courses of Action

This step is concerned with the question of what can be done to resolve the problem defined in the previous step. Generally, a number of alternative courses of action are available that could potentially help alleviate the problem condition. Three to seven is usually a reasonable number of alternatives to work with. Another approach is to brainstorm as many alternatives as possible initially and then reduce the list to a workable number.

Sound logic and reasoning are very important in this step. It is critical to avoid alternatives that could potentially alleviate the problem, but would create a greater new problem or require greater resources than the firm has at its disposal.

After serious analysis and listing of a number of alternatives, the next task is to evaluate them in term of their costs and benefits. Costs are any output or effort the firm must exert to implement the alternative. Benefits are any input or value received by the firm. Costs to be considered are time, money, other resources, and opportunity costs, while benefits are such things as sales, profits, goodwill, and customer satisfaction. The following checklist provides a guideline of questions to be used when performing this phase of the analysis.

Checklist for Formulating and Evaluating Alternative Courses of Action

1. What possible alternatives exist for solving the firm's problems?
2. What limits are there are on the possible alternatives? Competence? Resources? Management preference? Social responsibility? Legal restrictions?
3. What major alternatives are now available to the firm? What marketing concepts are involved that affect these alternatives?

4. Are the listed alternatives reasonable, given the firm's situation? Are they logical? Are the alternatives consistent with the goals of the marketing program? Are they consistent with the firm's objectives?
5. What are the costs of each alternative? What are the benefits? What are the advantages and disadvantages of each alternative?
6. Which alternative best solves the problem and minimizes the creation of new problems, given the above constraints?

4. Select and Record the Chosen Alternative and Implementation Details

In light of the previous analysis, the alternative is now selected that best solves the problem with a minimum creation of new problems. It is important to record the logic and reasoning that precipitated the selection of a particular alternative. This includes articulating not only why the alternative was selected but also why the other alternatives were not selected.

No analysis is complete without an action-oriented decision and plan for implementing the decision. The accompanying checklist indicates the type of questions that should be answered in this stage of analysis.

Checklist for Selecting and Implementing the Chosen Alternative

1. What must be done to implement the alternative?
2. What personnel will be involved? What are the responsibilities of each?
3. When and where will the alternative be implemented?
4. What will be the probable outcome?
5. How will the success or failure of the alternative be measured?

PITFALLS TO AVOID IN CASE ANALYSIS

Below is a summary of some of the most common errors analysts make when analyzing cases. When evaluating your analysis or those of others, this list provides a useful guide for spotting potential shortcomings.

1. *Inadequate definition of the problem.* By far the most common error made in case analysis is attempting to recommend a course of action without first adequately defining or understanding the problem. Whether presented orally or in a written report, a case analysis must begin with a focus on the central issues and problems represented in the case situation. Closely related is the error of analyzing symptoms without determining the root problem.
2. *The search for "the answer."* In case analysis, there are no clear-cut solutions. Keep in mind that the objective of case studies is learning through discussion and exploration. There is no one "official" or "correct" answer to a case. Rather, there are usually several reasonable alternative solutions.

HIGHLIGHT 4

An Operational Approach to Case and Problem Analysis

1. Read the case quickly to get an overview of the situation.
2. Read the case again thoroughly. Underline relevant information and take notes on potential areas of concern.
3. Review outside sources of information on the environment and the industry. Record relevant information and the source of this information.
4. Perform comparative analysis of the firm with the industry and industry averages.
5. Analyze the firm.
6. Analyze the marketing program.
7. Record the current situation in terms of relevant environmental, industry, firm, and marketing strategy parameters.
8. Make and record necessary assumptions to complete the situational framework.
9. Determine and record the major issues, problems, and their core elements.
10. Record proof that these are the major issues.
11. Record potential courses of actions.
12. Evaluate each initially to determine constraints that preclude acceptability.
13. Evaluate remaining alternatives in terms of costs and benefits.
14. Record analysis of alternatives.
15. Select an alternative.
16. Record alternative and defense of its selection.
17. Record the who, what, when, where, how, and why of the alternative and its implementation.

---

3. **Not enough information.** Analysts often complain there is not enough information in some cases to make a good decision. However, there is justification for not presenting *all* of the information in a case. As in real life, a marketing manager or consultant seldom has all the information necessary to make an optimal decision. Thus, reasonable assumptions have to be made, and the challenge is to find intelligent solutions in spite of the limited information.

4. **Use of generalities.** In analyzing cases, specific recommendations are necessarily not generalities. For example, a suggestion to increase the price is a generality, a suggestion to increase the price by $1.07 is a specific.

5. **A different situation.** Considerable time and effort are sometimes exerted by analysts contending that "If the situation were different, I'd know what course of action to take" or "If the marketing manager hadn't already fouled things up so badly, the firm wouldn't have a problem." Such reasoning ignores the fact that the events in the case have already happened and cannot be changed. Even though analysis or criticism of past events is necessary in diagnosing the problem, in the end, the present situation must be addressed and decisions must be made based on the given situations.

6. *Narrow vision analysis.* Although cases are often labeled as a specific type of case, such as "Pricing," "Product," and so forth, this does not mean that other marketing variables should be ignored. Too often analysts ignore the effects that a change in one marketing element will have on the others.

7. *Realism.* Too often analysts become so focused on solving a particular problem that their solutions become totally unrealistic. For instance, suggesting a $1 million advertising program for a firm with a capital structure of $50,000 is an unrealistic solution.

8. *The marketing research solution.* A quite common but unsatisfactory solution to case problems is marketing research; for example, "The firm should do this or that type of marketing research to find a solution to its problem." Although marketing research may be helpful as an intermediary step in some cases, marketing research does not solve problems or make decisions. In cases where marketing research is recommended, the cost and potential benefits should be fully specified in the case analysis.

9. *Rehashing the case material.* Analysts sometimes spend considerable effort rewriting a two- or three-page history of the firm as presented in the case. This is unnecessary since the instructor and other analysts are already familiar with this information.

10. *Premature conclusions.* Analysts sometimes jump to premature conclusions instead of waiting until their analysis is completed. Too many analysts jump to conclusions upon first reading the case and then proceed to interpret everything in the case as justifying their conclusions, even factors logically against it.

COMMUNICATING CASE ANALYSES

The final concern in case analysis deals with communicating the results of the analysis. The most comprehensive analysis has little value if it is not communicated effectively. There are two primary media through which case analyses are communicated—the written report and the oral presentation.

The Written Report

Since the structure of the written report will vary by the type of case analyzed, the purpose of this section is not to present a "one and only" way of writing up a case. The purpose of this section is to present some useful generalizations to aid analysts in case writeups.

A good written report starts with an outline that organizes the structure of the analysis in a logical manner. The following is a general outline for a marketing case report.

I. **Title Page.**
II. **Table of Contents.**
III. **Executive Summary. (A one- to two-page summary of the analysis and recommendations)**
IV. **Situation Analysis.**
  A. *Environment.*
    1. Economic conditions and trends.
    2. Cultural and social values and trends.
    3. Political and legal issues.
    4. Summary of environmental opportunities and threats.
    5. Implications for strategy development.
  B. *Industry.*
    1. Classification and definition of industry.
    2. Analysis of existing competitors.
    3. Analysis of potential new entrants.
    4. Analysis of substitute products.
    5. Analysis of suppliers.
    6. Analysis of buyers.
    7. Summary of industry opportunities and threats.
    8. Implications for strategy development.
  C. *Firm.*
    1. Objectives and constraints.
    2. Financial condition.
    3. Management philosophy.
    4. Organizational structure.
    5. Organizational culture.
    6. Summary of the firm's strengths and weaknesses.
    7. Implications for strategy development.
  D. *Marketing Strategy.*
    1. Objectives and constraints.
    2. Analysis of sales, profits and market share.
    3. Analysis of target market(s).
    4. Analysis of marketing mix variables.
    5. Summary of marketing strategy's strengths and weaknesses.
    6. Implications for strategy development.
V. **Problems Found in Situation Analysis.**
  A. *Statement of Primary Problem(s).*
    1. Evidence of problem(s).
    2. Effects of problem(s).
  B. *Statement of Secondary Problem(s).*
    1. Evidence of problem(s).
    2. Effects of problem(s).

  VI. Strategic Alternatives for Solving Problems.
   A. *Description of Strategic Alternative 1.*
    1. Benefits of alternative 1.
    2. Costs of alternative 1.
   B. *Description of Strategic Alternative 2.*
    1. Benefits of alternative 2.
    2. Costs of alternative 2.
   C. *Description of Strategic Alternative 3.*
    1. Benefits of alternative 3.
    2. Costs of alternative 3.
 VII. Selection of Strategic Alternative and Implementation.
   A. *Statement of selected strategy.*
   B. *Justification for selection of strategy.*
   C. *Description of implementation of strategy.*
 VIII. Summary.
  IX. Appendices.
   A. *Financial analysis.*
   B. *Technical analysis.*

Writing the case report entails filling out the details of the outline in prose form. Of course, not every case report requires all of the headings listed above and different headings may be required for some cases. Like any other skill, it takes practice to determine the appropriate headings and approach for writing up particular cases. However, good case reports flow logically from topic to topic, are clearly written, are based on solid situation analysis and demonstrate sound strategic thinking.

The Oral Presentation

Case analyses are often presented by an individual or team. As with the written report, a good outline is critical, and it is usually preferable to hand out the outline to each class member. Although there is no best way to present a case or to divide responsibility between team members, simply reading the written report is unacceptable since it encourages boredom and interferes with all-important class discussion.

The use of visual aids can be quite helpful in presenting class analyses. However, simply presenting financial statements contained in the case is a poor use of visual media. On the other hand, graphs of sales and profit curves can be more easily interpreted and can be quite useful for making specific points.

Oral presentation of cases is particularly helpful to analysts for learning the skill of speaking to a group. In particular, the ability to handle objections and disagreements without antagonizing others is a skill worth developing.

CONCLUSION

From the discussion it should be obvious that good case analyses require a major commitment of time and effort. Individuals must be highly motivated and willing to get involved in the analysis and discussion if they expect to learn and succeed in a course where cases are utilized. Persons with only passive interest who perform "night before" analyses cheat themselves of valuable learning experiences that can aid them in their careers.

ADDITIONAL READINGS

Bernhardt, Kenneth L., and Thomas C. Kinnear. *Cases in Marketing Management*. 5th ed. Homewood, Ill.: Richard D. Irwin, 1991, pp. 1–25.

Cravens, David W., and Charles W. Lamb, Jr. *Strategic Marketing Management Cases*. 4th ed. Homewood, Ill.: Richard D. Irwin, 1993, pp. 94–108.

O'Dell, William F.; Andrew C. Ruppel; Robert H. Trent; and William J. Kehoe. *Marketing Decision Making: Analytic Framework and Cases*. 4th ed. Cincinnati: South-Western Publishing, 1988, chaps. 1–5.

Financial Analysis for Marketing Decisions

FINANCIAL ANALYSIS

Financial analysis is an important aspect of marketing decision making and planning and should be an integral part of marketing problem and case analysis. In this section we present several financial tools that are useful for analyzing marketing problems and cases. First, we investigate break–even analysis, which is concerned with determining the number of units or dollar sales, or both, necessary to break even on a project or to obtain a given level of profits. Second, we illustrate net present value analysis, which is a somewhat more sophisticated tool for analyzing marketing alternatives. Finally, we investigate ratio analysis, which can be a quite useful tool for determining the financial condition of the firm, including its ability to invest in a new or modified marketing program.

Break–Even Analysis

Break–even analysis is a common tool for investigating the potential profitability of a marketing alternative. The *break–even point* is that level of sales in either units or sales dollars at which a firm covers all of its costs. In other words, it is the level at which total sales revenue just equals the total costs necessary to achieve these sales.

To compute the break–even point, an analyst must have or be able to obtain three values. First, the analyst needs to know the selling price per unit of the product (SP). For example, suppose the Ajax Company plans to sell its new electric car through its own dealerships at a retail price of $5,000. Second, the analyst needs to know the level of fixed costs (FC). Fixed costs are all costs relevant to the project that do not change regardless of how many units are produced or sold. For instance, whether Ajax produces and sells 1 or 100,000 cars, Ajax executives will receive their salaries, land must be purchased for a plant, a plant must be constructed, and machinery must be purchased. Other fixed costs include such things as interest, lease payments, and sinking fund payments. Suppose Ajax has totaled all of its fixed costs and the sum is $1.5 million. Third, the analyst must know the variable costs per unit produced (VC). As the name implies, variable costs are those that vary directly with the number of units produced. For example, for each car Ajax produces, there are costs for raw materials and components to build the car, such as batteries, electric motors, steel bodies and tires; there are labor costs for operating employees; there are machine costs, such as electricity and welding rods. Suppose these are totaled by Ajax, and it is determined that the variable costs for each car produced equal $3,500. With this information, the analyst can now determine the break–even point, which is the number of units that must be sold to just cover the cost of producing the cars. The break–even point is determined by dividing total fixed costs by the *contribution margin*. The contribution margin is simply the difference between the selling price per unit (SP) and variable costs per unit (VC). Algebraically,

$$BEP_{(in\ units)} = \frac{Total\ fixed\ costs}{Contribution\ margin}$$
$$= \frac{FC}{SP - VC}$$

Substituting the Ajax estimates,

$$BEP_{(in\ units)} = \frac{1,500,000}{5,000 - 3,500}$$
$$= \frac{1,500,000}{1,500}$$
$$= 1,000\ units$$

In other words, the Ajax Company must sell 1,000 cars to just break even (i.e., for total sales revenue to cover total costs).

Alternatively, the analyst may want to know the break-even point in terms of dollar sales volume. Of course, if the preceding analysis has been done, one could simply multiply the BEP (in units) times the selling price to determine the break-even sales volume (i.e., 1,000 units × $5,000/unit = $5 million). However, the BEP (in dollars) can be computed directly, using the formula below:

$$BEP_{(in\ dollars)} = \frac{FC}{1 - \dfrac{VC}{SP}}$$
$$= \frac{1,500,000}{1 - \dfrac{3,500}{5,000}}$$
$$= \frac{1,500,000}{1 - .7}$$
$$= \$5,000,000$$

Thus, Ajax must produce and sell 1,000 cars, which equals $5 million sales, to break even. Of course, firms do not want to just break even but want to make a profit. The logic of break-even analysis can easily be extended to include profits (P). Suppose Ajax decided that a 20 percent return on fixed costs would make the project worth the investment. Thus, Ajax would need 20% × $1,500,000 = $300,000 before-tax profit. To calculate how many units Ajax must sell to achieve this level of profits, the profit figure (P) is added to fixed costs in the above formulas. (We will label the break-even point as BEP′ to show that we are now computing unit and sales levels to obtain a given profit level.) In the Ajax example:

$$BEP'_{(in\ units)} = \frac{FC + P}{SP - VC}$$
$$= \frac{1,500,000 + 300,000}{5,000 - 3,500}$$
$$= \frac{1,800,000}{1,500}$$
$$= 1,200\ units$$

In terms of dollars,

$$BEP'_{(in\ dollars)} = \frac{FC + P}{1 - \dfrac{VC}{SP}}$$
$$= \frac{1,500,000 + 300,000}{1 - \dfrac{3,500}{5,000}}$$
$$= \frac{1,800,000}{1 - .7}$$
$$= \$6,000,000$$

Thus, Ajax must produce and sell 1,200 cars (sales volume of $6 million) to obtain a 20 percent return on fixed costs. Analysis must now be directed at determining whether a given marketing plan can be expected to produce sales of at least this level. If the answer is yes, the project would appear to be worth investing in. If not, Ajax should seek other opportunities.

Net Present Value Analysis

The profit-oriented marketing manager must understand that the capital invested in new products has a cost. It is a basic principle in business that whoever wishes to use capital must pay for its use. Dollars invested in new products could be diverted to other uses—to pay off debts, pay out to stockholders, or buy U.S. Treasury bonds—which would yield economic benefits to the corporation. If, on the other hand, all of the dollars used to finance a new product have to be borrowed from lenders outside the corporation, interest has to be paid on the loan.

One of the best ways to analyze the financial aspects of a marketing alternative is *net present value* analysis. This method employs a "discounted cash flow," which takes into account the time value of money and its price to the borrower. The following example will illustrate this method.

To compute the net present value of an investment proposal, the cost of capital must be estimated. The cost of capital can be defined as the required rate of return on an investment that would leave the owners of the firm as well off as if the project was not undertaken. Thus, it is the minimum percentage return on investment that a project must make to be worth undertaking. There are many methods of estimating the cost of capital. However, since these methods are not the concern of this text, we will simply assume that the cost of capital for the Ajax Corporation has been determined to be 10 percent.[1] Again, it should be noted that once the cost of capital is determined, it becomes the minimum rate of return required for an investment—a type of cutoff point. However, some firms in selecting their new product investments select a minimum rate of return that is above the cost of capital figure to allow for errors in judgment or measurement.

The Ajax Corporation is considering a proposal to market instant developing movie film. After conducting considerable marketing research, sales were projected to be $1 million per year. In addition, the finance department compiled the following information concerning the projects:

New equipment needed	$700,000
Useful life of equipment	10 years
Depreciation	10% per year
Salvage value	$100,000
Cost of goods and expenses	$700,000 per year
Cost of capital	10%
Tax rate	50%

To compute the net present value of this project, the net cash flow for each year of the project must first be determined. This can be done in four steps:

1. Sales − Cost of goods and expenses = Gross income

or

$$\$1,000,000 - 700,000 = \$300,000.$$

2. Gross income − Depreciation = Taxable income

or

$$\$300,000 - (10\% \times 600,000) = \$240,000.$$

---

[1]For methods of estimating the cost of capital, see Charles P. Jones, *Introduction to Financial Management* (Homewood, Ill.: Richard D. Irwin, 1992), chap. 14.

3. Taxable income − Tax = Net income

or

$$\$240,000 - (50\% \times 240,000) = \$120,000.$$

4. Net income + Depreciation = Net cash flow

or

$$\$120,000 + 60,000 = \$180,000 \text{ per year.}$$

Since the cost of capital is 10 percent, this figure is used to discount the net cash flows for each year. To illustrate, the $180,000 received at the end of the first year would be discounted by the factor $1/(1 + 0.10)$, which would be $180,000 \times 0.9091 = \$163,638$; the $180,000 received at the end of the second year would be discounted by the factor $1/(1 + 0.10)^2$, which would be $180,000 \times 0.8264 = \$148,752$, and so on. (Most finance textbooks have present value tables that can be used to simplify the computations.) Below are the present value computations for the 10-year project. It should be noted that the net cash flow for year 10 is $280,000 since there is an additional $100,000 inflow from salvage value.

Year	Net Cash Flow	0.10 Discount Factor	Present Value
1	$ 180,000	0.9091	$ 163,638
2	180,000	0.8264	148,752
3	180,000	0.7513	135,234
4	180,000	0.6830	122,940
5	180,000	0.6209	111,762
6	180,000	0.5645	101,610
7	180,000	0.5132	92,376
8	180,000	0.4665	83,970
9	180,000	0.4241	76,338
10	280,000	0.3855	107,940
Total	$1,900,000		$1,144,560

Thus, at a discount rate of 10 percent, the present value of the net cash flow from new product investment is greater than the $700,000 outlay required, and so the decision can be considered profitable by this standard. Here the *net present value* is $444,560, which is the difference between the $700,000 investment outlay and the $1,144,560 discounted cash flow. The present value ratio is nothing more than the present value of the net cash flow divided by the cash investment. If this ratio is one or larger than one, the project would be profitable for the firm to invest in.

There are many other measures of investment worth, but only one additional method will be discussed. It is the very popular and easily understood "payback method." *Payback* refers to the amount of time required to pay back the original outlay from the cash flows. Staying with the example, the project

---

HIGHLIGHT 1

Selected Present Value Discount Factors

Years	8%	10%	12%	14%	16%	18%
1	.9259	.9091	.8929	.8772	.8621	.8475
2	.8573	.8264	.7972	.7695	.7432	.7182
3	.7938	.7513	.7118	.6750	.6407	.6086
4	.7350	.6830	.6355	.5921	.5523	.5158
5	.6806	.6209	.5674	.5194	.4761	.4371
6	.6302	.5645	.5066	.4556	.4104	.3704
7	.5835	.5132	.4523	.3996	.3538	.3139
8	.5403	.4665	.4039	.3506	.3050	.2660
9	.5002	.4241	.3606	.3075	.2630	.2255
10	.4632	.3855	.3220	.2697	.2267	.1911

---

is expected to produce a stream of cash proceeds that is constant from year to year, so the payback period can be determined by dividing the investment outlay by this annual cash flow. Dividing $700,000 by $180,000, the payback period is approximately 3.9 years. Firms often set a maximum payback period before a project will be accepted. For example, many firms refuse to take on a project if the payback period exceeds five years.

This example should illustrate the difficulty in evaluating marketing investments from a profitability or economic worth standpoint. The most challenging problem is that of developing accurate cash flow estimates because there are many possible alternatives, such as price of the product and channels of distribution, and the consequences of each alternative must be forecast in terms of sales volumes, selling costs, and other expenses. In spite of all the problems, management must evaluate the economic worth of new product decisions, not only to reduce some of the guesswork and ambiguity surrounding marketing decision making, but also to reinforce the objective of trying to make profitable decisions.

Ratio Analysis

Firms' income statements and balance sheets provide a wealth of information that is useful for marketing decision making. Frequently, this information is included in marketing cases, yet analysts often have no convenient way of interpreting the financial position of the firm to make sound marketing decisions. Ratio analysis provides the analyst an easy and efficient method for investigating a firm's financial position by comparing the firm's ratios across time or with ratios of similar firms in the industry or with industry averages.

Ratio analysis involves four basic steps:

1. Choose the appropriate ratios.
2. Compute the ratios.
3. Compare the ratios.
4. Check for problems or opportunities.

1. Choose the appropriate ratios

The five basic types of financial ratios are: (1) liquidity ratios; (2) asset management ratios; (3) profitability ratios; (4) debt management ratios; and (5) market value ratios.[2] While calculating ratios of all five types is useful, liquidity, asset management, and profitability ratios provide information that is most directly relevant for marketing decision making. Although many ratios can be calculated in each of these groups, we have selected two of the most commonly used and readily available ratios in each group to illustrate the process.

Liquidity ratios. One of the first considerations in analyzing a marketing problem is the liquidity of the firm. *Liquidity* refers to the ability of the firm to pay its short-term obligations. If a firm cannot meet its short-term obligations, there is little that can be done until this problem is resolved. Simply stated, recommendations to increase advertising, to do marketing research, or to develop new products are of little value if the firm is about to go bankrupt!

The two most commonly used ratios for investigating liquidity are the *current ratio* and the *quick ratio* (or "acid test"). The current ratio is determined by dividing current assets by current liabilities and is a measure of the overall ability of the firm to meet its current obligations. A common rule of thumb is that the current ratio should be about 2:1.

The quick ratio is determined by subtracting inventory from current assets and dividing the remainder by current liabilities. Since inventory is the least liquid current asset, the quick ratio deals with assets that are most readily available for meeting short-term (one-year) obligations. A common rule of thumb is that the quick ratio should be at least 1:1.

Asset management ratios. Asset management ratios investigate how well the firm handles its assets. For marketing problems, two of the most useful asset management ratios are concerned with *inventory turnover* and *total asset utilization*. The inventory turnover ratio is determined by dividing sales by inventories.[3] If the firm is not turning its inventory over as rapidly as other

---

[2]See Eugene F. Brigham, *Fundamentals of Financial Management* (Hinsdale, Ill.: Dryden Press, 1986).

[3]It is useful to use average inventory rather than a single end-of-year estimate if monthly data are available.

HIGHLIGHT 2

Financial Ratios: Where to Find Them

1. *Annual Statement Studies*. Published by Robert Morris Associates, this work includes 11 financial ratios computed annually for over 150 lines of business. Each line of business is divided into four size categories.
2. Dun & Bradstreet provides 14 ratios calculated annually for over 100 lines of business.
3. *The Almanac of Business and Industrial Financial Ratios*. The almanac, published by Prentice Hall, Inc., lists industry averages for 22 financial ratios. Approximately 170 businesses and industries are listed.
4. *The Quarterly Financial Report for Manufacturing Corporations*. This work, published jointly by the Federal Trade Commission and the Securities and Exchange Commission, contains balance-sheet and income-statement information by industry groupings and by asset-size categories.
5. Trade associations and individual companies often compute ratios for their industries and make them available to analysts.

---

firms, it suggests that too many funds are being tied up in unproductive or obsolete inventory. In addition, if the firm's turnover ratio is decreasing over time, it suggests that there may be a problem in the marketing plan, since inventory is not being sold as rapidly as it had been in the past. One problem with this ratio is that, since sales usually are recorded at market prices and inventory usually is recorded at cost, the ratio may overstate turnover. Thus, some analysts prefer to use cost of sales rather than sales in computing turnover. We will use cost of sales in our analysis.

A second useful asset management ratio is total asset utilization. It is calculated by dividing sales by total assets and is a measure of how productively the firm's assets have been used to generate sales. If this ratio is well below industry figures, it suggests that marketing efforts may be relatively less effective than other firms or that some unproductive assets should be disposed of.

Profitability ratios. Profitability is a major goal of marketing and is an important test of the quality of marketing decision making in the firm. Two key profitability ratios are *profit margin on sales* and *return on total assets*. Profit margin on sales is determined by dividing profit before tax by sales. Serious questions about the firm and marketing plan should be raised if profit margin on sales is declining across time or is well below other firms in the industry. Return on total assets is determined by dividing profit before tax by total assets. This ratio is the return on the investment for the entire firm.

2. Compute the ratios

The next step in ratio analysis is to compute the ratios. Figure 1 presents the balance sheet and income statement for the Ajax Home Computer Company. The six ratios can be calculated from the Ajax balance sheet and income statement as follows:

Liquidity ratios:

$$\text{Current ratio} = \frac{\text{Current assets}}{\text{Current liabilities}} = \frac{700}{315} = 2.2$$

$$\text{Quick ratio} = \frac{\text{Current assets} - \text{Inventory}}{\text{Current liabilities}} = \frac{270}{315} = .86$$

Asset management ratios:

$$\text{Inventory turnover} = \frac{\text{Cost of sales}}{\text{Inventory}} = \frac{2,780}{430} = 6.5$$

$$\text{Total asset utilization} = \frac{\text{Sales}}{\text{Total assets}} = \frac{3,600}{2,400} = 1.5$$

Profitability ratios:

$$\text{Profit margin on sales} = \frac{\text{Profit before tax}}{\text{Sales}} = \frac{300}{3,600} = 8.3\%$$

$$\text{Return on total assets} = \frac{\text{Profit before tax}}{\text{Total assets}} = \frac{300}{2,400} = 12.5\%$$

3. Compare the ratios

While rules of thumb are useful for analyzing ratios, it cannot be overstated that comparison of ratios is always the preferred approach. The ratios computed for a firm can be compared in at least three ways. First, they can be compared over time to see if there are any favorable or unfavorable trends in the firm's financial position. Second, they can be compared with the ratios of other firms in the industry of similar size. Third, they can be compared with industry averages to get an overall idea of the firm's relative financial position in the industry.

Figure 2 provides a summary of the ratio analysis. The ratios computed for Ajax are presented along with the median ratios for firms of similar size in the industry and the industry median. The median is often reported in financial sources, rather than the mean, to avoid the strong effect of outliers.[4]

---

[4]For a discussion of ratio analysis for retailing, see Joseph B. Mason and Morris L. Mayer, *Modern Retailing: Theory and Practice,* 6th ed. (Homewood, Ill.: Richard D. Irwin, 1993), chap. 8.

Figure 1 *Balance Sheet and Income Statement for Ajax Home Computer Company*

AJAX HOME COMPUTER COMPANY
Balance Sheet
March 31, 1990
(in thousands)

Assets		Liabilities and Stockholders' Equity	
Cash	$ 30	Trade accounts payable	$ 150
Marketable securities	40	Accrued	25
Accounts receivable	200	Notes payable	100
Inventory	430	Accrued income tax	40
Total current assets	700	Total current liabilities	315
Plant and equipment	1,000	Bonds	500
Land	500	Debentures	85
Other investments	200	Stockholders' equity	1,500
Total assets	$2,400	Total liabilities and stockholders' equity	$2,400

AJAX HOME COMPUTER COMPANY
Income Statement
For the 12–Month Period Ending March 31, 1990
(in thousands)

Sales	$3,600
Cost of sales:	
Labor and materials	2,000
Depreciation	200
Selling expenses	500
General and administrative expenses	80
Total cost	2,780
Net operating income	820
Less interest expense:	
Interest on notes	20
Interest on debentures	200
Interest on bonds	300
Total interest	520
Profit before tax:	300
Federal income tax (@40%)	120
Net profit after tax	$ 180

4. Check for problems or opportunities

The ratio comparison in Figure 2 suggests that Ajax is in reasonably good shape financially. The current ratio is above the industry figures, although the quick ratio is slightly below them. However, the high inventory turnover ratio suggests that the slightly low quick ratio should not be a problem, since

Figure 2   *Ratio Comparison for Ajax Home Computer Company*

	Ajax	Industry Firms 1–10 million in Assets	Industry Median
Liquidity ratios:			
Current ratio	2.2	1.8	1.8
Quick ratio	.86	.9	1.0
Asset management ratios:			
Inventory turnover	6.5	3.2	2.8
Total assets utilization	1.5	1.7	1.6
Profitability ratios:			
Profit margin	8.3%	6.7%	8.2%
Return on total assets	12.5%	15.0%	14.7%

inventory turns over relatively quickly. Total asset utilization is slightly below industry averages and should be monitored closely. This, coupled with the slightly lower return on total assets, suggests that some unproductive assets should be disposed of. While the problem could be ineffective marketing, the high profit margin on sales suggests that marketing effort is probably not the problem.

CONCLUSION

This section has focused on several aspects of financial analysis that are useful for marketing decision making. The first, break-even analysis, is commonly used in marketing problem and case analysis. The second, net present value analysis, is quite useful for investigating the financial impact of marketing alternatives, such as new product introductions. The third, ratio analysis, is a useful tool sometimes overlooked in marketing problem solving. Performing a ratio analysis, as a regular portion of marketing problem and case analysis, can increase the understanding of the firm and its problems and opportunities.

ADDITIONAL READINGS

Brealey, Richard A., and Stewart C. Myers. *Principles of Corporate Finance*. 4th ed. New York: McGraw-Hill, 1991.

Campsey, B.J., and Eugene F. Brigham. *Introduction to Financial Management*. 2nd ed. Chicago: Dryden Press, 1989.

Day, George, and Liam Fahay. "Valuing Market Strategies." *Journal of Marketing,* July 1988, pp. 45–57.

Jones, Charles P. *Introduction to Financial Management*. Homewood, Ill.: Richard D. Irwin, 1992.

Ross, Stephen A.; Randolph W. Westerfield; and Jeffrey F. Jaffe. *Corporate Finance*. 3rd ed. Homewood, Ill.: Richard D. Irwin, 1993.

SECTION IV

Developing Marketing Plans

Imagine this scenario. After receiving your bachelor's or master's degree in marketing, you are hired by a major consumer goods company. Because you've done well in school, you are confident that you have a lot of marketing knowledge and a lot to offer to the firm. You're highly motivated and are looking forward to a successful career.

After just a few days of work you are called in for a conference with the vice president of marketing. The vice president welcomes you and tells you how glad the firm is that you have joined them. The vice president also says that, since you have done so well in your marketing courses and have had such recent training, he wants you to work on a special project.

He tells you that the company has a new product, which is to be introduced in a few months. He also says, confidentially, that recent new product introductions by the company haven't been too successful. Suggesting that the recent problems are probably because the company has not been doing a very good job of developing marketing plans, the vice president tells you not to look at marketing plans for the company's other products.

Your assignment, then, is to develop a marketing plan for the proposed product in the next six weeks. The vice president explains that a good job here will lead to rapid advancement in the company. You thank the vice president for the assignment and promise that you'll do your best.

How would you feel when you returned to your desk? Surely, you'd be flattered that you had been given this opportunity and be eager to do a good job. However, how confident are you that you could develop a quality marketing plan? Would you even know where to begin?

We suspect that many of you, even those who have an excellent knowledge of marketing principles and are adept at solving marketing cases, may not yet have the skills necessary to develop a marketing plan from scratch. Thus, the purpose of this section is to offer a framework for developing marketing plans. In one sense, this section is no more than a summary of the whole text. In other words, it is an organizational framework based on the text material that can be used to direct the development of marketing plans.

Students should note that we are not presenting this framework and discussion as the only way to develop a marketing plan. While we believe this is a useful framework for logically analyzing the problems involved in developing a marketing plan, other approaches can be used just as successfully.

Often, successful firms prepare much less detailed plans, since much of the background material and current conditions are well known to everyone involved. However, our review of plans used in various firms suggests that something like this framework is not uncommon.

We would like to mention one other qualification before beginning our discussion. Students should remember that one important part of the marketing plan involves the development of a sales forecast. While we have discussed several approaches to sales forecasting in the text, we will detail only one specific approach here.

Figure 1   *A Marketing Plan Format*

—Title page.
—Executive summary.
—Table of contents.
—Introduction.
—Situational analysis.
—Marketing planning.
—Implementation and control of the marketing plan.
—Summary.
—Appendix: Financial analysis.
—References.

A MARKETING PLAN FRAMEWORK

Marketing plans have three basic purposes. First, they are used as a tangible record of analysis to investigate the logic involved. This is done to ensure the feasibility and internal consistency of the project and to evaluate the likely consequences of implementing the plan. Second, they are used as roadmaps or guidelines for directing appropriate actions. A marketing plan is designed to be the best available scenario and rationale for directing the firm's efforts for a particular product or brand. Third, they are used as tools to obtain funding for implementation. This funding may come from internal or external sources. For example, a brand manager may have to present a marketing plan to senior executives in a firm to get a budget request filled. This would be an internal source. Similarly, proposals for funding from investors or business loans from banks often require a marketing plan. These would be external sources.

Figure 1 presents a format for preparing marketing plans. Each of the 10 elements will be briefly discussed. We will refer to previous chapters and sections in this text and to other sources where additional information can be obtained when a marketing plan is being prepared. We also will offer additional information for focusing particular sections of the plan as well as for developing financial analysis.

Title Page

The *title page* should contain the following information: (1) the name of the product or brand for which the marketing plan has been prepared—for example, Marketing Plan for Little Friskies Dog Food; (2) the time period for which the plan is designed—for example, 1993–94; (3) the person(s) and position(s) of those submitting the plan—for example, submitted by Amy Lewis, brand manager; (4) the persons, group, or agency to whom the plan is being submitted—for example, submitted to Lauren Ellis, product group manager, and (5) the date of submission of the plan—for example, June 30, 1993.

While preparing the *title page* is a simple task, remember that it is the first thing readers see. Thus, a title page that is poorly laid out, is smudged, or contains misspelled words can lead to the inference that the project was developed hurriedly and with little attention to detail. As with the rest of the project, appearances are important and affect what people think about the plan.

Executive Summary

The *executive summary* is a two- to three-page summary of the contents of the report. Its purpose is to provide a quick summary of the marketing plan for executives who need to be informed about the plan but are typically not directly involved in plan approval. For instance, senior executives for firms with a broad product line may not have time to read the entire plan but need an overview to keep informed about operations.

The executive summary should include a brief introduction, the major aspects of the marketing plan, and a budget statement. This is not the place to go into detail about each and every aspect of the marketing plan. Rather, it should focus on the major market opportunity and the key elements of the marketing plan that are designed to capitalize on this opportunity.

It is also useful to state specifically how much money is required to implement the plan. In an ongoing firm, many costs can be estimated from historical data or from discussions with other executives in charge of specific functional areas. However, in many situations (such as a class project), sufficient information is not always available to give exact costs for every aspect of production, promotion, and distribution. In these cases, include a rough estimate of total marketing costs of the plan. In many ongoing firms, marketing cost elements are concentrated in the areas of promotion and marketing research, and these figures are integrated with those from other functional areas as parts of the overall business plan.

Table of Contents

The table of contents is a listing of everything contained in the plan and where it is located in the report. Reports that contain a variety of charts and figures may also have a table of exhibits listing their titles and page numbers within the report.

In addition to using the table of contents as a place to find specific information, readers may also review it to see if each section of the report is logically sequenced. For example, situational analysis logically precedes marketing planning as an activity, and this ordering makes sense in presenting the plan.

Introduction

The types of information and amount of detail reported in the *introduction* depend in part on whether the plan is being designed for a new or existing product or brand. If the product is new, the introduction should explain the product concept and the reasons why it is expected to be successful. Basically, this part of your report should make the new idea sound attractive to management or investors. In addition, it is useful to offer estimates of expected sales, costs, and return on investment.

If the marketing plan is for an existing brand in an ongoing firm, it is common to begin the report with a brief history of the brand. The major focus here is on the brand's performance in the last three to five years. It is useful to prepare graphs of the brand's performance that show its sales, profits, and market share for previous years and to explain the reasons for any major changes. These exhibits can also be extended to include predicted changes in these variables given the new marketing plan. A brief discussion of the overall strategy followed in previous years also provides understanding of how much change is being proposed in the new marketing plan.

Also useful is to offer a precise statement of the purpose of the report as well as a "roadmap" of the report in the introduction. In other words, tell readers what this report is, how it is organized, and what will be covered in the following sections.

Situational Analysis

The *situational analysis* is not unlike the analysis discussed in Chapter 1 and Section 2 of this text. The focus remains on the most critical and relevant environmental conditions (or changes in them) that affect the success or failure of the proposed plan. While any aspect of the economic, social, political, legal, or cooperative environments might deserve considerable attention, there is seldom if ever a marketing plan in which the competitive environment does not require considerable discussion. In fact, the competitive environment may be set off as a separate section called *industry analysis*. The strengths and weaknesses of major competitors, their relative market shares, and the success of various competitive strategies are critical elements of the situation analysis.

Section 5 of the text offers some sources of information for analyzing the competitive environment, such as the *Audits and Surveys National Total-Market Index* and the *Nielson Retail Index*. In addition, trade association publications, *Fortune, Business Week,* and *The Wall Street Journal,* frequently have useful articles on competitive strategies. Firms' annual reports often provide considerable useful information.

Marketing Planning

Marketing Planning is, of course, a critical section of the report. As previously noted, it includes three major elements: marketing objectives, target market(s), and the marketing mix.

HIGHLIGHT 1

Some Questions to Consider in Competitive Analysis

Understanding an industry and the actions of competitors is critical to developing successful marketing plans. Below is a list of some questions to consider when performing competitive analysis. Thinking about these questions can aid the marketing planner in developing better marketing strategies.

1. Which firms compete in this industry, and what is their financial position and marketing capability?
2. What are the relative market shares of various brands?
3. How many brands and models does each firm offer?
4. What marketing strategies have the market leaders employed?

5. Which brands have gained and which have lost market share in recent years, and what factors have led to these changes?
6. Are new competitors likely to enter the market?
7. How quickly do competitive firms react to changes in the market?
8. From which firms or brands might we be able to take market share?
9. What are the particular strengths and weaknesses of competitors in the industry?
10. How do we compare with other firms in the industry in terms of financial strength and marketing skills?

Marketing objectives

Marketing objectives are often stated in plans in terms of the percentage of particular outcomes that are to be achieved; for example, 80 percent awareness of the brand in particular markets, increase in trial rate by 30 percent, distribution coverage of 60 percent, increase in total market share by 3 percent over the life of the plan. Similarly, there may also be objective statements in terms of sales units or dollars or increases in these. Of course, the reasons for selection of the particular objectives and rationale are important points to explain.

Target markets

The *target market(s)* discussion explains the customer base and rationale or justification for it. An approach to developing appropriate target markets is contained in Chapter 5 of this text, and a useful source of secondary data for segmenting markets is the *National Purchase Diary Panel*.

This section also includes relevant discussion of changes or important issues in consumer or industrial buyer behavior; for example, what benefits consumers are seeking in this products class, what benefits does the particular brand offer, or what purchasing trends are shaping the market for this product. Discussions of consumer and industrial buyer behavior are contained in Chapters 3 and 4 of this text.

Marketing mix

The marketing mix discussion explains in detail the selected strategy consisting of product, promotion, distribution and price, and the rationale for it. Also, if marketing research has been done on these elements or is planned, it can be discussed in this section.

Product. The product section details a description of the product or brand, its packaging and attributes. Product life-cycle considerations should be mentioned if they affect the proposed plan.

Of critical importance in this discussion is the competitive differential advantage of the product or brand. Here it must be carefully considered whether the brand really does anything better than the competition or is purchased primarily on the basis of image. For example, many brands of toothpaste have fluoride, yet Crest has the largest market share primarily through promoting this attribute of its brand. Thus, does Crest do anything more than other toothpastes, or is it Crest's image that accounts for sales?

Discussion of product-related issues is contained in Chapters 6 and 7, and services are discussed in Chapter 12 of this text. For discussion of marketing plans for products at the international level, see Chapter 13.

Promotion. The promotion discussion consists of a description and justification of the planned promotion mix. It is useful to explain the theme of the promotion and to include some examples of potential ads as well as the nature of the sales force if one is to be used. For mass-marketed consumer goods, promotion costs are clearly significant and need to be considered explicitly in the marketing plan.

Discussion of promotion-related issues is contained in Chapters 8 and 9 of this text. Secondary sources, such as *Standard Rate and Data, Simmons Media/ Market Service, Starch Advertising Readership Service,* and the *Nielsen Television Index,* provide useful information for selecting, budgeting, and justifying media and other promotional decisions.

Distribution. The distribution discussion describes and justifies the appropriate channel or channels for the product. This includes types of intermediaries and specifically who they will be. Other important issues concern the level of market coverage desired, cost, and control considerations. In many cases, the channels of distribution used by the firm, as well as competitive firms, are well established. For example, General Motors and Ford distribute their automobiles through independent dealer networks. Thus, unless there is a compelling reason to change channels, the traditional channel will often be the appropriate alternative. However, serious consideration may have to be given to methods of obtaining channel support, for example, trade deals to obtain sufficient shelf space.

Discussion of distribution-related issues is contained in Chapter 10 of this text. Useful retail distribution information can be found in the *Nielsen Retail Index* and the *Audits and Surveys National Total-Market Index.*

HIGHLIGHT 2

Stating Objectives: How to Tell a "Good" One from a "Bad" One

For the direction setting purpose of objectives to be fulfilled, objectives need to meet five specifications:

1. An objective should relate to a single, specific topic. (It should not be stated in the form of a vague abstraction or a pious platitude—"we want to be a leader in our industry" or "our objective is to be more aggressive marketers.")
2. An objective should relate to a result, not to an activity to be performed. (The objective is the result of the activity, not the performing of the activity.)
3. An objective should be measurable (stated in quantitative terms whenever feasible).
4. An objective should contain a time deadline for its achievement.
5. An objective should be challenging but achievable.

Source: Adapted from Arthur A. Thompson, Jr., and A. J. Strickland, *Strategic Management: Concepts and Cases.* 5th ed. (Homewood, Ill.: Richard D. Irwin, 1990), pp. 23–34.

Consider the following examples:

—Poor: Our objective is to maximize profits.

Remarks: How much is "maximum"? The statement is not subject to measurement. What criterion or yardstick will management use to determine if and when actual profits are equal to maximum profits? No deadline is specified.

Better: Our total profit target in 1994 is $1 million.

—Poor: Our objective is to increase sales revenue and unit volume.

Remarks: How much? Also, because the statement relates to two topics, it may be inconsistent. Increasing unit volume may require a price cut, and if demand is price inelastic, sales revenue would fall as unit volume rises. No time frame for achievement is indicated.

Better: Our objective this calendar year is

Price. The pricing discussion starts with a specific statement of the price of the product. Depending on what type of channel is used, manufacturer price, wholesale price, and suggested retail price need to be listed and justified. In addition, special deals or trade discounts that are to be employed must be considered in terms of their effect on the firm's selling price.

Discussion of price-related issues is contained in Chapter 11. In addition to a variety of other useful information, the *Nielsen Retail Index* provides information on wholesale and retail prices.

Marketing research. For any aspect of marketing planning, there may be a need for marketing research. If such research is to be performed, it is important to justify it and explain its costs and benefits. Such costs should also be included in the financial analysis.

If marketing research has already been conducted as part of the marketing plan, it can be reported as needed to justify various decisions that were reached.

to increase sales revenues from $30 million to $35 million: we expect this to be accomplished by selling 1 million units at an average price of $35.

—Poor: Our objective in 1994 is to boost advertising expenditures by 15 percent.

Remarks: Advertising is an activity, not a result. The advertising objective should be stated in terms of what result the extra advertising is intended to produce.

Better: Our objective is to boost our market share from 8 percent to 10 percent in 1994 with the help of a 15 percent increase in advertising expenditures.

—Poor: Our objective is to be a pioneer in research and development and to be the technological leader in the industry.

Remarks: Very sweeping and perhaps overly ambitious; implies trying to march in too many directions at once if the industry is one with a wide range of technological fron-

tiers. More a platitude than an action commitment to a specific result.

Better: During the 1990s, our objective is to continue as a leader in introducing new technologies and new devices that will allow buyers of electrically powered equipment to conserve on electric energy usage.

—Poor: Our objective is to be the most profitable company in our industry.

Remarks: Not specific enough by what measures of profit—total dollars or earnings per share or unit profit margin or return on equity investment or all of these? Also, because the objective concerns how well other companies will perform, the objective, while challenging, may not be achievable.

Better: We will strive to remain atop the industry in terms of rate of return on equity investment by earning a 25 percent aftertax return on equity investment in 1994.

To illustrate, if research found that two out of three consumers liked the taste of a new formula Coke, this information would likely be included in the product portion of the report. However, the details of the research could be placed here in the marketing research section. Discussion of marketing research is contained in Chapter 2.

Implementation and Control of the Marketing Plan

This section contains a discussion and justification of how the marketing plan will be implemented and controlled. It also explains who will be in charge of monitoring and changing the plan should unanticipated events occur and how the success or failure of the plan will be measured. Success or failure of the plan is typically measured by a comparison of the results of implementing the plan with the stated objectives.

HIGHLIGHT 3

Some Questions to Consider in Consumer Analysis

Knowledge of consumers is paramount to developing successful marketing plans. Below is a list of questions that are useful to consider when analyzing consumers. For some of the questions, secondary sources of information or primary marketing research can be employed to aid in decision making. However, a number of them require the analyst to do some serious thinking about the relationship between brands of the product and various consumer groups to better understand the market.

1. How many people purchase and use this product in general?
2. How many people purchase and use each brand of the product?
3. Is there an opportunity to reach nonusers of the product with a unique marketing strategy?
4. What does the product do for consumers functionally, and how does this vary by brand?
5. What does the product do for consumers in a social or psychological sense, and how does this vary by brand?
6. Where do consumers currently purchase various brands of the product?
7. How much are consumers willing to pay for specific brands, and is price a determining factor for purchase?
8. What is the market profile of the heavy user of this product, and what percentage of the total market are heavy users?
9. What media reach these consumers?
10. On average, how often is this product purchased?
11. How important is brand image for consumers of this product?
12. Why do consumers purchase particular brands?
13. How brand loyal are consumers of this product?

For a marketing plan developed within an ongoing firm, this section can be quite explicit, since procedures for implementing plans may be well established. However, for a classroom project, the key issues to be considered are the persons responsible for implementing the plan, a time-table for sequencing the tasks, and a method of measuring and evaluating the success or failure of the plan.

Summary

This *summary* need not be much different than the executive summary stated at the beginning of the document. However, it is usually a bit longer, more detailed, and states more fully the case for financing the plan.

(**HIGHLIGHT 4**)

Some Questions to Consider in Marketing Planning

Below is a brief list of questions to ask yourself about the marketing planning section of the report. Answering them honestly and recognizing both the strengths and weaknesses of your marketing plan should help you improve it.

1. What are the key assumptions that were made in developing the marketing plan?
2. How badly will the product's market position be hurt if these assumptions turn out to be incorrect?
3. How good is the marketing research?
4. Is the marketing plan consistent? For example, if the plan is to seek a prestige position in the market, is the product priced, promoted, and distributed to create this image?

5. Is the marketing plan feasible? For example, are the financial and other resources (such as a distribution network) available to implement it?
6. How will the marketing plan affect profits and market share, and is it consistent with corporate objectives?
7. Will implementing the marketing plan result in competitive retaliation that will end up hurting the firm?
8. Is the marketing mix designed to reach and attract new consumers or increase usage among existing users or both?
9. Will the marketing mix help to develop brand-loyal consumers?
10. Will the marketing plan be successful not just in the short-run but also contribute to a profitable long-run position?

Appendix — Financial Analysis

Financial analysis is a very important part of any marketing plan. While a complete business plan often includes extensive financial analysis, such as a complete cost breakdown and estimated return on investment, marketing planners frequently do not have complete accounting data for computing these figures. For example, decisions concerning how much overhead is to be apportioned to the product are not usually made solely by marketing personnel. However, the marketing plan should contain at least a sales forecast and estimates of relevant marketing costs.

Sales forecast

As noted, there are a variety of ways to develop sales forecasts. Regardless of the method, however, they all involve trying to predict the future as accurately as possible. It is, of course, necessary to justify the logic for the forecasted figures, rather than offer them with no support.

One basic approach to developing a sales forecast is outlined in Figure 2. This approach begins by estimating the total number of persons in the selected target market. This estimate comes from the market segmentation analysis

---

HIGHLIGHT 5

Some Questions to Consider in Implementation and Control

Implementation and control of a marketing plan require careful scheduling and attention to detail. While some firms have standard procedures for dealing with many of the questions raised below, thinking through each of the questions should help improve the efficiency of even these firms in this stage of the process.

1. Who is responsible for implementing and controlling the marketing plan?
2. What tasks must be performed to implement the marketing plan?
3. What are the deadlines for implementing the various tasks, and how critical are specific deadlines?
4. Has sufficient time been scheduled to implement the various tasks?

5. How long will it take to get the planned market coverage?
6. How will the success or failure of the plan be determined?
7. How long will it take to get the desired results from the plan?
8. How long will the plan be in effect before changes will be made to improve it based on more current information?
9. If an ad agency or other firms are involved in implementing the plan, how much responsibility and authority will they have?
10. How frequently will the progress of the plan be monitored?

---

and may include information from test marketing and from secondary sources, such as *Statistical Abstracts of the United States*. For example, suppose a company is marketing a solar-powered watch that is designed not only to tell time but to take the pulse of the wearer. The product is targeted at joggers and others interested in aerobic exercise. By reviewing the literature on these activities, the marketing planner, John Murphy, finds that the average estimate of this market on a national level is 60 million persons and is growing by 4 million persons per year. Thus, John might conclude that the total number of people in the target market for next year is 64 million. If he has not further limited the product's target market and has no other information, John might use this number as a basis for starting the forecast analysis.

The second estimate John needs is the annual number of purchases per person in the product's target market. This estimate could be quite large for such products as breakfast cereal or less than one (annual purchase per person) for such products as automobiles. For watches, the estimate is likely to be much less than one since people are likely to buy a new watch only every few years. Thus John might estimate the annual number of purchases per person in the target market to be .25. Of course, as a careful marketing planner, John would probably carefully research this market to refine this estimate. In any event, multiplying these two rough numbers gives John an estimate of the

Figure 2   *A Basic Approach to Sales Forecasting*

Total number of people in target markets *(a)*	*a*
Annual number of purchases per person *(b)*	× *b*
Total potential market *(c)*	= *c*
Total potential market *(c)*	*c*
Percent of total market coverage *(d)*	× *d*
Total available market *(e)*	= *e*
Total available market *(e)*	*e*
Expected market share *(f)*	× *f*
Sales forecast (in units) *(g)*	= *g*
Sales forecast (in units) *(g)*	*g*
Price *(h)*	× *h*
Sales forecast (in dollars) *(i)*	= *i*

total potential market, in this case, 64 million times .25 equals 16 million. In other words, if next year alone John's company could sell the watch to every jogger or aerobic exerciser who is buying a watch, the company could expect sales to be 16 million units.

Of course, the firm cannot expect to sell every jogger a watch for several reasons. First, it is unlikely to obtain 100 percent market coverage in the first year, if ever. Even major consumer goods companies selling convenience goods seldom reach the entire market in the first year and many never achieve even 90 percent distribution. Given the nature of the product and depending on the distribution alternative, John's company might be doing quite well to average 50 percent market coverage in the first year. If John's plans call for this kind of coverage, his estimate of the total available market would be 16 million times .5, which equals 8 million.

A second reason why John's plans would not call for dominating the market is that his company does not have the only product available or wanted by this target market. Many of the people who will purchase such a watch will purchase a competitive brand. He must, therefore, estimate the product's likely market share. Of all the estimates made in developing a sales forecast, this one is critical, since it is a reflection of the entire marketing plan. Important factors to consider in developing this estimate include: (1) competitive market shares and likely marketing plans; (2) competitive retaliation should the product do well; (3) differential advantage of the product, such as lower price; (4) promotion mix and budget relative to competitors; and (5) market shares obtained by similar products in the introductory year.

Overall, suppose John estimates the product's market share to be 5 percent, since other competitive products have beat his company to the market and because the company's differential advantage is only a slightly more stylish watch. In this case, the sales forecast for year one would be 8 million times .05, which equals 400,000 units. If the manufacturer's selling price was $50, then the sales forecast in dollars would be 400,000 times $50, which equals $20 million.

This approach can also be used to extend the sales forecast for any number of years. Typically, estimates of most of the figures change from year to year, depending on changes in market size, changes in distribution coverage, and changes in expected market shares. The value of this approach is that it forces an analyst to carefully consider and justify each of the estimates offered, rather than simply pulling numbers out of the air. In developing and justifying these estimates, many of the sources listed in Section 5 provide a good place to start searching for information—for example, *Selling Areas Marketing Inc.* or SAMI data.

Estimates of marketing costs

A complete delineation of all costs, apportionment of overhead, and other accounting tasks usually are performed by other departments within a firm. All of this information, including expected return on investment from implementing the marketing plan, is part of the overall business plan.

However, the marketing plan should at least contain estimates of major marketing costs. These include such things as advertising, sales-force training and compensation, channel development, and marketing research. Estimates may also be included for product development and package design.

For some marketing costs, reasonable estimates are available from sources such as *Standard Rate and Data*. However, some cost figures, such as marketing research, might be obtained from asking various marketing experts for the estimated price of proposed research. Other types of marketing costs might be estimated from financial statements of firms in the industry. For example, Morris's *Annual Statement Studies* offers percentage breakdowns of various income statement information by industry. These might be used to estimate the percentage of the sales-forecast figure which would likely be spent in a particular cost category.

References

This section contains the sources of any secondary information that was used in developing the marketing plan. This information might include company reports and memos, statements of company objectives, and articles or books used for information or support of the marketing plan.

References should be listed alphabetically using a consistent format. One way of preparing references is to use the same approach as is used in marketing journals. For example, the format used for references in *Journal of Marketing* articles is usually acceptable.

CONCLUSION

Suppose you're now back sitting at your desk faced with the task of developing a marketing plan for a new product. Do you believe that you might have the skills to develop a marketing plan? Of course, your ability to develop a quality plan will depend on your learning experiences during your course work and the amount of practice you've had; for example, if you developed a promotion plan in your advertising course, it is likely that you could do a better job on the promotion phase of the marketing plan. Similarly, your experiences in analyzing cases should have sharpened your skills at recognizing problems and developing solutions to them. But inexperience (or experience) aside, hopefully you now feel that you understand the process of developing a marketing plan. You at least know where to start, where to seek information, how to structure the plan, and what are some of the critical issues that require analysis.

ADDITIONAL READINGS

Ames, Charles B. "How to Devise a Winning Business Plan." *Journal of Business Strategy,* May/June 1989, pp. 26–30.

Cohen, William A. *Developing a Winning Marketing Plan.* New York: John Wiley & Sons, 1987.

Czepiel, John A. *Competitive Marketing Strategy.* Englewood Cliffs, N.J.: Prentice Hall, 1992.

Hirschhorn, Larry, and Thomas Gilmore. "The New Boundaries of the Boundaryless Company." *Harvard Business Review,* May-June 1992, pp. 104–15.

Lehmann, Donald R. and Russell S. Winer. *Analysis for Marketing Planning.* Plano, Tex: Business Publications, 1988.

Nonaka, Ikujiro. "The Knowledge Creating Company." *Harvard Business Review,* November-December 1991, pp. 96–104.

Onkvisit, Sak, and John J. Shaw. "Myopic Management: The Hollow Strength of American Competitiveness." *Business Horizons,* January-February 1991, pp. 15–19.

Sandy, William. "Link Your Business Plan to a Performance Plan." *Journal of Business Strategy,* November/December 1990, pp. 4–8.

Schnaars, Steven P. *Marketing Strategy: A Customer-Driven Approach.* New York: Free Press, 1991.

SECTION V

Secondary Data Sources

In analyzing and presenting cases and developing marketing plans, it is often very useful for analysts to be able to find outside data sources as a means of supporting their recommendations or conclusions. The data referred to here are from secondary sources and can be located in most business libraries. The purpose of this section is to list and briefly describe some of the key data sources that are available to analysts. The references are listed under eight specific headings: selected periodicals, general marketing information sources, selected marketing information services, selected retail trade publications, financial information sources, basic U.S. statistical sources, general business and industry sources, and indexes and abstracts.[1]

SELECTED PERIODICALS

Advertising Age
American Demographics
American Economist
Bank Marketing
Brandweek
Business America
Business Economics
Business Horizons
Business Marketing
Business & Professional Ethics Journal
Business Quarterly
Business and Society Review
Business Week
California Management Review
Columbia Journal of World Business
Conference Board Record
Direct Marketing
Distribution
Forbes
Fortune
Global Trade
Harvard Business Review
Health Marketing Quarterly
Inc.
Industrial Marketing Management
Industry Week

---

[1]Some of the listed references included in this section were adapted excerpts from: Gilbert A. Churchill, Jr., *Marketing Research: Methodological Foundations,* 5th ed. (Chicago: Dryden Press, 1991); Barry Berman and Joel R. Evans, *Retailing Management,* 5th ed. (New York: Macmillan, 1992); William Davidson, Daniel J. Sweeney, and Robert Stampfl, *Retailing Management,* 5th ed. (New York: John Wiley & Sons, 1984); and Lorna M. Daniells, *Business Information Sources: Revised Edition* (Berkeley, Calif.: University of California Press, 1985).

Journal of the Academy of Marketing Science
Journal of Advertising
Journal of Advertising Research
Journal of Asia-Pacific Business
Journal of Business Ethics
Journal of Business and Industrial Marketing
Journal of Business Research
Journal of Business Strategy
Journal of Business-To-Business Marketing
Journal of Consumer Research
Journal of East-West Business
Journal of Euromarketing
Journal of Experimental Psychology
Journal of Food Products Marketing
Journal of Global Marketing
Journal of Hospital Marketing
Journal of Hospitality & Leisure Marketing
Journal of International Business Studies
Journal of International Consumer Marketing
Journal of Macro Marketing
Journal of Marketing
Journal of Marketing and Public Policy
Journal of Marketing Channels
Journal of Marketing Research
Journal of Multinational Financial Management
Journal of NonProfit & Public Sector Marketing
Journal of Personal Selling and Sales Management
Journal of Pharmaceutical Marketing Management
Journal of Professional Services Marketing
Journal of Promotion Management
Journal of Psychology
Journal of Restaurant & Foodservice Marketing
Journal of Retailing
Journal of Travel & Tourism Marketing
Marketing (Maclean Hunter)
Marketing and Media Decisions
Marketing Briefing
Marketing Communications
Marketing In Action
Marketing Information Guide
Marketing Insights
Marketing News
Marketing Perspectives
Market Research Facts & Trends
Market Research Society
Marketing Science
Marketing Times
Michigan Business Review

Michigan State University Business Topics
Money
Nations Business
Organizational Dynamics
Sales Management
Sales and Marketing Management
Strategic Management Journal
Survey of Current Business
The Journal of Business
The Review of Business and Economic Research
Time

GENERAL MARKETING INFORMATION SOURCES

Commercial Atlas and Marketing Guide. Skokie, Ill.: Rand-McNally. Statistics on population, principal cities, business centers, trading areas, sales and manufacturing units, transportation data, and so forth.

Editor and Publisher "Market Guide." Market information for 1,500 American and Canadian cities. Data include population, household, gas meters, climate, retailing, and newspaper information.

Guide to Consumer Markets. New York: The Conference Board. This useful annual compilation of U.S. statistics on the consumer marketplace covers population, employment, income, expenditures, production, and prices.

Market Guide. New York. This guide compiles market data for over 1,600 U.S. and Canadian newspaper cities.

Marketing Economic Guide. New York: Marketing Economics Institute. Statistics in this guide are similar to those published in Sales and Marketing Management. Data covers 1,500 U.S. cities, 3,100 counties, and all metro areas.

Marketing Information Guide. Washington, D.C.: Department of Commerce. Annotations of selected current publications and reports, with basic information and statistics on marketing and distribution.

Milutinovich, J.S. "Business Facts for Decision Makers: Where to Find Them." *Business Horizons,* March–April 1985, pp. 63–80.

Population and Its Distribution: The United States Markets. J. Walter Thompson Co. New York: McGraw-Hill. A handbook of marketing facts selected from the *U.S. Census of Population* and the most recent census data on retail trade.

Sales and Marketing Management. (Formerly *Sales Management,* to October 1975). This valuable semimonthly journal includes four useful annual statistical issues: *Survey of Buying Power* (July), *Survey of Buying Power, Part II* (October); *Survey of Industrial Purchasing Power* (April); *Survey of Selling Costs* (January). These are excellent references for buying income, buying power index, cash income, merchandise line, manufacturing line, and retail sales.

Small Business Bibliography Series. U.S. Small Business Administration. Concise annotated bibliographies of subjects of interest to a small business owner.

Standard Directory of Advertisers. National Register Publishing Co. Directory of 17,000 companies that advertise nationally, arranged by industry with alphabetical index.

The Dartnell Sales Manager's Handbook. Dartnell Corporation. A practical one-volume reference work for concise information about the sales policies and practices of American companies.

SELECTED MARKETING INFORMATION SERVICES

Audits and Surveys National Total-Market Index. Contains information on various product types, including total market size, brand market shares, retail inventory, distribution coverage, and out of stock.

Directory of U.S. and Canadian Marketing Surveys and Services. C.H. Kline & Co. Contains a list of almost 3,000 marketing reports and continuing services available from 191 consulting firms.

Dun & Bradstreet Market Identifiers. Relevant marketing information on over 4.3 million establishments for constructing sales prospect files, sales territories, sales territory potentials, and isolating potential new customers with particular characteristics.

FINDEX, The Directory of Market Research Reports, Studies and Surveys (Bethesda, Md.: Cambridge Information Group). This publication provides a directory of more than 10,000 research reports produced by 500 top U.S. and international research firms.

Handbook of Marketing Research. Amsterdam: European Society for Opinion and Marketing Research. Provides a list of European market research societies and organizations, arranged by country.

International Directory of Published Market Research. London. Contains almost 7,000 published market research studies. Over 100 countries are represented.

Membership Roster and International Buyers' Guide to Marketing Services. Chicago. Provides a list of AMA members which contains an index by affiliation for each member.

National Purchase Diary Panel (NPD). Monthly purchase information based on the largest panel diary in the United States with detailed brand, frequency of purchase, characteristics of heavy buyers, and other market data.

Nielson Retail Index. Contains basic product turnover data, retail prices, store displays, promotional activity, and local advertising based on a national sample of supermarkets, drugstores, and mass merchandisers.

Nielson Television Index. Well-known index which provides estimates of the size and nature of the audience for individual television programs.

Selling Areas Marketing, Inc. Reports on warehouse withdrawals of various food products in each of 42 major markets covering 80 percent of national food sales.

Simmons Media/Marketing Service. Provides cross referencing of product usage and media exposure for magazine, television, newspaper, and radio based on a strict national probability sample.

Standard Rate and Data. Nine volumes on major media which include a variety of information in addition to prices for media in selected markets.

Starch Advertising Readership Service. Measures the reading of advertisements in magazines and newspapers and provides information on overall readership percentages, readers per dollar, and rank when grouped by product category.

SELECTED RETAIL TRADE PUBLICATIONS

American Druggist (monthly), The Hearst Corporation, 959 Eighth Avenue, New York, N.Y. 10019.

Auto Chain Store Magazine (ACS) (monthly), Babcox Publications, Inc., 11 South Forge Street, Akron, Ohio 44304.

Body Fashions & Intimate Apparel (monthly), Harcourt Brace Jovanovich Publications, 757 Third Avenue, New York, N.Y. 10017.

C. Store Business (10 times/year), Maclean Hunter Media, 1351 Washington Boulevard, Stamford, Conn. 06902.

Catalog Showroom Business (monthly), Gralla Publications, 1515 Broadway, New York, N.Y. 10036.

Catalog Showroom Merchandiser (monthly), CSM Marketing, Inc., 1020 West Jericho Turnpike, Smithtown, N.Y. 11787.

Chain Drug Review (biweekly), Racher Press, Inc., 1 Park Avenue, New York, N.Y. 10016.

Chain Store Age—Executive Edition (monthly), Lebhar-Friedman, Inc., 425 Park Avenue, New York, N.Y. 10022.

Chain Store Age—General Merchandise Edition (monthly), Lebhar-Friedman, Inc., 425 Park Avenue, New York, N.Y. 10022.

Chain Store Age—Supermarkets Edition (monthly), Lebhar-Friedman, Inc., 425 Park Avenue, New York, N.Y. 10022.

CompetitivEdge (monthly), National Home Furnishings Association, 405 Merchandise Mart, Chicago, Ill. 60654.

Consumer Electronics Monthly (monthly), CES Publishing Corporation, 135 West 50th Street, New York, N.Y. 10020.

Convenience Store Merchandiser (monthly), Associated Business Publications, Inc., 41 East 42nd Street, New York, N.Y. 10017.

Convenience Store News (monthly, with additional issues in March, April, August, and October), BMT Publications, Inc., 254 West 31st Street, New York, N.Y. 10001.

Daily News Record (daily), Fairchild Publications, 7 East 12th Street, New York, N.Y. 10003.

Decorating Retailer (monthly), National Decorating Products Association, 1050 North Lindbergh Boulevard, St. Louis, Mo. 63132.

Decorative Products World (monthly, except January), 2911 Washington Avenue, St. Louis, Mo. 63103.

Direct Marketing (monthly), Hoke Communications, Inc., 224 Seventh Street, Garden City, N.Y. 11530.

Discount Merchandiser (monthly), Schwartz Publications, 2 Park Avenue, New York, N.Y. 10016.

Discount Store News (biweekly except May and December), Lebhar-Friedman, Inc., 425 Park Avenue, New York, N.Y. 10022.

Drug Store News (biweekly), Lebhar-Friedman, Inc., 425 Park Avenue, New York, N.Y. 10022.

Drug Topics (biweekly), Medical Economics Company, Inc., 680 Kinderkamack Road, Oradell, N.J. 07649.

Earnshaw's Infants Girls Boys Wear Review (monthly), Earnshaw Publications, Inc., 393 Seventh Avenue, New York, N.Y. 10001.

Electronics Retailer (monthly, except combined issues in January–February, and June–July), Fairchild Publications, 7 East 12th Street, New York, N.Y. 10003.

Floor Covering Weekly (weekly), Hearst Business Communications, Inc., 645 Steward Avenue, Garden City, N.Y. 11530.

Food Merchandising for Nonfood Retailers (quarterly), Lebhar-Friedman, Inc., 425 Park Avenue, New York, N.Y. 10022.

Furniture/Today (biweekly), Communications/Today Ltd., 200 S. Mai Street, High Point, N.C. 27261.

Garden Supply Retailer (monthly), The Miller Publishing Company, 2501 Wayzata Blvd., Minneapolis, Minn. 55440.

Giftware Business (monthly), Gralla Publications, 1515 Broadway, New York, N.Y. 10036.

Hardware Age (monthly), Chilton Company, Chilton Way, Radnor, Pa. 19089.

Hardware Merchandiser (monthly), The Irving-Cloud Publishing Company, 7300 North Cicero Avenue, Lincolnwood, Ill. 60646.

Home & Auto (semimonthly except November and December), Harcourt Brace Jovanovich Publications, 757 Third Avenue, New York, N.Y. 10017.

Home Center (monthly), Vance Publishing Corporation, 300 West Adams, Chicago, Ill. 60606.

Housewares (semimonthly plus January, July, and December issues), Harcourt Brace Jovanovich Publications, 757 Third Avenue, New York, N.Y. 10017.

Lawn & Garden Marketing (10 times annually), Intertec Publishing Corporation, 9221 Quivira Road, Overland Park, Kan. 66212.

Mart (monthly), Morgan-Grampian Publishing Co., 2 Park Avenue, New York, N.Y. 10016.

Men's Wear (semimonthly), Fairchild Publications, 7 East 12th Street, New York, N.Y. 10003.

Merchandising (monthly), Gralla Publications, 1515 Broadway, New York, N.Y. 10036.

NARDA News (monthly), NARDA, Inc., 2 North Riverside Plaza, Chicago, Ill. 60606.

Nation's Restaurants News (biweekly), Lebhar-Friedman, Inc., 425 Park Avenue, New York, N.Y. 10022.

National Jeweler (bimonthly), Gralla Publications, 1515 Broadway, New York, N.Y. 10036.

National Mall Monitor (bimonthly), National Mall Monitor, 2280 U.S. 19 North, Suite 264, Clearwater, Fla. 33575.

National Petroleum News (NPN) (monthly), Hunter Publishing Company, 950 Lee Street, Des Plaines, Ill. 60016.

Non-Foods Merchandising (monthly), Charleson Publishing Co., 124 East 40th Street, New York, N.Y. 10016.

Non-Store Marketing Report (biweekly), Maxwell Sroge Publishing Inc., Sroge Building, 731 North Cascade Avenue, Colorado Springs, Colo. 80903.

Outdoor Retailer (bimonthly), Pacifica Publishing Corporation, 31652 Second Avenue, South Laguna, Calif. 92677.

Private Label (monthly), E. W. Williams Publishing Co., 80–88th Avenue, New York, N.Y. 10011.

Professional Furniture Merchant (monthly), Vista Publications, Inc., 9600 W. Sample Road, Coral Springs, Fla. 33065.

Progressive Grocer (monthly), Maclean Hunter Media, 1351 Washington Boulevard, Stamford, Conn. 06901.

Restaurants & Institutions (semimonthly), Cahners Publishing Co., 221 Columbus Avenue, Boston, Mass. 02116.

Retail Control (monthly except April–May, and June–July when bimonthly), NRMA—Financial Executives Division, 100 West 31st Street, New York, N.Y. 10001.

Retailing Home Furnishings (weekly), Fairchild Publications, 7 East 12th Street, New York, N.Y. 10003.

Shopping Center World (monthly), Communications Channels, Inc., 6255 Barfield Road, Atlanta, Ga. 30328.

Sporting Goods Business (monthly), Gralla Publications, 1515 Broadway, New York, N.Y. 10036.

Sporting Goods Dealer (monthly), The Sporting News Publishing Company, 1212 North Lindbergh Boulevard, St. Louis, Mo. 63132.

Sports Retailer (monthly), National Sporting Goods Association, 1699 Wall Street, Mt. Prospect, Ill. 60056.

Stores (monthly), National Retail Merchants Association, 100 W. 31st Street, New York, N.Y. 10001.

Supermarket Business (monthly), Fieldmark Media, Inc., 25 West 43rd Street, New York, N.Y. 10036.

Supermarket News (weekly), 71 West 35th Street, Suite 1600, New York, N.Y. 10001.

Teens and Boys Magazine (monthly), 71 West 35th Street, Suite 1600, New York, N.Y. 10001.

Tire Review (monthly), Babcox Publications, 11 South Forge Street, Akron, Ohio 44304.

Toys Hobbies & Crafts (monthly except June), Harcourt Brace Jovanovich Publications, 1 East First Street, Duluth, Minn. 55802.

Video Store (monthly), Hester Communications, Inc., 1700 East Dyer Road, Suite 250, Santa Ana, Calif. 92705.

Visual Merchandising & Store Design (monthly), Signs of the Times Publishing Company, 407 Gilbert Avenue, Cincinnati, Ohio 45202.

Women's Wear Daily (daily), Fairchild Publications, 7 East 12th Street, New York, N.Y. 10003.

FINANCIAL INFORMATION SOURCES

Almanac of Business and Industrial Financial Ratios. Prentice Hall. Provides financial and operating ratios for about 160 industries.

Annotated Bibliography of Corporate Finance. Toronto: Macmillan Company of Canada. Classified, annotated bibliography on the theory and practice of corporate finance. Includes 26 subject sections from corporate finance in general to international financial management.

Annual Statement Studies. Robert Morris Associates. Provides financial and operating ratios for about 300 lines of businesses.

Blue Line Investment Survey. Quarterly ratings and reports on 1,000 stocks; analysis of 60 industries and special situations analysis (monthly); supplements on new developments and editorials on conditions affecting price trends.

Commercial and Financial Chronicle. Variety of articles and news reports on business, government, and finance. Monday's issue lists new securities, dividends, and called bonds. Thursday's issue is devoted to business articles.

Dun's Review. Dun & Bradstreet. This monthly includes very useful annual financial ratios for about 125 lines of business.

Encyclopedia of Banking and Finance. Boston: Bankers Publishing Co. One-volume encyclopedia covers the whole area of banking and finance.

Expenses in Retail Business. NCR Corp. Includes operating ratios for over 17 lines of retail businesses.

Fairchild's Financial Manual of Retail Stores. Information about officers and directors, products, subsidiaries, sales, and earnings for apparel stores, mail order firms, variety chains, and supermarkets.

Federal Reserve Bulletin. Board of Governors of the Federal Reserve System. The "Financial and Business Statistics" section of each issue of this monthly bulletin is the best single source for current U.S. banking and monetary statistics.

Financial Executive. Financial Executives Institute. Includes articles for the financial manager.

Financial Planning. Atlanta: International Association of Financial Planning. Provides articles on a wide range of topics of interest to financial planners.

Financial Studies of the Small Business. Financial Research Associates. Includes financial and operating ratios for 50 lines of small businesses.

Financial World. Articles on business activities of interest to investors, including investment opportunities and pertinent data on firms, such as earnings and dividend records.

Industry Norms and Key Business Ratios. Dun & Bradstreet Credit Services.

Mergers & Acquisitions. Information for Industry. Contains lists of rosters of U.S. mergers and acquisitions, of joint ventures and cooperation agreements.

Moody's Bank and Finance Manual; Moody's Industrial Manual; Moody's Municipal & Government Manual; Moody's Public Utility Manual; Moody's Transportation Manual; Moody's Directors Service. Brief histories of companies and their operations, subsidiaries, officers and directors, products, and balance sheet and income statements over several years.

Moody's Bond Survey. Moody's Investors Service. Weekly data on stocks and bonds, including recommendations for purchases or sale and discussions of industry trends and developments.

Moody's Handbook of Widely Held Common Stocks. Moody's Investors Service. Weekly data on stocks and bonds, including recommendations for purchases or sale and discussions of industry trends and developments.

Quarterly Financial Report for Manufacturing, Mining, and Trade Corporations. U.S. Federal Trade Commission. U.S. Government Printing Office. Details quarterly income statement/balance sheet data and financial/operating ratios classified by industry.

Security Owner's Stock Guide. Standard & Poor's Corp. Standard & Poor's rating, stock price range, and other helpful information for about 4,200 common and preferred stocks.

Security Price Index. Standard & Poor's Corp. Price indexes, bond prices, sales, yields, Dow Jones averages, etc.

Standard Corporation Records. Standard & Poor's Corp. Published in looseleaf form, offers information similar to Moody's manuals. Use of this extensive service facilitates buying securities for both the individual and the institutional investor.

Yearbook on Corporate Mergers, Joint Ventures, and Corporate Policy. Cambridge Corporation. Arranged by industry and often includes date, price, the business of the acquired company, sales or earnings, and price/earnings ratio.

BASIC U.S. STATISTICAL SOURCES

American Statistics Index. Congressional Information Service. Detailed, descriptive guide and index to statistics published by all government agencies, congressional committees, and statistics-producing programs.

Business Service Checklist. Department of Commerce. Weekly guide to Department of Commerce publications, plus key business indicators.

Business Statistics. Department of Commerce. (Supplement to *Survey of Current Business.*) History of the statistical series appearing in the *Survey.* Also included are source references and useful explanation notes.

Census Catalog and Guide. Provides a listing of the programs and services of the Census Bureau. Lists reports, diskettes, microfiche, and maps.

Census of Agriculture. Department of Commerce. Data by states and counties on livestock, farm characteristics, values.

Census of Manufacturers. Department of Commerce. Industry statistics, area statistics, subjects reports, location of plants, industry descriptions arranged in Standard Industrial Classification, and a variety of ratios.

Census of Mineral Industries. Department of Commerce. Similar to *Census of Manufacturers.* Also includes capital expenditures and employment and payrolls.

Census of Retail Trade. Department of Commerce. Compiles data for states, SMSAs, counties, and cities with populations of 2,500 or more by kind of business. Data include number of establishments, sales, payroll, and personnel.

Census of Selected Services. Department of Commerce. Includes data on hotels, motels, beauty parlors, barber shops, and other retail service organizations.

Census of Transportation. Passenger Transportation Survey, Commodity Transportation Survey, Travel Inventory and Use Survey, Bus and Truck Carrier Survey.

Census Tract Reports. Department of Commerce, Bureau of Census. Detailed information on both population and housing subjects.

Census of Wholesale Trade. Department of Commerce. Similar to *Census of Retail Trade*—information is for wholesale establishment.

County and City Data Book. Department of Commerce. Summary statistics for small geographical areas.

Current Business Reports. Department of Commerce. Reports monthly department store sales of selected items.

Economic Indicators. U.S. Council of Economic Advisors. Source for statistical tables and charts of basic economic indicators.

Economic Report of the President. Transmitted to the Congress, January (each year), together with the *Annual Report* of the Council of Economic Advisers. Statistical tables relating to income, employment, and production.

Federal Reserve Bulletin. Washington, D.C.: Federal Reserve System Board of Governors. Published monthly, this publication is an important source of financial data, including statistics on banking activity, interest rates, savings, the index of industrial production, an index of department store sales, prices, and international trade and finance.

Handbook of Basic Economic Statistics. Economic Statistics Bureau of Washington, D.C. Current and historical statistics on industry, commerce, labor, and agriculture.

Handbook of Cyclical Indicators. Washington, D.C.: U.S. Department of Commerce. Published monthly, this publication contains at least 70 indicators of business activity designed to serve as a key to general economic conditions.

Merchandising, "Statistical and Marketing Report." New York: Billboard Publications. This annual report, contained in the March issue, includes statistical information related to sales, shipments, imports, exports, and more for certain consumer durables, including home electronics and major appliances.

Predicasts Basebook. Predicasts, Inc. Comprehensive, 29,000 time series, arranged by a modified 7-digit SIC number and includes statistics for economic indicators.

Predicasts Forecasts. Predicasts, Inc. Reports short- and long-range forecast statistics for basic economic indicators and for individual industries/products. Each forecast includes date and page reference.

Social Indicators. U.S. Bureau of the Census. Includes statistics and charts for a variety of U.S. social conditions and trends.

Standard & Poor's Corporate Records. New York: Standard & Poor's Corporation. *Corporate Records* provides current financial statistics for companies as well as background information and news items.

Standard & Poor's Industry Surveys. New York: Standard and Poor's Corporation. These surveys provide analyses of all major domestic industries, including outlooks for the industry, trends and problems, and statistical tables and charts. A basic analysis is published yearly and offers a comparative company analysis of the leading companies in an industry. Current analyses are published three times per year and include important developments and available statistics for the industry, market, and company, as well as investment outlook for the industry.

Standard & Poor's Statistical Service. New York: Standard and Poor's Corporation. This publication presents monthly statistical data (current and historical) for several areas, including banking and finance, production and labor, and income and trade.

Statistical Abstract of the United States. Department of Commerce. Summary statistics in industrial, social, political, and economic fields in the United States. It is augmented by the *Cities Supplement, The County Data Book,* and *Historical Statistics of the United States.*

Statistical Reference Index. Congressional Information Service. Selective guide to American statistical publications available from sources other than the U.S. government.

Statistical Service. Standard & Poor's Corp. Reports coverage of current and basic statistics arranged in three parts: the white current statistics gives latest annual figures; the yellow monthly issue provides latest figures covering the current year; and the basic statistics section.

Statistics of Income: Corporation Income Tax Returns. Internal Revenue Service. Balance sheet and income statement statistics derived from corporate tax returns.

Statistics of Income: U.S. Business Tax Returns. Internal Revenue Service. Summarizes financial and economic data for proprietorships, partnerships, and small business corporations.

Statistics Sources. Gale Research. Provides a guide to general sources for statistics on industrial, business, social, education, financial, and other subjects.

Survey of Current Business. Department of Commerce. Facts on industrial and business activity in the United States and statistical summary of national income and product accounts. A weekly supplement provides an up-to-date summary of business.

U.S. Industrial Outlook. U.S. Bureau of Industrial Economics, Department of Commerce. Contains information on recent trends and outlook in 250 individual industries.

GENERAL BUSINESS AND INDUSTRY SOURCES

Aerospace Facts and Figures. Aerospace Industries Association of America.

Almanac of the Canning, Freezing, Preserving Industries. E. E. Judge & Sons. Includes general industry information and a directory of the industry.

America's Corporate Families: The Billion Dollar Directory. Dun & Bradstreet. Similar to Million Dollar Directory.

Annual Statistical Report. American Iron and Steel Institute.

Appliance. Dana Chase Publications. Includes statistical reviews, purchasing directory, and general information.

Beverage Industry. Magazines for Industry, Inc. Publishes a separate Annual Manual in three segments: relevant statistics, manual of operations, and a buyer's guide.

Bibliographic Guide to Business and Economics. Boston: G.K. Hall. A comprehensive author/title/subject listing of all business and economic materials cataloged during one year by the Library of Congress and the Research Libraries of the New York Public Library.

Business Information Sources. Daniells. University of California Press. A book complete with bibliographies representing almost every aspect of business.

Chemical Marketing Reporter. Schnell Publishing. Includes lengthy, continuing list of "Current Prices of Chemicals and Related Materials."

Computerworld. Computerworld, Inc. Last December issue includes "Review and Forecast," an analysis of computer industry's past year and the outlook for the next year.

Construction Review. Department of Commerce. Current statistics on construction put in place, costs, and employment.

Directory of Corporate Affiliations. National Register Publishing Co. Lists over 4,000 major American parent companies' line of business, approximate sales, number of employees, ticker symbol, top officers, subsidiaries, divisions and/ or affiliates.

Directory of Industry Data Sources. Information Access Co. Provides a listing of industry-intensive data for U.S., Canada, and Europe.

Distribution Worldwide. Chilton Co. Special annual issue, *Distribution Guide,* compiles information on transportation methods and wage.

Drug and Cosmetic Industry. Drug Markets, Inc. Separate publication in July, *Drug and Cosmetic Catalog,* provides list of manufacturers of drugs and cosmetics and their respective products.

Electronic News Financial Fact Book & Directory. Fairchild Publications. A detailed financial manual covering electronic companies; includes a ranked list of top companies.

Electrical World. January and February issues include two-part statistical report on expenditures, construction, and other categories by region; capacity; sales, and financial statistics for the electrical industry.

Encyclopedia of Business Information Sources. Paul Wasserman et al., eds., Gale Research Company. A detailed listing of primary subjects of interest to managerial personnel, with a record of sourcebooks, periodicals, organizations, directories, handbooks, bibliographies, and other sources of information on each topic. Two vols., nearly 17,000 entries in over 1,600 subject areas.

Forest Industries. Miller Freeman Publications, Inc. The March issue includes "Forest Industries Wood-Based Panel," a review of production and sales figures for selected wood products; extra issue in May includes a statistical review of the lumber industry.

Implement and Tractor. Intertec Publishing Corporation. January issue includes equipment specifications and operating data for farm and industrial equipment. November issue includes statistics and information on the farm industry.

Industry Surveys. Standard & Poor's Corp. Continuously revised analysis of leading industries (40 industries made up of 1,300 companies). Current analysis contains interim operating data of investment comment. Basic analysis features company ratio comparisons and balance sheet statistics.

Kline Guide to the Chemical Industry. 4th ed. C.H.Kline & Co. An economic analysis of the chemical industry.

Middle Market Directory. Dun & Bradstreet. Inventories approximately 18,000 U.S. companies with an indicated worth of $500,000 to $999,999, giving officers, products, standard industrial classification, approximate sales, and number of employees.

Million Dollar Directory. Dun & Bradstreet. Lists U.S. companies with an indicated worth of $1 million or more, giving officers and directors, products, standard industrial classification, sales, and number of employees.

Modern Brewery Age. Business Journals, Inc. February issue includes a review of sales and production figures for the brewery industry. A separate publication, *The Blue Book,* issued in May, compiles sales and consumption figures by state for the brewery industry.

Motor Vehicle Facts & Figures. Manufacturers Association of the United States. Contains statistics on automobile and truck production, sales and registrations, ownership and usage, economic and social impact of the automobile.

National Petroleum News. McGraw-Hill, Inc. May issue includes statistics on sales and consumption of fuel oils, gasoline, and related products. Some figures are for 10 years, along with 10-year projections.

Operating Results of Department and Specialty Stores. National Retail Merchants Association.

Packaging. Cahners Publishing Co. Industry publication that includes special annual issues "Packaging Encyclopedia" and "Buyer's Guide and Directory."

Paper Trade Journal. Vance Publishing Corp. Includes: Financial Review: North America's Paper Industry Outlook, Who's Who in North America Paper-making, and general industry information.

Petroleum Facts and Figures. American Petroleum Institute.

Poor's Register of Corporations, Directors, and Executives of the United States and Canada. Standard & Poor's Corp. Divided into two sections. The first gives officers, products, sales range, and number of employees for about 30,000 corporations. The second gives brief information on executives and directors.

PROMPT. Predicasts, Inc. Predicasts Overview of Markets and Technology. A continuing abstracting index to worldwide articles of 28 industries.

Publishers Weekly. R.R. Bowker Co. Includes general discussions of the industry, an annual summary and highlights publication, and industry statistics.

Quick-Frozen Foods. Harcourt Brace Jovanovich Publications. October issue includes "Frozen Food Almanac," providing statistics on the frozen food industry by product.

Retail Trade. Provides a survey of retail sales, retail inventories, purchases, gross margins, and account receivable by type of retail store and form of legal organization.

Statistical Sources. Paul Wasserman et al., eds. Gale Research Corp., 4th ed., 1974. A subject guide to industrial, business, social, educational, financial data, and other related topics.

The Super Market Industry Speaks. Super Market Institute.

Vending Times. February issue includes "The Buyers Guide," a special issue providing information on the vending industry; June issue includes "The Census of the Industry," a special issue containing statistics on the vending industry.

Who Owns Whom: North America. Dun & Bradstreet. A directory of U.S. and Canadian parent companies listing their subsidiaries and associates outside the U.S. or Canada.

INDEXES AND ABSTRACTS

Accountants Digest. L. L. Briggs. A digest of articles appearing currently in accounting periodicals.

Accountants Index. American Institute of Certified Public Accountants. An index to books, pamphlets, and articles on accounting and finance.

Accounting Articles. Commerce Clearing House. Loose-leaf index to articles in accounting and business periodicals.

Advertising Age Editorial Index. Crain Communications, Inc. Index to articles in *Advertising Age*.

American Statistical Index. Congressional Information Service. A comprehensive two-part annual index to the statistical publications of the U.S. government.

Applied Science & Technology Index. (Formerly *Industrial Arts Index* to 1958). H. W. Wilson Co. Reviews over 300 periodicals relevant to the applied sciences, many of which pertain to business.

Battelle Library Review. (Formerly *Battelle Technical Review* to 1962.) Battelle Memorial Institute. Annotated bibliography of books, reports, and articles on automation and automatic processes.

Bulletin of Public Affairs Information Service. Public Affairs Information Service, Inc. (Since 1915—annual index.) A selective list of the latest books, pamphlets, government publications, reports of public and private agencies, and periodicals relating to economic conditions, public administration, and international relations.

Business Education Index. McGraw-Hill Book Co. (Since 1940—annual index.) Annual author and subject index of books, articles, and theses on business education.

Business Index. Los Altos, Calif.: (Microfilm Reel) Information Access Co. An index that includes 650 business periodicals or selected articles from non-business journals.

Business Periodicals Index. H. W. Wilson Co. A subject index to the disciplines of accounting, advertising, banking, general business, insurance, labor, management, and marketing.

Business Publications Index and Abstracts. Prepared by Management Contents. Gale Research Co. A two-part monthly subject/author index to all articles in over 700 English language business/management periodicals, plus some proceedings, study courses, and a few books.

Canadian Business Index. Toronto: Micromedia Ltd. An index to 150 Canadian periodicals and a few newspapers.

Catalog of United States Census Publication. Washington, D.C.: Dept. of Commerce, Bureau of Census. Indexes all available at Census Bureau Data. Main divisions are: agriculture, business, construction, foreign trade, government, guide to locating U.S. census information.

Computer and Information Systems. (Formerly *Information Processing Journal* to 1969.) Cambridge Communications Corporation.

Conference Board. Cumulative Index. A subject index to a wide range of studies, pamphlets, and articles in the areas of: consumer research, corporate relations, economic and policy analysis, human resources, international business management, and management functions.

Cumulative Index of NICB Publications. The National Industrial Conferences Board. Annual index of NICB books, pamphlets, and articles in the area of management of personnel.

Current contents: Social & Behavioral Sciences. Institute for Scientific Information. A collection of tables of contents from 1,300 periodicals in the social and behavioral sciences. Business, finance, economics, management, and many other related areas of sociology and social issues are covered.

Engineering Index Monthly. Engineering Information, Inc. A subject list of abstracts, significant technological periodicals, and other literature.

Financial Times Index. Financial Times Business Information Ltd. A three-part index for corporate information in the U.K. and worldwide, including institutions, associations, and so on.

Funk and Scott Index Europe. Predicasts, Inc. Indexes articles on U.S. companies, products, and industries from over 750 business, industrial, and financial periodicals. Includes a third section of articles arranged by region and country.

Funk and Scott Index International. Predicasts Inc. Indexes articles on foreign companies and industries from over 1,000 foreign and domestic periodicals and documents.

Funk and Scott Index United States. Predicasts, Inc. Indexes articles on U.S. companies, products, and industries from over 750 business, industrial, and financial periodicals.

Guide to U.S. Government Publications. McLean, Va., Documents Index. Annotated guide to publications of various U.S. government agencies.

International Abstracts in Operations Research. Operations Research Society of America.

International Journal of Abstracts of Statistical Methods in Industry. The Hague, Netherlands: International Statistical Institute.

Management Contents. A collection of tables of contents for a selection of over 300 business / management journals.

Management Information Guides. Gale Research Company. Bibliographical references to information sources for various business subjects.

Management Review. American Management Association.

Monthly Catalog of U.S. Government Publications. U.S. Government Printing Office. Continuing list of federal government publications.

Monthly Checklist of State Publications. U.S. Library of Congress, Exchange and Gift Division. Record of state documents received by Library of Congress.

National Newspaper Index. An assortment of citations to articles and news appearing in leading newspapers nationwide.

New York Times Index. New York. Very detailed index of all articles in the *Times*, arranged alphabetically with many cross-references.

Psychological Abstracts. American Psychological Association.

Public Affairs Information Service. Public Affairs Information Service, Inc. A selective subject list of books, pamphlets, and government publications covering business, banking, and economics as well as subjects in the area of public affairs.

Reader's Guide to Periodical Literature. H. W. Wilson Co. Index by author and subject to selected U.S. general and nontechnical periodicals.

Research Index. Dorking, Surrey, Eng.: Business Surveys, Ltd. Indexes news of financial interest on industries and companies, appearing in over 100 British (and a few European) trade and economics journals as well as several newspapers.

Sociological Abstracts. American Sociological Association.

The Wall Street Journal Index. Dow Jones & Company, Inc. An index of all articles in *The WSJ* grouped in two sections: corporate news and general news.

Name Index

Subject Index